Mezz Mezzr

was born in Chicago in 1899 and was one of that city's leading clarinettists during the twenties, golden age of the blues. Many of Mezzrow's records from his 1933 big band, through faultless sessions with Tommy Ladnier and Sidney Bechet in 1938, to post-war Mezzrow–Bechet masterpieces on his King Jazz label, are marvellous, revealing his deep feeling for the blues, well-thought lines, frequent agility and appealing acid tone. Following his appearance at the Nice Jazz Festival, 1948, Mezzrow became a big star in Europe, touring regularly with various bands and with Louis Armstrong. For a white musician, Mezzrow was acclaimed for his exceptional feel for jazz, but his most important contribution is this autobiography, *Really the Blues*, written with Bernard Wolfe and first published in 1946, for its unbounded vitality that so captures the revolution that jazz represented to the youth of Chicago in the twenties and even more of Harlem in the thirties and forties.

MEZZ MEZZROW
WITH BERNARD WOLFE

Really the Blues

Flamingo
An Imprint of HarperCollins*Publishers*

Flamingo
An Imprint of HarperCollinsPublishers,
77–85 Fulham Palace Road,
Hammersmith, London W6 8JB

A Flamingo Modern Classic 1993
9 8 7 6 5 4 3 2 1

First published in the USA by
Random House 1946

The Author asserts the moral right to
be identified as the author of this work

Author photograph by Redferns

A CIP catalogue record for this book
is available from the British Library

ISBN 0 00 654691 9

Set in Garamond 3

Printed in Great Britain by
HarperCollinsManufacturing Glasgow

To all hipsters, hustlers and fly cats tipping along The Stroll.

(Keep scuffling.)

To all the cons in all the houses of many slammers, wrastling with chinches.

(Short time, boys.)

To all the junkies and lushheads in two-bit scratch-pads, and the flophouse grads in morgue iceboxes.

(R.I.P.)

To the sweettalkers, the gumbeaters, the high-jivers, out of the gallion for good and never going to take low again.

(You got to make it, daddy.)

★

To Bessie Smith, Jimmy Noone, King Oliver, Louis Armstrong, Zutty Singleton, Johnny Dodds, Sidney Bechet and Tommy Ladnier.

(Grab a taste of millennium, gate.)

Contents

APPENDICES

Introduction to the Flamingo Edition

THE END OF RASCISM

One of my favorite places to go when I was a kid in Chicago was Riverview, the giant amusement park on the North Side. Riverview, which during the 1950s was nicknamed Polio Park, after the reigning communicable disease of the decade, had dozens of rides, including some of the fastest, most terrifying roller coasters ever designed. Among them were The Silver Streak, The Comet, The Wild Mouse, The Flying Turns, and The Bobs. Of those, The Flying Turns, a seatless ride that lasted all of thirty seconds or so, and required the passengers in each car to recline consecutively on one another, was my favorite. The Turns did not operate on tracks but rather on a steeply banked, bobsled-like series of tortuous sliding curves that never failed to engender in me the sensation of being about to catapult out of the car over the stand of trees to the west of the parking lot. To a fairly manic kid, which I was, this was a big thrill, and I must have ridden The Flying Turns hundreds of times between the ages of seven and sixteen.

The Bobs, however, was the most frightening roller coaster in the park. Each year several people were injured or killed on that ride; usually when a kid attempted to prove his bravery by standing up in the car as it jerked suddenly downward at about a hundred miles per hour. The kids liked to speculate about how many lives The Bobs had taken over the years. I knew only one kid, Earl Weyerholz, who claimed to have stood up in his car at the top of the first hill more than once and lived to tell about it. I never doubted Earl Weyerholz because I once saw him submerge his arm up to the bicep in an aquarium containing two piranhas, just to recover a quarter Bobby DiMarco had thrown into it and dared Earl to go after. Earl was eleven then. He died in 1958, at the age of fourteen, from the more than two hundred bee stings he sustained that year at summer camp in Wisconsin. How or why he got stung so often was never explained to me. I just assumed somebody had dared him to stick his arms into a few hives for a dollar or something.

Shoot The Chutes was also a popular Riverview ride. Passengers rode in boats that slid at terrific speed into a pool and everybody got soaking wet. The Chutes never really appealed very much to me, though; I never saw the point of getting wet for no good reason. The Parachute was another one that did not thrill me. Being dropped to the ground from a great height while seated on a thin wooden plank with only a narrow metal bar to hold onto was not my idea of a good time. In fact, just the thought of it scared the hell out of me; I didn't even like to watch people do it. I don't think not wanting to go on The Parachute meant that I was acrophobic, however, because I was extremely adept at scaling garage roofs by alleyway drainpipes and jumping from one roof to the next. The Parachute just seemed like a crazy thing to submit oneself to, as did The Rotor, a circular contraption that spun around so fast that when the floor was removed riders were plastered to the walls by centrifugal force. Both The Parachute and The Rotor always had long lines of people waiting to be exquisitely tortured.

What my friends and I were most fond of at Riverview was Dunk The Nigger. At least that's what we called the concession where by throwing a baseball at a target on a handle and hitting it square you could cause the seat lever in the attached cage to release and plunge the man sitting on the perch into a tank of about five feet of water. All of the guys who worked in the cages were black, and they hated to see us coming. Between the ages of thirteen and sixteen my friends and I terrorized these guys. They were supposed to taunt the thrower, make fun of him or her and try to keep them spending quarters for three balls. Most people who played this game were lucky to hit the target hard enough to dunk the clown once in every six tries; but my buddies and I became experts. We'd buy about ten dollars worth of baseballs and keep these guys going down, time after time.

Of course they hated us with a passion. "Don't you little motherfuckers have somewhere else to go?" they'd yell. "Goddam motherfuckin' white boy, I'm gon' get yo' ass when I gets my break!" We'd just laugh and keep pegging hardballs at the trip lever targets. My pal Big Steve was great at Dunk The Nigger; he was our true ace because he threw the hardest and his arm never got tired. "You fat ofay sumbitch!" one of the black guys would shout at Big Steve as he dunked him for the fifth pitch in a row. "Stop complaining," Steve would yell back at him. "You're getting a free bath, aren't ya?"

None of us thought too much about the fact that the job of taunt-and-dunk was about half a cut above being a carnival geek and a full cut below working at a car wash. It never occurred to us, more than a quarter of a century ago, why it was that all of the guys on the perches were black, or that we were racists. Unwitting racists, perhaps; after all, we were kids, ignorant and foolish products of White Chicago during the 1950s.

One summer afternoon in 1963, the year I turned sixteen, my friends and I arrived at Riverview and headed straight for Dunk The Nigger. We were shocked to see a white guy sitting on a perch in one of the cages. Nobody said anything but we all stared at him. Big Steve bought some balls and began hurling them at one of the black guys' target. "What's the matter, gray?" the guy shouted at Steve. "Don't want to pick on one of your own?"

I don't remember whether or not I bought any balls that day, but I do know it was the last time I went to the concession. In fact, that was one of the last times I patronized Riverview, since I left Chicago early the following year and Riverview was torn down not long after. I don't know what Big Steve or any of my other old friends who played Dunk The Nigger with me think about it now, or even if they've ever thought about it at all. That's just the way things were.

* * *

Mezz Mezzrow lived in the same neighborhood on the North Side of Chicago as I did. His father owned a drugstore, as did mine. He reputedly became a bootlegger, as was my father. I figure he must have discovered the iniquity of racism much in the manner I did. Mezzrow may have been a better reefer dealer than he was a jazz musician, but he understood both the music and the race that spawned it.

The saxophonist Bud Freeman, who knew Mezz in Chicago in the 1920s, and who was involved in Mezzrow's attempt to organize the first integrated band in New York in 1930—before John Hammond succeeded in the same endeavor—said, "Mezz was a very strong human being and knew things about the black people, their way of thinking and their music, that very few white people did." Indeed, when he was jailed on Riker's Island for two years for selling marijuana, Mezz insisted on being classified as a Negro inmate and considered it a great honor to be housed in the Negro section of the prison.

The fact that Mezzrow married a black woman and fathered a son by her may not seem all that remarkable in 1990, but to have done this more than a half-century ago and live in Harlem on what Jack Kerouac called "The Great American Negro Sidewalk of the World," was to spit directly into the face of the demon. Mezz translated the experience for young cats of the '40s and '50s like Kerouac, Allen Ginsberg, Neal Cassady and John Clellon Holmes, and inspired them not only in their lives but their writing, a valuable legacy.

I bought my copy of *Really the Blues* for a dime in a used bookshop on Clement Street in San Francisco in 1967. It's still worth reading, not just for the history but for the point of view. Perspective is a small animal crawling alone through the night jungle. Sooner or later, though, as Mezz knew, it must go to the stream, lower its head and drink, just like all the other animals.

Barry Gifford
Berkeley, 1990

Barry Gifford, who was born in Chicago and worked as a musician, is the author of the novels *Wild at Heart, Port Tropique* and *Landscape with Traveler*, among many other books. He is also co-author, with Lawrence Lee, of *Jack's Book: An Oral Biography of Jack Kerouac.*

Book 1 (1899–1923)

A Nothin'
But a Child

When I was a nothin' but a child,
When I was a nothin' but a child,
All you men tried to drive me wild. . . .

Bessie Smith's Reckless Blues

1

DON'T CRY, MA

Music school? Are you kidding? I learned to play the sax in Pontiac Reformatory.

Pontiac was called "The School" on account of the kids who were sent there. I've been to a mess of schools like that—ones you won't find on the approved list of any Parent-Teacher Association. Guess I learned more tricks there than a spider monkey does on a trapeze. Took my public-school training in three jails and a plenty of pool-rooms, went to college in a gang of tea-pads, earned my Ph.D. in more creep joints and speakeasies and dancehalls than the law allows. Pontiac was just a kindergarten to me.

Pontiac was thirty years ago. I'm forty-six now and in pretty good shape, except for a little gas on the stomach and a slight neurosis before coffee in the morning. What they piled into this knowledge-box of mine hasn't brought me down any. I still get my kicks out of the music I picked up in that reform school; it's been a primer and catechism and Bible to me, all rolled up in one.

More than once I strayed off from the music and did my share of evil, and served my time. Other times the opium had me so strong it turned me every way but loose—then I packed away the sax and the clarinet and cut right out of this world. Messy. But I always crawled out of the fog and latched on to my horns and began to blow again. I always came back to the music. I was cut out to be a jazzman the way the righteous are chosen for the church.

I've been in the stir and I've had my miseries, but all in all life's been good to me. I fly right now. The other cats from the corner of Division and Western didn't do so good. Bow Gistensohn shot it out with his best pal in a gang war and wound up in the morgue. Mitter Foley, who gave it to Bow, was laid to rest on a slab too. As for Emil Burbacher, he messed with the law some kind of way and got twenty years in Joliet. Those boys didn't live healthy.

I did all right, considering. In spite of jail and drugs and bad times my skin's still in one piece. Today I've got my good friends all over the world, from Lenox Avenue and Sugar Hill to Java and the South Seas. I used to walk in the shade but I'm on that sunny side now. When I get off on my horn the joint still jumps, and that's a good feeling. Old Lady Fortune sure laid it on me when she handed me that tinny old sax in Pontiac jailhouse.

They taught me the blues in Pontiac—I mean the blues, blues that I felt from my head to my shoes, really the blues. And it was in Pontiac that I dug that Jim Crow man in person, a mother-feryer that would cut your throat for looking. We marched in from the mess hall in two lines, and the colored boys lockstepped into one side of the cell block and we lockstepped into the other, and Jim Crow had the block, parading all around us, grinning like a polecat. I saw my first race riot there, out in the prison yard. It left me so shaky I almost blew my top and got sicker than a hog with the colic. Jim Crow just wouldn't get out of my face.

But out in Pontiac I got my first chance to play in a real man-size band, with jam-up instruments, and it was a mixed band at that, Negroes and whites side by side busting their conks. During those months I got me a solid dose of the colored man's gift for keeping the life and the spirit in him while he tells of his troubles in music. I heard the blues for the first time, sung in low moanful chants morning, noon and night. The colored boys sang them in their cells and they sang them out in the yard, where the work gangs massaged the coal piles.

I've played the music in a lot of places these last thirty years, from Al Capone's roadhouses to swing joints along 52nd Street in New York, Paris nightclubs, Harvard University, dicty Washington embassies and Park Avenue salons, not to mention all the barrel-house dives. It's the same music I learned in Pontiac. The idiom's still with me. That's what I'm going to tell about in this book.

Poppa, have you got any idea how a man took to jazz in the early days? Do you know how he spent years watching the droopy chicks in cathouses, listening to his cellmates moaning low behind the bars, digging the riffs the wheels were knocking out when he rode the rods—and then all of a sudden picked up a horn and began to tell the whole story in music? I'm going to explain about that. And about how he fought across the no-man's-land between the races, outing Jim Crow as he went, to get where he had to go. And how it felt when he got there. I'll tell about that too, especially that. Listen hard, now. This is a story that happened in the U. S. of A.

I was born on a windy night in 1899, along with the Twentieth Century. . . .

Don't get the idea I was born a criminal. I wasn't one of these raggedy slum kids who have to use a sewer grating for a teething ring. Nothing like that. My family was as respectable as Sunday morning, loaded with doctors, lawyers, dentists and pharmacists, and they all worked hard to make a solid citizen out of me. They almost did it, too. The law didn't catch up with me until I was sixteen years old.

The streets of Chicago's Northwest Side were like a magnet to me; all the honey in a beehive couldn't keep us kids indoors. There was something in the air that whispered of big doings you wouldn't want to miss. The sidewalks were always jammed, big gamblers and racketeers, dressed sharp as a tack, strutted by with their diamond stickpins, chicks you heard stories about would tip up and down the avenue real cool, the cops toured the neighborhood in big Cadillacs filled with shotguns. Anything and everything could happen on the Northwest Side—and usually did.

Our gang made its headquarters at "The Corner," the intersection of Division and Western Avenues, after Emil Glick opened his poolroom there. We used to do crazy things together. We had a yen, every time we got away from home and school, to strut and act biggity and shoot the works, live our whole lives out before the sun went down. We picked fights and robbed candy stores. We sat around a fire on a vacant lot until all hours, roasting pota-

5

toes and giving mouth-organ concerts to stray cats and dogs. Sometimes we'd hop a freightcar to St. Louis or Cape Girardeau, Mo., for a poor man's Cook's Tour. When we'd come down the street the girls would tear out for the other side—we were known to be the wildest gang this side of hell. In school we chewed tobacco and snuff, using the inkwells in our desks for cuspidors. Most of us stole .22 rifles or .38 bulldog revolvers from our fathers and roamed through the streets and alleys like desperados, loud-checked caps with three-inch visors pulled down over our eyes. We got our sport by taking potshots at sparrows and the glass insulators on telephone poles. We came on like Jesse James.

It took just a whispered "kike" or "Jew bastard" from a member of some rival Polish or Irish gang, and fists were flying between us. One time in Humboldt Park Leo "Bow" Gistensohn, our leader, didn't like the way a cop down by the lake called him "sheeny." The next thing we knew Bow had him in a bear-hug, swinging him off the ground. The cop yanked his .38 out and let Bow have it in the stomach, but Bow didn't even loose his grip. With that bullet in him and blood spurting out like water from a faucet, he lifted that two-hundred-pound cop clear over his head and heaved him in the lake. They took the bullet out of him and he lived, just to spite that cop, I guess.

At fifteen I was all jammed up full of energy, restless as a Mexican jumping bean. Something was all puffed up in me, but I couldn't dig what it was or give it a name. All the sights and sounds of the Northwest Side, the balalaika chords my father used to strum, the tunes we blew on our mouth organs, the gang fights and the poolrooms, the gats we packed in our hip pockets and aimed at each other for fun, Bow Gistensohn and Murph Steinberg and Emil Burbacher and the colored boy Sullivan, the squealing girls—they were all jumbled up in my head. I went around humming and whistling all the time, trying to straighten out all this jumble. When we hung out at The Corner, I'd keep working my fingers like I was playing the piano or the balalaika or maybe a sax, anything that would make the right patterns of sounds when you worked over it hard with plenty of feeling. Sometimes I patted the pavement with my foot, or beat the top of a garbage can with a couple of sticks, making time the way I'd seen Sullivan do when the spirit hit him. It got me so bad most of the time I couldn't sit still. I felt like I wanted to jump out of my skin, hop off into space on a C. & A. locomotive, anything but stay put.

I wasn't much interested in girls yet, but girls wouldn't have helped. It was a lot more than a mere sex flash that kept me all keyed up. I was maneuvering for a new language that would make me shout out loud and romp on to glory. What I needed was the vocabulary. I was feeling my way to music like a baby fights its way into talk.

Music was my kind of talk. I didn't get that straight before Pontiac, but my instincts were on the right track.

What landed me in the reformatory was a big shiny Studebaker touring car. Sammy "O'Brien" rolled up to The Corner in this job one afternoon and asked me to go riding with him.

We called this kid O'Brien because his beak was so big and hooked it kept the sun out of his face and got caught on clothes lines. "Sammy," we used to say to him, "if we had your nose full of nickels we'd be rich." Sammy bummed his way from the ghetto on New York's Lower East Side and hung around the poolroom doing odd jobs and camping on the pool tables at night. He was in the wrong pew behind the wheel of that Studebaker, sporting all around town.

In those days, when automobiles were still a novelty, we got a big kick out of joyriding in somebody else's car. We knew every make of car on the road, and we knew that cars didn't have locks but only needed standard magneto keys to turn on the current. Every one of us had his pockets stuffed with a collection of popular keys—Bosch, Remy and Delco. We could take Mr. Anybody's car any time we had a mind to.

While we were touring around I asked Sammy how come he was driving this car and he said he was driving for some bigshot doctor, but later he confessed that Emil Burbacher had taken the car from in front of a church. That soft seat got hard to me before the words were out of his mouth. When the car stalled in front of a gang of cops waiting for a streetcar, I felt that hardwood jail bench under me, and creosote filled the air. Sammy took one look at the cops and flew, leaving me to hold the bag.

"Whose car is this, son?" one of the cops asked. I told him it was mine. "Sure it is," he said. "That's why I've got the number listed here as a stolen car."

"Well, you see, sir, I can tell you about that," I said real quick. "Dad took the car to church this morning and I had a date with my girl this afternoon so, while he was in church, I just took it and went on my date. I just this minute left my girl's house and I'm on my way home now."

The cop wasn't in a believing mood. He thought that even so, we ought to drop over to the station house, just to check my story. I handled that car as though the tires were soapbubbles, because I didn't want him to guess I never drove before in my life.

I didn't want no part of jail; I kept wondering how the hell I was going to get out of this mess. Then I got a brainstorm. This car was so open, all you had to do was put one foot out and you were running. I figured that if I swung up over the curbstone, the cop naturally would have to grab for the wheel instead of his gun and I could run. I worked it all out, with my heart pounding so loud I couldn't even hear the motor. When I had the plan all set in my mind, I waited for just the right spot, then swerved hard and ran up on the sidewalk—to find myself right outside the station house, knee-deep in brass buttons.

Inside, the sergeant asked what my name was, and I said, "Milton Mezzrow." A minute later he was talking to the license bureau on the phone and writing on a slip of paper. By stretching my neck I could read the words: "Edward Mikelson, 2715 Logan Blvd., no phone." The sergeant asked sarcastically for my name again.

"Sir, now I'm really going to tell you the truth," I said, putting on the weeps as though I figured the game was up. "My name is Milton Mikelson and I live at 2715 Logan Boulevard. I didn't want to tell you that before because I was afraid my father might whip me for getting into trouble and I'd never get the car again, so I lied about my name. Please leave me go home and I promise you I'll never do it again."

The sergeant looked up at the cop, then back at the slip of paper on his desk. "That's the name, all right," he said. "I guess the kid's O.K. Listen, you, get the hell out of here and don't pull any more stunts on your father or we'll lock you up the next time."

"Thank you, sir," I said, with gratitude that came straight from the heart, "yes, sir, thanks a million." I cut out from that place every way but slow, and was just climbing into the Studebaker when I heard something that made my stomach drop down to my socks. Somebody called me by my right name.

"Hey, Mezzrow, what you doing in this part of town?" It was a lieutenant I knew from my neighborhood. He came over with a big smile, glad to see me getting so prosperous. Right there on the station-house steps was the cop who had brought me in.

"What's that name, Lieutenant?" the cop said. I began to smell that creosote again.

"Mezzrow," the lieutenant said. "Why, he's from my old neighborhood. Knew him years ago when I pounded the beat on Division Street."

"We-ell," the cop said, grabbing me by the neck. "We'll put *this* bird back in the cage." He yanked me out of the car and kicked me so hard with his bulldog toe, I flew right into the precinct house. Five minutes later I was booked and locked up with a couple of drunks.

My education began right then and there. In the county jail, where they put me to wait for my trial, I shared a cell with a German named Schneider who said he was an alien prisoner of war. He had worked for the Humboldt Safe Company before his arrest, and he took a shine to me. In one week flat, just to pass the time, he taught me all the secrets of safecracking and the art of making skeleton keys to fit any type of lock. That's one business I never did find time to go into, but those lessons came in handy later, when I was always losing my keys to apartment and hotel rooms.

At my trial there was a long discussion between the judge and my uncle, who brought his lawyer to court to represent me. He sure did some representing. The three of them went into a huddle and decided it would be good for me to get a dose of reformatory medicine. A few days later I was on the train, bound for The School at Pontiac.

I wasn't as lonely as I thought I was going to be. With our gang on the train, handcuffed right to me, was Emil Burbacher. He had stolen a car, he told me, and was sentenced to the reformatory for it. Bow and Murph, I found out, were already enrolled as star pupils in The School for breaking into a candy store and trying to steal some mouth organs. It wasn't like going to jail at all. Somebody just picked up the corner of Division and Western and moved it out to Pontiac, gang and all; the only things left behind were Emil Glick's pool tables and a pair of dice.

After the fingerprinting routine and short-arm inspection at Pontiac, we were given numbers and sent to the barber shop, where I got my first lesson in jailbird humor. When it came my turn they sat me in the chair and asked me how I wanted my hair cut. "Straight down in the back," I said, "and no clippers on the side." "Oh, no," the barber said, "we never do that." He went to work with his comb and shears while I huddled there kind of bewildered, wondering how I'd find Murph and Bow. All of a sudden I felt a pair of clippers starting at the nape of my neck and chugging like a locomotive straight over to my forehead. The way that barber ploughed over my head, it's a wonder he missed my eyebrows. "Oh, oh," one of the inmates working around the shop said sympathetically, "now ain't that too bad, and him with such nice pretty hair and everything." This was a great joke to the keeper, but not to me. "Well," the keeper said, "you might as well take it all off now. We don't want him looking like that around here." The barber took his advice. When he got finished a fly would slip and break his neck where my hair used to be.

I had no trouble looking up my pals. Word buzzed through the grapevine about the new "fish," and it didn't take a day before one of the "politicians" (that was what we called the trustees) slipped me a folded piece of toilet paper. It was a note from Murph. "I'm in the band," he wrote. "Try and make it."

At my interview a few days later I practically convinced the officials that I was the impresario of the Chicago Opera, picked up by mistake. They took me at my word and assigned me to the cell block that housed the band members. Here I saw Murph again. He was the bugler for the block, waking us with reveille every morning and sending us to bed with taps every night.

In the band room I met Professor Scott, a friendly sort of man with a pleasant face and a nice, easygoing manner about him. He started to warm up as soon as he heard I had studied the piano and could read music.

"I used to play solo trombone in Arthur Pryor's band," he told me. "Look, Milton, we've got a pretty good band here, but there are two instruments we miss a whole lot because the boys don't want to study them, and they're the flute and the piccolo. Now, then. You asked me could you learn to play the saxophone, so I'll make a deal with you. You learn the flute and I'll teach you the sax too. It won't be hard because the fingering's about the same on both."

I sweated over that flute like it was an overgrown tuba, and after I learned my daily exercises I'd shoot for the alto sax. I guess I blew enough wind into those two instruments to fill the Graf Zeppelin. The clarinets were all assigned to other inmates, but they didn't hold my interest just yet.

The band was mixed. I liked two of the colored boys especially, one named Yellow who played cornet and another, King, who played the alto horn. They were the boys who started our jam sessions at Pontiac, the first ones I ever played in. Man, it was wonderful to see the look in Murph's eye when Yellow was blowing up a breeze on the cornet. It hit me just as hard. He played from the side of his mouth, with his left cheek puffed out like a balloon, and when he played the blues he really knocked us out. After we got friendly he told me about the bands he had played with in circuses all through the South, even though he couldn't read a note of music.

After band rehearsal Murph, Yellow and I would get in a corner with a bass player and King on the alto horn and start to jam, forgetting all the written music, just letting our instincts take over. The blues came so natural to Murph and me, and we began to play them so good, that the Professor couldn't stay in his office when he heard us. Pretty soon he was giving us special attention.

Bow never got to make the band; he was stuck in the yard gang on account of his size and strength. Just across the railroad tracks that ran alongside the band room was the powerhouse, and here the coal cars would pull up to be unloaded. It would really send you to watch the yard gang unload those cars. The best unloading team was made up of three guys who commanded a lot of respect in the prison, a colored boy named Georgia, a white boy named Joe Kelly, and the great Bow himself. They held the record for getting a car cleaned out, and they liked for us to play the blues in a medium tempo to keep time with their shovels. We accompanied them for hours at a time, playing the blues slow and easy while they kept heaving and chanting out loud. Their shovels slid into the coal pile with a long *sssshhhh* sound, and every time the boys pulled them out they grunted "Ho." All day long they went on like that: "Sssshhhh. . . . *Ho.* . . . Sssshhhh. . . . *Ho.* . . ."

Many a time, when we were blowing away on the blues, Professor Scott would break out his trombone and join in. What a beautiful tone that cat had. Listening to Murph trying to imitate Yellow's half-valve inflections and slurs, he got an idea. One day he showed up in the band room with a slide cornet, something that amazed us all because we'd never seen anything like it before. Murph couldn't catch on to Yellow's technique, and the Professor thought he might get those slurs and inflections better if he used the slide, because it gives you quarter tones and certain notes a little sharp, just the way you need them in the blues. The Professor could see how our eyes gleamed when Yellow played those beautiful phrases of his, and his paternal instinct began to jump. Yellow would make up a phrase and then give us some notes to play like an organ background, calling out "Hey, you make this."

That boy was really a bitch, even though he was never taught to play music. He had more music in him than Heinz has pickles.

One morning, all excited, the Professor called us into his private office, where he had a victrola standing in the corner. "Where you git that, Professor?" Yellow said, his face all lit up. The Professor put his finger to his lips to shut us up and put a record on. The music we heard like to outed all of us. It was the *Livery Stable Blues* by the Original Dixieland Jazz Band, now a real collectors' item. Man, what a thrill I got out of Larry Shield's clarinet weaving through the music, and the subtle trumpet that sounded just a little like Yellow's. It gave us the courage of our convictions to hear that kind of playing from a record—if you're on a record, we figured, you must be great, and here was a guy who didn't even play as much horn as Yellow, right there on the wax. We spent a gang of mornings after that trying to learn the number, with Professor Scott jotting down the parts for the different instruments, but we never did get it straight.

Night after night we'd lie on the corn-husk mattresses in our cells, listening to the blues drifting over from the Negro side of the block. I would be reading or just lying in my bunk, eyeballing the whitewashed ceiling, when somebody would start chanting a weary melody over and over until the whole block was drugg. The blues would hit some colored boy and out of a clear sky he'd begin to sing them:

> *Ooooohhhhh, ain't gonna do it no mo-o,*
> *Ooooohhhhh, ain't gonna do it no mo-o,*
> *If I hadn't drunk so much whisky*
> *Wouldn't be layin' here on this hard flo'.*

This would get to one of the other cats, and he'd yell, "Sing 'em, brother, sing 'em," trying to take some weight off himself. Then the first one, relieved of his burden because somebody has heard him, as though the Lord had heeded his prayer, answers back with a kind of playful resentment—he'd been admitting he had the blues but he's coming out of it now and can smile a little. So

13

he comes back with, "You may make it, brother, but you'll never be the same." And now some third guy, who'd been listening to this half-sad, half-playful talking back and forth, would feel the same urge and chime in, "You might get better, poppa, but you'll never get well."

Those chants and rhythmic calls always struck a gong in me. The tonal inflections and the story they told, always blending together like the colors in an artist's picture, the way the syllables were always placed right, the changes in the words to fit the music—this all hit me like a millennium would hit a philosopher. Those few simple riffs opened my eyes to the Negro's philosophy more than any fat sociology textbook ever could. They cheered me up right away and made me feel wonderful towards those guys. Many a time I was laid out there with the blues heavy on my chest, when somebody would begin to sing 'em and the weight would be lifted. Those were a people who really knew what to do about the blues.

The white man is a spoiled child, and when he gets the blues he goes neurotic. But the Negro never had anything before and never expects anything after, so when the blues get him he comes out smiling and without any evil feeling. "Oh, well," he says, "Lord, I'm satisfied. All I wants to do is to grow collard greens in my back yard and eat 'em." The white man can't feel that way, usually. When he's brought down he gets ugly, works himself up into a fighting mood and comes out nasty. He's got the idea that because he feels bad somebody's done him wrong, and he means to take it out on somebody. The colored man, like as not, can toss it off with a laugh and a mournful, but not too mournful, song about it. It's easy to say he's shiftless and happy-go-lucky and just doesn't give a damn. That's how a lot of white people explain away this quality in the Negro, but that's not the real story. The colored man doesn't often get sullen and tight-lipped and evil because his philosophy goes deeper and he thinks straight. Maybe he hasn't got all the hyped-up words and theories to explain how he thinks. That's all right. He knows. He tells about it in his music. You'll find the answer there, if you know what to look for.

In Pontiac I learned something important—that there aren't many people in the world with as much sensitivity and plain human respect for a guy as the Negroes. I'd be stepping along in the line, feeling low and lonesome, and all of a sudden one of the boys in the colored line, Yellow or King or maybe somebody I didn't even know, would call out, "Hey, boy, whatcha know," and smile, and I'd feel good all over. I never found many white men with that kind of right instinct and plain friendly feeling that hits you at the psychological moment like a tonic. The message you get from just a couple of ordinary words and the smile in a man's eyes—that's what saved me many a time from going to the shady side of the street in that jailhouse. I had plenty to thank those colored boys for. They not only taught me their fine music; they made me feel good.

Jim Crow made himself plenty scarce around the band room and the work gang, but he was standing close by, biding his time. When he finally showed himself he came on like a funky rat.

On Saturday afternoons and Sundays we were allowed in the yard for some ball playing and a much needed breath of air. The yard was divided into two factions—the colored and white boys who hung out together, and the Southern white boys who were always throwing sneers at us when we passed. Mitter Foley, Joe Kelly, Johnny Fredricks, Georgia, Big Six, Yellow and Bow were the leaders on our side. The other gang was led by some mean, stringy guys who always looked hard and never cracked a friendly smile. They all had names like Texas and Tennessee, as though they were clippings from some geography-book map instead of flesh-and-blood human beings.

The real trouble between the two gangs was caused by the fact that Big Six, a colored boy, had a white "punk." A punk, if you want it in plain English, is a boy with smooth skin who takes the place of a woman in a jailbird's love life. I'm not going to apologize for Big Six; I'm just saying that the Southern boys had their punks too, plenty of them, but they resented a Negro doing the same things they did with a white boy. It was the same evil that white

Southerners have about a Negro man and a white woman. Those Southern boys meant to draw the color line around their punks too.

One afternoon, when Big Six was walking around the yard with his punk by his side, the Southern boys ganged up on him and began to cuss him out. That's how it started. At first it was just another fist fight, but in a couple of minutes every cat in the yard was at it in a free-for-all race riot. The guards began to blow whistles, shoot their revolvers in the air; a lot of knives came into sight before it was over, and they were put to use. When the riot was finally put down a lot of cats were cut up like stuck hogs and others had broken arms, bloody noses and gimpy legs. Our privileges were taken away for a long time and the silent system took over. The ringleaders were put in solitary.

Right after the fight I landed in the hospital with dysentery and I almost checked out. It wasn't just the germs that made me so sick—my nervous system was so upset that for a while they thought I wouldn't come out of it. All the time I was stretched out on the infirmary cot I kept looking at the blank walls and seeing the mean, murdering faces of those Southern peckerwoods when they went after Big Six and the others with their knives. It couldn't have been worse if they'd come after me. I felt so close to those Negroes, it was just like I'd seen a gang attack on my own family.

I began to realize right there what the Civil War really meant. I'd been in plenty of tough fights back in Chicago, but never anything as bad as this one. The Tennessees and Texases wanted to *kill* every Negro they could lay their mitts on—you could see it in their faces. I'd never seen such murdering hate before.

When I got better I began to talk with Yellow and King in the band room. After what they told me I have never wanted to cross the Mason-Dixon line and almost never have, except for one date in Baltimore that I played with my eyes shut.

"Man," Yellow said, "they'd cut your nuts out for lookin', where those motherferyers come from." King was a more dignified and scholarly kind of guy. All he said was, "Milton, in my home town I couldn't even walk down the street less'n I got off in the gutter to let some white man pass." When I told him about my buddy

Sullivan back in Chicago, the colored boy who hung out with us all the time and played catch on our ball team, his eyes opened wide and a wonderful happy expression spread over his face. He gave me the kind of look an artist might give you when he never dreams you'll understand his painting and then you dig everything in it, down to the last brush-stroke. King and I understood each other.

While I was in the hospital my mother came to visit me. She was crying when she came in with Judge Graves, the warden.

"Don't cry, Ma," I said. "You must not understand or you wouldn't be crying like that. This is a wonderful place and I'm learning to play the flute and piccolo and saxophone and I like it here. They treat us swell, and besides, Murph, Bow and Emil are here, so I'm not lonesome. I only spoiled my stomach and I'll be all right." She left feeling a lot better.

I had an indeterminate sentence of one to ten years. When I came up before the parole board to have my time set they made it one year. Judge Graves said, "Milton, do you know why you got such a light sentence? It's because of the way you acted toward your mother when she visited you."

On a cold February day in 1918 they gave me a prison-made suit (it cost me ten sacks of Bull Durham to keep the tailors from making one leg twice as long as the other), put a railroad coach ticket in my hand, and told me to go down to the Pontiac station and take a train to Chicago. That was one of the first coach tickets I ever owned. It almost seems as if I had to graduate from The School to stop riding rods, tops, blinds and boxcars.

Riding the cushions on my way home made me think of another train ride I once took with Murph and Bow. It was right after the sinking of the big excursion boat, *The Eastland*, when over eight hundred people were drowned off a downtown pier in the Chicago River. We bought up a stack of photos of the disaster and hopped a freight to St. Louis for a little adventure, fixing to pay our way by selling the pictures as we bummed around. When we hit Cape Girardeau, Mo., dirty from riding the rails and dark-complexioned to begin with, we fell into a lunch-counter to knock out some vittles. For a long time the waiter jigged us, while all the other customers kept gunning us with their eyes. Finally the owner came over to us and said, "Where the hell did you come from? We don't serve niggers in here." We were given the bum's rush to the sidewalk, our breadbaskets empty and our nerves jumping. In small towns we hit after that, whenever we saw a sign saying "Nigger don't let the sun shine on your head" we knew it meant us too, although we didn't know why.

That experience began to mean a lot to me when I thought it over on my way home from Pontiac. We were Jews, but in Cape Girardeau they had told us we were Negroes. Now, all of a sudden, I realized that I agreed with them. That's what I learned in Pontiac. The Southerners had called me a "nigger-lover" there. Solid. I not only loved those colored boys, but I was one of them—I felt closer to them than I felt to the whites, and I even got the same treatment they got. I remembered that when Sullivan visited our synagogue back in Chicago, the rabbi told him that Moses, King Solomon, and the Queen of Sheba were all colored, and maybe the whole world was once colored. This made me feel good because Sullivan was such a wonderful ball player. They were right for kicking me out of that beanery in Cape Girardeau. I belonged on the other side of the track.

By the time I reached home, I knew that I was going to spend all my time from then on sticking close to Negroes. They were my kind of people. And I was going to learn their music and play it for the rest of my days. I was going to be a musician, a Negro musician, hipping the world about the blues the way only Negroes can. I didn't know how the hell I was going to do it, but I was straight on what I had to do.

Most of my skullbusters got solved at The School. I went in there green but I came out chocolate brown.

2

Not Too Far Tangent

The First World War was jumping then, and one day on Michigan Boulevard I saw a big recruiting parade that would have made Benedict Arnold sign up. There must have been five hundred pieces in the Navy band that led the procession, blasting away on a Sousa march. The blare of the trumpets and the moans of the slide trombones got under my skin, and as soon as I spotted the saxophones I hit on a bright idea. That night I told my parents I was going to join the Navy—they'd teach me to play the sax real good and I'd keep far away from any stray bullets.

I dreamed about it all that night. Man, I could see myself in a sharp uniform, strutting down the main drag blowing my sax while the chicks lined up along the curb, giving me the eye all the way. The enemy was nowhere to be seen.

Bright and early the next morning I shot down to the recruiting station to become a musician at the government's expense. But when I took my physical the doctor put his stethoscope to my chest and shook his head. I expected the man to show up any minute with his tape measure to outfit me with a wooden kimono. "You'll have to go home, son," the doc said. "You've got a slight murmur in your heart."

That was a bringdown. My mother almost fainted when I showed up on the doorstep without even a middy blouse, but she made a quick recovery and cooked up a big pot of borscht for her returning hero. From the reception she gave me you would have thought I'd come home from the wars with the Kaiser in my vest pocket.

That night I tore out for The Corner, to take up my old civilian post in the poolroom.

At first I just made myself useful around Emil Glick's place, helping to rack up the balls and run the chuck-luck game, but before long I was promoted. You see, when prohibition came on every piss-ant and his brother suddenly fell into big money, and a romping crap game took over on our billiard table every night. I was made the lookout man and told to stick around out front with my eyes peeled for any signs of John Law. When a paddy showed himself I would tap on the window with a key, and in five seconds a billiard tournament was going full blast, with spectators lined up around the table digging all the fine points of each player. I got two dollars an hour, plus a bust in the jaw from the law every now and then.

Thousand-dollar bills were passed around like stage money every night at Glick's place; the bank was known to be made up of no less than $25,000. A lot of the guys who hung around were squares who worked for their gold, more gamblers than gangsters, so there weren't any shootings or killings around our corner. They were Jewish expressmen, cutters in the garment trade, cab drivers —easygoing guys who spent half their lives playing klabiasch, pinochle, and tarok, a funny game that was played with thick Hungarian pasteboards the size of postcards. Once these guys got hip to themselves and went into the bootlegging game, big money started to show up. In the crowd almost any night you could find such bigtime gamblers as Red Tell, Big Izzy, Nick the Greek, Joe Tuckman, Cincy Norton, Sam Cohen, George Turner, and Bon Bons. One of these guys made the front page when he ran seven bucks up to $43,000 one night and bought the Boulevard Hotel on South Michigan Boulevard. A few weeks later he hit the headlines again, this time after a police raid. That hotel turned out to be a dirty whorehouse under his auspices.

By this time Bow and Emil Burbacher were sprung from The School and showed up on The Corner again. Murph had joined a circus band after his release and was barnstorming around the country some place. One night Bow came up with a story about some barrels of whisky he'd spotted in the cellar of a poolroom, just a block away. His problem was a lock on the basement door he couldn't force open. I went along with him and Emil just to show off what I'd learned about picking locks from old Schneider in the county jail. I opened the lock with a buttonhook, and Bow carried a fifty-gallon barrel out to a cab all by himself. At the Bucket of Blood, a café on Madison Street, we sold the juice for close to $200.

About that time Sid Barry blew in from New York and went into partnership with Emil Glick. That cat was a born gambler and get-rich-quick operator—he could locate gold like a good hustling chick. He got himself a wholesale drug license, because wholesale druggists were the only ones allowed to handle liquor. The best bonded bourbon whisky sold for $23 a case to the druggist, but the price was jumped to $123 for a bootlegger or saloonkeeper. Nobody argued about price then because any case of booze could be run up to a barrel by mixing in alcohol and distilled water, plus a little burnt sugar.

Once Sid got a shipment of a hundred cases of booze on the legit, and that's when he showed up as nervous as some jello-pudding. There was a government record of those cases, but Sid would sooner have his throat cut than push them at legit prices to the drugstores. He came running into the poolroom one night and said, "Come on, you guys, I want you to beat me up, make a cripple out of me, tear my clothes off and make my nose bleed." The gang took him at his word: they took turns trying to crack his jaw, laid black eyes on him, and put knots in his head with a billiard cue. Then Sid shimmied to his feet, thanked his friends, and wobbled down to the police station to squawk about how some hoodlums gave him the works and hijacked all his whisky. After that he sold the stuff at bootleg prices. For a busted smeller, a couple of shiners, and a few creases in the knowledge-box he made himself ten grand.

I got my kicks out of rubbing elbows with all those bigtime gamblers and muscle men, and the easy money didn't run me away. But I didn't want to go too far tangent—I kept looking for my kind of music in all the joints we hit in our cruising around. That's just where I finally found it.

Almost every night after the poolroom closed we'd load up a cab and head for the Roamer Inn on 119th near Western, a famous whorehouse that belonged to Al Capone's syndicate. We were always sharp, with our expensive Hannan or Johnson-&-Murphy shoes and our "pussywillow" silk shirts from Capper-&-Capper—one-inch candy stripes were all the go then, and those shirts made us look like a gang of barber poles topped with slickum. Even before I was in the money I togged like a fashion plate, so I could run with the hip cats who hung around the poolroom. I was always as ready as they were, although sometimes I never had a blip in my poke.

The Roamer Inn was like a model of all the canhouses I ever saw around Chicago, the granddaddy of them all. There was a big front room with a long bar on one side and quarter slot machines lined up along the wall. In back there was a larger room, with benches running all around the walls but no tables. The girls sat there while the johns (customers) moped around giving them the once-over. Those girls were always competing with each other: one would come up to you, switching her hips like a young duck, and whisper in your ear, "Want to go to bed, dear, I'll show you a good time, honey, I'm French," and a minute later another one would ease along and say coyly, "Baby, don't you want a straight girl for a change?" They were like two rival sororities; they hung out in separate cliques and threw dirty looks at each other.

The girls we knew were all on the dogwatch, from four to twelve in the morning. It used to tickle me to see how they dolled themselves up for the trade. They paraded around in teddies or gingham baby rompers with big bows in the back, high-heel shoes, pretty silk hair ribbons twice as big as their heads, and rouge an inch thick all over their kissers. When a john had eyeballed the parade and made his choice he would follow her upstairs, where the landlady sat at a little desk in the hall. This landlady would hand out a metal check and a towel to the girl, while the customer forked over two bucks. Then the girl was assigned a room number. All night long you could hear the landlady calling out in a bored voice, like a combination strawboss and timekeeper, "*All* right, Number Eight, *all* right, Number Ten—somebody's waiting, don't take all night." She ran that joint with a stopwatch.

The girls explained to me that they got eighty cents a trick, one payment for each metal check—"turning a trick" was how they described one session with a john. Twenty cents went for protection, and the other dollar belonged to the house. But the girls didn't keep their eighty cents. That fee went to the pimps, or macs, who kept wandering around downstairs. The girls used to fight over their macs. "That coffee-an' mac you got," a French girl would crack to a straight one, and then it was on—hair came out by the handful, some bleached and some unbleached.

Those girls worked hard—some of them didn't even knock off for a single night, hiding their condition with tricks I won't go into now. One girl I met, the daughter of a Baptist minister from Valparaiso, Indiana, had been working for three solid months. I asked her how come and she said in a quiet way, "My man borrowed a thousand bucks from the syndicate and I'm gonna stay here until I work it out." When you were in the red with them people it wasn't healthy to think about vacations, with or without pay.

I couldn't see going upstairs until I met Marcelle. She was a tall redhead, with a shape that would make you jump for joy and a reputation as the best French girl in the place. Maybe I better explain about something here—I was really kind of timid and ashamed on my first visits to the Inn, but I never showed it. In fact, the smooth, know-it-all act I put on was so strong that a lot of the girls took me for a bigtime pimp. Marcelle must have figured me for a fly cat too, and her curiosity was aroused.

The johns lined up for Marcelle like it was payday. I didn't go upstairs with her much, but we used to smile at each other and there was a real close feeling between us. The way we hit it off began to be noticed. One night the bartender (he must have took me for a mac too) called me over and whispered, "I'd lay off if

I was you, bud—that's Al Capone's girl." I used to see Scarface around there and jawblock with him sometimes. He was sharp, young and ready in those days, with a couple of trigger men always trailing along at his elbows. He was friendly enough, and that was how I wanted him to keep on feeling.

My answer to that bartender was simple and straight. I didn't like to see a nice guy like that so upset. I stopped going there.

But Marcelle wouldn't give up just like that. It didn't take her long to dig where I hung out. One night a yellow cab pulled up in front of the poolroom and word was sent in to me that a lady was waiting outside. That made my vanity jump, but when I hit the curb and saw it was Marcelle my nerves didn't feel like they were taking any rest cure either. "Hey look, baby," I said, "I know you're Capone's old lady—uh, uh, I ain't coming on this tab." She pouted, kind of brought down because I didn't rush off and shoot Scarface full of holes so I could move in.

It wasn't all fear or bashfulness that kept me from really going after Marcelle. As much as I liked her, I couldn't often bring myself to follow her upstairs. Everything was too mechanical that way, like playing a two-dollar shot machine—you invest heavy but you come out light. Maybe I was too sensitive, I don't know. Anyhow, I always felt that it was just like chewing a steak in tempo with a metronome. I didn't like to do my loving on schedule, with one eye closed and the other on the clock. I like both my eyes closed.

There was another reason I stopped going to the Roamer Inn: they didn't have any music there. But pretty soon I caught up with another syndicate house at 119th and Wood, where I found what I was looking for. They had a Creole jazz band there, straight from the bayou, and I used to sit by the piano all night long, listening to them knock out the blues. I never went upstairs once in that place. Women were a dime a dozen, but where could you find a good New Orleans jazz band?

It was George Turner, the gambler, who steered me to the South Side and my millennium. One night, when we were drinking in a saloon after a crap game, George buzzed the bartender and asked for the key to the piano in the back room. I didn't pay him much mind when he disappeared. In those days every beer joint had a player piano with that mandolin effect, sometimes with drums and cymbals that played automatically as the roll wound around. I thought George was going to knock out some of the usual corn.

But a minute later I was sprinting for the back room. George had unlocked the piano and was playing the blues as though he was born in the gallion. Where did he ever learn this music? He must have been in jail, I thought. There didn't seem to be any other place where a man could latch on to that kind of music.

I stood by that beat-up old tinklebox in a hypnotic state, like a bird charmed by a snake. This music gave me a mental orgasm—I couldn't have felt closer to this man if he'd been my own father. When he was finished I asked him did he know the *Sweet Baby Blues*. He was so tickled to find that I went for the blues, he almost fell off the piano stool. "No kidding, Milton, do you like this music?" he said. "Come on, I'm going to take you where you'll really hear a lot of it." Five of us piled into a cab and cut out for the colored district on the South Side.

The first place we dug was the De Luxe Café at 35th and State, above the saloon and billiard parlor of the same name. We had to wait outside in line because there was standing room only, but finally the headwaiter at the top of the stairs snapped his fingers and the doorman let us in. As we took our seats near the bandstand, a light-skinned red-headed girl was circling around the dance floor wrapping up a song that went like this: "It takes a long, tall, brown-skin gal to make a preacher lay his Bible down." The way she explained it, I could see exactly what bothered that preacher. Every time she shouted the word *lo-ong*, the gal she was singing about stretched another foot. Right after that she sang another lowdown blues:

> *Leave me be your side track, poppa,*
> *Till your main line comes,*
> *Leave me be your side track, poppa,*

Till your main line comes,
I can do better switchin'
Than your main line ever done.

After listening to one chorus of that number I decided that girl could run my locomotive down her side track any old time.

The next blues she went to work on had the same kind of down-to-earth, simple story in it that always excited me so much. Even then the popular songs of the day were so full of sentimental foolishness, they made you feel the whole goddamned world was turned into a mess of love-sick calves. And when you tried to cut loose from this fog of romantic trash by running to the white cafés, you found vocalists there who acted like they were on leave from a whorehouse. The way the white singers tried to deliver their message of sex was tough and brutal and called for two bucks on the line. Twinkle didn't come on with that jive. She sang:

Baby, see that spider climbin' on that wall,
Baby, see that spider climbin' on that wall,
He's goin' up there for to get his ashes hauled.

How many whites would ever think of making sex as downright simple and hygienic as getting your ashbin cleaned out?

The crowd went wild over Twinkle and she had to keep on giving encores, but when Alberta Hunter hit the floor singing "He may be your man but he comes to see me sometime," the house came down. Alberta kept working her way around the floor, stopping to sing a chorus at each table, so that by the time she was through she'd gone over the one song ten or fifteen times, giving it a new twist every time. "Sing it, you sweet cow!" some fellow shouted from the table next to ours. The chick that was with him capped this with "Yeah baby, he can't help it, it's the way you do it." Across the floor a stout brown-skinned woman yelled, "Aaawww, sing it baby," throwing her hands over her head and snapping her fingers on the offbeat. Alberta really sent that audience singing *Some Sweet Day*. Finally, for the last chorus, she got up on a small platform in front of the bandstand and did "her num-

26

ber." Every entertainer would wind up that way, doing a becoming little time step and break all her own.

What hit me about Twinkle, Alberta, and another fine singer in the place named Florence Mills, was their grace and their dignified, relaxed attitude. Florence, petite and demure, just stood at ease and sang like a humming bird. A lot of white vocalists, even some with the big name bands today, are either as stiff as a stuffed owl or else they go through more wringing and twisting than a shake dancer, doing grinds and bumps all over the place, throwing it around the way it should be thrown around in only one place, which isn't a public dancehall.

A good colored singer doesn't have to wrap her sex in a package and peddle it to the customers like a cootch dancer in a sideshow. She seldom goes in for the nympho kick—she can take it easy and be more genuine, because she isn't doing any high-pressure selling. The music really moves her, and she passes it on to the audience with the lazy way she handles her body. To me there's more natural suggestion in the snap of a colored singer's fingers than you get from all the acrobatic routines of these so-called "hot" singers.

The most action a solid Negro singer will give you is a subdued touch of the boogie, hardly moving anything closer to home than her index fingers. Most of the time she'll just stand still and concentrate on putting real meaning and feeling into the song itself. A woman who really knows how to sing and means it can make your love come down even if she's buried in a block of cement up to her neck—all she needs are healthy vocal cords and a soul, not a chassis with the seven-years'-itch. Most white singers made me feel their message was full of larceny, but when I heard these songbirds at the De Luxe I almost blew my top. Sex was all clean and simple and good, the way it came out of them.

You could see most of the celebrities of the day, colored and white, hanging around the De Luxe. Bill Robinson, the burlesque comedian Harry Steppe, comedian Benny Davis, Joe Frisco, Al Jolson, Sophie Tucker, Blossom Seeley, a lot of Ziegfeld Follies actors, famous colored teams like Moss and Fry and Williams and

Walker, Eva Tanguay, Eddie Cantor, who was then Bert Williams' protegé—all kinds of showpeople used to head for this place whenever they were in town. Word had spread through the Orpheum Circuit that a real New Orleans jazz band was playing there, and you had to fight your way in every night in the week.

That band really put me in a trance. It was the Original New Orleans Creole Jazz Band, led by clarinet-playing Lawrence Dewey (Duhé). With him were Sugar Johnnie and Freddie Keppard on cornet; Roy Palmer, trombone; Sidney Bechet, clarinet and curved soprano sax; Lil Hardin, piano; Tubby Hall, drums (substituting for his brother Minor, who had just been drafted); Jimmy Palao, violin; Bab Frank, piccolo; Wellman Braud, bass fiddle. This band really upset the town and paved the way for the rest of the New Orleans jazzmen in good old Chi.

The duets that Bechet and Dewey played on their clarinets left me breathless, and so did Bab Frank's exciting piccolo trills and improvised arpeggios that could be heard above all the rest of the band like little white mice scampering over the tops of the notes. Freddie Keppard fanned his horn with a battered old derby in a way that would astound the trumpeters of today. That was the first time I ever saw that done, and before he was through Freddie really broke it up. Before Harmon wah-wah mutes were even thought of, he was getting his glissandos and quarter-tones with a water glass and a beer bottle too. Lil Hardin always had a grin a mile wide as she bent over the keyboard—the way she came on with a steady four-four rhythm and the right inversions of chords helped rock the band. Braud was a showman with the bass, picking a tone round as a bell and slapping rhythm all the way through.

But it was Freddie's horn and Bechet's clarinet that really floored me. Freddie's cornet was powerful and to the point; the way he led the ensemble, breathing at the right breaks and carrying the lead all the time, there never was any letdown. He kept the band paced better than a jockey does a racehorse. Bechet's slurs and moans and his true conception of counterpoint harmony were wonderful. Later on he explained to me that his tonal inflections were suggested by the moo-cow and the barnyard.

Once in a while I noticed the couples who were jammed on the dance floor, all doing the bunny hug. Sweet nothings hit my ears like sounds from another world: "Perculate you filthy bitch," some sweet man yelled to his partner while the band played a slow drag, and a little later another cat called out to some chick on the other side of the hall, "Hey baby, where you been keepin' your beefsteak at?" (These phrases stuck with me so hard that when I got together my first band I named it "Milton Mezzrow and His Perculatin' Fools.") My mind kept telling me that this was where I really belonged. I had found my utopia and I began scheming to come back every night, including Sundays and holidays.

Pretty soon one o'clock rolled around, closing time. George Turner went over to the bandstand, with me trotting along at his heels. I began to talk with Bab Frank about piccolos, and found out he played the Albert system while I played the Boehm. Bechet showed me his curved soprano, which I handled like it was the Kohinoor diamond. I almost fell out when he invited me to come along with the musicians to the Royal Garden (later the Lincoln Garden), where they had their after-hours sessions.

I sat through that whole night listening to them playing music from Scott Joplin's *Red Book*, a collection of instrumental arrangements that revolutionized the whole jazz world. For the first time I heard all those great numbers that were spreading a spirit you never found in ragtime and regular band music, the real spirit of the colored musician—pieces like *Gold Dust, Skeleton Jangle, Sassafras, Apple Sass Rag,* and *Ole Miss.*

That was my big night, the night I really began to live. On my first visit to the South Side I managed to hit the two spots that were making history in the jazz world and I met some of the musicians who were already legends. I figured I had found something bigger and better than all the chicks and bankrolls in the world.

Sidney Bechet's curved soprano put a bug in my head. I went right down to take my old flute out of hock and traded it in for a soprano sax. As soon as I could blow three notes on it I began to practice the *St. Louis Blues.* Many a time I'd just sit around looking at my horn—I could hardly believe I had one of my own. I wanted to shout out to the whole world, "You all look out now, here I come, everybody step aside, I'm gonna show you where from! I'm gonna blow in this horn and make you know that jazz is the king and let it be so!"

One day while I was practising it got so good to me that I put my horn under my arm and cut out for the South Side. I didn't know where I was going; I guess I just had the feeling that a man who plays a horn ought to go where people really understand about horns. I was wandering up and down State Street, carrying that case like it was my passport, when I passed a shoeshine parlor and heard something that attracted me. Some kids in there were making riffs with their rags as they massaged the shoes. It sounded like tapdancing, and it drew me inside.

"Boy, what you got in that case?" one of the kids asked, as though he didn't know. It looked like I got the case open before he was through talking, I was so tickled. "You play that thing?" he said. As much as I had played it at home and as good as I thought I was, when I put the horn together and blew on it I couldn't make a sound, I was so nervous. That was my first case of stage-fright. Finally I got going on *St. Louis Blues*, while all these kids began to clap their hands and pat their feet, some keeping time with their rags. When I finished a chorus they all smiled and looked friendly. They were like a group of adults standing around a baby that's just spoken its first word. One of them asked could he blow the sax, and when he put it to his mouth he didn't even know how to place his fingers on the keys but he blew a tone so full and natural it knocked me out. I had really come to the right place.

I wanted to buy some music, and these boys directed me to Clarence Williams' music store on State Street. Clarence was sitting out in front, sunning himself. He was a very congenial-looking guy, with a big broad smile and wide eyes that said he was willing to help you anytime you asked. This fine man was a music publisher (he put the great Bessie Smith on records) and the composer of a lot of numbers that are jazz standards today—old stand-bys like *Sugar Blues, Royal Garden Blues, I Ain't Gonna Give Nobody None of My Jelly Roll, I Wish I Could Shimmy Like My Sister Kate, I Found a New Baby, Everybody Loves My Baby,* and plenty more. He took me in as though he had known me for years and sat down at the piano to play *Royal Garden* and *Sister Kate* for me. Before I left he gave me the sheet music and wouldn't take any money for it.

What struck me about *Royal Garden* was the way the bass worked as a sort of masculine counterpoint against the harmonies and melodies of the right hand. I felt at last I had found the secret of jazz, just what I'd been looking for all along. These little inflections of Clarence's are something the greatest musicians of today have missed. He gave me a rendition of the lyrics too. The comp he played was just like the style of the old guitar players—bass and chord, bass and chord, with the hands alternating most of the time. The main thing all through was the inversion of chords in the true jazz idiom, which gives the improvising soloist just the right foundation to build his variations on.

Solid. I was all set now. I had the sax, and music to practise with, and good, friendly people to help me when I needed it. All I wanted to do was to work on my sax all day, then hang around the De Luxe and the Royal Garden all night, visiting Clarence in between to keep me straight. I'd made it at last, I figured—I was really a musician now.

Don't look for no chitlin's before you kill your hawg. Wham, I woke up to find myself in jail again. It was getting to be a drag.

3

THE BAND HOUSE, THE BAND HOUSE

I AIN'T done nothing, judge, Your Honor. Honest, I was just sitting in that hashhouse, smacking my chops on a egg sandwich, minding my business. . . . Joe Tuckman felt like balling that night cause he beat Big Izzy for ten grand in the crap game, and he took us all out for some sport. After catching the show at the Royal Garden and a couple other spots, we wound up in this restaurant for some breakfast, with the cab driver tagging along. We just began to eat when in breezed these two pounders on the bloodhound tip, hunting down the owner of the cab parked out front. The driver told them he was their man and what about it. "This about it," one of the cops said pleasantly. "You wouldn't by any chance know where we could find the owner of these guns, would you? It just so happens they were snuggled up under the back seat of your cab." Out from his pocket came a gang of .22's and .38's, enough steel utensils to open a hardware store.

I didn't know who belonged to those pistols, and today, twenty-seven years later, I still don't. In those days guys packed rods like women do lipstick; practically every hip pocket in town was a walking arsenal. I couldn't figure out why a copper would go poking his nose under the seat of a respectable-looking cab at six in the A.M. It goes to show you what comes out of minding other people's business. Snoop and ye shall find. I wonder what do cops want to be that way for? It just gets people in trouble.

You could have heard yourself think in that beanery—a pin dropped then would have made an explosion like a cannon cracker. Everybody got busy at once, some studying their fingernails and the cab driver shoveling food in so fast that when the cop tapped him on the shoulder he coughed up a spoon. "You're sure a gabby bunch of guys," the cop said. "I hear better conversation down at the morgue." He sighed. "O.K., *O*. K., come along then, I'll take you to a place where you'll have plenty of time to sit down and write out your speeches."

After we were booked at the precinct station house Joe Tuckman put up our bail, and two days later we showed up for trial. If you pleaded guilty to carrying concealed weapons the usual fine was twenty-five bucks and costs, but when the judge asked who owned the guns we all got tongue-tied again. Bop, he hit us with the whole book, $200 and costs or six months in the house of many slammers. I was the kid in the group, so after paying everybody else's fine the boys said, "We'll come and get you out tomorrow, Milton, just sit tight now and don't worry." Off I went to Chicago's city prison at 26th and California, the Bridewell, known as "The Band House" in the underworld. I tried hard not to worry but I didn't make out so good.

When we stripped naked and lined up for our numbers and prison clothes, my morale hit zero and kept sinking. Jack, the drapes they handed me a jungle bum wouldn't wear on weekdays. Long underwear that looked like the housing project of some gophers on a fresh-air kick, about ten sizes too big and five quarts of creosote too funky. A blue-and-white striped rag that they called a shirt, faded and torn and built for a humpy giant to begin with. Socks made from some kind of stiff string, with less give than a stinchy miser. Hobnailed, high-topped gunboats weighing about ten pounds each, with one-inch soles as flexible as a petrified tree. Those excuses for shoes were handed to us after being put through a sterilizing process, with impressions dug into their inner soles by the toes of all the lousy bums who wore them before. When you stood up and put your weight on those violin cases you thought you were standing barefoot over the iron grating of a subway ventilator. A busted ragpicker would have given those togs the go-by.

We were hustled off to the south cell block, where I was locked up in a cage that would have cramped a canary. In the corner I spied a bucket coated with two inches of lime inside and out, with no cover; from the tip-off my nose gave me, I figured this was the can. The bed was about two feet wide and six feet long, with an inch-thick straw mattress stretched over some rusty, sagging old springs. It would have been more restful kipping on a pile of hardtack, unbuttered. At mealtime they marched us to the mess hall and dished out some cold baked beans with a hunk of salt pork that had seen better days about the time Dewey took Manila. Then we lockstepped back to our cells and about nine o'clock the lights were switched off. I was really in the dumps, but I finally dozed off because the social life was so boring.

Maybe misery doesn't love company but it sure seems to attract it. A minute later I was hopping around that cell entertaining more company than Elsa Maxwell. Hundreds of the largest bedbugs I have ever seen (and I've been a blood donor for many a prizewinner in my time) had opened up transfusion offices all over my body and were feasting on plasma-an'. There must have been something wrong with their thyroid glands, they were so overgrown. They were so cocky and drunk with power, not to mention my blood, that they didn't bother to play fair—they just maneuvered into position on the ceiling and dropped down on me like dive-bombers on a target. It was insulting, the way they paid the rules of the game no mind. Most of them were so large and bloated that when you smacked one on your face or arm it would pop like the cork on a wine bottle. I found out then that chinches never die. When they get tired of scuffling for their chow and want to retire, they just go and live happily forever after in The Band House.

I called the guard and he brought me some matches and a newspaper to burn them out. "Be sure you get them cracks, bud," he told me, pointing to the blistered and scaling whitewash on the walls, but there wasn't much hope in his voice. I lit the paper at each hole and they marched out in squads—grandma, grandpa, and the whole family, generation after generation all the way back to the Ark. Later on, the guard, maybe out of a sense of fair play, slipped me a blowtorch to make the battle a little less one-sided. It would have took a flamethrower to even up the score.

No rest for the weary—between the bugs and the food they dished out to us I was put in mind of a song the kids used to sing in the streets of my neighborhood:

The Band House, The Band House,
I'll never go there any more.
They give you bread as heavy as lead,
They give you soup that'll make you puke,
They give you meat that stinks like feet,
I'll never go there any more.

"Occupation?"

"I'm a musician, sir."

"Musician, hey." That deputy warden made it sound like it was lower than whaleshit, and that's at the bottom of the ocean. "Huh, you goddamn Jews and niggers are always duckin' work. Well, the only kind of music you'll make around here'll be with a pick and banjo." Before I could dig what he meant he turned to his stooge and yelled, "Brickyard!"

My job was to load up a wheelbarrow with smoking bricks from the kilns and haul them over to the stockpiles. But I never did any manual labor before, on account of some lung trouble when I was a kid, and when I went to lift that loaded wheelbarrow it wouldn't budge; it felt like it was riveted to the ground. After a couple of tries I tipped the whole works over, spilling the bricks on the ground.

"Hey, you Jew bastard!" The keeper came trotting over with a club in his hand. "So you're one of these sheenies that won't work, hey. Well, we'll see about that." I was led back to the deputy, who asked what the trouble was and then, before I had a chance to open my yap, said, "Shut up or I'll bust you in the nose. You're goin' back to the brickyard, and this time you're gonna get a pick and banjo." I began to dig that they weren't planning to make me the star boarder around there.

Back in the brickyard I was assigned to the clay hole. Here came that wheelbarrow again, but this time I had to load it with clay and push it up a plank incline to the brick machine. I never got as far as the planks; every time I tried to pick up the handles and push, I dumped the whole load. The screw got disgusted with me and yelled, "Get the hell over there and help those cons pile up them bricks, but believe me if it was up to me you'd be down in that quarry with a sledgehammer, makin' little ones out of big ones." That's how The Band House got its name, I found out. In the quarry a pick was called a pick and a shovel was a banjo. You should have heard the special arrangements the picks and banjos played, and the riffs the sledgehammers laid down. That was one band I didn't want to hear nor see. Those instruments didn't belong to my music school.

I had to stand on top of the pile, trying to catch four or five bricks at a time when the man below heaved them at me. The first batch caught me right in the breadbasket and bounced square on my toes, and the next shipment almost mashed my fingertips off. I quit then and there, so back to the office I was marched, to stand with my face to the wall for two hours. Next day I was shifted to the pottery yard, where they made me bounce fifty-pound wads of clay on a concrete floor to make them compact. Those soggy chunks kept slipping out of my hands before I got them two inches off the ground. Slap my wrist and call me Butterfingers. It looked like I just wasn't going to make it on the slave tip—the spirit was willing but the flesh said uh, uh.

That night my back felt like it had been run through a wringer and massaged with a sledgehammer. Worse yet, it looked like I was in for six solid months of this routine, because my pals kept on not showing up with the ransom money. I wasn't on any health kick and I didn't go for the body-building program they had mapped out at all. Who wants to be a corpse with muscles?

The only way to keep my health, I figured, was to get into the prison hospital, where they had nice clean beds, good chow, and no straw bosses. I began to study over all the pains and diseases known to man, to see which ones I could come down with the fastest. There were a lot of doctors and druggists in my family, and I used to hear a lot of medical jive when I apprenticed in my uncle's drugstore, so I knew which symptoms went with what sickness.

Just before lights-out I began to moan like a pup with the stomach-ache, and when I heard the keeper coming I stuck my hand down my throat practically to the elbow and began to throw up. "Oh, my side, my side, it's killing me," I groaned. The head keeper came on the run and sure enough I was rushed to the hospital. I had all the right pains in all the right places, so when the doctor looked me over he diagnosed appendicitis. They cleaned my bowels out and put me to bed to wait for an operation in the morning.

That night the famous race riots of July, 1919, broke out on the South Side. The whole city must have become a slaughter-house because people were getting shot up all over the place, and all the hospitals in town were turned into emergency stations. Every hour or so they brought in guys who had been used for target practice. When the head doctor made his rounds I told him I was feeling pretty good, so he said maybe they'd hold up my operation and treat just the emergency cases. He was such a smooth talker, he convinced me. The nurse was given orders to keep me cleaned out in case I took a turn for the worse and had to be cut open in a hurry. I decided not to take a turn in any direction; I didn't want to be no trouble.

There weren't enough doctors or nurses to go around, so I got up out of bed to help the emergency patients. One guy was brought in with a double-barrel load of buckshot in his back. We had some job removing all the pieces of lead—his hide looked like the moon's surface seen through a telescope, it had so many lumps and craters. We took a big paint brush and plastered him with iodine, then yanked out the pieces one by one with some large tweezers and forceps. The poor guy squirmed and wriggled like a jellyfish with the d.t.'s. Another man had had a kind of freak accident: he'd been driving through the South Side, holding onto the wheel with both hands, when a stray bullet passed clean through almost all his fingers.

There was open warfare on the streets of Chicago that night. The trouble started, they told us, down at Jackson Park beach in the

Negro district, when some white guys beat up some colored boys who wanted to go swimming. It must have spread like a prairie fire, because the victims were carted in from all over town. That was one night I was glad not to be out on the streets. One race riot was all my belly could hold.

For three or four days I lived on fluids, and I got so raving hungry I was ready to chew on the bedclothes. Finally I buzzed Big Buster, a colored boy who worked in the hospital kitchen, and he took pity on me. Buster had been Jack Johnson's sparring partner and you could see why—he was about six foot five, with a wonderful nature, and as good as he was he was just that tough. As soon as he saw the fix I was in, he made up a triple-decker sandwich a couple stories shorter than the Empire State, with chicken and bacon and all the trimmings, and slipped it to me in an ice-pan, under a towel. My jaws were going so fast I almost ate right through the pan.

An hour later I was wheeled into the operating room. That head doctor must have had an itchy scalpel that day.

All I remember, after they gave me a shot in the arm and shaved me, is the smell of burnt rags when I sniffed the ether. When I opened my eyes again the doctor and a gang of nurses were standing around my bed looking like pallbearers. I was hid from the ward by a white screen. Now every time I'd seen that screen before, it meant some poor cat was bowing out for keeps. Gee, I really fooled these people, I thought, I'm not dying and I better tell them. "Take that screen away, Doc," I said, "because if you're going to stand around until I stop inhaling and exhaling you sure going to have a long wait." The doctor smiled and ordered the screen removed.

One nurse stayed with me, holding a small curved pan shaped like a cucumber near my chin. I looked down and saw big chunks of clotted blood in it. My mouth felt like it had been coated with varnish. "Water," I said. That nurse was feeling contrary. "No," she said, "ice." I sucked on some chipped ice, then I felt sharp pains in my stomach and started to moan. The nurse tried to take my mind off my misery by holding up my appendix and giving me a spiel about it, like a guide taking some sightseers through the Grand Canyon. She showed me a big cherry pit on one side and a couple of other points of interest, but I wasn't in the mood for a travelogue.

I blew my top for seven days—I couldn't eat or pass water or move my bowels in all that time. Then the doc showed up with a tube and a wire and wanted to catheterize me. "Nothing doing, Doc," I said. "You moved my insides around like you were playing checkers with them, and threw out all my spare parts, and I didn't kick, but this is sure one part of me I'd like to keep just about the way it is, so lay off, Doc." A man has got to protect his interests some of the time. He gave up and went away.

Then one of the head nurses came to my bed and said, "Milton, I think I know how to relieve you of those gas pains, but you mustn't breathe a word about it even if it works because it's against doctor's orders. Are you game?" I told her I was ready to try anything. Right away she mixed up a mess of olive oil, glycerine, soap and turpentine (I don't remember whether or not she threw in the kitchen sink) and gave me the whole works for an enema. When it was over I was so relieved that I cried like a baby, while she held my hand and stroked my hair.

During a talk with the doctor I found out what had caused my internal bleeding, and he told me how close I came to paying Saint Peter a visit. That sandwich had caked up in my stomach like a block of cement and almost killed me; it looked like the chicken in that triple-decker wanted to roost in my stomach for the rest of her days.

On the ninth day my stitches were pulled out and I began to feel halfway alive again, thanks to that cure-'em-or-kill-'em enematic cocktail. The nurse asked me if I could ever look a chicken in the face again, and I told her I felt about that sandwich the way the Spanish Queen in that poem felt about other forms of pleasure:

> It's a hell of a life, said the Queen of Spain,
> Three minutes' pleasure and nine months' pain,
> Two weeks' rest and you're back at it again,
> It's a hell of a life, said the Queen of Spain.

My parents came to see me in the hospital and told me they didn't have the money to get me out and my rich uncles wouldn't come through because they thought some discipline would do me good. Those uncles of mine sure saved a pile of dough feeding me all that discipline at the state's expense. Mom bawled her head off when she saw me stretched out so thin and weak in that bed. She must have got a funny impression of the prison system in the Commonwealth of Illinois, because every time she came to see me in jail I was flat on my back, looking like I was passing out of the picture. "Mom," I said, whispering in her ear, "I don't want you to get the wrong idea because I really am in great shape. I just pretended to be sick so I could lay around in the hospital and stuff myself on all the fine food they got here." She felt a lot better when she left, but this time I didn't get my sentence reduced for being a Boy Scout. They were a hard lot of oscars in the Bridewell.

Every afternoon the nurses ganged up around my bed and begged me to sing the blues for them. I was the life of the party in that ward, and always got some special dessert for my singing. One number they were all crazy about was *Hesitation Blues*, which I rendered with real feeling:

> Oh, ashes to ashes and dust to dust,
> If the whisky don't get you then the women must.
> Oh tell me how long, how long must I wait,
> Oh can I get it now, or must I hesitate.
>
> You're playin' in my orchard, now don't you see,
> If you don't like my peaches stop shakin' my tree.
> Oh tell me how long, etc.

I really meant those words. The girls hung around my bed all day long, giving me sponge-baths and fixing my linen until my tree was shook so much, all the peaches were ready to drop. Nobody ever tramped around so much in my orchard before.

Everything was rolling along until I got some news that brought me down—they were figuring on shipping me back to the regular prison in a few days. It looked like I was getting too goddamn healthy.

Curtains. I suspected it would be tough making them believe I had appendicitis twice in the same place. My mind began to work fast. Then I remembered that in the rear of the hospital there was a TB ward. Now TB is a disease on which I am a specialist, because I'd once been in a sanatorium on account of pleurisy, and I still had some rales that would come in handy. Overnight I developed a hacking cough and a pain in my left lung. I could already taste those fat steaks and the milk, butter, eggs and fresh fruit those cats feasted on in the TB ward. I coughed harder and harder, with my mouth watering.

One of the colored porters, who used to sing the blues with me, was a pal of mine. "Hey boy, come over here," I said to him. "I want you to do something for me. Tomorrow I'll give you a paper sputum cup and I want you to go back in the TB ward and slip it to the sickest cat in there and tell him to cough up a lunger. Bring it back to me and be sure it's full, hear?" He flashed me a big broad grin that meant: Good as did.

Next afternoon when the interne made his rounds I hacked and coughed and told him about the sticking pain in my left lung, the one that was affected when I went to the sanatorium. He ordered a sputum box and urine bottle for tests. When I woke up next morning about six, I saw a box on my table and when I picked it up it was so full I was scared of it. My friend the porter told me one of the TB boys had obliged me by coughing up some sputum a few minutes before, the morning being the best time to really get results. The porter had picked the sickest guy in the ward, some poor cat who had it so bad he kicked the bucket a few days later.

It didn't take long before the whole staff of doctors was lined up around my bed, pounding on my chest like a flock of woodpeckers. The slide showed up positive and I had been pronounced a TB patient. Brickyard, my back you'll never break—I got me a date with a two-inch steak.

A guy really began to live in the Bridewell when he had TB. I strutted around the hospital like Poppa De-Da-Da, then was transferred to the west cell house back in the prison, a brand-new modern building. Here the cells, instead of being built in block form without windows, were arranged all around the cell house, making up the walls. Each cell was bright and clean, with a window, a modern wash basin and a honest-to-God toilet bowl. It was like the Waldorf-Astoria compared to the louse-trap I'd been in first. In this place you'd never wake up to find yourself in a clinch with Mr. Chinch. We had clean sheets and hospital beds with springs, real bounce-springs, and decent chow, and no work. On the top tier a dozen cells were set aside for us TB sufferers. They gave us our own dishes and silverware and fed us right in our cells. Maybe they weren't so hard in the Bridewell, after all. You just had to show them you were dying and they got real kind.

On the tier below ours, just across from me, was a big colored boy named Red. He was a straw boss in the brickyard, and came in every night after work all covered with yellow dust. With that round, pleasant face of his, and his clean-shaven skull, and his barrel chest so big it made him topheavy, he looked like a guy you wanted to have on your side. Every night he'd come plodding back singing some chain-gang blues, the kind of wail the colored country folks call river music. He was dogtired but so happy to see another day gone that he'd chant,

> Short time, poppa, short time for you and I,
> Short time, Jew kid, another one's gone by.

The "Jew kid" was me, and I didn't mind it at all, the way he said it. "Hey Jew kid," he'd call out to me, "how you feel today?" and it always made me happy because he really wanted to know.

It wasn't long before we had a quartet going in the block, entertaining the inmates and keepers 'most every night. The way it happened, Red started to sing *'Way Down Upon the Swanee River* one night, and a gang of us joined in. We kept on singing and the bad voices just dropped out one by one, without anybody ever telling them to, till at the end we had a perfect quartet. I got my biggest thrill when Red took off on *Go Down, Moses* and some other spirituals, and the other colored boys chimed in. I couldn't hold myself back, even though I didn't know the words or the music—those plaintive laments got me so bad I had to lift up my voice and speak my piece too. I fitted in with such ease, slurring to the different harmonies like they were part of me, that they all crowed with glee afterwards and Red called out, "Jew kid's really in there too." That was a wonderful feeling.

During the last part of my sentence they put me on the front gate of the jail, to help out the keeper there. I didn't do much except stand around and lend a hand sliding the big gates open once in a while. Sometimes, when I pushed open the gate to the women's prison, the chicks would rush to the window and look out at me longingly, like I was the last man left in the world. We got real friendly after a while. They were so lonely and I was so bored that we began smuggling red-hot notes back and forth. One of the girls would write, "If I could only explain how good you look to me out there. I love you." Or another one would say, "Honey, I don't know your name but I sure like your style. We could have some fun together. Where can I find you when we get loose from here?" I had those jailbird blues too, and I wrote back things like, "Baby, I sure could use you tonight, why don't you drop around?" Other times, when the girls were sneaking a look, I'd feel in a serenading mood, so I'd wrap up my comb in a piece of toilet paper and blow on it like a kazoo, playing *Ain't Gonna Give Nobody None of My Jelly Roll*. But it was only a kind of joke, I sure didn't mean what it said in the song. I wasn't that stir-happy.

My six months rolled by and I was turned loose. I walked through the gates, took one last look at the Bridge of Sighs that led over the canal to The Band House, and hopped a trolley for home. After being cooped up in a world of killjoy grays for so long, it made my head swim to see all the colors in the trolley ads and on the civilian clothes of the passengers. The sudden stops and starts, the loud clanging of the motorman's bell, the bright sunlight and the cars rushing by, all made me dizzy. I figured I'd better shoot for The Corner fast and get my bearings.

I was curious about what was waiting for me, and a little unsure of myself. There was a gang of things I had to get with again.

What next?

4

QUIT FOOLIN' WITH THAT COMB

I DON'T want to sound braggadocious, but for awhile I was doing so good I almost hired Wells-Fargo to haul my gold around. Back on The Corner I became manager of the poolroom, and with the chuck-luck and Indian-dice games at the cigar counter I was coining at least two C-notes a week. Some nights I'd try my luck in the crap game and wind up with a grand or more in my kick. Small-fry politicians began dropping around and handing me big fat cigars, and one time a rookie cop called me mister.

Now that I was in the money and had done two bits in the pen, I got more respect from the gang. Almost every night that I could, I'd get them together and ride them up to the South Side, instead of tagging along with them to the whorehouses. I began to collar that all the evil I ever found came from ounce-brain white men who hated the Negroes and me both, while most all the good things in life came to me from the race. Whenever I needed something so bad my life depended on it, it was always the race that came through for me. A song or a smile, a chicken sandwich or a sputum cup—all I had to do was look like I needed it and it came to me like Aladdin rubbing his magic lamp. I always felt good when I was around those people.

We started to go to the Pekin Inn a lot, a joint at 28th and State where the sporting crowd and the money guys hung out. Two detectives had been killed in there, and the place had been closed up a couple of times, so the gang was kind of touchy about going there at first, especially after the race riot. Feeling was still running high after that undeclared war, and the South Side wasn't exactly a picnic-ground for whites.

Who should turn up as doorman at the Pekin one night but Big Buster, my boy who slipped me the sandwich in the Bridewell. He stood outside, towering a head or two over the crowd, smiling in a friendly way and keeping one eye peeled for the cops and ugly customers. Everything was in order for blocks around when Buster was on the scene; even the cab drivers, who were shooting and ramming each other all over town in a taxi war (the one Bow Gistensohn got killed in), got very polite and began tipping their caps when they drove up in front of Buster. The gang lost all their fears about the Pekin when they dug how friendly I was with that solid he-man, who took no stuff from nobody and whose heart was as big as his muscles. He really laid it on State Street.

At the Pekin they had Tony Jackson, a New Orleans musician, one of the greatest blues piano players that ever pounded a joybox. Tony could play the blues out of this world, yet and still he had a sweet and lyrical way of doing the pop tunes requested by white squares who only knew Sophie Tucker and the get-hot mob. Tony had a natural musical sense I've hardly ever seen equalled, and he wrote a number called *Pretty Little Baby* that really knocked me out.

A favorite piece of Tony's, a kind of bawdyhouse blues that the crowd could never get enough of, went like this:

> *Keep a-knockin' but you can't come in,*
> *I hear you knockin' but you can't come in,*
> *I got an all-night trick agin,*
> *So keep a-knockin' but you can't come in.*

> *Keep a-knockin' but you can't come in,*
> *I'm busy grindin' so you can't come in,*
> *If you love me you'll come back agin,*
> *Or come back tomorrow at half-past-ten.*

That number is a wonderful example of what happened to the blues when they moved out of the gallion, the work-gang and the levee and rode the rods into big towns like New Orleans, Charleston, Memphis and Chi. The Negroes who hit these cities found themselves on the bottom of the pile, on an even level with practically nobody but whores and sporting people, who had less prejudice, fake morals and intellectual stench about them. Besides, it often happened that a man who migrated into town couldn't eat unless his woman made money off of other men. But these people didn't get nasty about it; anyway they were half a step out of the gallion, and they were philosophical, and many a guy kept on loving his woman and camping outside her door until she could let him in, and they made up a lot of simple, plain-speaking songs that even had a chuckle or two in them about the trouble they saw.

Songs like Tony Jackson's show the Negro's real artistry with his prose, and the clean way he looks at sex, while all the white songs that ever came out of whorehouses don't have anything but a vulgar slant and an obscene idiom. These blues from the South taught me one thing: You take the weight off a good man a little and his song will start jumping with joy. You can't get a good man really down. Why, some of those work-gang blues and half-humorous whorehouse songs, once they got up North, even wound up as tender love ballads.

Joe "King" Oliver was killing them after hours at the Pekin with the same band that played with him at the Dreamland, the New Orleans Creole Jazz Band. Joe himself handled the trumpet, and with him he had Johnny Dodds on the clarinet; Honoré Dutrey, trombone; Ed Garland, bass; Minor Hall, drums; and on the piano, Lil Hardin (later Lil Armstrong, the wife of Louis Armstrong).

This band sounded entirely different from Lawrence Dewey's outfit. Joe set straight and simple patterns on his horn that were like the spice added to a dish by a master chef to make its flavor just right. When Joe played, the man improvising out in front had freedom to move around, yet there was a foundation under him as solid and steady as the Rock of Gibraltar. That's why Johnny Dodds' clarinet sounded so wonderful with Joe behind him. Whether Joe played open horn or with a mute, the effect was the same.

Nobody could improve on Joe's way of coming in for his own solos just before the chorus started, taking off from a solid riff with the ease and sureness of a graceful diver sailing out from a springboard. Dewey's band played Scott Joplin's arrangements, so their music was more organized and according to the book, with less real collective improvisation; but Joe's men always picked tunes and harmonies right out of their heads, making it up all the way. It was Joe's free style that inspired Clarence Williams to write *Royal Garden Blues.*

I ran into Clarence again at the Pekin, and when I told him where I'd been during the riot he took me over to his music store to show me something. On the wall outside there was a big grease-spot where his head always rested when he sunned himself, and all over it was a gang of bullet holes. "I was down in New Orleans when all that stuff happened," Clarence told me. "Looked like the Lord must have been with me and sent me away, Milton, 'cause I'd a sure been sittin' here and you know the answer."

About five o'clock one morning Joe Oliver finished up at the Pekin and took me out to eat. He steered me around to a bakery, where he bought three big loaves of hot bread, then over to a Chinese chop-suey joint. All he ordered was a big pot of tea for a nickel, and then he got fidgety and began to look all around the place. The waiters all seemed to be ducking him. Finally Joe cornered the boss himself and said, "Man, what's your story, bring on that sugar."

I saw right away why all the sugar went into hiding when Joe showed up in that place. As soon as the sugar bowl arrived he tore a whole loaf of hot bread in half, poured most of the sugar into it, and ate it like a sandwich, sipping the tea to wash it down. He would eat two or three loaves at a time, with as many bowls of sugar. "Man," he told me, "this is what I call real eatin'. Moms always used to make sugar sandwiches for me when I was a kid." Clarence Williams must have seen Joe fussing with the Chinaman one night when all the sugar was hid on him, and got the idea for *Sugar Blues.*

I got to be part of the fixtures at the Pekin and a lot of other South Side spots—Elite Number One, Elite Number Two, the Dreamland, Entertainers' Café, and the Lorraine Gardens, where

Jimmy Noone played clarinet with Freddie Keppard, Jimmy Bertrand, and Tony Jackson. Making friends with Jimmy Noone, and Sidney Bechet and Joe Oliver and Clarence Williams, I began to feel like I owned the South Side. When I stood around outside the Pekin, beating up my chops with Big Buster, and he put his arm around my shoulder in a friendly way, I almost busted the buttons off my vest, my chest swole up so much. Any time I breezed down the street, cats would flash me friendly grins and hands would wave at me from all sides, and I felt like I was king of the tribe. I was really living then.

Guess I had a real talent for being at the wrong place at the right time. This particular day I was climbing up the back stairs of a house in the Italian section, going to see a friend of mine, when I heard shots coming from the yard. Some guy was trying to hop the fence and a cop was chasing him, firing in the air. When the policeman saw me up on the porch he covered me with his gun and yelled, "Come on down here!" The other guy and me were marched down to the station house and thrown into the county jail. It seemed that a case of stolen silks had turned up under the stairs of that building, and I was held on suspicion for a couple weeks.

When we were let out of our cells to exercise in the bull pen, I got together a quartet and we sang *Down Among the Sheltering Palms* and *Back Home Again in Indiana*. We had something better than a metronome to keep time for us—the hammering in a corner of the bull pen, where a gang of carpenters were throwing up a scaffold to hang Smiling Jack O'Brien, I think it was, for some famous murder. At night after we were locked in our cells they kept testing the trap door with sandbags. Every time the slap of that door echoed through the cell block, I felt my neck jerk and my breathing went bad. It was very quiet in the cells. Nobody even cleared his throat, for fear of disturbing the peace.

One night they moved us to the other side of the cell block and locked us in early. A little later Smiling Jack came through the door between the blocks, walking that last long mile like he was taking a stroll in the park. With a mirror I rigged up so I could see the door and the scaffold, I had a ringside seat for the whole show. There was a priest at Jack's side when he passed through, but Jack didn't pay him no mind—he kept singing *Dear Old Girl* in a high falsetto tenor, and when he got close to the scaffold he lit a cigarette and stuck it between his lips. He never stopped smiling.

After the priest mumbled a prayer the black hood was slipped over Jack's head and he was led to the trap door. Then the trap was sprung, with a bang I felt down to my toenails, and Jack dangled there. Hell broke loose in the block then; cups were rattled between the bars, keepers ran up and down the gallery threatening to turn the fire hoses on us.

They didn't have anything on me, so after a few days my case was nolle prossed and I was sprung. But that scene stuck with me. I've never played *Dear Old Girl* since then without thinking of Smiling Jack O'Brien and the sound of that trap door cracking open, and of the way his legs looked as he hung there, kind of squirming and snaking around at first, then quiet all of a sudden, with his shoes swinging easy in space like a couple of tired crows.

Most of the famous and up-and-coming performers of the day —Ted Lewis, Sophie Tucker, Benny Davis, Eddie Cantor, Dolly Kaye, Al Jolson (they even gave him the title of "The Jazz Singer") —were heebs, and the boys had the feeling that we should all stick together and not knock the big names of "our" race. I didn't go for that jive at all; being a Jew didn't mean a thing to me. Around the poolroom I defended the guys I felt were my real brothers, the colored musicians who made music that sent me, not a lot of beat-up old hamfats who sang and played a commercial excuse for the real thing. I never could dig the phony idea of a race—if we were a "race"—sticking together all the way, even when it meant turning your back on what was good or bad.

Joe Oliver and Freddie Keppard made me love the trumpet, but that wasn't my instrument. The notes that kept singing in my head were the notes that came weaving out of Sidney Bechet's curved soprano and clarinet, and the clarinets of Jimmy Noone and

49

Johnny Dodds. But all of a sudden Murph Steinberg blew into town again, after his barnstorming tour, and knocked me off the beam. Murph was a professional musician now, and he knew the score, so when he told me I couldn't get a job with the curved sax I traded it in for a tenor. I blew on that horn until my lungs yelled ouch, and I felt I was getting close to the blues and the jazz idiom. My old man came home from work one night when I felt I was coming on, and I grabbed the horn to show off while he was eating his supper, but he screamed "Stop blowing so loud—you sound like a fog-horn!" He was suffering from a migraine headache that day, and the notes must have beat on his eardrums like a triphammer. That killed my ardor for the tenor sax, because Pops knew so much about music I figured I must be wrong. I sold the horn before I could even play *Come to Jesus* on it.

One night Murph came tearing into the poolroom as winded as Paul Revere's horse. "Boy," he said, "get yourself together and come with me. We're gonna meet a guy who really plays the clarinet." We hopped into Harry Shapiro's cab and took off for the LaSalle Street Station to hand Leon Rappolo the twisters to the city.

Rapp was a little hyped-up Italian guy, with pop-eyes and a bullet-shaped head perched on top of his puny frame. Dig this outfit: a shepherd-plaid suit with strides that hit him about an inch above his shoe-tops, so tight he must have worked his way into them with a shoehorn; black patent-leather shoes with high cloth tops and pearl buttons; white silk socks, a black derby hat, and a yellow walking stick. He was so sharp he would have made Lucius Beebe look like he was togged in a barrel.

Harry Shapiro was crazy about musicians so we headed straight for his dommy. We woke his folks up about 1:30 in the morning, but they were a very congenial lot and loved music so they got up and joined the party. What a jam session we put on that night. Murph dragged out his trumpet, Rapp put his clarinet together, Frank Snyder set up his drums, I worked up enough guts to sit down at the piano—and look out, sister, *Royal Garden* began to romp. Rapp was sort of in there, the first oscar I ever heard who sounded a little like Bechet on the clarinet. He bent over almost double when he played, with his horn practically on the floor, so he could hear himself better. We must have beat out about thirty choruses before the neighbors were on our necks and the cops broke it up.

The famous New Orleans Rhythm Kings were just getting their band together, including Rapp, and Elmer Schobel on the piano, and I followed them all around town, listening to them rehearse and play one-nighters. I'd never heard any white band come so close to the New Orleans style before—they stole Joe Oliver's riffs and they stole them good, like Robin Hood. Over in the Friars Inn, at Wabash and Jackson, where they later opened, they'd rehearse one chorus all afternoon till they got it just right, and it would knock me out when they showed up on the bandstand that night and forgot every note. Not a living ass in that band could read a note except Elmer Schobel. Elmer would give them their notes from the piano, and what a scramble there would be when one guy stole another guy's notes. Rapp and I got to be good friends, and my job at the poolroom was interfering with my hanging around with him, so I quit working. Potatoes without gravy don't mash good.

One night during intermission at the Friars Inn Rapp took me into his dressing room, where he felt around on the molding and came up with a cigarette made out of brown wheatstraw paper. When he lit it up a funny odor came out that reminded me of the cubebs I smoked when I was a kid. He sounded more like he was sighing than smoking, sucking air in with the smoke and making a noise like an old Russian sipping tea from a saucer. After he got a lungful he closed his lips tight and held it in till he about choked and had to cough. "Ever smoke any muggles?" he asked me. "Man, this is some golden-leaf I brought up from New Orleans, it'll make you feel good, take a puff." The minute he said that, dope hit my mind and I got scared—working in my uncle's drugstore had made me know that messing with dope was a one-way ticket to the graveyard. I told him I didn't smoke and let it go at that, because I looked up to him so much as a musician.

Rapp used to carry me to his apartment and we'd come on like gangbusters playing together. He'd light up and get real high, and when he was groovy as a ten-cent movie he'd begin to play the blues on a beat-up guitar. I would wrap my comb in toilet paper and sing through it while he backed me up. It used to tickle Rapp right down to his toes to hear a Yankee really come on with the blues. Many a time he'd say to me, "Boy, you mean to tell me you ain't never been down South and blow that way? Why don't you get yourself a horn and quit foolin' with that comb?"

His birthday happened around this time, and I felt so warm towards him that I decided to buy him a new guitar. Down to the Jewish ghetto on Maxwell Street I went, to look around in the second-hand stores. I came to one store where an old Jewish man with a long beard and a little yomelkeh stood in the doorway, and I heard something there that knocked me out. An old-fashioned victrola setting out on the curb was playing a record, Blind Lemon Jefferson's *Black Snake Moan,* and the old Jewish man kept shaking his head sadly, like he knew that evil black snake personally:

> *Oh-oh, some black snake's been*
> *suckin' my rider's tongue.*

I bought that record right away, then picked up a sharp guitar for Rapp for only eight bucks. The next day Rapp and I went out to Lincoln Park and got into a rowboat. Rapp smoked his muta while he played the new guitar, and I blew on my kazoo. We really had a ball that day, paddling around in the sun playing *Black Snake Moan* and a gang of other blues. Muggles make you hungry as a chinch in a storage house, and Rapp gobbled up about ten boxes of crackerjacks, shoveling so fast he even ate the prizes in a couple of them.

What happened to Rapp is a sad story. Two or three years later paresis caught up with him, and all the salvarsan shots in the world couldn't get him straight. It finally went to his head and they had to bug him. All the time he was in the asylum he kept waiting for a big train to pull in with a carload of muta just for him, and when they let him out in the yard he would go down to the railroad tracks and begin flagging all the trains that passed, looking for a package of joy that never showed up. Poor Rapp. He was a musician from the heart, a solid viper. I hope he finally caught that Muggles Special and rode it straight on to glory, high as a Georgia pine, feasting on a ton of crackerjacks and picking the blues on his guitar.

Knocking around with Rapp and the Rhythm Kings put the finishing touches on me and straightened me out. To be with those guys made me know that any white man, if he thought straight and studied hard, could sing and dance and play with the Negro. You didn't have to take the finest and most original and honest music in America and mess it up because you were a white man; you could dig the colored man's real message and get in there with him, like Rapp. I felt good all over after a session with the Rhythm Kings, and I began to miss that tenor sax.

Man, I was gone with it—inspiration's mammy was with me. And to top it all, I walked down Madison Street one day and what I heard made me think my ears were lying. Bessie Smith was shouting the *Downhearted Blues* from a record in a music shop. I flew in and bought up every record they had by the mother of the blues—*Cemetery Blues, Bleedin' Hearted*, and *Midnight Blues*—then I ran home and listened to them for hours on the victrola. I was put in a trance by Bessie's moanful stories and the patterns of true harmony in the piano background, full of little runs that crawled up and down my spine like mice. Every note that woman wailed vibrated on the tight strings of my nervous system; every word she sang answered a question I was asking. You couldn't drag me away from that victrola, not even to eat.

What knocked me out most on those records was the slurring and division of words to fit the musical pattern, the way the words were put to work for the music. I tried to write them down because I figured the only way to dig Bessie's unique phrasing was to get the words down exactly as she sang them. It was something I had to do; there was a great secret buried in that woman's genius that I had to get. After every few words I'd stop the record to write the lyrics down, so my dad made a suggestion. Why didn't I ask my sister Helen to take down the words in shorthand? She was doing secretarial work and he figured it would be a cinch for her.

If my sister had made a table-pad out of my best record or used my old horn for a garbage can she couldn't have made me hotter than she did that day. I've never been so steamed up, before or since. She was in a very proper and dicty mood, so she kept "correcting" Bessie's grammar, straightening out her words and putting them in "good" English until they sounded like some stuck-up jive from *McGuffy's Reader* instead of the real down-to-earth language of the blues. That girl was schooled so good, she wouldn't admit there was such a word as "ain't" in the English language, even if a hundred million Americans yelled it in her face every hour of the day. I've never felt friendly towards her to this day, on account of how she laid her fancy high-school airs on the immortal Bessie Smith.

Inspiration's old lady gave birth to a new brainchild one afternoon at a Rhythm Kings rehearsal, when I took a few choruses on Jack Pettis' C-melody sax while he was out humoring his bladder. My head began to buzz while I played. I had to cut loose some way, to turn my back once and for all on that hincty, killjoy world of my sister's and move over to Bessie Smith's world body and soul. My fingers itched for a horn, so I could sit around and blow with my real friends for the rest of my life. I was so hyped-up I couldn't sit still; every nerve in my body had St. Vitus' Dance and sweat popped out all over my face. Now-or-never was the play.

Finally, without knowing for sure what I was going to do, I ran home. I sneaked into the house and stole my sister's Hudson-seal fur coat out of the closet, then I beat it down to a whorehouse and sold it to the madam for $150. With the dough I made for the Conn Music Company and bought an alto sax for cash. Then I began to breathe easier—my sister had paid for her fine-lady act and put me in a business where they said "ain't" all the day long and far into the night. Great deal.

The Rhythm Kings were rehearsing all afternoon, and Rapp made me break out my brand-new horn and sit in with them. Every note I blew that day was a blast at my sister and her book-learning. I couldn't go home after that, naturally, so the same day I moved into a room across from the poolroom. Come to think of it, I *ain't* been home since.

I didn't want to work in the poolroom again because I needed my evenings free to practise and run with Rapp. Then one day I ran into Mottel Rovech, an old friend of the family's, and he asked me would I like to work for him in his phonograph factory, the Linerphone Talking Machine Company on Union Street. I told him sure, and the next day I was made superintendent of the whole plant. Mottel was a walking ledger—he ran a million-dollar business out of his pockets, keeping all his records in Yiddish on little cards and scraps of paper that he carried around with him. I straightened out his bookkeeping system and paid some attention to the business at first, but the music finally got the better of me and I started to clown around the place. I brought my sax to work and practised the blues all day in the office, while all the workers left their benches and stood around listening. I guess that was the first time in history that an audience ever got paid union wages for listening to a jazz concert. Mottel and I both decided that it would be better if I stayed home to do my practising, so the job came to an end.

That was the last job I ever took that went tangent to the music, except for the stretches when I peddled marihuana. Seeing me on the loose, Murph gave me the idea of dropping around to see a booking agent, and when I wandered out of that office in a daze I was a professional musician with my own band. My job was to get together a four-piece outfit under my own name ("Milton Mezzrow and His Perculatin' Fools," it was called) to play a stage-show date in a burlesque house. Our program was made up of three numbers, *Royal Garden*, *Jelly Roll*, and *Panama*, which we took over from the Rhythm Kings. That date lasted for two weeks and my feet never came near the ground in all that time.

Then a banjo player named Fuzzy Greenfield made me an offer to play in a roadhouse band with him for thirty-five bucks a week, "good tips," and room and board. But there was a catch: I had to join the union first, and that took gold. I went to see my gambler friends at The Corner and told them my story, and right away they dug up the initiation fee and sent me to a pal of theirs on the union's board of examiners. I answered some questions and signed some papers and man, what you know, I was in.

I was sure one perculatin' fool that day. There in black and white on the card it said Milton Mezzrow was now a member in good standing of Local 10 of the Chicago Federation of Musicians of the American Federation of Labor. The date was December 11, 1923. That's my birthday, buddy; that's the day I was born with a silver sax in my yap, after being bounced around in Lady Luck's belly for twenty-four long years.

Yes sir, I came into the world that day with a stamped and sealed birth certificate in my hand, by courtesy of the A. F. of L. Jack, I finally made it, I was a musician. If you'll pardon my beat-up English—Ain't that a bitch!

CHICAGO, CHICAGO

Chicago, Chicago,
That toddlin' town, toddlin' town,
Chicago, Chicago,
I'll show you around. . . .

CHICAGO

THEY FOUND THE BODY IN A DITCH

BURNHAM was a small town on the Illinois boundary line, not far from Hammond, Indiana, a hop and a skip from Chicago. If the census man ever counted up all the dishwater hair and Timkin rear ends that swung around that place, he would have found more whores per square foot than in any town in the good old U.S.A. The houses they worked in never played shut-eye, and they did more business than a free-lunch counter on the Bowery, with about two hundred girls who worked eight-hour shifts on weekdays and twelve hours straight on Saturdays and legal holidays. The town was better known to tourists than Niagara Falls—it *was* a kind of Niagara Falls, strictly the one-night-stand type—and important visitors from every state in the Union dropped around to snag a honeymoon between trains. Pimps and simps would fall in from here and there and everywhere, grabbing thousand-dollar advances from the madames and leaving their lady friends in pawn. The girls stayed put until they ground out the thousand or got a slap from Mr. Clap.

Burnham's real business center was made up of these pleasure houses—this was one place where business and pleasure were buddies —and it was a block from the Arrowhead Inn, where we played. Business jumped all the time at the Inn from the traffic going and coming. You could always dig whether a cat was on his way to or coming from a workout at one of the houses when he dropped in at the Arrowhead for a bracer. If he was all hopped up, cracking wise, acting big buying drinks for the house, he was on his way. But if he came in with his haunches dragging the ground and his chin in his lap, looking to drink up all the whisky on the bar, you could gamble he'd been there and gone. Sugar plums became salt mackerel fast in that town.

The girls leaving the eight P.M. and four A.M. shifts would stop off at the cabaret for some sport, and they were good-natured and sociable, even after eight hours of grinding at the mill. I used to walk from table to table, playing request numbers on my horn while one of the entertainers sang. I never in my life saw a flock of chicks who could turn on the weeps so fast when we played their favorite tearjerkers—songs like *Ace in the Hole, My Gal Sal*, and *Melancholy Baby*. One girl always asked for Victor Herbert's *Kiss Me Again* and began to rain in the face like a professional mourner every time she heard it. All these chicks went to Weep City when they heard the words to *The Curse of an Aching Heart*:

> *You made me what I am today,*
> *I hope you're satisfied,*
> *You dragged and dragged me down*
> *Until my soul within me died.*
> *You shattered each and every dream,*
> *You fooled me from the start,*
> *And though you're not true*
> *May God bless you,*
> *That's the curse of an aching heart.*

That was the Number One song on their Fit Parade.

Al Capone's syndicate owned a piece of the Arrowhead, as well as the whole town, including the suburbs, but there was a part owner living on the premises with his wife, a tall, husky well-built guy named Frank Hitchcock who looked like ready money. We were one big happy family at first, the musicians and girl entertainers and the Hitchcocks, all living upstairs in separate rooms and small apartments.

The piano player in the band was an old maid about forty-five who knew every song that had been published in the last hundred years and could play in any key you named, each one cornier than the other. Fuzzy Greenfield, a tall gawky kid with heavy horn-rimmed glasses, handled the plectrum banjo, a five-stringed instrument with a long neck. Fuzzy was a studious guy, never hit a bad chord, and always had himself a good time. Ray Eisel, the drummer, was a thin and wiry fly cat who really beat his tubs. He was raised in the colored district on the South Side, where drums could talk.

Ray and Fuzzy were salty with our unhip no-playing piano player, because she broke time on the piano so bad that the strings yelled whoa to the hammers. The three of us got along fine. The first time we began to jawblock we found out that we all were from the jazz school, and that made us friends right away. When I dragged out my music library and showed them the copies of *Royal Garden* that I got from Clarence Williams in person, my stock became preferred to them. We began to rehearse like mad, and walked around so chesty we would have made Miss Peacock pull a fade-out.

One afternoon I went into Chicago to pick up some music at the Melrose Brothers' Publishing Company. Somebody was playing the piano in one of the rehearsal rooms in a way that made me know he was colored, and when I busted in I came face to face with Jellyroll Morton, the composer of many a jazz classic. Nobody ever played just like him—he was lyrical and didn't have as much of a beat as some guys, but his delicate and flowery touch was Jelly's trademark. We got to be pals fast, and he gave me the orchestrations for his famous tunes, *King Porter Stomp* and *Wolverine*. When I brought that music back to the Inn the boys jumped on it like mice on cheese.

If you could catch a couple of cats that just met each other talking about certain musicians they know or humming a riff or two to each other, before you could call a preacher they'd be practically married. Don't forget that in those days our music was called "nigger music" and "whorehouse music" and "nice people" turned their noses up at it. Jazz musicians were looked down on by the so-called respectable citizens as though they were toads that crawled out from under a rock, bent on doing evil. We could roam around a town for weeks without digging another human who even knew what we were talking about.

When I told Ray Eisel I knew those two great colored drummers, Tubby Hall and Baby Dodds, he jumped for joy because they had inspired him to play the drums and were his ideals. We got so close to each other that we made the Siamese twins look like they were standing on opposite sides of the Grand Canyon. I really went for Ray's press roll on the drums; he was the first fay boy I ever heard who mastered this vital foundation of jazz music. After a while Ray and I even had our suits made of the same material and cut in the same style by the same tailor, to show we belonged to the same hip school.

Our little band shaped up fine, especially after we outed that nickelodeon piano player and got Eddie Long, a kid who had a very heavy touch but a wonderful ear and a gift for transposing like Old Man Rudiments himself. We sopped up a lot of learning at Capone's University of Gutbucket Arts. The entertainers mooched from table to table singing fifteen or twenty choruses each, most of them howling in ungodly keys, and none of them ever had any written music so we backed them up by ear and it was collective improvisation all night long.

Pretty soon I was made leader of the band and put in charge of the entertainers, doing the hiring and firing. I guess I took my work to heart because inside of a month they were calling me "The Professor" around that University, and meant it.

One day along about noon Frank Hitchcock yanked us all out of our pads and took us downstairs. There was a lot of excitement around the place and we were called out to the back yard, where we saw some men putting up a large circus tent. I figured some carnival was coming to town and we were going to play for it.

Carnival hell. When we went inside the tent we saw barrels of beer being lined up in long rows, and a large icebox being built off to one side. I didn't dig this set-up at all until a man named Jack, one of Capone's lieutenants, came along. He gave us a brace and bit, a box of sticks like the butcher uses to peg meat with, and some galvanized pails. Then he yelled, "One of you guys drill holes in these barrel plugs and let three-quarters of a pail of beer run out of each barrel. Then another guy plugs up each hole with these here wooden sticks, to stop the beer from running out."

It was just about that time that Capone bought up the Blackhawk

Brewery in Chicago, but he couldn't brew anything stronger than near beer there because the Feds had his water on and it was boiling. So these barrels of near beer were trucked out to the Arrowhead to be spiked.

After we let out the right amount from a barrel, another guy came along with a large pail that had a pump and gauge attached to it. In this pail was a concoction of ginger ale and alcohol, just enough to equal the amount of beer that was drawn off. This mixture was pumped into each barrel, plus thirty pounds of air, and you had a barrel of real suds. I think they got as high as seventy-five bucks a barrel for this spiked stuff.

Jack showed up then for the next maneuver. That cat was stronger than Samson after a raw steak dinner. He would roll a barrel over so the plug was facing up, then break off the meat stick and place a new plug over the old one. With one mighty swing of a big wooden sledgehammer he would drive the new plug all the way in, forcing the old one clean into the barrel. In all the time I understudied at this spiking routine, I never saw Jack take a second swing at a plug.

I began to get better acquainted with the rest of the mob, including Mr. Shot himself. Al always showed up surrounded by a gang of trigger men—they sat in a corner, very gay and noisy but gunning the whole situation out of the corners of their eyes. Al's big round face had a broad grin plastered on it and he was always good-natured, which didn't annoy me at all.

Al's youngest brother Mitzi, then about eighteen years old and studying to be a Romeo, used to hang around the place whenever he had time. His job was to follow the beer trucks out to Burnham, riding in a small Ford coupé with Little Dewey, another protection man, to make sure the load wasn't hijacked. Their cute little Ford tagged along behind those big trucks like a harmless pup, nobody ever guessing that it was loaded up with tommy guns. Mitzi was handsome and streamlined, and he really broke it up with one of the entertainers, Lillian, a sandy-haired, pleasant girl who was more sedate than the other chicks, more the clean-cut small-town type. Mitzi went all the way for her, and big brother Al didn't like it at all.

Al pitched a boogie-woogie about Mitzi's romance, and that's how I got my nickname of The Professor. "Fire that girl," he told me. "Get her out of here. If I hear any more stuff about her and Mitzi you're booked to go too."

I should have had my head examined—all of a sudden I got interested in talking it over. "I won't fire her," I said. "She's one of the best entertainers we got around here. Why don't you keep Mitzi out of here, if that's the way you feel about it?" I was so hot under the collar, I forgot that you need something to wrap a collar around.

"She can't sing anyway," Al said.

"Can't sing," I yelled. "Why, you couldn't even tell good whisky if you smelled it and that's your racket, so how do you figure to tell me about music."

All of a sudden I remembered that I was talking to Mr. Fifty Caliber himself, and lockjaw came on. I began to wonder how many bounces my head was going to take crossing the street.

Five or six of Al's henchmen were standing around and they began to laugh. I guess I managed to put up a kind of feeble grin myself, while I waited for their typewriters to begin pounding out their farewell notes to me. Might as well go out smiling, I figured. Happy as the day is long. Die laughing.

Al busted out howling himself. "Listen to the Pro-fes-sor!" he said. "Haw! haw! The kid's got plenty guts." But then he got serious again, and so did I—it was funny how my moods began to run right after his. "But if I ever catch Mitzi fooling around here it won't be good for the both of you, see." I saw. I could even see the goosepimples on my goosepimples.

That's how I got my nickname, without so much as a bruise. But for a long time after that I wasn't so good at conversation—you never saw a Professor with less gift of gab.

Romance began to romp all over the Inn. Frank Hitchcock called me outside one day and swore me to secrecy, then handed me the keys to his big McFarland sedan and told me to run over to Hammond and pick up Millie Smith, the best-looking and singinest gal we had in our crew. On the way back Millie asked me to help her out of the mess she had gotten into. Mrs. Hitchcock was hip to her romance with Frank and that eternal triangle was about to be squared. "I want to quit, Milton," she said, "but Frank is so much in love with me that he threatens to hunt me down to the end of the world if I leave Burnham. Oh, Milton, what am I going to do?"

Millie was a fine-looking girl with sweet ways about her, but I couldn't see how I would fit into this picture. If I didn't play ball with Frank he would be frantic, yet Mrs. Hitchcock was all right with me because she always looked out for us. She kept the books for the syndicate, checked the cash registers, and gave the musicians a break when she figured up our tabs for drinks. Things were messy.

One night a waiter winked me off the bandstand and said the boss wanted to see me in the back yard. I found that big slob sitting out there on a beer barrel, bawling like a two-year-old. "Millie and me have been fussing," he said, "and she's sitting on a log out there in the woods and won't come back. You got to do something, you just got to." It seemed like the syndicate was beginning to get hot about his affair with Millie—Mrs. Hitchcock was threatening to leave and Al's boys were trying everything in the books to break it up. They needed Mrs. Hitchcock because they knew they could trust her bookkeeping. A bigtime pimp was sent in to Millie and tried to lean his affection on her; he kept her sitting up after work until high noon, fruiting her, and the plan worked. Frank got wind of this heavy romancing and had a brawl with Millie out in the woods. Seemed as if Scarface was in there when it came to psychology too.

Frank had a proposition to make me. "Look, Milton," he said, "I've got a big bankroll socked away in a vault in Chicago, and I want you to come to Mexico with Millie and me. I got plenty of connections down there. All we got to do is take the McFarland and drive down and go in the dope-smuggling racket. In a few months we'll clean up a million bucks and then we'll quit and go to Europe and lead a wonderful life. It's no use, Milton, I love Millie so much I can't help myself."

I began to think that sure was no lie and told him I would think it over, just to quiet him down. He asked me to take the car and go over to the woods to get Millie.

Right here is where we pulled a boner. I didn't know at the time that I was being followed, but my leaving the bandstand out of a clear sky and taking Frank's car called for a tail. The mob figured that Frank and I were cooking up something, and before the night was over I was called to the bar and put on the carpet by Johnny Patten, the Boy Mayor of Burnham.

Johnny Patten was known from coast to coast in the underworld. He was a sharp cat, about twenty-five; a fashion plate, always jolly and full of stuff, with a real Irish wit. Johnny took me outside and came right to the point. "Kid," he said, "I like you and I don't want to see you get in wrong, so stay away from Frank and Millie. We'll take care of that." The pat on the back he gave me was friendly enough, but it could have been a shillelagh just as well. Johnny could get away with murder if he wanted to, and I mean murder. There never was a town sewed up as tight as Burnham was under the syndicate. The chief of police was our bartender, and all the waiters were aldermen, so we never had any trouble with the law. The only time the board of aldermen ever had a meeting was when enough of the waiters ganged up around the bar to talk about the laines they clipped, and the police chief was too busy mixing drinks to bust himself under the prohibition act.

Things began to happen fast. First Mrs. Hitchcock packed up and took a powder, and there was hell to pay. There was nobody to run the Inn and keep the books—that is, nobody without sticky fingers. After a conference of the syndicate I was called in by Johnny Patten again. "Kid, can you keep books?" he asked. "Not much, just for the joint and like that." I'd studied a little bookkeeping in school, and I'd done that kind of work for Mottel Rovech, so I told him yes.

Johnny threw up his hands and exclaimed, "Well, you guys, our worries are over—The Professor's gonna keep school now. Now look kid, all we want around here is a 60-40 break. Don't say a word if you catch these mugs stealing; so long as we get sixty cents on the dollar we'll call it even." He showed me how to operate the cash registers and slipped me the combination to the safe.

Things went along good for a while, and then I was summoned before the council again. "We've bought the Roadside Home on the road to Joliet," Johnny told me, "and we want to know if you will take your band and some of your entertainers out there and run the place for us? We're putting the joint in Millie Smith's name because that's the only way to get her out of here and get Mrs. Hitchcock back. We know you'll give us a break and make yourself some nice dough too. How about it?"

It was O.K. with me and I told him so—I was getting fed up with all the plotting and buzzing around the Arrowhead anyhow. "You won't have any headaches," Johnny assured me. "Little Dewey will be out with the beer every day and you can get together with him and leave us know how things are going." Just like that I was in business.

The Roadside Home was a pretty sort of restaurant with a semi-circular driveway in front, a nice flower garden, and sharp land-scaping. It was built on the style of old English architecture, three stories high, with gabled roofs all around, real fancy. There was a large screened-in porch out in front, and the whole place looked more like somebody's mansion than a cabaret. The joint had been closed down for a year by the government, on account of a murder being committed there and some booze being found on the premises.

I loaded up the band, four of the entertainers, and Bonnie, the checkroom girl, and off we went. The reason I took Bonnie along was because I liked her; in fact, we got married later. She was a dark-haired, attractive kid, always full of spirit and very congenial, and she had ambitions to be an entertainer. Whenever I looked over at her from the bandstand during a number, she'd put her thumb in her mouth and blow her cheeks out, making fun of me, and it always gave me a laugh. I taught her the words to *Nobody's Sweetheart* and *Lots O' Mamma*, plus a little Charleston step like I'd seen on the South Side, and she was a performer. I had to play Svengali to her Trilby all the time—she couldn't follow when anybody else played the piano, so I backed her up when she sang.

One night two new entertainers showed up at the Roadside, and I took them upstairs to their rooms. One of them had a gang of beautiful evening gowns but couldn't sing a lick, and I wondered why the agent sent her out. Her name was Ann Brown. I didn't know anything was up until Little Dewey spotted her one night and almost crawled into a beer barrel. "What's *she* doin' here?" he yelled.

"Hell, that's one of the new entertainers," I said. "Don't tell me she's one of *your* loves." By this time I was ready to believe everybody was romancing everybody else. I'd already caught Frank Hitchcock up in Millie's room in the Roadside, which didn't help my nervous indigestion any.

"One of *my* loves!" Little Dewey exploded. "Christ, that's the big boss's *wife*." The boss, naturally, was Capone himself.

I was right in the middle of a meal but I ate no more, even though we had our famous dish that night, milkfed spring chicken. It seemed that Ann had heard about one of the boys being mixed up with an entertainer in Burnham and didn't know it was Frank Hitchcock, not Al, so she was doing a little snooping on her own. I decided to separate myself from that place right quick.

I called Burnham and told Frank to get another band, and he almost climbed into the telephone making me all kinds of propositions, because he didn't trust anybody else with Millie. I was a safe thirty miles away, so I told him I was leaving inside of a hour and I didn't want to get mixed up in any kind of swindle that the boss wouldn't be happy about. The only tense I ever wanted from Al Capone when he mentioned The Professor was the present tense.

Bonnie got her things together and piled in, and we cut out for Chicago. That was the last I saw of Burnham and the Roadside Home. A couple of years later Frank Hitchcock's body was found in a ditch on one of those lonely roads. Some musician married Millie Smith, and she got TB.

6

THEM FIRST KICKS ARE A KILLER

I GUESS I must be the sociable type—my list of associates was beginning to look like a Barbary Coast police blotter on Saturday night. On my next job, besides meeting Leon "Bix" Beiderbecke, "the young man with a horn," I found myself running with a literary ex-pug, a pistol-packing rabbi, and a peewee jockey whose onliest riding crop was a stick of marihuana.

Monkey Pollack was a frantic cat, small, tough and game as they make them. I knew him from way back, because we'd both been roustabout kids on the Northwest Side. For a long time he made out good as a welterweight prizefighter, which explained the mashed-up nose that detoured all over his map and those sagging Ubangi chops. Monkey could really mess with the King's English, and later on he went to work as a reporter on some East Chicago newspaper. He used to hang around the Arrowhead Inn when I was playing there, and for a pencil-pusher he sure could flash plenty of Uncle Sam's I.O.U.'s. That cat had enough gold to pay the whole Newspaper Guild's liquor bill for a year.

One night Monkey came over to me at the Arrowhead and buzzed in his happy-go-lucky way, "Milton, how'd you like to come and work for me?" He puffed on the big cigar that he always had stuck in his face and posed back like a big butter-and-egg man. "I'm a big-time cabaret owner now—I took over a big joint in Indiana Harbor that I'm gonna run as a high-class club, and your band would cinch it in that town. We can't miss, we got everything. Boy, what a sweet set-up, I even got a two-gun rabbi for a bartender."

After we cut out from the Roadside Home I got to thinking

about that Yiddish Buffalo Bill and the idea tickled me so much that I looked Monkey up. In the late Summer of 1924 I got the band together and we headed for the Martinique Inn at Indiana Harbor, righteous and ready.

Monkey wasn't jiving about that bartender. He wasn't exactly a rabbi, yet and still Mac was an honest-to-God Jewish root-toot-tooting cowboy straight from Peckerville, Texas, pardner, and itchy in the trigger finger. He was one of the best marksmen that ever came out of the Panhandle, and he had a gang of medals and cups for his sharpshooting, plus a Dead-Eye Dick control on the trigger and nerves like high-tension coiled springs. For our afternoon sport we'd go out in the back yard and watch him pick dimes off beer bottles with a six-shooter at fifty paces, whooping as though Indians were biting the dust by the gross. Sometimes he would twirl his lasso and rope the whole bunch of us in with one flick of his wrist, yelling "Yippee-i-yip!" like it was round-up time on the range. One of the funniest things I ever heard was Mac spieling in Yiddish, because he spoke it with a thick Southern drawl, piling on more "you-all's" than a Geechee senator. "*Was macht ir*, you-all?" he'd say with his nasal twang, and he had us rolling on the floor. We called him "Ragtime Cowboy Jew" and Monkey nicknamed him "Yiddle." Mac was always sitting out in the yard, sunning himself and twirling his guns lazily at the hip, so I made up a little doggerel song about him that went, "Don't fiddle with the Yiddle, or he'll riddle you in the middle."

Mac was about medium height, lean and wiry, one of those Arrow-Collar-ad guys with slick black hair and sharp features. Indiana Harbor was a drinking town, and he must have shoved enough rot-gut across the bar to fill Lake Michigan, but he never touched the juice himself. Maybe he figured he had to keep his wits about him because things wound up in a brawl almost every night at the Martinique. One guy leaning on the bar would make a friendly remark about his neighbor's tie or the style of his haircut, and in nothing flat each one was cussing up a breeze about the other's mother until they began to rumble. Mac would conk the ugly customers on the top and carry them outside to become acquainted with the good earth, all without getting one hair on his Romeo head out of line. When he was tending bar he always wore a ten-gallon cowboy hat and high-heeled boots, tight-legged pants and a white collar stiff as a plaster-of-Paris cast. A pair of pearl-handled blue-steel pistols always hung from his waist as though they grew there. Mac had about six revolvers to his name, all won in shooting contests, plus two Winchester repeating rifles and a shotgun. The guy was a walking Wild West show.

Indiana Harbor was small but it jumped like mad. It was a steel town, not far from Gary, Indiana, and a lot of the Poles who worked in the mills used to come down to the Martinique to wet their tonsils or maybe dissolve them altogether. Those hunkies were lush crazy and could they drink. They would stick around all night until six in the morning, bending their elbows like they were doing setting-up exercises, then go straight to work. Some of them practically lived in the place, carrying on all their personal business from the bar. I once found a letter on the barroom floor that one of the millhands had been trying to write, and this is what it said: "Dear Mary, I wuz be riting on you for 2 weeks you wuz anser me never, are you mad or wot." The note was signed "Stanislaus Kawajzak." Love, you funny thing.

It was that flashy, sawed-off runt of a jockey named Patrick who made a viper out of me after Leon Rappolo failed. Back in the Arrowhead Inn, where I first met Patrick, he told me he was going to New Orleans and would be back one day with some marihuana, real golden-leaf. He asked me did I want some of the stuff, and coming up tough I said sure, bring me some, I'd like to try it. When Patrick marched into the Martinique one night I began to look for the nearest exit, but it was too late. "Hi ya, boy," he said with a grin bigger than he was hisself, "let's you and me go to the can, I got something for you." That men's room might have been a death-house, the way I kept curving away from it, but this muta-mad Tom Thumb latched on to me like a ball-and-chain and steered me straight inside.

As soon as we were alone he pulled out a gang of cigarettes and handed them to me. They were as fat as ordinary cigarettes but were rolled in brown wheatstraw paper. We both lit up and I got halfway through mine, hoping they would break the news to mother gently, before he stopped me. "Hey," he said, "take it easy, kid. You want to knock yourself out?"

I didn't feel a thing and I told him so. "Do you know one thing?" he said. "You ain't even smokin' it right. You got to hold that muggle so that it barely touches your lips, see, then draw in air around it. Say *tfff*, *tfff*, only breathe in when you say it. Then don't blow it out right away, you got to give the stuff a chance." He had a tricky look in his eye that I didn't go for at all. The last time I saw that kind of look it was on a district attorney's mug, and it caused me a lot of inconvenience.

After I finished the weed I went back to the bandstand. Everything seemed normal and I began to play as usual. I passed a stick of gauge around for the other boys to smoke, and we started a set.

The first thing I noticed was that I began to hear my saxophone as though it was inside my head, but I couldn't hear much of the band in back of me, although I knew they were there. All the other instruments sounded like they were way off in the distance; I got the same sensation you'd get if you stuffed your ears with cotton and talked out loud. Then I began to feel the vibrations of the reed much more pronounced against my lip, and my head buzzed like a loudspeaker. I found I was slurring much better and putting just the right feeling into my phrases—I was really coming on. All the notes came easing out of my horn like they'd already been made up, greased and stuffed into the bell, so all I had to do was blow a little and send them on their way, one right after the other, never missing, never behind time, all without an ounce of effort. The phrases seemed to have more continuity to them and I was sticking to the theme without ever going tangent. I felt I could go on playing for years without running out of ideas and energy. There wasn't any struggle; it was all made-to-order and suddenly there wasn't a sour note or a discord in the world that could bother me. I began to feel very happy and sure of myself. With my loaded horn I could take all the fist-swinging, evil things in the world and bring them together in perfect harmony, spreading peace and joy and relaxation to all the keyed-up and punchy people everywhere. I began to preach my millenniums on my horn, leading all the sinners on to glory.

The other guys in the band were giggling and making cracks, but I couldn't talk with my mouthpiece between my lips, so I closed my eyes and drifted out to the audience with my music. The people were going crazy over the subtle changes in our playing; they couldn't dig what was happening but some kind of electricity was crackling in the air and it made them all glow and jump. Every so often I opened my eyes and found myself looking straight into a girl's face right in front of the bandstand, swinging there like a pendulum. She was an attractive, rose-complexioned chick, with wind-blown honey-colored hair, and her flushed face was all twisted up with glee. That convulsed face of hers stirred up big waves of laughter in my stomach, waves that kept breaking loose and spreading up to my head, shaking my whole frame. I had to close my eyes fast to keep from exploding with the joy.

It's a funny thing about marihuana—when you first begin smoking it you see things in a wonderful soothing, easygoing new light. All of a sudden the world is stripped of its dirty gray shrouds and becomes one big bellyful of giggles, a spherical laugh, bathed in brilliant, sparkling colors that hit you like a heatwave. Nothing leaves you cold any more; there's a humorous tickle and great meaning in the least little thing, the twitch of somebody's little finger or the click of a beer glass. All your pores open like funnels, your nerve-ends stretch their mouths wide, hungry and thirsty for new sights and sounds and sensations; and every sensation, when it comes, is the most exciting one you've ever had. You can't get enough of anything—you want to gobble up the whole goddamned universe just for an appetizer. Them first kicks are a killer, Jim.

Suppose you're the critical and analytical type, always ripping things to pieces, tearing the covers off and being disgusted by what you find under the sheet. Well, under the influence of muta you don't lose your surgical touch exactly, but you don't come up evil and grimy about it. You still see what you saw before but in a different, more tolerant way, through rose-colored glasses, and things that would have irritated you before just tickle you. Everything is good for a laugh; the wrinkles get ironed out of your face and you forget what a frown is, you just want to hold on to your belly and roar till the tears come. Some women especially, instead of being nasty and mean just go off bellowing until hysteria comes on. All the larceny kind of dissolves out of them—they relax and grin from ear to ear, and get right on the ground floor with you. Maybe no power on earth can work out a lasting armistice in that eternal battle of the sexes, but muggles are the one thing I know that can even bring about an overnight order to "Cease firing."

Tea puts a musician in a real masterly sphere, and that's why so many jazzmen have used it. You look down on the other members of the band like an old mother hen surveying her brood of chicks; if one of them hits a sour note or comes up with a bad modulation, you just smile tolerantly and figure, oh well, he'll learn, it'll be better next time, give the guy a chance. Pretty soon you find yourself helping him out, trying to put him on the right track. The most terrific thing is this, that all the while you're playing, really getting off, your own accompaniment keeps flashing through your head, just like you were a one-man band. You hear the basic tones of the theme and keep up your pattern of improvisation without ever getting tangled up, giving out with a uniform sequence all the way. Nothing can mess you up. You hear everything at once and you hear it right. When you get that feeling of power and sureness, you're in a solid groove.

You know how jittery, got-to-be-moving people in the city always get up in the subway train two minutes before they arrive at the station? Their nerves are on edge; they're watching the clock, thinking about schedules, full of that high-powered mile-a-minute jive. Well, when you've picked up on some gauge that clock just stretches its arms, yawns, and dozes off. The whole world slows down and gets drowsy. You wait until the train stops dead and the doors slide open, then you get up and stroll out in slow motion, like a sleep-walker with a long night ahead of him and no appointments to keep. You've got all the time in the world. What's the rush, buddy? Take-it-easy, that's the play, it's bound to sweeten it all the way.

I kept on blowing, with my eyes glued shut, and then a strange thing happened. All of a sudden somebody was screaming in a choked, high-pitched voice, like she was being strangled, "Stop it, you're killing me! Stop! I can't stand it!" When I opened my eyes it seemed like all the people on the dance floor were melted down into one solid, mesmerized mass; it was an overstuffed sardine-can of an audience, packed in an olive-oil trance. The people were all pasted together, looking up at the band with hypnotic eyes and swaying—at first I saw just a lot of shining eyes bobbing lazily on top of a rolling sea of flesh. But off to one side there was discord, breaking the spell. An entertainer, one of the girls who did a couple of vocals and specialized in a suggestive dance routine, was having a ball all to herself. She had cut loose from her partner and was throwing herself around like a snake with the hives. The rhythm really had this queen; her eyes almost jumped out of their sockets and the cords in her neck stood out stiff and hard like ropes. What she was doing with the rest of her anatomy isn't discussed in mixed company.

"Don't do that!" she yelled. "Don't do that to me!" When she wasn't shouting her head off she just moaned way down in her soundbox, like an owl gargling.

Then with one flying leap she sailed up on the bandstand, pulled her dress up to her neck, and began to dance. I don't know if dance is the right word for what she did—she didn't move her feet hardly at all, although she moved practically everything else. She went through her whole routine, bumps and grinds and shakes and breaks, making up new twists as she went along, and I mean twists. A bandstand was sure the wrong place to do what she was trying to do that night. All the time she kept screaming, "Cut it out! It's murder!" but her body wasn't saying no.

It was a frantic scene, like a nightmare walking, and it got wilder because all the excitement made us come on like gangbusters to accompany this palsy-bug routine. Patrick and his gang of vipers were getting their kicks—the gauge they picked up on was really in there, and it had them treetop tall, mellow as a cello. Monkey Pollack stood in the back, moving a little less than a petrified tree, only his big lips shaking like meatballs with the chills, and the Ragtime Cowboy Jew was staring through the clouds of smoke as though he was watching a coyote do a toe-dance. That girl must have been powered with Diesel engines, the way she kept on going. The sweat was rolling down her screwed-up face like her pores were faucets, leaving streaks of mascara in the thick rouge. She would have made a scarecrow do a nip-up and a flip.

The tension kept puffing up like an overstuffed balloon, and finally it broke. There was the sharp crack of pistol shots ringing through the sweat and strain. Fear clamped down over the sea of faces like a mask, and the swaying suddenly stopped.

It was only Mac, our gunplayful cowboy bartender. Whenever he got worked up he would whip out his pistols and fire at the ceiling, catching the breaks in our music. The excitement that night was too much for him and to ease his nerves he was taking potshots at the electric bulbs, with a slap-happy grin on his kisser. Every time he pulled the trigger another Mazda crossed the Great Divide—he may have been punchy but his trigger finger didn't know about it.

The girl collapsed then, as though somebody had yanked the backbone right out of her body. She fell to the floor like a hunk of putty and lay in a heap, quivering and making those funny noises way down in her throat. They carried her upstairs and put her to bed, and I guess she woke up about six weeks later. Music sure hath charms, all right, but what it does to the savage breast isn't always according to the books.

The bandstand was only a foot high but when I went to step down it took me a year to find the floor, it seemed so far away. I was sailing through the clouds, flapping my free-wheeling wings, and leaving the stand was like stepping off into space. Twelve months later my foot struck solid ground with a jolt, but the other one stayed up there on those lovely soft clouds, and I almost fell flat on my face. There was a roar of laughter from Patrick's table and I began to feel self-conscious and nauseous at the same time. I flew to the men's room and got there just in time. Patrick came in and started to laugh at me.

"What's the matter, kid?" he said. "You not feeling so good?" At that moment I was up in a plane, soaring around the sky, with a buzz-saw in my head. Up and around we went, saying nuts to Newton and all his fancy laws of gravitation, but suddenly we went into a nosedive and I came down to earth, sock. Ouch. My head went spattering off in more directions than a hand grenade. Patrick put a cold towel to my temples and I snapped out of it. After sitting down for a while I was all right.

When I went back to the stand I still heard all my music amplified, as though my ear was built right into the horn. The evening rolled away before I knew it. When the entertainers sang I accompanied them on the piano, and from the way they kept glancing up at me I could tell they felt the harmonies I was inventing behind them without any effort at all. The notes kept sliding out of my horn like bubbles in seltzer water. My control over the vibrations of my tones was perfect, and I got a terrific lift from the richness of the music, the bigness of it. The notes eased out like lava running down a mountain, slow and sure and steaming. It was good.

The Martinique was right on the highway between Gary and Chicago, so we used to get a lot of transient trade and college kids from South Bend dropping in, besides the local guzzlers. Not long after we opened, a fine youngster named Fats Morris started to come around. He was a student at Notre Dame, a robust Joe-College kind of kid, husky and tall and always dressed in plus-four knickers. Fats seemed to be well off and he had only one passion in life, jazz music. He used to bring along a gang of college kids who just sat around drinking and listening to the band with expressions that showed how much they were wrapped up and down with it. It never struck us funny that these youngsters didn't bring any girls with them, even though they were a pretty manly bunch of guys. Like practically all jazz disciples they really came to listen, not to dance or gumbeat around the table.

That kind of single-minded attitude always strikes a gong in us musicians. A guy who's really serious about this music likes to take it straight, without getting it all tangled up with sex. One thing at a time, as they say. The musicians I worked and ran with never fooled with women either, not enough to amount to anything. When we saw one of our buddies blowing his top over some chicken dinner we pitied him for going tangent and we hoped he'd get himself straight soon. You can't mix up the sweet talk and high-pressure fruiting with blowing jazz music out of your guts. I know, because I've tried it.

One night Fats invited me to have a drink at his table, and he asked me did I ever hear a kid named Beiderbecke play the cornet. He was surprised when I told him I had heard some of the Wolverines' records but never met Bix, because the only musicians I knew personally and cared much about were Joe Oliver, Sidney Bechet, Jimmy Noone, Baby Dodds and guys like that. "You've got to hear this boy," Fats said. "He's playing not far from here, at Gary Beach."

I didn't pay this talk much mind, but it led to my meeting with a cat that became one of my best friends later on. A few nights later Fats walked into the Martinique with Leon Bismarck "Bix" Beiderbecke.

Musicians get keyed-up and complexy when a brother of the same school drops in to hear them get off. Whether you know the visitor or not, you can dig him just by looking at him; you know right away that this cat is hip and that one isn't. When somebody solid is present and makes you know it, it sets all the performers on edge and sometimes they render a very sad solo trying to send him. The night Bix came in that's what happened. I dug right away that this big overgrown kid, who looked like he'd been snatched out of a cradle in the cornfields, knew what the score was.

We were playing when he came in, and he took a seat with Fats in front of the bandstand. When we looked down at him he just smiled in a friendly way, to show he appreciated what we were doing, and went on watching us, his chin resting in one hand and a glass of beer snuggled in the other like it was a second thumb. There was a dead-serious, concentrated look on his face that I got to know later as his trademark—I've never seen such an intense, searching expression on anybody else. With that pokerface mask of his and his left eye half closed, he looked like a jeweler squinting at a diamond to find out whether it's phony or not. He seemed to be looking right through us.

Bix was a rawboned, husky, farmboy kind of kid, a little above average height and still growing. His frog-eyes popped out of a ruddy face and he had light brown hair that always looked like it was trying to go someplace else. In those days he had an air of cynicism and boredom about most things, just sitting around lazy-like with his legs crossed and his body drooping, but it wasn't an act with him. Even in his teens he had worked out the special tastes and interests that he carried all through his short life—his shying-away from things showed that what got most people worked up left him completely cold.

Not that he was dull or sluggish; nothing like that. That kid could get as lively and hopped-up as anybody you ever saw, but it took something really stirring, something really good, to get a rise out of him. Music is what did it mostly. When something got him all tense and aroused he would keep chuckling "Ha! Ha! Ha!" deep down in his throat and his arms would fly around like a windmill. Music was the one thing that really brought him to life. Not even whisky could do it, and he gave it every chance. The kid must have been born with a hollow leg, the way he gulped the stuff down. But he always had a tight grip on himself, until some music came along that made him want to relax and let go.

When I met Bix he was a star member of the Wolverines, and that little white band had already made some recordings that cause record collectors to foam at the mouth today. The music they were turning out, thanks to Bix's head arrangements, was ten years ahead of its time, and two of their recordings, *Copenhagen* and *Riverboat Shuffle*, were already on their way to becoming classics. Bix's horn work in those numbers was amazing for a kid of schoolboy age.

That night, as soon as we finished the number we were playing for an entertainer, I called *Royal Garden Blues*, our old standby. We had a trick way of playing the breaks in the interlude following the verse and this time we gave it all we had, for Bix's benefit. He sat there like a mummy, not moving a muscle. Then, just as we finished the first break, he jumped to his feet, his face all lit up, grabbed his horn and hopped on the bandstand.

Bix played a cornet that he carried without a case, a short, stubby, silver-plated horn that looked like it came from the junkpile and should never have left there. He stood facing me as he played, because we were the two lead instruments, and the whisky fumes that he blew out of that beat-up old cornet almost gassed me. The music that came out, pickled in alcohol, hit me even harder. I noticed that some of his inflections were like Joe Oliver's and Freddie Keppard's —what he tried to do was to play Joe's half-valve inflections with Freddie's hard drive. All in all, it was more a polished riverboat style than anything else. That style was second nature to Bix because he'd grown up in Davenport, Iowa, and always hung around the waterfront.

I have never heard a tone like he got before or since. He played mostly open horn, every note full, big, rich and round, standing out like a pearl, loud but never irritating or jangling, with a powerful drive that few white musicians had in those days. Bix was too young for the soulful tone, full of oppression and misery, that the great Negro trumpeters get—too young and, maybe, too disciplined. His attack was more on the militaristic side, powerful and energetic, every note packing a solid punch, with his head always in full control over his heart. That attack was as surefooted as a mountain goat; every note was sharp as a rifle's crack, incisive as a bite. Bix was a natural-born leader. He set the pace and the idiom, defined the style, wherever he played, and the other musicians just naturally fell into step.

With his half-valve inflections he produced little quarter-tones, in glissandos that blended into just the right harmonies. He felt his way into those harmonies, groped his way towards them, with a judgment that never failed. In musical chords some notes are supposed to be sharp and some flat, and the whole secret of our music was that in our slurs we instinctively worked towards those notes, without knowing the ABC's of musical theory. A lot of us, including Bix, never learned to read much music until later. Bix had the most perfect instincts of all. He was born with harmony in his soul, and chords instead of corpuscles.

When we finished playing that set we all gathered around Bix and began to pop questions about his recordings. "Gee," I said, "I'd sure like to learn *Riverboat Shuffle*." Without a word he sat down at the piano and started to play it, while we stood around with our mouths hanging open. His touch knocked us all out, it was like his horn playing so much in metric pattern. To a man we forgot we were working. So far as we were concerned there was no such animal as a boss or an audience.

"Get your horn," Bix said to me, reaching for his own. Then he started to blow the introduction to *Riverboat Shuffle*. "You take this note and do this," he told me, blowing the second harmony part. I played it back for him and he yelled, "That's it! That's it!" All worked up, he turned and played Eddie Long a part on the piano, and one by one the pieces began to fit together like the parts of a jigsaw puzzle. Right then and there was one of the early examples of a real "head arrangement," as the colored musicians call it, orchestrated not on paper but by ear. Everybody got their parts straight and Bix gave us a downbeat with his horn to his mouth. "Ha! Ha! Ha!" was all he said when we finished, and all he had to say. His eyes told us the rest.

Monkey Pollack was climbing all over the stand by this time, hardly able to believe his ears. "This kid want a job, Milton?" he said. "Let him start Saturday night!"

From then on Bix and I were pals. He played with us until closing and came back every chance he got. I never stopped being astounded by the things he could do on his horn; a favorite trick of his that always got me was to grab a sheet of music and hold it in front of his horn, flat up against the bell, to give him what we called a "buzz tone." He'd picked up this twist from the colored boys on the South Side and the musicians on the riverboats.

Playing with Bix was one of the great experiences in my life. The minute he started to blow I jumped with a flying leap into the harmony pattern like I was born to it, and never left the track for a moment. It was like slipping into a suit made to order for you by a fine tailor, silk-lined all through. When two musicians hit it off like that right from the start, a fine glow of ease and contentment creeps over them. They've reached a perfect understanding through their music; they're friends, seeing eye to eye. Maybe there's a parable here for the world. Two guys, complete strangers, face each other, and while one takes off on the lead the other feeds the accompaniment to him, helping him to render his solo and making the solo richer, spurring him on and encouraging him all the way. One feeds harmony while the other speaks his piece on his horn, telling the world what's on his mind, supported every inch of the way by his pal. It's like a congregation backing up the minister's words with whispered "Amen's" at the right places. The congregation never stands up and hollers "Shut up! You're a liar!" while the minister's preaching—that would be discord, the whole spell of being together and united in a common feeling would be broken. That's how it is when you play music with a man you understand and who understands you. You preach to him with your horn and he answers back with his "Amen," never contradicting you. You speak the same language, back each other up. Your message and his message fit together like pie and ice cream. When that happens, man, you know you've got a friend. You get that good feeling. You're really sent.

Even when we talked to each other it was the same way, each guy echoing the other. The words could have been dropped altogether; we might just as well have kept nodding at each other. Once in a while, when business was slow at the Martinique, I would knock off early and Bix and I would pile into a cab, bound for the South Side in Chicago to hear some of our favorite musicians. Bix always had a jug of raw corn with him, and while he guzzled we would talk back and forth.

"What do you think about the longhaired musicians?" I asked him once, as we were riding along.

"Most of them are corny," he said, "but it's the composers I like —that is, the modern ones."

"Boy," he told me another time, "it's such a relief to get to the South Side and hear Joe Oliver and Jimmy Noone and Bessie. I miss those old riverboat bands down around Davenport." He got serious for a moment. "I wonder," he said, thinking hard, "why white musicians are so corny? Hell, you even feel better physically when you get in a colored café. The people all seem to be enjoying everything in a real way. The band always has something that keeps your ear cocked all the time. The dancers all feel the music, and the expression on their faces when somebody takes off really gives me a lift. Goddamn, those people know how to live."

It's hard to put into words, but my friendship with Bix was one of the fine things in my life. It's probably tough for anybody outside of the jazz world to latch on to its real meaning. When you're a kid and your first millennium falls on you—when you get in a groove that you know is *right* for you, find a way of expressing something deep down and know it's *your* way—it makes you bubble inside. But it's hard to tell outsiders about it. It's all locked up inside you, in a kind of mental prison. Then, once in a million years, somebody like Bix comes along and you know the same millennium is upon him too, it's the same with him as it is with you. That gives you the courage of your convictions—all of a sudden you know you aren't plodding around in circles in a wilderness. No wonder jazz musicians have an off-center perspective on the world. You can't blame them for walking around with a superior air, partly because they're plain lonely and partly because they know they've got hold of something good, a straight slant on things, and yet nobody understands it. A Bix Beiderbecke will. He knows where to put the "Amen's."

Monkey and all the boys piled into my car one day for a drive into Chicago, and when we came back towards evening we found the place sealed up tighter than a submarine, with padlocks on all the doors. There was an ugly rumor going around that Monkey had been dispensing alcoholic beverages at the Martinique, and the government got upset about it. While we were gone some Feds had swooped down on the place and shut it up.

7

TEA DON'T DO YOU THAT WAY

THE next place I worked in, on Randolph Street in downtown Chicago, was called the Deauville, pronounced Doughville. You had to pull up in a diamond-studded limousine. with solid gold fenders and ermine upholstery, before the doorman would even reach for the twister to your slammer. This new club was what the French call *intime* and we call a closet; there wasn't enough room in it for a midget to swing an underfed kitten, or even for a flea to do the lindyhop, but it was full up with Parisian atmosphere, a telephone booth with French dressing. The owner nixed big crowds out; he never allowed more than five or six parties in the place at one time, and they had to be packed up with loot. Many a night we put on the whole floor show, chorus and all, for a party of six or eight, and they were usually too blind to see it.

It wasn't like the joint went broke for being so hincty. Even the smallest party couldn't get out of there without dropping at least two grand for the night. The boss catered mostly to Indians who had struck oil on the reservation, beefy cattlemen who were sure to be milked, sugar daddies with their sable-sporting chicken dinners, and butter-and-egg men with plenty of bacon. He wasn't exactly doing without. The Deauville was such a mint that he even considered making it smaller.

In this dicty corral I learned that the great American public likes nothing better than to be roped in, and the tighter you squeeze 'em the more you please 'em. The main attraction at the club was Frank Libuse, the famous vaudevillian, who gave the suckers a workout they never forgot. Frank used to pose as a waiter, with baggy pants falling down over his shoes, a Prince Albert coat six sizes too big, and a tablecloth folded over his arm for a napkin. When a party was lucky enough to pass the doorman, the head-waiter would lead them to a table and then Frank went to work. He'd pull the chair out from under some dignified dowager and catch her just before she went to fall on her daniel; leaning over to brush some crumbs off the table, he'd bump up against some pretty young frail with his rear end and send her flying; he spilled soup all over the table, poured drinks into the customers' laps, mussed the ladies' hair as he served them, dropped loaded trays on the floor, yanked the cigar out of some railroad magnate's mouth and ducked it in an ashtray, snatched an uppity dame right up from her seat and waltzed her out on the dance floor, pince-nez and all. With his sunken cheeks, deadpan kisser and wig that looked like a Fuller brush, he used to give us hysterics up on the band-stand, but we had to sit through it pokerfaced and act like we weren't hip. Finally, when the cash customers were hotter than a pussy with the pox, he would knock over the whole goddamn table, then jump out on the dance floor just in time to escape being washed away. Mabel Walzer, his partner, tipped out then, all dolled up like a little girl, and sang some grand opera while Frank trilled delicate little runs offkey on his flute, butchering the aria.

When the customers dug the comedy that had been put on at their expense—and I mean expense—they didn't have guts enough to do anything about it, so they just grinned like a mule eating green tomatoes and tipped all the help heavy to show they were good sports. I guess the moral is that if you want to entertain an American audience good, just beat their brains out and they'll always come back for more.

I got this job in the Deauville from Irving Rothchild, the famous violin player who led Sophie Tucker's band for so many years. The grapevine in the jazz world would make Western Union look like the pony express, and while I was at the Martinique word got around that I was a good "hot man," with a real colored style. When I hit town again after Indiana Harbor I knocked around for a few months playing club dates, but one day Irving looked me up at union headquarters and said he'd heard about my playing and could I get a six-piece band together for this new club.

I got some men together, including Murph Steinberg on the trumpet and a teen-age kid named Eddie Condon on the banjo. Eddie, or Slick, as we called him, never went near a campus but he was strictly the Joe-College type, togged in plus-fours and a polka-dot bow tie and sporting a crew haircut that was one step away from total baldness. Eddie thought the company was too fast for him, especially after he found out the job paid $115 a week, but I finally talked him into it and we got to be good friends after a while.

We finished at the Deauville in the late Spring of 1925 and Irving landed us a summer job at the North Shore Pavilion in South Haven, a resort across the lake from Chicago. Eddie Condon had another vacation job lined up and couldn't make it so I took along his brother Pat on the banjo. Trouble was waiting for us at South Haven—as soon as we hit the place we run smack into that phony race issue. The Pavilion catered mostly to Gentiles, and when the manager found out that three of us musicians were Broadway arabs from the tribe of Israel he wouldn't even leave us blow note one.

This made us hotter than tabasco sauce but Irving wasn't stumped. "If we're smart," he said to us, "we can put that Pavilion guy right out of business. There's a big summer house for rent here, with a porch that's bigger than a regular dance floor, so why don't we take it over and run our own café? I always wanted to be a night-club impresario anyhow." The idea of squatting there for the summer suited us fine, because we all wanted to shake the café sunburn we got in the Deauville. The whole gang of us went to work with hammers and saws, screening in the porch, fixing the leaks in the roof, painting and polishing all over the place. We got hold of a piano somewheres, put up some tables on the porch, and inside of two weeks we had the joint jumping.

That place never did have a name—we forgot to think one up ahead of time, and after our gala opening we never had time to hang a handle on it. We gave the customers a ham-and-cheese sandwich and a bottle of pop for a dollar, and they had the right to hang around all night to cut some rug or dig the band. Irving never got to touch his fiddle all summer long because he had to play host and waiter. If you'd of seen him juggling those plates and bottles around you would have thought that he schooled Frank Libuse, only his act wasn't on purpose. His valet, a little East Side Jewish boy called Dinky, doubled as Chef Cook-'Em-Up. Soon as we got going in the evening, folks down at the beach would hear our horns and up they'd come boogity-boogity, like we were a bunch of Pied Pipers. We never did any advertising—we didn't even have a menu—but the standing-room-only sign would have been out every night, if anybody ever got around to painting a sign. All us nightclub owners lived upstairs with our families and we had ourselves a ball all summer.

We hung out on the beach all day long, jamming our heads off while the people gathered around us like sandflies. The mermaids would come up out of the water, drawn by the music, and in no time at all every pebble on that beach that wasn't dancing the Charleston was doing the Black Bottom. The manager of the Pavilion couldn't see us for looking that summer, especially after he counted up his season's take. Little Dinky did better than any of us at South Haven. He was always playing the horses, and one time he caught a couple of long shots and run his small bankroll up to a couple grand. Right quick he pulled a fade-out on us, and a couple days later, when we already had the cops out looking for him, he showed up again togged like Esquire and driving a big limousine. Bull Durham was his sidekick before, but he couldn't see nothing but corona-coronas now. He gave Irving a fit posing all over the place, then cut out for Florida, where he became a bigtime bookmaker. I hear that he's sitting pretty now, with a big string of horses and a valet of his own. From rags to racehorses, that was Dinky's story.

My struggle-buggy was getting to look like a rinky-dink old tin can on wheels, so when I got back to Chicago that Fall I traded it in for a Willys Knight brougham sedan. One night I got the urge to dig the cats at The Corner and show them how good I was doing, so I pulled up in front of the poolroom and leaned my car against the curb. They sure gave me the glad-hand when they laid their peepers on my new car. "Some car, Milton, where'd you steal it? You won't go to Pontiac this time," one guy said. "Hell no, he'll make the Big House with this one," said another. Then they all got a bright idea. "Hey Milton, what do you say we pile in and make the canhouses." You would have thought I'd left them that morning, the way their minds kept running down that same old alley. You can't teach a dotey cat new tricks.

We made the rounds that night just like it was old times, and at the Four Deuces, one of the big syndicate houses, I met a cute little chick named Jane who had a sad story to lay on me. Jack, I swear, I'm no sky-pilot, but a creep pad turns into a confession booth as soon as I squat in it—the chicks really run their mouths some spieling their life histories in my face. My ears are bent in half from the tales of woe I've listened to in Lulu's parlors on both sides of the Atlantic. "Well, it's a long story," Jane said, taking a deep breath, and then she shot it at me right from Year One, and it was long. Tune out if you've heard this one before. . . .

Born: Des Moines. Married at seventeen, had a baby girl. Husband drinking man, walked out on her. Tough going. Worked as waitress in beanery to keep body and soul together. In walks traveling salesman, promises job in Chicago, stakes her to railroad ticket. Big hopes, going to make fresh start, send for kid. In the big town, no job, has to deal 'em off the arm in hashhouse again, sad. Homesick, tired, bored. Another snake shows up, smooth talker, feeds her line about good job. Final step: he places her in Four Deuces, girls show her the ropes. Humiliation, despair; trapped, no way out. Pimp's a hard man, threatens her, she's scared to leave. Oh, life isn't worth living, what's she to do? She's so miserable, misses the baby. Oh, Milton. . . .

Corny? Sure, the husks are still on it—the oldest profession in the world is jammed up with the oldest stories in the world. What brings you down in a tale like that is not that it's phony but that it's so *true*. That's just the way it does happen in the U.S.A., nine times out of ten, starting right there in Des Moines, or Butte, or

Valparaiso, Indiana. Our national anthem should be *The Curse of an Aching Heart*, played on the G-string.

Could be I'm soft but I always fall for that kind of jive, especially when it rings true, and this time it sure did. The routine was so unhip that she couldn't have made it up. She was a very delicate little thing, sweet and refined, and she seemed so out of place around all those simple whores that my heart went out to her. I began to think fast. That damsel-in-distress sob-story had me buckling on my shining armor and manicuring my white charger, making ready to stage a Keystone-comedy rescue scene in the red-light district.

I was feeling a little restless myself; greener pastures were in my face. Stories from other musicians who'd been off to Detroit and New York kept drifting back to Chicago, making us know that King Jazz was romping up and down the land, and the wanderlust began to get me. The stampede of the Chicagoans, which was to make jazz an international phenomenon ten years later, was just getting under way; a lot of Windy City musicians were packing up their instruments and toothbrushes and setting out to bring the gospel of riff to the citizens of Main Street. Detroit was one place in particular I wanted to dig because the office for all the Gene Goldkette bands was there, Ray Miller's band was at the Addison Hotel, McKinney's Cotton Pickers were jumping at the Arcadia, and Fletcher Henderson was barnstorming around the neighborhood too. My wife Bonnie was putting up with some relatives and I knew she was O.K., so I made up my mind to travel gay—that was the play, all the way.

"Look baby," I said, "if you want to cut out of this joint so bad, I'll take you to Detroit. I had it in my mind to drive over there anyway, so you meet me tomorrow and we'll go places." The halo that started to shape up around my conk was so big and bright, I felt like an overgrown glow-worm. Guys get promoted to the holy-man class for good deeds like that, I figured—I could see the great day coming when Milton Mezzrow would be a legend in all the whorehouses across the country, the patron saint of every women's pen and every home for wayward girls in the U.S.A.

"Oh Milton," Jane said, her face lit up like Old Sol in July, "will you really take me? Really?" She was all set to do a cart wheel and a double flip, and my halo began to eat up more voltage.

In the morning she snuck out of the Four Deuces, leaving all her togs, and I picked her up in front of the LaSalle Street station. Off we drove, zigzagging all around town to make sure we weren't being tailed, and on the way we began to cook up our plans—we were both going to work like hell in Detroit and run up big bank accounts, then Jane would make a beeline for Des Moines and her bouncing baby girl. I got feeling so good that I started to sing some riffs, knocking out a tricky Baby Dodds beat on the steering wheel with my palms: bib-*bop*, bip-*bop*, bip-a-di-dee, bip-*bam*. Pretty soon Jane caught the spirit and began to drum on the dashboard with her knuckles. She latched on to that South Side rhythm real good, catching all the breaks and never messing up the time; when we hit Detroit that night her beat was so solid she was ready to join the union. That little girl had cadence in her cuticles and tempo in her toes.

In Detroit I found lodging for her with a nice respectable elderly couple (I camped solo on a studio couch in the parlor, just me and my halo). Next day I dropped around to the Goldkette office and got the kind of welcome an escaped con does from the warden— they'd heard about me through the grapevine and it looked like I was in. That same night they sent me on a club date with Tommy Dorsey in a pick-up band, where we played opposite McKinney's Cotton Pickers, one of the best-known big colored bands of the day. The corny stocks and jumbled-up special arrangements we had to read at sight must have sounded pretty cute to those colored boys, whose numbers were all fixed by solid arrangers like Don Redman. Outside of Fletcher Henderson's band, the Cotton Pickers were about the first big jazz unit to tour the East, and they came on with a steady rock that was really groovy.

In '26 Detroit was as wide open as a politician's pocket on election day; the town was having itself a ball all around the clock. Even if you had your collar on backwards you weren't safe walking down Bobian, Elizabeth and Adams Streets, where the whorehouses jumped and capered. The girls would sit themselves at the windows in come-on poses and tap on the glass with Chinese chopsticks, to catch your eye—I guess it was what you might call drumming up trade. In the summertime they'd reach out and snatch the straw hat right off your head, and if you were fool enough to go after it your poke was bound to be lighter when you came out. On Saturday nights there were lines a block long outside some of these houses, way before the era of the double feature, and squads of cops turned out to keep the customers in order. The hot-dog man had to make five or six trips home every night to get a fresh supply of franks for these pleasure-seekers.

The real aristocrats of the sporting world in Detroit were the madams—there were so many of them trucking around town with thousand-dollar bills tucked in their stockings, having struck it rich in this new gold rush, that some of the nightclubs had to set aside a special night just for their entertainment. The Club Alabam, on Adams Street in the colored district, used to send a horse-and-wagon touring around town once a week, sporting a big sign that shouted, "LANDLADIES' NIGHT AT THE CLUB ALABAM!—FUN AND FROLIC! —COME ONE AND ALL!" They came by the dozens, loaded down with ice like it was rock candy, leaving their houses operating at full capacity. The only thing that could close down those houses was a quarantine for smallpox.

The Club Alabam was really brawling one night when I dropped around. The landladies were having a field day in that cellar; I could hardly fight my way inside, there were so many buxom madams of both races jammed in there, sporting big sparklers and fancy corsages, each one surrounded by a gang of her chicks and swilling champagne like it came from the kitchen sink. The beef trust was out in full force—these landladies were all shaped up like barrels, wherever there wasn't a crease in their meat there was a dimple. Some fly cat chased a girl right up the stairs, trying to sweettalk her until one of the fellows from the Cotton Pickers hit him in his jaw and knocked him right down again. People coming and going kept stepping over his body like he was a doormat. If a corpse was dropped on the dance floor at the Club Alabam that night, nobody would have even sent for the garbage wagon.

A few musicians I knew were on the stand when I came in, Tommy Dorsey among them, and some of the Cotton Pickers joined them for a light session. That was an eye-opener to me. I began to know what a difference there was between the New Orleans style that I was so hopped-up about and the so-called Eastern style of jazz—the Eastern musicians had a pretentious, flashy, mechanical way of taking a chorus, but very little of their playing had any color or distinction at all; it was only a good tonal quality with slick technique that kept these cats in the limelight, as far as I could see. To this day there hasn't been one of them able to set a pace or establish a definite style in either the jazz or the swing idiom. The real jazz, like the real marihuana, comes from the bayou country.

Before long the Goldkette office steered me to a steady job, playing with a small hot band in a ritzy joint called Luigi's Café. It struck me funny how the top and bottom crusts of society were always getting together during the prohibition era. In this swanky club, which was run by the head of the notorious Purple Gang, Detroit's bluebloods used to congregate—the Grosse Pointe mob on the slumming kick, rubbing elbows with Louie the Wop's mob. That Purple Gang was a hard lot of guys, so tough they made Capone's playmates look like a kindergarten class, and Detroit's snooty set used to feel it was really living to talk to them hoodlums without getting their ounce-brains blown out.

Just by a freak it turned out that the man I rented a room from, a wholesale kosher chicken dealer, was Louie the Wop's father-in-law. It's a small underworld.

A lot of the hot men around Detroit began to drop in at Luigi's, so that the band was usually twice the size our contract called for. Tommy Dorsey was playing at the Book-Cadillac, while his brother Jimmy was at the Greystone, and both of them were regular visitors; so were Bob Chester and Gene Prendegast of the Goldkette Orange Blossom Band (directed by Glen Gray, who later got famous with his Casa Loma orchestra). I don't know if those upper-crust Grosse Pointers ever appreciated it or not, but under Louie the Wop's auspices they were treated to jam sessions night after night by practically all the top-notch musicians who later made jazz history in this country. A list of the guys who played gratis for the customers at Luigi's would make the Music Corporation of America look like its total assets were one small-size shoestring.

I was not without my muta at the time, and some of the boys (I won't mention any names) used to drop by to sit in and get high with me, because I always had the best stuff that could be found. We would have jam-up sessions, playing until we all fractured our toupees, the music getting more frantic and freakish all the time, and then we'd go and stuff ourselves with fine vittles. A couple of times I had to make a trip back to Chi to pick up a fresh supply from my connection, a little Mexican named Pasquale. In those days we used to get a Prince Albert tobacco-can full of marihuana, clean and without any sticks or seeds in it, for two dollars. The grefa they pushed around Detroit was like the scrapings off old wooden bridges, compared with the golden-leaf being peddled in Chicago, and tasted twice as bad.

Every one of us that smoked the stuff came to the conclusion that it wasn't habit-forming and couldn't be called a narcotic. We found out that at one time the government had discussed it as a drug and tried to include it in the Harrison Anti-Narcotic Act but never could dig up any scientific reason for it. There being no law against muta then, we used to roll our cigarettes right out in the open and light up like you would on a Camel or a Chesterfield. To us a muggle wasn't any more dangerous or habit-forming than those other great American vices, the five-cent Coke and the ice-cream cone, only it gave you more kicks for your money.

Us vipers began to know that we had a gang of things in common: we ate like starved cannibals who finally latch on to a missionary, and we laughed a whole lot and lazed around in an easygoing way, and we all decided that the muta had some aphrodisiac qualities too, which didn't run us away from it. All the puffed-up strutting little people we saw around, jogging their self-important way along so chesty and chumpy, plotting and scheming and getting more wrinkled and jumpy all the time, made us all howl, they struck us so weird. Not that we got rowdy and rough about it. We were on another plane in another sphere compared to the musicians who were bottle babies, always hitting the jug and then coming up brawling after they got loaded. We liked things to be easy and relaxed, mellow and mild, not loud or loutish, and the scowling chin-out tension of the lushhounds with their false courage didn't appeal to us.

Besides, the lushies didn't even play good music—their tones became hard and evil, not natural, soft and soulful—and anything that messed up the music instead of sending it on its way was out with us. We members of the viper school were for making music that was real foxy, all lit up with inspiration and her mammy. The juice guzzlers went sour fast on their instruments, then turned grimy because it preyed on their minds.

When you run into hop, Jim, skip and jump. Hop is strictly for hamfats.

Detroit must have been built in a poppy field, there was so much opium going up in smoke in that town. I kept hearing stories from friends about all the hopdogs that lived in Detroit. A musician friend of mine named Mike who kipped in one of these hotels had to mugg with a lot of hophead gangsters who roomed near him, especially with a tough oscar named Frankie Riccardi. This Frankie, a sociable guy with a yen for company, used to drop in on Mike to beat up his chops a while. Mike would have felt happier playing host to a headhunter with his toolkit under his arm.

Frankie Riccardi was always shooting his mouth off to Mike about how great his hop was and how it made our muta look about as strong as ladies' cigars. One day while he was spieling about his dope, Mike called me over to straighten this gunman out with some golden-leaf and lowrate him once and for all. We tipped Frankie off on the routine and he burned up two sticks of gauge real fast, putting on a Samson act, sneering all the time. "These things got as much kick as some corn silk," he said. "Ain't you guys got something real strong, like a malted milk or maybe some farina? *Strunz!*"

Then the tea hit him—all of a sudden he jumped up from his chair and began to squeal like a monkey with his tail cut off. It was really something to see, this bad trigger man running over to the window, tearing at his collar and yelling, "Oh my God, I'm dyin', I'm dyin', call the doctor! For Christ's sake, get me a doctor!" I felt like asking him didn't he want some more of that farina but my P.A. system blew a tube.

We knew that Frankie's gargling and gagging wasn't exactly a death-rattle. He was just having a stomach attack from over-eating or constipation, and the most he needed was some bicarbonate of soda and a physic, not a croaker. You see, when you get high off of gauge it dries up the saliva in your mouth and your stomach fills up with gas and presses against your ticker, till for the first time in your life you feel every beat your heart is making without looking for it. It's the strangest sensation you ever had since you were old enough to know better, like somebody was using your eardrums for tomtoms. At first you hear your heart beat fast, then it begins to come on slow with loud accentuated beats that confuse you so much you can't hear them at all. That's when the fun begins. It's like there's an alarm clock buried under your ribs, ticking off the seconds and reminding you that the shroud-tailor has designs on you. Then it stops. The next thing you think of is, Lord, I must be dying, I can't hear my heart beat any more. It's really on then.

It's funny how the toughest gorilla gets tame and whimpers like a young pup when he begins to hear his own pump riffing. A guy who's got a bad conscience likes to keep away from timepieces. Trigger men don't want to think that everybody goes when the wagon comes and they have to wind up six feet under the sod too, just like all the rest of us, when the clock runs down. The more guys they wash away, the more they get to feeling like they're immortal or something. Never remind a gangster of his pulse, unless you want to lose yours fast.

Frankie's hard crust mightn't ever have been punctured by the hop, but it sure turned to lard fast after those two sticks of tea got a hold of him. Muta takes all the goddamn hardness and evil out of you, cuts down the tush-hog bullying side of your personality and makes you think straight, with your head instead of your fists; it digs the truth out and dangles it right in front of your nose. Everything comes out in the wash starched and clean. A viper doesn't like lies—he's on the up-and-up and makes you get on the ground floor with him. You call your shots all the way in viperland. Frankie probably began to see the faces of all the guys he plugged full of daylight and figured it was Judgment Day instead of an ordinary bilious attack. At first he was squinch-eyed but now his eyes blew up like soapbubbles and panic danced all over his face.

That prize gunman was one sick rooster that day. He may have been hip to his hop, but the muta made him fly right for a hot minute.

A gang of gay sporting people used to come up to Luigi's and pretty soon I found myself hanging out with them. They were mostly gamblers and big spenders, flashy good-natured Jews, dressed in loud checked suits and open-necked sports shirts. At first I took them to be bigtime businessmen and we had some fine times together, eating in private restaurants run by Mrs. Come-And-Get-It and getting our bones cracked in the Russian baths. One of them was a happy-go-lucky guy called Sam "Trombanick" (that means "bum" in Russian), who owned The Oriental Rest on Division Street, where they broiled rib steaks over a charcoal fire and served them on wooden platters.

One Sunday morning, after a workout at the Russian boiler room where they steamed us down to a low gravy, I tagged along with this gang to somebody's apartment in the Charlotte Hotel. In the large living room most of these guys climbed out of their jackets, got a stranglehold on their coronas with their molars, and settled down to a game of knock rummy, with me sitting in. But three of them beat it into the next room without a word and shut the door. Pretty soon a funny smell took charge of the room, and one of the fellows at the table got a wet bath towel, rolled it up, and squeezed it against the crack at the bottom of the bedroom door.

I couldn't dig this mess but I kept my mouth shut and tried to play hip. Nobody else seemed to be paying any mind and I figured I'd be out of line if I cracked my jaw. I kept sniffing that odor and I began to feel queer and out of place, kind of like a Hottentot who wanders into the Union League Club looking for a nickel's worth of betel nuts.

A little later two of the fellows who did the disappearing act came back and joined the game, while a couple more left the table and went into the bedroom. When the door opened I could see a wet sheet hanging on the inside of it, and my skull began to play a quiz game. "What the hell's going on in there?" I asked.

"Send him in here and let him find out for himself," somebody yelled from the bedroom. I began to wish I didn't have such a gift of gab, but now I had to keep up my front. I got up and strolled into the next room, not knowing whether to shake or grin and doing a little of both.

That was one walk I sure wish I had never taken. It took me five seconds to get into that room and, later on, damn near five years to crawl all the way out again, on my hands and knees.

The smell in that room was enough to knock you out. It was sort of sweet, with a punch in it, heavy as an insomniac's eyelids, so thick and solid it was like a brick wall built all around you. It made my smeller tingle, got me scared and excited me too, put me on edge—it promised a rare jam-up kick, some once-in-a-life-time thrill. The three guys were stretched out crossways on the bed, one of them facing the other two, and between them was a round brass tray full of funny little gadgets, with a small lamp burning right in the center of it. There was a bowl of fruit laying on the bed too. It looked like a scene straight out of the Arabian Nights, with the thieves and princes disguised in pinchback sports jackets. I was looking for the carpet to flap and take off any minute now and sail out of the window, bed and all, with the four of us sprawled out on it.

I had introduced one of these borscht-guzzling oriental potentates to muta, and he spoke up. "Come over here," he said, "and lay down with your head on my chest and I'll let you smoke something that'll make you throw your muggles in the ashcan. There ain't nothin' to them weeds, kid, try this and you'll put them up for keeps. This is something you're gonna enjoy."

"Jesus, what is it?" I asked, and my heart began to make sounds like an outboard motor running out of gas. "Lay down and try it— I wouldn't give you anything that could hurt you, kid. We do this every two weeks or so. This is called pleasure smoking, the rich man's kind, it's hop and it's good for what ails you." They all came on with kyaw-kyaw over this brilliant dialogue.

Grefa was kid-stuff to me, but opium meant dope and I was really scared of it. Hell, I thought, Detroit is really a hoppy town— people must order their opium along with their groceries. That bed might have been a cold marble slab, the way I eased down on it until the opium layout was right square in my chops. The guy opposite us was cooking the stuff. In one hand he held the long ebony pipe (a fancy one, sporting a big diamond on the stem), with a bowl stuck on it where he did his cooking.

"So you're a musician, hey?" he said. "All you horn-tooters smoke them weeds, don't you? What does it do, make you get hot when you play? You know it's a funny thing, come to think of it, this very same pipe was made by one of your musician guys only he quit playing and now he makes flutes and clarinets. Looks like a flute, don't it? But wait'll you hear the song this little pill sings with it. You play the flute too?" he asked me, signifying to the others, and they all fell out at this funny gag.

In this comedian's right hand was the yen hok, a wire about as long and thin as a hatpin, with finer wire wound around the handle. He would dip the point of the yen hok into a jar of dark-brown gooey stuff that looked like tar, then hold a drop over the flame until it began to swell up like a tiny balloon, adding more to it now and then. Over and over he kept heating this small hunk of hop, rolling it on the thumb of his left hand until it was compact and looked like a tight little wad of brown cotton. Then he held the pipe bowl close to the top of his special lamp and stuck the pill on the edge of the bowl, drawing the yen hok round and round to stretch the opium, which was now golden-brown in color. . . .

(I'll skip the rest of the details because right now I'm not supposed to be writing an instruction manual on how to become a dope fiend in three easy lessons.)

Several times the master of ceremonies stuck the pill close to my nose and told me to smell it. Poppa, you never laid your sniffer on anything so fine in all your life. It made me feel like I wanted to waller all in it, chew on it, plaster it all over my fine body and then lick it off inch by inch. I just took a deep breath, sighed, and whispered "Mmmmmmm, that sure smells good, Jack." For a second I was really for it.

"This is what you call shyin', kid," the cook said. "This cooks all the poison out of the pill." Finally the gummy pill was given another going-over until it was shaped like a cone, then it was stuck into a small eye in the center of the bowl. When the pipe was passed to the man behind me he drew on it—the stuff began to dance and curl a little around the edges, making a sizzling sound, and then it ran into the bowl and disappeared. The chef fixed up another pill and passed it to the next man. After a couple of centuries my turn came around. The chairman of the meeting began to pass me the pipe, but then he drew it back and laid it down on the tray.

"This your first pill, kid?" he asked. I told him yes, wondering if maybe they were giving me a last-minute reprieve. "I'll be damned if I'll give it to him," he said, and called out for one of the fellows in the next room. "Hey Jake," he yelled, "come on and give this Johnny-Come-Lately his first pill. You know I got a habit." I found out later a man that's hooked on hop will never lay the first pill on a beginner, because he doesn't want it on his mind in case you become a hophead. This is a strong superstition among the "legion of the condemned." Dope fiends are full of nice little rules and regulations like that; Emily Post could write a book just on hophead etiquette.

Jake came in, glad to lend a helping hand, and passed me the pipe. "Keep puffin' in short jerks," he said, "and swallow the smoke at the same time." I felt like I couldn't even swallow my own tonsil-juice without gagging then, but I tried to follow instructions the best I could, wondering how many of my old pals would miss me after I was gone.

Goddamn if I didn't live through it. Man, I even liked it. Before I finished one pill a heatwave heaved up out of my stomach and spread all through me, right down to my toes, the most intense and pleasant sensation I have ever felt in all my life. At first it tipped easy-like through my main line, then it surged and galloped down all my sidestreets; and every atom in my body began to shimmy in delight. That fiery little pill was toe-dancing up and down every single strand of my nervous system, plucking each one till it hummed a merry song, lighting up a million bulbs in my body that I never knew were there—I didn't even know there were any sockets for them. I glowed all over, like the sun was planted in my breadbasket. Man, I was sent, and I didn't want to come back.

"How'd you like that, kid?" the cook asked. "Better than your muggles?"

"I'll say it is," I said, beaming at him. "Gee, you feel it way down to your crunchers. Tea don't do you that way." They all began to laugh and that put me on a complex towards the whole situation, but in a minute I was pulling on my second pill. This time my stomach began to growl a little—not in protest, not kicking up any fuss about it, but like an old hounddog having his flea-bites scratched and moaning low in pleasure. After a while, when my belly rhumba stopped, I laid back with not a care or a worry in this world. I was a skinful of contentment, a bundle of happiness in a blue serge suit. I found myself watching the cook dreamily, as though he had some magic formula. I didn't ever want to lose that warmth and tingling ease in my body. My blood had turned to hot rum-and-butter, my skull was crammed full of sunbeams.

When I smoked about five pills they told me I had had enough and should eat some of the fruit in the bowl. "Eat an orange, Milton," the cook said. "Fruit and hop go together, and it's good for you." I don't think an orange ever tasted any sweeter to me; it was like some nectar the angels juice up on in the driftsmoke neighbor-hood, not anything that ever came off a lousy old tree.

We finally got up and went back to the rummy game. My eyelids seemed to have weights on them and the lights sort of dazzled me at first; I felt self-conscious because I knew all these guys were gunning me and grinning. Pretty soon I began to feel sick at the stomach and tore out for the bathroom. In a couple of minutes it was all over and I had that grand and glorious feeling again, all sunny and mellow, with ultra-violet rays playing hide-and-seek all through my frame. The gang told me to lay down for a while, and when I stretched out on the couch I felt as satisfied as a cat under a hot stove. It was too good to be true. Muta never came on like that. But then I got to thinking that this stuff was the real thing, and if I had to keep on using it I would be a dope fiend, and that kind of brought me down.

I didn't work that night—I sent a substitute in my place and drove straight for home, to stash my frame between a deuce of lily-whites. All night long I slept sounder than an Egyptian mummy. When I finally got back to work I felt a little shaky and hazy, and took everything easy; the stuff didn't affect my playing much except that I felt sluggish and went around in a sort of halfway stupor. This doesn't compare with muggles when it comes to play-ing, I told myself, and I made up my mind not to mess with it again. That's one resolution I sure wish I had kept.

Years later, when I was living in New York, I finally found out who all my hophead friends were. One day I saw Sam Trom-banick's mug staring at me from the front page of a Manhattan paper—he was one of the leaders of the Purple Gang and he had just been bumped off. That Purple Gang must have included in its membership the whole goddamned population of Detroit. After that, one by one, I saw the kissers of most all those good-natured sporty guys in the papers, including the yen hok expert and Jake, who gave me my initiation to hop—they all got theirs sooner or later. One day even Frankie Riccardi's pan jumped out at me. He was Louie the Wop's brother; until he made his exit he was head torpedo for the mob.

Oh, about Jane—her wind-up was sad. I never got to see her very often after I started at Luigi's because I brought my wife and her kid (by a former marriage) out to Detroit. But once when I ran into her she told me she was doing real good, working in ˄ restaurant and living in a small apartment of her own. She came up with a bankbook that had a balance of close to a thousand bucks, better than I could show myself. Tips must be good, I thought.

Tips, hell—taps would have been more like it. One evening I was walking down Bobian Street, igging the girls in the windows. The chopstick arrangement they were beating out on the glass panes didn't attract my attention none. But then I heard something that made me put on the brakes and look up. It was a tricky syncopated beat that doesn't usually come from a whorehouse window—bip-*bop*, bip-*bop*, bip-a-di-dee, bip-*bam*—that steady solid Baby Dodds break, straight from the South Side. Suddenly it stopped. Sitting there in the window was sweet innocent little Jane, togged in a now-you-see-it-now-you-don't kimono, looking first like one thing and then another. She held those chopsticks in her grabbers with her arms raised in front of her, frozen stiff, looking like a mechanical doll waiting to be wound up. I didn't say anything. I looked up, and she looked back at me, and that was all that happened. Then I hunched my shoulders and walked away. That was the last I saw of Jane—a little later my wife got homesick for Chicago and we headed back to the big city. I kept thinking to myself, O.K. Jane, all right, I'm not mad, it's your life and you got to live it—only why did you have to beat on the window that particular way? Why did she have to use Baby Dodds that way? She didn't have to do that. It kept worrying me.

It's a lot of things you got to skip and forget in life, is what I keep telling myself. You got to be built like Master Pangloss, Jack. By the way, I still believe that little girl's story—every word of it, all the way back to Des Moines, bouncing baby, traveling salesman, and all.

8

GOT THE HEEBIES, GOT THE JEEBIES

IN 1926, St. Vitus was doing a marathon buck-and-wing through the country, accompanied by the stutter of sub-machine guns. From sundown to sunup life was one romping, rollicking bath in a 22-karat gold tub filled with spiked milk-and-honey. All day long, to accommodate those who needed a pick-me-up, the corner druggist dished out quart bottles of short-order salvation from under the counter, disguised with hair-tonic labels. The cotton-mouthed hangover became America's occupational disease; hair-of-the-dog was adopted as the national morning-after beverage. Rotgut and remorse trickled through Uncle Sammy's veins. . . .

There was a revolution simmering in Chicago, led by a gang of pink-cheeked high-school kids. These rebels in plus-fours, huddled on a bandstand instead of a soap-box, passed out riffs instead of handbills, but the effect was the same. Their jazz was only a musical version of the hard-cutting broadsides that two foxy studs named Mencken and Nathan were beginning to shoot at Joe Public in the pages of *The American Mercury*—a collectively improvised nose-thumbing at all pillars of all communities, one big syncopated Bronx cheer for the righteous squares everywhere. Jazz was the only language they could find to preach their fire-eating message.

These upstart small-fries were known as the Austin High Gang, and gumption was their middle name. It was on Chicago's West Side that they started hatching their plots, way out in Austin, a well-to-do suburb where all the days were Sabbaths, a sleepy-time neighborhood big as a yawn and just about as lively, loaded with shade-trees and clipped lawns and a groggy-eyed population that never came out of its coma except to turn over. In all their scheming these kids aimed to run out of town the sloppy, insipid, yes-we-have-no-bananas music of the day, which seemed to echo the knocked-out spirit of their sleepwalking neighbors. They wanted to blast every highminded citizen clear out of his easy chair with their yarddog growls and gully-low howls.

Before they even collared their diplomas at Austin High they had all been swept up and carried away by the tidal wave of hot music that was searing and singeing its way from the Gulf of Mexico up to the Great Lakes, cutting the country right up the middle with a smoky belt of jazz. These juvenile cats were gone with it; they meant to pave the way for that flood from the Mississippi delta and speed it on to glory. Out of the belly spasms of this frenzy-jammed country a brand-new voice sang out to them, rumbling and rolling answers to all their questions, and they liked what it said. It was the voice of jazz, making itself heard above the rattle of machine guns and the clink of whisky bottles. That lowdown call came hammering at their ears all the way from New Orleans, wrapped in a wail and a husky lament, and it hit them just like it did me a few years earlier. They listened hard, and naturally, they got restless. At night, instead of hugging the fireside and boning up on algebra and Louie the Fourteenth, they snuck out and beat it into town to tour the South Side, studying its flicker and frolic. There they got a liberal education that lowrated all the book-learning and Sunday-school sermons they had thrown at them out where the pretty lawns got a weekly finger-wave.

They heard the real jazz too, coming up from the South Side like a heartbeat. Joe Oliver taught them how to cut their musical eye-teeth; Jimmy Noone and Johnny Dodds helped them dig their gutbucket ABC's; Louis Armstrong riffed and scatted them through many an after-hours lesson in night school, until they were all honor students. Their greedy ears drank in the music like suction pumps. The sprawling outside world, they found, was raw and bubbling, crude, brutal, unscrubbed behind the ears but jim-jam-jumping with vital spirits; its collar might be grimy and tattered, but it was popping with life and lusty energy, ready for anything and everything, with a gusto you couldn't down. And jazz, the real jazz, was its theme song. These kids went for that unwashed, untidy world, and they made up their minds to learn its unwashed, untidy music.

As they roamed around town in their knee-britches, sniffing for signs of life like a scavenger snagging cigarette butts, they bumped into other defiant, music-starved kids like themselves—Floyd O'Brien, Muggsy Spanier, Eddie Condon, Gene Krupa, Joe Sullivan, Herman Foster. From time to time they came across up-and-coming young musicians just starting out full of pound and pep, guys like Bix Beiderbecke, Joe Marsala, Bill Davison, Danny Polo, Jack Teagarden, Jess Stacy, Pee Wee Russell; and they sat funnel-eared and google-eyed at the feet of older, more seasoned music-makers like Leon Rappolo and the other white cats in the New Orleans Rhythm Kings.

All these different strands of music kept snaking around in their heads, and these kids finally began to weave them together, working out their own styles and techniques as a blend of everything they heard. They started to play hot music themselves, stuttering towards a language that would let them speak out what was on their whirlpool minds. They got the ingredients a little mixed up, sure; some of their music was spotty and fumbling, reaching out in too many directions at once, each note ready to bust with a dozen different ideas stuffed in it. But they were headed right, and the spirit was in them. That was plenty for a starter.

While they were still messing with their schoolbooks they got together a high-school jazz band called the Austin Blue Friars (in honor of the Rhythm Kings who were featured at the Friars Inn), and they played their skullbusting music, mixed in with limp-as-lard pop tunes, at Parent-Teacher-Association dances and open-air affairs in the local park, and once in a while a gig at a small café that their mothers never knew about. After they graduated from school, or got thrown out on their ears, the Austin High Gang stuck together. Finally they organized a professional outfit called Husk O'Hare's Wolverines—this time lifting the name from Bix's old band. Then they were on their way.

Who were these frantic kids? Their ringleaders, the ones who really went places afterwards, were Frank Teschemacher, first alto sax and clarinet; Jimmy MacPartland, cornet, and his brother Dick on guitar; Dave North, piano; Jim Lannigan, bass; Dave Tough, drums; and Lawrence "Bud" Freeman on tenor sax. Another Chicago youngster, Floyd O'Brien, was added on the trombone to fill out the band, and later on, when I joined up with them, I made the third sax. I first met up with the whole crowd when I breezed back from Detroit. Most of the kids were still in their teens, but the South Side had already tattooed its special mark all over them. I had started to think that the South Side was my own personal property, and that no other white musicians, except for a tiny handful, would ever vibrate to its tune the way I did. Those kids made my homecoming a red-letter day in the Mezzrow calendar.

They were a high-spirited, eager, try-anything bunch of kids, these teen-age refugees from the sunny suburbs, as frisky as a herd of prancing fillies, yet and still they had their dead-serious side, pledged body and soul to the gospel of jazz, and they formed the nucleus of a great crew of jazzmen who have gone down in history as the Chicagoans. The Austin High Gang had among its charter members some of the finest and most dedicated white artists this country has ever coughed up. They may have been a drag and a headache to their mothers, but they were sure a jumping joy to me.

"Hey, Mezzrow!"

I gunned the kid—I'd never seen him before in my life. He was a tall blond good-looking youngblood, with dimples and a frame that might have hopped out of a physical-culture magazine. He got in my face just as I stepped into the lobby from the elevator at union headquarters.

"You're Milton Mezzrow, aren't you?" He seemed too honest for a bill-collector or a process-server, so I admitted it. "Just the one I want to see," he said with a big grin. "Are you doing anything? I've heard a lot about you and I know the fellows would be glad to have you play in our band." The band was Husk

O'Hare's Wolverines and they were working for the summer out at White City, a roller-coaster amusement park out on the far South Side.

It looked like my press-agent Mr. Grapevine was on the job again for me, and it didn't hurt my ego none. I didn't mind copping a slave just then because I could use the gold, and besides, the kid laid his racket so smooth that I warmed up to him. His name was Jimmy MacPartland, the cornet player who later became famous for his work on the Chicagoans' recording of *Nobody's Sweetheart*. This was really my first job with another band, because up to then I always got my own units together, but it made me feel sort of biggity to be hired that way. I told him yes.

The first night I showed up for work they threw a Frank Black arrangement of *Kamenoi Ostrow* at me and I knew I was going to have plenty trouble trying to play the notes the way they were written down. I figured this was just another wood-sawing dance band where the musicians kept their noses buried in cornfed stock arrangements, so I decided to try and play it as is to keep them happy. I had made up my mind in advance that these cats weren't from doodlely-squat.

Well, I had another think coming. The next minute it was like I was hearing things—a little old half-pint kid was squatted behind the big bass drum, with just his head sticking up, knocking out the rhythm of Baby Dodds! He was a cat named Dave Tough, and he was the only white drummer I ever heard, outside of Ray Eisel, who had mastered that South Side beat. My mouth flew open wider than a trapdoor and Dave, bobbing up and down like a piston, rocking and rolling with a rhythm that wouldn't quit, grinned back at me. The way they swung that arrangement sent me so much that when I took my chorus I forgot all about the written music and really ran wild.

Could it be true? Here was a bunch of strange kids, and white ones at that, playing the music I loved, music I thought nobody knew except a chosen few. When we finished the arrangement I was all red in the face because I had made so many mistakes, but Bud Freeman had messed it up some too and that made me feel a little better. Tesch was the boy who could really read. He had studied the violin when he was young and had such a legitimate schooling, he would even read a fly-speck if it got on the paper. He played first alto and clarinet; Bud played tenor, and I played third alto. I didn't bring my clarinet and soprano sax along because Jimmy had raved so much about Tesch's clarinet playing, and I could see why. Tesch had a big forceful tone on the alto, too, and he really could lead a sax section.

They all looked at me when we stopped, to see how I liked it, and I said "Whew, I'll have to woodshed this thing awhile so I can get straight with you all." Then, maybe for my benefit, Jimmy called *Dinah*, which was right in my alley. This was strictly a head arrangement and we began to jam awhile. Pretty soon Jimmy gave me a chorus, and when I began to play Dave Tough fell right in with me and we took the place over. What a difference there was playing this way, instead of crawling across a line of man-made fly-specks. I let myself go on this one—it was one of those great moments, when the walls between you and other people suddenly melt away and you all fuse together. Bud Freeman and Frank Teschemacher kept their eyes pinned on me, shaking their heads as if they didn't believe it, and that made me blow even more. Before a word was spoken it was understood that we were all going to be great friends. A mutual-assistance pact was signed and sealed between us before we even sat down at the conference table and brought out the fountain pen. Each man laid down another riff for his signature. Every note we blew added another clause to the agreement.

When we finished the first set Bud jumped up and yelled, "Hey, did you hear that—he plays just like the colored boys!" Tesch flashed me a big grin, and I began to swell up with joy. This was the first time in my life that a whole group of white musicians had ever cheered me for sticking to the pure Negro jazz style. What knocked me out was that by this time the Austin High Gang had practically moved into the South Side and were schooled so good they could identify almost every riff and trick break I threw at them. Tesch couldn't get over it when I told him how Bix used to come and sit in with our band at the Martinique, because Bix was his god, mentor and all-round idol. "Yeah, yeah," he kept saying, with his eyes open wide as camera shutters and shining through his thick hornrimmed glasses, "I want to meet that guy some day."

Tesch and Dave were the two that attracted me most, because their music was heading for the real jazz idiom and their temperaments fitted mine like the bark does a tree. Jimmy MacPartland could get on the beam too—he had a subtle tone that showed he had listened hard to Bix, and some of his passages were straight from Louis Armstrong. Then there was Floyd O'Brien, whose New Orleans trombone was really in there. Man, 'tain't no crack but a solid fact—these kids from Austin, some of them still wet behind the ears, had latched on to the spirit of hot jazz so good, you would have thought sometimes that they came out of the gallion instead of Chicago's manicured and well-groomed suburbs.

Dave Tough was my boy. He was a little bit of a guy, no chubbier than a dime and as lean as hard times, with a mop of dark hair, high cheekbones, and a nose ground fine as a razor blade, and he popped with spirit till he couldn't sit still. It always hit me to see that keyed-up peanut crawl behind the drums, looking like a mouse huddled behind a elephant, and cut loose with the solid rhythm he had picked up from the great colored drummers—the beat really moved him and he jumped from head to toe, then back again. Once some of the Austin boys were invited out to a society dame's salon to put on a show for her distinguished guests, and Dave beat his tubs so hard and threw himself around with so much pep that the hostess came trotting over, glared down at him over her lorgnette, and snorted, "Take—that—cannibal—out—of—here!" Dave and I got to be bosom pals.

It was little Dave who gave me a knockdown to George Jean Nathan and H. L. Mencken, two guys who could mess with the King's English too. Dave used to read *The American Mercury* from cover to cover, especially the section called "Americana" where all the bluenoses, bigots, and two-faced killjoys in this land-of-the-free got a going-over they never forgot. That *Mercury* really got to be the Austin High Gang's Bible. It looked to us like

Mencken was yelling the same message in his magazine that we were trying to get across in our music; his words were practically lyrics to our hot jazz. I dug him all the way, because *The Mercury* gave you the same straight-seeing perspective that muta does—to me that hard-cutting magazine was a load of literary muggles.

Tesch, a medium-sized, sober-pussed, studious cat with eyes barricaded behind thick glasses, was the most philosophical member of the gang. He almost became a lushhound but I put him on muta, and it was he who coined the phrase, "everything gets in your mouth," that got so popular among viper jazzmen. Tesch was very cynical and downhearted about our music; he always thought we'd go to our graves without being appreciated, and he kept telling me about all the great composers and musical trailblazers who never got recognized until after they were dead. "What's the use, Milton?" he'd ask me, his face as long as a sigh and just as mournful. "You knock yourself out making a great new music for the people, and they treat you like some kind of plague or blight, like you were offering them leprosy instead of art, and you wind up in the poorhouse or the asylum. That's always the way it goes with a real artist who won't put his talents on the auction-block to be sold to the highest bidder." In spite of his gloomy slant, though, Tesch was all wrapped up in his music, and never let himself get sidetracked. He went around for months at a time in one raggedy old suit, looking like a ragpicker on vacation, and he wouldn't wear a hat even in a hurricane.

Late at night Tesch and I would hop in my car and travel over to the outer drive in Grant Park, where we'd pull up in back of Soldier's Field, near the water fountain. All night long we'd play clarinet duets in the style of Jimmy Noone and Doc Poston, getting high on gauge and blowing until we were blue in the face. One night, just after we parked and started our open-air concert, we saw a motorcycle cop driving towards us from the highway, and Tesch said pessimistically, with a I-told-you-so tone, "This is it, Milton. Will we ever have any peace and be able to play as we feel? Won't they ever let us alone?" We both figured John Law was bearing down on us like a messenger from all the decent, respectable citizens who were home in bed having decent, respectable nightmares instead of braying through their horns at the stars. When the bloodhound got alongside our car, he parked his motorcycle and strolled over to us. "Go ahead, boys, keep on playing," he said. "That sounded real good. A guy doesn't get to hear much of that music on this beat." He nodded his head approvingly, like an old concert-goer in the first row at Carnegie Hall.

Ho! Ho! What you know—a bluecoat with the soul of an artist! Tesch and I almost fell through the floor of the car. A minute later, when we recovered from the shock, this music-lover from the Chicago Motorcycle Squad had the honor of hearing the world's premier of Teschemacher's and Mezzrow's chamber music for two clarinets, interpreted by the composers themselves.

After that we knew there was one safe place to go early in the morning when we wanted to jam for a while. Night after night Bud, Dave, Tesch and as many others as could squeeze in my car would broom over to this hide-out in Grant Park and blow our tops under the twinklers, shooting riffs at the moon through the courtesy of the Windy City Police Force. At least once in my life I met a copper who was a human being. That is a miracle that deserves to go down in history, like the waters parting for the Israelites or Lazarus rising from the dead, so right here and now I want to record for posterity that I saw it with my own two eyes, so help me God.

In those days, if you pried the lid off my skull with a can-opener, you might have spotted some weird eels snaking through the whirlpool I lugged around under my hat. Maybe, for one thing, you would have scooped out some why-and-wherefore of the thick Southern accent I was developing. It's a fact—I wasn't putting my mind to it, but I'd started to use so many of the phrases and intonations of the Negro, I must have sounded like I was trying to pass for colored. Every word that rolled off my lips was soft and fuzzy, wrapped in a yawn, creeping with a slow-motion crawl. I was going on to twenty-seven, a Chicago-born Jew from Russian parents, and I'd hardly ever been south of the Capone district, but I sounded like I arrived from the levee last Juvember.

Dave Tough, who tipped delicately over his words like they were thin ice, always used to lecture me on how important it was to keep your speech pure, pointing out that the French and people like that formed their vowels lovingly, shaping their lips just right when they spoke, while Americans spoke tough out of the corners of their mouths, clipping and crunching all the sounds. I always came back with the argument that the Negroes were one exception; their speech was full and rounded to my ears, and they never twisted their lips up like a gangster on an alum diet. I thought Dave's careful way of talking was too precise and effeminate. He thought I was kind of illiterate, even though he admired my musical taste and knowledge. He was always making me conscious of the way I talked because he kept on parodying the slurs and colloquial kicks in my speech, saying that I was just trying to ape the colored man. That got me steamed up.

"Dave," I told him, "you know all the music we care anything about comes from the Negro, and if you want to dig our music you got to dig the guys who made it up. You can't get to know what a people are like, can you, unless you really learn and know their language?" I tried to show him how I spent weeks studying Bessie Smith's slaughter of the white man's dictionary, analyzing all her glides and slippery elisions, before I could figure out the secret of her blues singing. It turned out, though, that Dave had never heard Bessie sing, so the gab-session wound up one night with our breezing over to the Paradise Gardens on 35th near Calumet, to listen to the queen of the blues pour her great heart out. She was featured there with Jimmy Noone's band.

Bessie had such a ringing vibration in that voice of hers, and her tones boomed out so clear and clanging full, you could hear her singing all the way down the street. There was a traffic jam out in front of that café; cats and their kittens blocked up the sidewalk, hypnotized by the walloping blues that came throbbing out of Bessie's throat. She was putting away *Young Woman Blues*, one of her greatest numbers, when we eased in:

Woke up this mornin' when chickens was crowin' for day,
Felt on the right side of my pillow, my man had gone away.
By his pillow he left a note
Readin' "I'm sorry Jane you got my goat,
No time to marry, no time to settle down."
I'm a young woman and ain't done runnin' roun',
I'm a young woman and ain't done runnin' roun'.
Some people call me a hobo, some call me a bum,
Nobody knows my name, nobody knows what I've done,
I'm as good as any woman in your town.
I ain't no high yaller, I'm a beginner brown,
I ain't gonna marry, ain't gon' settle down,
I'm gon' drink good moonshine and run these browns down.
See that long lonesome road, Lawd, you know it's gotta end,
And I'm a good woman, and I can get plenty men.

Dave and I just melted together in the blaze of Bessie's singing; that wasn't a voice she had, it was a flame-thrower licking out across the room. Right after that Bessie launched into another one of the numbers that made her famous, *Reckless Blues*:

When I was a nothin' but a child, when I was a nothin' but a child,
All you men tried to drive me wild.
Now I'm growin' old, now I am growin' old,
And I got what it takes to get all of you men told,
My momma says I'm reckless, my daddy says I'm wild,
My momma says I'm reckless, my daddy says I'm wild,
I ain't good-lookin' but I'm somebody's angel child.
Daddy, momma wants some lovin,' daddy, momma wants some
   huggin',
Hand it pretty poppa, momma wants some lovin' I found,
Hand it pretty poppa, momma wants some lovin' right now.

Bessie was a real woman, all woman, all the femaleness the world ever saw in one sweet package. She was tall and brown-skinned, with great big dimples creasing her cheeks, dripping good looks—just this side of voluptuous, buxom and massive but stately too, shapely as a hour-glass, with a high-voltage magnet for a personality. When she was in a room her vitality flowed out like a cloud and stuffed the air till the walls bulged. She didn't have any mannerisms, she never needed any twirls and twitches to send those golden notes of hers on their sunshiny way. She just stood there and sang, letting the love and the laughter run out of her, and the heaving sadness too; she felt everything and swayed just a little with the glory of being alive and feeling, and once in a while, with a grace that made you want to laugh and cry all at once, she made an eloquent little gesture with her hand. Bessie maybe never practised her scales in any conservatory of music, wrestling with arpeggios, but she was an artist right down to her fingertips—a very great artist, born with silver strings for vocal cords and a foaming, churning soul to keep them a-quiver.

Her style was so individual that nobody else ever grasped it. The way she let her rich music tumble out was a perfect example of improvisation—the melody meant nothing to her, she made up her own melody to fit the poetry of her story, phrasing all around the original tune if it wasn't just right, making the vowels come out just the right length, dropping the consonants that might trip up her story, putting just enough emphasis on each syllable to make you really know what she was getting at. She *lived* every story she sang; she was just telling you how it happened to her.

Jimmy Noone's band was too much. Playing with him then were Teddy Weatherford on piano, Tubby Hall on drums, Johnny St. Cyr on guitar and banjo, Little Mitch (George Mitchell) on trumpet, and Kid Ory on trombone; and what Jimmy didn't do with that clarinet of his, weaving in and through and all around those cats like an expert hackie in heavy traffic, just ain't been invented yet. Jimmy's clarinet was the most beautiful I have ever heard in my whole life, even better than Johnny Dodds', and if I can play that instrument at all today it's thanks to his inspiration. He played strictly New Orleans style, with a soulful tone instead of the shrill twittering effects you hear today, and he played all over that instrument from top to bottom, hitting every register but the cash one. The little flourishes he came up with "in the windows," fill-ins at the ends of phrases where the other players took a breath, were really amazing. He was always inventing new things, but they were in the New Orleans idiom every time.

A few months later, when Jimmy's band was playing in the Apex Club, some distinguished visitors dropped in to catch him. Word had got to the Chicago Symphony guys that the clarinetist at the Apex could do more things on his instrument than the law allows, and the famous composer Maurice Ravel, who was in town to be guest conductor for the symphony, showed up at the Apex one night with the first clarinetist of that longhair crowd. His mouth dropped open at the first riff Jimmy played, and stayed that way all night long; and that classical clarinetist thought he was hearing things too. "Amazing," Ravel would say to his pal, and the guy would answer "Incredible," and they see-sawed back and forth on their unbelief like that until the joint closed up. Ravel spent hours writing down Jimmy's riffs as he played, and the clarinetist swore over and over that he couldn't understand how Jimmy could get those effects out of the instrument. When he left, the composer said he was going to write a symphony around the phrases he had heard. I don't know whether he ever got around to doing it, because I ain't kept in touch with the highbrow world, but I'll bet that if he tried he sure had trouble.

After her number that night, Bessie and Jimmy came over to our table for a few drinks. When I told her how long I had been listening to her records, how wonderful I thought they were and how *Cemetery Blues* inspired me to become a musician when I was a kid, she was very modest—she just smiled, showing those great big dimples of hers, fidgeted around and said, "Yeah, you like that?" I asked her would she do *Cemetery Blues* for me and she busted out laughing. "Boy," she said, "what you studyin' 'bout a cemetery for? You ought to be out in the park with some pretty chick." That night, and every time I saw her from then on, Bessie kept kidding me about the kinky waves in my hair; she'd stroke my head once or twice and say, "You ain't had your hair fried, is you, boy? Where'd you get them pretty waves? I get seasick every time I look at them." Many's the time I almost peeled my whole goddamn scalp off, to hand to her on a silver platter.

You ever hear what happened to that fine, full-of-life female woman? You know how she died? Well, she went on for years, being robbed by stinchy managers who would murder their own mothers for a deuce of blips, having to parade around in gaudy gowns full of dime-store junk and throw away her great art while the lushes and morons made cracks about her size and shape. She drank a lot, and there must have been plenty of nights when she got the blues she couldn't lose, but she went on singing, pouring out the richness and the beauty in her that never dried up. Then one day in 1937 she was in an automobile crash down in Mississippi, the Murder State, and her arm was almost tore out of its socket. They brought her to the hospital but it seemed like there wasn't any room for her just then—the people around there didn't care for the color of her skin. The car turned around and drove away, with Bessie's blood dripping on the floor-mat. She was finally admitted to another hospital where the officials must have been color-blind, but by that time she had lost so much blood that they couldn't operate on her, and a little later she died. *See that lonesome road, Lawd, it got to end,* she used to sing. That was how the lonesome road ended up for the greatest folk singer this country ever heard—with Jim Crow directing the traffic.

I cried when I heard about it. A lot of people did. She was mother, sister, friend and lovin' woman to me and to a lot of guys, and she taught us most all we knew and gave us the courage to keep straight with our music, and they took her and murdered her down South—murdered her in cold blood because, like she said, she wasn't no high yaller, just a beginner brown, and more real woman than those Jim Crow mammyjamming whites would know what to do with.

Wolverines? We were more like night owls. Night after night, soon as we finished work at White City, we'd shoot over to my house for a record-playing session, and we never broke up until the teen-inetsy hours of the morning. I was beginning to collect hot records like some guys collect telephone numbers, and the ones I had would make a record-fan's head spin around like a turntable. My landlady finally got her claws on that collection to make up for some back rent. What some people won't stoop to for the stuff with the dead ones' pictures.

We had a ritual for these music-appreciation classes: first we dragged out some bottles of gin and made sure a can of golden-leaf was handy, so everybody could gain altitude in his own way. A paper bag was wrapped around the overhead glimmer to curb the brightness, and then we all hunched over my old hand-wound victrola like a committee of voodoo witch doctors in confab over some herbs. The incantations came fast and furious. "Did you hear *that*?" one guy would whisper when he heard some extra-special riff, and another would exclaim "Get a load of that—let's put it back!" We were always jumping up and putting the needle back to play a good passage over. Every time there was an explosive break in the music we'd all raise our arms high, like a calisthenics class, then bring them down in unison, yelling "BAM!" so loud the whole house shook. We must have looked like a gang of Arabs in shirtsleeves and suspenders, bamming and salaaming towards some Decca-Mecca. We sure used to scoff back some during those sessions—my wife Bonnie would come on with a mess of green-apple pies and buttercrust strawberry tarts that were really killers. The way we kept shoveling all that fine pastry into our faces while we listened to the music was double kicks.

Chumps who have to rise and shine in the morning, slaves to the alarm clock, sure don't understand us creative artists none. Every time we got the victrola under way, a strong rhythm section would start jumping in the background, beat out on the walls and ceilings with broom-handles and shoes by our groggy neighbors. We didn't mind their horning in that way but it sure as hell both-ered us that they couldn't keep time better than they did—early risers just never seem to have any get-up for music at all. To stop their corny anvil chorus we'd take the needle off and play the records with our fingernails, leaning over so close to catch the riffs that we were all practically inside the machine. Later on, Josh Billings, one of our sidekicks, came up with a tricky homemade muffler that was a gangbuster—one phonograph needle stuck halfway into the top of a pencil eraser, and another shoved into the bottom with its point out. When we screwed this gadget into the tone-arm it would play a record real soft, so the early-to-bed citizens could catch up with their bad dreams and everybody was happy. Muggles is the mother of invention. Those early birds always scrambling to catch that worm really puzzled us. Man does not live by worms alone.

Funny how you can get all wrapped up in music, especially when you've got some muta to tie the bundle. One night after one of these sessions we grabbed our horns and drove out towards the outer drive along Grant Park, figuring to stage a gay open-air jam session under the auspices of that music-loving motorcycle cop. Most of us were high on muggles and Dave Tough had a bottle of gin, and we rolled along chirping riffs and weaving the car from side to side. Suddenly a red light blinked at us, and we pulled up in back of another car at the crossing to wait for the go-ahead. Time gumshoed by, walking in his sleep. It was about a half hour later that Dave began wondering about that light—"You know something?" he said. "I don't want to seem impatient or anything like that, I'm not in any rush exactly, but I have a feeling those lights aren't changing as fast as they used to."

We all gave him the horse laugh and went on singing; it looked to us like little Dave had midges in his britches. After fifteen minutes or so, when Dave brought up the subject again, I decided to humor him by leaning out and looking the situation over. Goddamn if that car up ahead wasn't empty as a confessional on Saturday night—it was just parked against the curb, and what we took for a traffic signal was only its rear lamp.

We must have been squatting there for an hour, all told, waiting for a plenty stubborn tail-light to change. When tea grabs your glands you've got time on your hands—years and years on every fingertip.

I was always on the lookout for new records to pep up those wax-fests of ours. One day, thanks to a chick I was chummy with in the Okeh Distributing Company, I got hold of one that almost washed me away. It was a dealer's advanced pressing of Louis Armstrong's famous *Heebie Jeebies*, a milestone in recording history because it marked the first time Old Gatemouth ever put his scatting on wax. Later on Louis tipped us off to how it happened: he'd been mugging at the mike during the recording, just starting to sing his vocal, when he dropped the music with the lyrics on it, so he had to make up some for the rest of the chorus. We thought we were dreaming when we heard him begin singing the words—*I got the heebies, I mean the jeebies*—and then sail into a sequence of riffs that sounded just like his horn-playing.

If you want an idea of how to tear a lyric limb from limb, maul it, mangle it, and then make mince-meat out of it, take a look first at the words Louis was supposed to sing:

> *I've got the heebies, I mean the jeebies,*
> *Talk 'bout a dance the heebie jeebies,*
> *You'll see girls and boys,*
> *Faces lit with joys, if you don't know it*
> *You ought to learn it, don't feel so blue,*
> *Some one will teach you,*
> *Come on now let's do that prance*
> *Called the heebie jeebies dance,*
> *You will like it, it's the heebie jeebies dance.*

Right after the phrase, *if you don't know it*, the music slipped out of Louis' hand. He wasn't stumped, not that cat. On he went, remembering a couple more phrases here and there, and then he forgot about the words entirely, making up syncopated scats that were copied right from his horn tones. Here's a rough idea of how it came out:

> *Say I've got the heebies, I mean the jeebies,*
> *Talkin' about, the dazza heebie jeebies,*
> *You'll see goils and boys, faces wit' a little bit a joy,*
> *Say don't you know it, you don't dawduh,*
> *Daw fee blue, come on we'll teach you,*
> *Come on, and do that dance, they call the heebie jeebies dance*

Yes ma'am, poppa's got the heebie jeebies bad, ay,
Eef, gaff, mmmff, dee-bo, duh deedle-la bahm,
Rip-bip-ee-doo-dee-doot, doo,
Roo-dee-doot duh-dee-dut-duh-dut,
Dee-dut-dee-dut-doo, dee-doo-dee-doo-dee-doo-dut,
Skeep, skam, skip-bo-dee-dah-dee-dat, doop-dum-dee,
Frantic rhythm, so come on down, do that dance,
They call the heebie jeebies dance, sweet mammo,
Poppa's got to do the heebie jeebies dance.

Right then and there, when Louis dropped that sheet of paper and gave his improvising genius the floor, he started a musical craze that became as much a part of America's cultural life as Superman and Post-Toasties. All the hi-de-ho, vo-de-o-do, and boop-boop-a-doo howlers that later sprouted up around the country like a bunch of walking ads for Alka-Seltzer were mostly cheap commercial imitations of what Louis did spontaneously, and with perfect musical sense, on that historic record.

This record of Louis' took all of Chicago by storm as soon as it was released. When I brought a copy of it down to union headquarters it caused a stampede to the Okeh office, and inside of a week the copies were all sold out. For months after that you would hear cats greeting each other with Louis' riffs when they met around town—*I got the heebies*, one would yell out, and the other would answer *I got the jeebies*, and the next minute they were scatting in each other's face. Louis' recording almost drove the English language out of the Windy City for good.

I brought the record home to play for the gang, and man, they all fell through the ceiling. Bud, Dave and Tesch almost wore it out by playing it over and over until we knew the whole thing by heart. Suddenly, about two in the A.M., Tesch jumped to his feet, his sad pan all lit up for once, and yelled, "Hey, listen you guys, I got an idea! This is something Bix should hear right away! Let's go out to Hudson Lake and give him the thrill of his life!"

A scramble was on and it was most mad, old man. Bix was fifty miles away, but we were all halfway down the stairs before Tesch's chops got together again. We dove every whichaway into that green monster of mine (that's what the boys called my chariot) and started off like gangbusters for Hudson Lake, a summer resort where Bix, Pee Wee Russell and Frankie Trombauer were playing with Gene Goldkette's Greystone Dance Orchestra. All the way there we kept chanting Louis' weird riffs, while I kept the car zigzagging like a roller-coaster to mark the explosions. The other drivers on the road must have known that we were musicians because they sure scampered for the ditch fast when we heaved into sight.

It was three in the morning when we busted into that yarddog's stash that Bix and Pee Wee used for a cottage. Jim, the funk in that dommy was so thick you could cut it with a butterknife, and them cats had the whole insect population of Indiana for their roommates. It was here that Bix composed his famous piano solo, *In a Mist*, but once you laid your peepers on the joint you wondered why that composition wasn't named *In a Garbage Can*.

In their large living room the boys had collected a gang of furniture from the Year of the Flood, trash that Noah threw out without any regrets—chairs with more legs off than on, a sofa with all its springs sticking up through the upholstery and stuffing that kept oozing out like toothpaste, a table that laid on its side because it wouldn't stand up. There wasn't sheet one on the beds in this part of the pigpen. I couldn't tell you if there were any rugs under the dirt, but the room did have an upright piano with a bad list to keyboard standing in the middle of the floor. Bix would sit at that old tinklebox in the early hours of the morning, beads of 100-proof sweat slithering down his face, knocking out beautiful weird music in the middle of this junkheap. Imagine Paderewski squatting in a city dump, craunching Opus Number Seventeen out of a wheezy organ-grinder's box, and you get the idea.

Pee Wee and Bix shared a small room off the kitchen that would have made any self-respecting porker turn up his snout and walk away. They slept in their clothes most all the time, stretched out with King Kong. The first thing they did when they unglued their lamps each day was to reach for the gallon of corn that always leaned against the bedpost and wash out their mouths. Those cats used corn mash like it was Lavoris. Whenever you tipped into their room you had to pile through big stacks of empty sardine and baked-bean cans; those two canned delicacies made up the whole menu in this establishment. The back porch was loaded with thirty or forty quarts of milk, some of them over a month old. Every day the milkman left two quarts and sometimes the boys would remember to drink a bottle but most of the time they forgot. They kept saying they were going to leave the milkman a note telling him to nix out the moo-juice, but they never did find a pencil and paper at the same time so the deliveries went on for two whole summers.

The back yard held the overflow from the junkpile. Out there was a pump and a washtub where the boys made their toilet, such as it was—if you batted your eye once you missed it entirely. When they shaved they just set up a mirror on the fender of an old Buick, or something that was rumored to have been a Buick once, that stood out there developing more sags and slumps each day. That rattle-trap was rigor mortis on wheels, and there was a story behind it. One day, it seems, Bix and Pee Wee decided they needed some rubber, so they bought up this struggle-buggy for thirty-five bucks. It wasn't running then—so far as any of us knew, it never *did* run—but those two Barney Oldfields weren't stumped. They pushed it all the way out to their cottage and there it squatted forever after; nobody even tried to budge it again. It made a good sturdy shaving rack, though, and the boys were happy with it. They figured to live right in the country you had to have a car.

That morning, as soon as we grabbed those cats out of their pads and played *Heebie Jeebies* for them, they all fractured their wigs. "Ha! Ha! Ha!" Bix kept chuckling as the record played over and over, and his long bony arms beat out the breaks, flailing through the air like the blades of a threshing machine. He never did get over Louis' masterpiece. Soon as it was over he grabbed it from the machine and tore out of the house, to wake up everybody he knew around Hudson Lake and make them listen to it. It was this same record that inspired Bix and Frankie Trombauer, a little later that same year (1926), to make two discs of their own that are now collectors' items—*Royal Garden Blues* and *Singin' the Blues*.

The occasion called for a party, but when Bix went prowling for his jug of corn he found it was drained dry. He looked accusingly at Pee Wee and his face got all wrinkled with disgust. "Uh, uh," he said, "the Ghost was at it again. We better go down to The Old Maids' and get us some more juice to celebrate with—hell, I'm so dry I couldn't even spit cotton."

Off we flew in my brougham to a rickety old farmhouse about ten miles down the road, a place haunted by two barefooted raggedy old hags who must have been witches retired on a pension. When you drove up in front of their lopsided henhouse you had to stay put in your car—about a dozen lean and mangy man-eating hounds roamed around the yard, baring their fangs and trying to leap over the picket fence to sample the meat on your buttocks. Sitting in the car, we blew the horn and yelled, "Hey there! Anybody home? You got some cash customers!" until those two shriveled-up ghosts in gingham dresses came tottering out. When we gave them our order one of these apparitions took a shovel and hobbled out to the fields to dig up some of the gallon jugs of corn they had buried there. We laid in a real supply of that poison, at two bucks per crock, and cut out fast. On the way back we ran out of gas, so all the guys had to get out and push the car home. Bix cussed up a breeze and threatened to pour some of that corn in the gas tank. "If it does the same thing in that motor that it does in my stomach," he panted, "this old buggy ought to take off and coast home on the treetops."

They told me this place was called Hudson Lake because there's a body of water somewhere around there. I must have gone out there twenty times to see Bix, but I still have to see anything that looked like a lake—there was always so much excitement in the air, and so much drinking and jamming and fooling around, that the time flew by like in a dream and we hardly knew the world existed outside of that greasy shack. Maybe we just weren't the outdoor type. Anyhow, on this particular night, like all the other times we visited him, Bix sat at that beat-up piano for hours, sometimes making our kind of music and sometimes drifting off into queer harmony patterns that the rest of us couldn't dig. The rest of the world melted away; we were the last men left on earth, skidding on a giant billiard-ball across a green felt vacuum with no side-pockets, while Bix crouched over his keyboard in a trance, barleycorned and brooding, tickling bizarre music out of the ivories.

Bix was already reaching out beyond the frontiers of jazz, into some strange musical jungle where he hoped to find Christ-knows-what; he had the explorer's itch but he couldn't tell you what new flora and fauna he was trailing. We didn't want to tag along, but he kept urging us to follow. During those long drunken nights, when everything real looked like a pipe-dream and the wildest fantasies seemed so substantial and alive you could almost reach out and touch them, he kept straining at the leash, trying to break away from jazz into some entirely new musical language. Over and over he would play the peculiar "modern" music that was like a signpost to him, showing him where he thought he had to go—Stravinsky's *Firebird*, Dukas' *The Sorcerer's Apprentice*, Debussy's *Afternoon of a Faun*, Eastwood Lane's *Adirondack Sketches* (the one called "Dirge to Indian Joe" was a favorite of Bix's), some of the compositions of McDowell, and Gustav Holst's symphony *The Planets*, the one where human voices represent the different heavenly bodies. These musical tangents, leading to a dozen different detours, were all scrambled up with the jazz in Bix's head, and that mess finally led him to compose *In a Mist*. "Hey, get a load of this," he called out to us that night, and then he played his new composition through.

It made us all a little uncomfortable, because so much of it was out of our idiom. Some parts were pretty, maybe, but it didn't send me like Earl Hines always did. We humored Bix along for a while, to let him get that hightony stuff out of his system, and then we all yelled "*Royal Garden*! How about *Royal Garden*?" When he switched to the blues, hunching over the keyboard and jerking his shoulders rhythmically as he beat out the good solid chords we knew, we relaxed and had a good time. Then he was back in the groove, the one we all belonged in.

Get this straight, we pure-and-simple jazzmen didn't scoff the "serious" composers exactly, but they weren't in our school, they didn't express our feelings and ideas and we didn't want to change like Bix was beginning to. One thing about symphony music that really tickled us, made us bust our conks laughing, was the way the pompous director posed up front with his stick, as ungraceful and mechanical as an epileptic metronome, especially when he'd break out during a heavy overture and put on a frantic scene, his long hair fluttering up a breeze and his arms pumping like he was a pitcher winding up to shoot a spitball over the plate. Never mind about the composer's ideas when he wrote the music down. We were all music-*makers* too, instrumentalists as well as creators—to us the two things were one, a guy composed *as* he played, the creating and the performing took place at the same time—and we kept thinking what a drag it must be for any musician with spirit to have to sit in on a symphonic assembly-line. Could a musician really stand up and tell his story, let his guts come romping out, when he had to keep one eye glued on a dancing puppet and the other on his music? That's like handcuffing an anarchist to a billy-swinging cop on one side and a gospel-spieling preacher on the other and then telling him to be happy because he's a free man. A creative musician is an anarchist with a horn, and you can't put any shackles on him. Written music is like handcuffs; and so is the pendulum in white-tie-and-tails up on the conductor's stand. Symphony means slavery in any jazzman's dictionary. Jazz and freedom are synonyms.

Once, back in Chicago, a bunch of us went over to the Wurlitzer store and there in the window we saw our whole philosophy on display. They had a kind of animated-doll symphony orchestra set up there, run by some hidden electrical clockwork—the leader was planted up on the rostrum jerking his arms like they were twin windshield wipers, the violinists pumped back and forth like they were sawing wood, and all the other musicians bobbed and twitched the same way, with the clipped military precision of a goose-stepping army. One-two, one-two—take their clock away and they'd go around in circles, like travelers without a compass. Well, a creative musician doesn't need compasses or guides or maps or signposts; goddamn that stuff, the spirit's in him and it'll show him the way. One-hundred-men-with-a-fuehrer, a musical battalion hypnotized by a dictator's baton—that's no kind of a set-up for a man's inspired soul to shake loose and jump out of his instrument in a flood of carefree, truth-speaking, right-from-the-heart music.

"Wonderful!" Dave Tough said when he caught sight of that window exhibit. "There it is—that's the answer." We all laughed like hell. But when we tried to tell Bix about it later our story only got a feeble grin out of him. There had always been a touch of the militaristic, the highly disciplined and always-under-control, in his horn technique, and it was showing up stronger in his attitude towards music all the time, till he finally couldn't see what was so funny in that puppet-orchestra with its mechanical-doll conductor. He was a virtuoso technically, that's the truth, but jazz didn't mean for him what it meant for real hotmen, especially Negro ones—a geyser of boiling emotions, opening all your windows and letting your feelings flood out in a rush and a roar, instinct and spirit taking over. Jazz wasn't riot-in-music to him; his head always gave orders to his heart. The jazz wasn't the end for him, it was just a spring-board to something else, some new kind of expression that would let him say different things. Till the day he died he never did find that "something else." And he looked plenty hard too, until the effort finally killed him, or anyhow made him drink himself to death. (He died in 1931.)

That same frantic day at Hudson Lake, Bix nearly got run over by a locomotive. Long after the sun came up we ran out of corn, and Bix, with a tricky look in his eyes, called me and Pee Wee aside, along with a couple of the other guys. "I just remembered," he whispered, "that I got a spare gallon buried up on the hill, and if we sneak over there without these other lushes, there'll be enough to go around." We crept out Indian-file, with Bix leading the way like an old frontier scout.

Down the path we followed him, across some fields, then over a railroad track and a high fence topped with barbed wire. Sure enough, he dug out a jug, handed it to Pee Wee, and started back. But as we were hopping the fence Pee Wee, frail as a nail and big as a minute, got stuck on the wire and just hung there, squealing for help and hugging the jug for dear life. If he let go of that crock he could have pulled himself loose, but not Pee Wee—what's a guy's hide compared to a gallon of corn? By this time Bix, having staggered down to the railroad tracks, found he had a lot of sand between his toes, so he sat down on the rail and yanked his shoes off to empty them. Just then we saw a fast train coming round the bend. All of us began screaming at Bix to get the hell out of there, but he thought we were just kidding him and he threw some stones at us. That train wasn't more than a hundred feet away when he finally woke up to what was happening. Then he just rolled off the track and tumbled down the bank head first, traveling so fast he didn't have time to snatch his shoes off the rail. Those funky oxfords got clipped in half as neatly as if they'd been chopped with a meat-cleaver. "That just goes to show you," Bix told us, "it's dangerous for a man to take his shoes off. First time I took those things off in weeks and you see what the hell happens. It just ain't safe to undress."

We had some wonderful, out-of-the-world times with Bix at Hudson Lake, whole days and nights when the clock stopped and we blew our tops playing music and clowning. They were some of the best times I ever had; I'll never forget them. But Bix was growing away from us—finally he drifted clean out of our sphere, never to come home again. Losing his head over "serious" modern music made him go way tangent, until it changed his whole life and personality. He wasn't so regular with us any more after he joined up with Whiteman's band in 1928—why, when he came on to New York he started wearing wing collars, got himself cleaned up, sprouted a moustache and an English accent, and even began washing his socks. We never did dig this change in him; a lot of the music he tried to sell us seemed like something second-grade, and some of it was really corny.

When you come right down to it, what brought about the whole change in American music? What spread the gospel of jazz far and wide across the country, pulling at least one part of our native music free at last from European influences? It was the rebel in us. Our rebel instincts broke music away from what I'd call the handcuff-and-straitjacket discipline of the classical school, so creative artists could get up on the stand and speak out in their own honest and self-inspired language again. There had been a rebel in Bix too—

but a pint-sized one, a little stunted and gimpy, afraid to bust out and romp all over the place. It got even frailer and more anemic when the schooled musicians got after him.

American jazz lost one of its greatest disciples when Bix strayed away. He should have kept his dirty socks on, and never started sleeping between sheets.

Good news: test records of two numbers, *Royal Garden Blues* and *Singin' the Blues*, expected by Bix and Frankie Trombauer from New York any day. Why didn't I shoot over and dig them? R.S.V.P., and bring your own gunja.

Good deal; Dave Tough and I hopped into my chariot and shoved off for Bix's happy hunting grounds without even changing our shirts. I swear, we were making the run between Chicago and Detroit like a couple of Pullman porters. But this trip didn't pan out like the others.

It all started after we heard the tests. Dave sat in with the Greystone band, and Danny Polo, the clarinetist, almost blew his fuse when he heard him. No sooner did Danny get off the bandstand than he began to high-pressure us with a Chamber-of-Commerce spiel about Europe, where he'd once toured with some college-kid band. "Now there's a place where a musician really begins to live," he told us, that silver tongue of his shifting into high gear. Right then he could have sold us the Brooklyn Bridge without a money-back guarantee, his jive ran so smooth. "Why, it's a musician's paradise—the hotter you get, the more they'll rave about you, nobody ever turns out the lights and yells for the cops. Then you take the dames, say, those continental women don't put on any fancy airs, they know what the score is and they let you know it. And besides, nobody cares about the color of a man's skin over there, so their blood-pressure doesn't shoot up if somebody tells them that jazz is colored man's music. Jim Crow never went barnstorming across the Atlantic."

Europe? That wasn't Europe, it was a cloudland made-to-order for jazzmen that flashed through Danny's hot skull in a muta-dream. Dave and I sure thought his imagination was in the saddle and riding high that night, galloping straight for the millennium. . . . It was just a gumbeating session at first; we were just jawblocking to pass the time. But that Danny laid down a super hype, and blow my nose and call me Snorty if we didn't wind up with him giving notice to the Goldkette office so all three of us could pack our toothbrushes and catch the next boat for that joy-country. Back to Chicago we drove that very night to prepare for our grand tour of the Continent, Danny coaching us in the Frog lingo all the way home so we could gab with the parlay-voo's when we landed in good old Paree.

Uh-uh: we hit a petticoated snag. The minute Dave's wife Dorothy heard about Paris she set her heart on going too. Now we had fixed it to work our way over, and the quota for the ship's band was three, so I was left out in the cold. "Don't worry, Milton," they told me. "Soon as we hit that town and get set we'll send for you, no stuff." I was really in the dumps, but fate had me by the thin hairs and wouldn't turn me loose.

The night before they left for New York to catch their ship, Dave let me know he was having trouble with his room rent and needed my help to sneak his luggage out from under the hotel manager's bloodhound snout. Feeling lower than a toadstool, I drove my car down the alley in back of his place and he lowered his grips into the rumble seat with the aid of a clothesline; then I dropped him and Dorothy at the station and off to Europe they went. By the time I finally got to Paris myself, he was on the high seas heading for the States.

Our old gang was busting up fast, and it wasn't wedding bells that did it because wedding bells had a way of getting jammed up whenever we were around. No, what got into everybody was plain ordinary wanderlust and a yearning for greener pastures. The Chicagoans, including some of the Austin High Gang, were pulling a creep in a dozen different directions, each one trailing his own personal rainbow, and nothing could stop their migration. What with Dave on the other side of the drink and Tesch playing at the Midway Gardens with Muggsie Spanier and Jess Stacy, Bud Freeman and I were two lonesome oscars. About the only consolation we had was that young hopeful, Frank "Josh" Billings.

Josh, a talented young artist who shaped up like a young spruce and never wore a hat on his sandy head, didn't play music but always hung out with us. His parents were both doctors, and he was brought up in a very free-and-easy atmosphere, so he was with us all the way; wherever we went he tagged along and danced on all settings. A natural-born Bohemian, he was always trying to capture the rhythm of the Negro in his drawings.

Everything seemed to be going wrong for me and Bud—the whole town jumped stink on us. We weren't working much because the only bands with openings in them concentrated on sugar-coated ballads and pop tunes. To make it worse, the notes on my chariot were way overdue, and I figured I needed it more than the dealer because he had a lot more cars than I did. It looked like the road I had to hit, to keep from being slapped with a replevin writ.

Inspiration's old lady finally conked me with a one-two. Bud always used to strut around for us, doing a Ronald Colman or an Adolph Menjou while his younger brother Arnie played the straight-man opposite him, feeding him cues. (Arnie, who was stagestruck even worse than his brother, really made the grade later on, when he turned out to be a Shakespearean actor.) "Hey, what do you guys think of this?" I said while I watched them do their stuff one evening. "How about jumping in my car and let's take off for Hollywood? Bud's the matinee-idol type and he's a cinch to become a big actor in the movies, and he'll clean up and look out for us. A friend of mine is an actor out there and he could really set us in." If the rest of us couldn't make it as great lovers on the silver screen, I figured we could always connect with some band out there.

They all ate up the idea. Bud was already counting up his box-office receipts, and he promised that as soon as he took over Rudy Valentino's place he would never forget his old pals—we wouldn't have to worry about a thing. We all began to dream about that special swimming pool a hundred yards long, filled with imported champagne, that he was going to set up on his estate just for us. A squad of butlers would be assigned to do nothing but roll muggles all day long, each one five foot long, just for Josh and me. The whole Ziegfeld chorus, from the ponies to the showgirls, would be hired to fan us with palm leaves as we lounged around in the sun, reading H. L. Mencken and playing Louis Armstrong records over a P.A. system. Bud intended that we shouldn't want for nothing. Later on he would bring the whole Austin High Gang out to Hollywood and set them up, each one with a hand-picked harem of bathing beauties to manicure his toenails and shampoo his moss. Life was going to be one long clambake, out there in Uncle Sam's dream factory.

California look out, here we come—with more tricks in our pate than grandma had at eighty-eight! We were all set to bust open that Golden Gate, as we started out with twenty-five bucks between us, plus a couple of clean shirts, our horns, and a tube of toothpaste. All day and night we had a ball, singing Louis' *Heebie Jeebies* and *Muskrat Ramble* while Bud played on his tenor and the other guys beat time on the side of the car. At Kansas City, Kansas, to us just a milk-stop on the road to our sun-kissed utopia, we piled into the best hotel in town real chesty, as though we had passports to paradise in our hip pockets, and took over the best suite in the joint.

Next morning, when the house dick began to gun us, we went into a huddle about our change. I had a check for a double sawbuck coming from a booking office in Chi, so I wired for it while Bud and Billings wired home for some loot too. All day long we haunted the Western Union office, looking over our shoulders to see if that flatfoot was trailing us, but no gold showed up. We kept signing those dining-room checks, but our handwriting was getting a little shaky.

Good old Western Union. Next morning my twenty flew in out of the ozone, plus twenty-five more from Bud's father. We were in gravy once more, and we looked that gumshoe square in the eye again. When we checked out of the hotel and started for the garage, we could already feel those soft Pacific breezes tiptoeing across our maps. More trouble: no car. "Sorry," the bossman said, not even bothering to get up off his rooster. "The sheriff dropped over and took your car and left this replevin writ for you. Sorry. Can't do a thing about it."

I got the whole picture—my booking agent, who was friends with the guy that sold me the car, must have put the skids right under me as soon as he got my wire.

That was a solid drag, and to top it off, when we drooped back to the hotel I found that my last can of muta was empty. You should have seen me scraping together the sticks and seeds, then choking on the oily taste when I lit up on that mess. What a bringdown. It began to look like we were going to pull into paradise riding the rods, with me smoking grefa that a raggedy peon would have thrown in the garbage can.

Well, going back was out anyhow—you don't detour off the glory road just because some stinchy simp repossesses your buggy. "I got an idea," I said. "Let's hock our instruments and buy us a Ford and go on from here. I sure as hell want to get a look at that old Pacific Ocean before I die." Five minutes later we were lined up at uncle's, beefing about the measly ninety bucks he shoved across the counter for the whole lot of horns. Later, in the used-car lot, the only thing the man had for our short money was a rinky-dink old Ford. Yet and still, it was a five-passenger touring car, and that was all we wanted to know. "You boys are getting a bargain," the dealer told us. "This Lizzie may not look good but she'll run over the top of them mountains like a mountain goat." He forgot to tell us he was talking about a dead mountain goat.

Popping with the old pioneer spirit and ready for anything, we set out once more for the land of orange groves and quick money. By the time we wound up in Menlo, Kansas, we were traveling on four rims, minus the top to our chassis, and the engine coughed so bad on its one good lung that Billings beat us into town on foot and hiked halfway back to greet us. Poor Lizzie. We pushed her rear end into the only garage for miles around, a blacksmith's shop, and parked her next to a broken-down old horse as swaybacked as she was.

No Hotel Ritz for us this time; our stash was over some kind of feed store, where the nice old landlady took pity on us and gave us the best room in the place, one that almost had four walls. Acting big, I tipped her off as to how we were bigtime musicians from Chicago, headed for Hollywood to make our fortunes. In nothing flat, while we were brushing an inch of dust off the furniture (it was harvest time and the chaff blew in from the wheat fields by the bushel), the local sheriff showed up in our mouse-trap leading a posse of the town's first citizens, most of them with necks so full of moss they looked like buffaloes.

"Stranger," the sheriff drawled, "how come you claim to be from Chicago when your license plates have got Kansas writ all over them big as daylight?" I flashed my bill-of-sale but they still looked sceptical, eyeing us like we were a bunch of outlaws fresh in from the hills and fixing to make the local bank. When I explained that we were temporarily without funds, just by accident, understand, nothing that a few million bucks wouldn't take care of, kyaw-kyaw, they all got excited and spoke up at once: "Say, did any of you fellers ever harvest wheat? There's a mighty big crop out there and we sure as blazes could use a couple of extry hands."

I had my mouth open, ready to explain that we were all recuperating from yellow fever and the bubonic plague and couldn't do any physical labor by doctor's orders, but the ham actor in Bud got the best of him. "Oh," he sang out, "how *int*eresting. Why, I'd love to do that, I'm sure, and without a doubt my friends would fancy the idea too. If you don't mind my asking, hm, perhaps I could inquire, how much would it pay?"

A guy could make a slow-motion killing around here—they were willing to fork over all of five dollars a day for our blood, sweat and tears. "You can start tomorrow most any time," one of the farmers said. "You probably will be needing to catch up on your sleep, so don't rush to get there early—say about five o'clock." I asked did he mean P.M. He said he meant A.M.

When we got Bud alone we almost jumped down his throat. "You're crazy, Milton," he said. "Just think, we'll be getting all that fine sunshine and exercise and they'll pay us for it besides." He began to do a strongman act for us, flexing his biceps like Charles

Atlas. Bud was vain about his figure and always kept his belly button glued to his spine when he stood up.

Next morning he was gay as a jay, and so anxious to get out in the fields that he rolled us out of our pads and practically carried us outside. The thermometer read 120 in the shade that day, so we stripped down to the waist. Billings, always quick on the draw, beat us to the driver's seat of the horse-and-wagon behind the threshing machine and grabbed the reins, so the rest of us went to work with the pitchforks. I wrastled plenty with my first load, but I haven't thrown it up yet—every time I heaved the fork it twisted round in my hands and the wheat flew every place but in the wagon. Bud wouldn't wear any of the straw hats they gave us; he was a he-man and thought the farmers were sissies to worry about sunstroke. We carried him home and he came to in about an hour or so.

Never a dull moment in Hicksville; that night, while we were unraveling the kinks in our weary bones, a delegation of about ten yokels suddenly showed up in our room and I'll be goddamned if their spokesman didn't shove a real, honest-to-God soprano sax right in our faces. "Play," he said, and what he meant was, play or else. We latched on to that horn like it was a bottle of Sloane's Liniment, fighting among ourselves for the chance to blow it first. It sure knocked those rubes out when they heard us play the blues, and before we knew it we were signed up to entertain at a party they decided to give in our honor.

The following night the whole town declared a holiday and every man, woman and child turned up in the hall, a long shed with some wobbly wooden benches here and there for chairs. They moved an old piano in from Zeb's parlor, pitched about three tones below 440, and after I made a speech about how the artists entertaining tonight were famous on five continents, we went into our act. Bud did a comedy pantomime on how to kill yourself with no other props but a pitchfork and a stack of wheat, and then we played *Royal Garden* and a gang of other blues, with me spanking the piano while Bud blew the soprano and Josh and Art banged on the benches to make up the rhythm section. There never was an act went over half as big at the Palace. The farmers got so excited that at one point they even tried to do a square dance to our music, but the blues tempo messed up their geometry and they had to quit.

Back to the Western Union I went, this time to send a frantic SOS to Joe Tuckman, the gambler, explaining how I needed fifteen bucks to get my band out of hock and buy somè more tires, so how about it? I hadn't seen Joe for about four years, but he came through all the same. When we pulled out of Menlo, after a gala send-off from the townsfolk, we had a tankful of gas but mighty few blips left in our pockets.

Somewhere on our travels, after Josh had given up and gone back home, I remembered a cat named Stew Miller, good old Stew Miller, who lived in Trinidad, Colorado, where his old man owned some big copper mines or something. Young Stew, a real jazz fan who went to school around Chicago and haunted the South Side when I was making the rounds, knew Bix and the Wolverines and he sure would be happy to see us again. "Boys," I announced, "grab your hats, here we go again. Mush! We're off to Trinidad, Colorado, and all points west!" Through Western Union the Freemans had lucked up on a sawbuck from home, so we were in the chips again.

In Pueblo, Colorado, Lizzie got car-sick. This was one trip where you never could figure out who was carrying who; we staggered into town pushing Lady Lizz again. Bud thought her attitude was downright inconsiderate, and this time it got him so hot that he said we might as well sell the damned thing, because we had all we could do to carry ourselves. As soon as we managed to get rid of the buggy for forty bucks (we used that mountain-goat line on some sucker and it worked fine), I bought a can of tea from some Mexicans and we grabbed a bus and started off for Trinidad. By the time the bus creaked into town I was so high on the weed I couldn't tell which Trinidad we were in, the Colorado one or the one in the West Indies; I half expected all those lean hombres in miners' caps to break into a hot rhumba and begin chanting calypso songs at us. Finally, though, I remembered Stew Miller's name, and when we tracked him down what a welcome we got from the kid. It was old-home week for us.

Stew's folks were over in Denver and he put us up in his house that night. "You couldn't have showed up at a better time," he told us gleefully. "Boy, tomorrow night it's really going to jump around here—we're having a jamboree at Ratoon Pass, way up in the mountains, and it's going to be some party." He wasn't lying. This festival was supposed to celebrate the good old days of the wild and woolly West; all the men had let their beards and hair grow long, to show how the West looked at its woolliest, and they dressed up in the clothes of their forefathers, with mean-looking shooting irons buckled around their hips. I lit up for this big deal, and was higher than those mountains before we even got up there.

Man, what a shindig that was. Give me a barrelhouse joint on the South Side any day, where it's quiet as a church-mouse outing compared to the social life in the Rockies. Talk about the *wild* West; this was ferocious. When they started shooting it up in the big barn, setting fire to one corner of the building, we told Stew we had had enough. "Aw, stick around," he said. "These guys haven't even started yet. There's going to be some fighting going on in a minute—each one of the fellows takes the part of some historical figure and they re-enact some scene from the past, so it gets pretty lively."

Lively nothing; it was lethal. Before we could crawl out of that homicidal little clam-bake, half of the barn was on fire and the gun-smoke was so thick it almost blinded us. They sure wasted a lot of valuable ammunition at those festivals of theirs: it would have been more economical to line up the whole population of the town and mow them down with a machine gun. If the wild West needs any labor-saving device, it sure as hell is a firing squad.

That night Bud and Art wired home for fare, and next day they cut out for Chicago. I almost cried when I saw them pull out of the station. All of a sudden I didn't want to be out in the wide open spaces any more, where men are men if only they live that long. I had a hankering to be back on home territory, rubbing elbows with gentle people like Capone's sissy-boys and the Purple Gang goody-goodies. It wasn't healthy in these parts—they pulled jamborees on you when you weren't looking.

Western Union, I love you. As soon as my wife got my wire she sold all the furniture and sent me a ticket to come home. I rode all the way back on The Chief, the crack train on the Santa Fe, ducking in my seat like a psychoneurotic rabbit every time I saw a ten-gallon hat meandering down the aisle.

9

FORGOTTENEST MAN IN TOWN

FEASTING-TIME was over and Joe Famine, a no-tooth scant-singer with a breadbasket full of mites and scrimps, took to dogging us round. While we were busy looking the other way, the Jazz Era's heyday had been here and gone. History was laying some trickeration on us.

By 1927-28 we were getting our last earful of real Storyville jazz; that was the tail-end of New Orleans' golden age. It was just about the last time that hot musicians, still jumping with that oldtime Basin Street spirit and Storyville romp, had much chance to come on with their inspired, free-and-easy collective improvisation. Storyville was fast becoming just another chapter in the jazzman's storybook, a fable about some mythical land-of-dreams. Tin Pan Alley was soon to be the main stem in the music world, and Basin Street just a one-way road to the poorhouse.

Of all the great delta-bred music-makers, it wasn't but a few outside of Jimmy Noone, Sidney Bechet, Zutty Singleton, Louis Armstrong, King Oliver, Tubby Hall, Baby Dodds, Johnny St. Cyr and such who were still beating it out around Chicago, and not all of them were playing their original ad-lib style with small musical units. The wind was being sucked out of the Windy City. Before long the founding fathers of jazz weren't to be found no-way. The day of the big name-bands was coming up. Louis Armstrong now had an eleven-piece band behind him, and King Oliver had augmented his Plantation orchestra with three saxes (in place of the one clarinet), and the real big orchestras of Fletcher Henderson and McKinney's Cotton Pickers were going places, building up a national reputation for themselves, while the small romping combinations were getting lost in the scuffle. All the white bands making the grade swole up so big they could hardly fit on a regular cabaret bandstand any more: Paul Whiteman's orchestra, and Ben Pollack's and Gene Goldkette's too, looked and sounded like symphony groups to us, because five-piece and six-piece bands had always spelled jazz in our language. Jazz meant one thing to us, New Orleans. No matter how many pieces and whole sections the big commercial dance bands were sprouting, they didn't have anything to do with our kind of music and we just laughed them off. We were the keepers of the faith, the purists, the cats who stayed with it. The others were out to make money, not music. But chances go around, and we figured our time was sure to come.

If we'd a had a second-hand crystal ball to look into, we'd have seen the lean and gripy times ready to smack us in our chops by the year the depression rolled around, when the big commercial outfits got complete control of the popular-music business. We should have spotted the warning signals, telling us how music was slated to become a dull production-line grind, cutting everything to the same standard pattern, turning out notes like a meat packer turns out pork sausages, making the musicians dribble out stock and special arrangements of sweet pop tunes and corny show numbers, mixed in with some hammy clowning up on the bandstand to tickle the simpy customers. But maybe it's just as well we jazzmen didn't creep up on Father Time and take a peek around the bend in the calendar. What was waiting for us up ahead, if we'd got a preview, would have given us the creeps. Maybe it was better that we kept marching towards that poorhouse like it was a dicty country club built especially for us, complete with an air-conditioned marihuana bin in the cellar and hot-and-cold running corn mash.

On a dark and evil night in January, 1932, Wild Bill Davison the trumpet-player was driving Frank Teschemacher from work and the door flew open and Tesch fell clear out, right under a speeding taxi that killed him on the spot. That was a couple of months after Bix passed away in New York. When Wild Bill finally got over the shock all he could do was shake his head and say, "Where are we gonna get another sax player like Tesch?"

He could have saved his breath. There was no sense asking the question by then. Sure, there weren't any more fay sax men around with even a touch of the New Orleans style, but that was all right too. There wasn't going to be much demand for hot sax men from then on. New Orleans was dead and buried by 1932. It was just a legend. Old Tesch's death just put a period to the death-sentence of hot jazz, and to the whole saga of the Chicagoans, the last group of white musicians in this country who tried to keep even a little bit of the New Orleans spirit alive.

In the Fall of 1927, when I ankled back to Chicago from my barnstorming and barn-burning tour of the West, we were still living in a fool's paradise. What gave us a false feeling of security was that the hot man—and that meant mostly the cats in our gang, the Chicagoans who still looked to New Orleans for their inspiration—was really Mr. Kingpin in the music world. Straight musicians had worked up some real solid respect for us by then, because when one of us was shoved into a run-of-the-mill commercial band he electrified the whole group, having the same effect on it that a supercharger does on an airplane engine. So once in a while there was a demand for our services. We figured there'd always be a hambone or two around for us.

It's the same old story whenever the box-office boys, the strictly commercial big-business operators, take over any creative field and begin coining gold. First they try to buy up the serious, pure, really gifted artists in their field, the ones who stayed devoted and single-minded and never got dazzled by the Almighty Simolion. The uncommercial artists have prestige value, lend dignity to the phony package that's put up for sale. In this money-mad high-pressure-salesmanship country especially, the real artist is always having tempting cash offers dangled in front of his nose, if he'll only sign the papers and go commercial. Too often the guy, no matter how talented he is, is having too much trouble eating regular on the proceeds of his own creative work. He feels he's not getting the recognition he deserves from the public, and while he's knocking himself out the vulgarizers of his art go touring around town in limousines. Like as not, he's a cinch to put his John Henry on the dotted line.

I'm not saying that a jazz musician is a genius, or a remarkable fellow, or even that he deserves an extra pat on the back just because he stays honest and devoted, sticks with the original uncorrupted New Orleans style. Each guy has to go into a huddle with his own conscience to decide about that, and he doesn't deserve any cheers if he wants to keep his hands clean. All I'm getting at is this: the "pure" musician has added prestige, and the entrepreneurs and promotors in the music world, who are a little ashamed of their being so mercenary, recognize that fact. The pure artist's talents have been kept working, they're not blunted. He's traveling uphill all the time, but up, and he hits on all cylinders. He's that special touch in any musical organization, the something-new-that's-been-added. And the smart boys in the business realized early that he was an asset, and liked to inject him into a mechanical no-spirit big band for his hypodermic value.

And they were right. A hot man gave any orchestra, and the dancers as well, a new spirit and a stimulating pulse. His tone would stand out clear, full and firm, and his hard attack and phrasing added new inspiration to the saggy-souled men around him. As soon as he took off on a solo the whole band seemed to scramble out of its stupor, shook off the sleeping sickness, snapped back into alertness and showed some real sparkle for once. Listen hard to the first recordings Bix made with Paul Whiteman, when he still had some of the riverboat spirit left in him, see how his force and drive push the whole band along in spite of their straitjacket arrangements, and you'll dig what I mean. I swear, one good hot man was a tonic, a shot-in-the-arm, a musical hotfoot to fifteen knocked-out slaves with their noses buried in written music. The minute a hot jazzman busted loose, all the guys who were resting would start to clap their hands and beat time with their feet and swing their bodies behind the soloist, swaying from side to side, really stirred into feeling and come-alive expression at last.

Come to think of it, that's how the word "swing" was coined among us. When we talked about a musician who played hot, we would say he could swing or he couldn't swing, meaning what kind of effect did he have on the band. This word was cooked up after the unhip public took over the expression "hot" and made it corny by getting up in front of a band and snapping their fingers in a childish way, yelling "Get hot! Yeah man, get hot!" like a bunch of kids at the ringside yelling instructions to Joe Louis on how to use his right. That happened all the time, and it got us embarrassed and irritated all at once. It used to grate on our nerves because it was usually slung in our faces when we were playing our hottest numbers. Things got so bad, after a while, that when the squares yelled "hot" to us we turned cold on them right away. That's the reason we hot musicians are always making up new lingo for ourselves. Whenever the outsiders pick up the jazzman's colloquialisms they kick them around until the words lose all their real fresh meaning. Just look at what's happened to the word "swing" in the last fifteen years, if you want an example. Now the term is slapped on any corn you want to sell to the unsuspecting public. It's a gaudy label to plaster on an inferior, adulterated product, and there sure ought to be a pure-music law to regulate its use and abuse.

Well, like I say, things looked good. Didn't take no time at all, after I hit town, before a trumpet player named Leo Schuken came up to me at union headquarters and popped the usual question—"Milton, are you doing anything?" When I answered no he asked did I want to go into the Rendezvous, a gaudy high-class joint at Clark and Diversey Boulevard, with a new band. The place was owned by Leo's uncle, and Leo wanted me to round up the men for the band, which was to be called The Immigrants, because he knew I was in with the real hot contingent. I asked him what type of band did he have in mind. "Sweet and hot," he answered.

As soon as I heard that he wanted some hot men I started on a manhunt, and before long I had a pretty good line-up: Tesch on tenor sax and clarinet, Floyd O'Brien on trombone, Herman Foster on guitar, Leo Schuken on trumpet and his brother Phil on third alto and flute, and myself on first alto and clarinet. Then Eddie

Condon tipped us off that he had come across a bright and studious kid with real big hands, who had all the makings of a good pianist if we took him under our wing, and that was how we got Joe Sullivan on the ivories. Joe had a good classical schooling on the piano, but he was green to our idiom. I used to go over to his house a lot, bringing him Bessie Smith records so he could dig the piano accompaniments of Fletcher Henderson and James P. Johnson, and he studied hard.

Now all that was missing was a drummer. Seemed like every cat I went after just then was out of town or already tied up, but finally I got the phone number of a kid who was supposed to be cleancut, intelligent, and very ambitious, and who could make a fine drummer if he was given a chance. They told me he needed a little coaching; he had a gang of talent and it could be brought out easy. His name was Gene Krupa.

Sure enough, when I finally tracked the kid down he was thrilled at the opportunity to play with this band, because he knew all about the other guys in it and had plenty of respect for them. He was a neat, well-dressed, very good-looking youngster, hardly more than seventeen at the time; never talked much, shy and serious, and we liked him fine. We took him in hand right away, and not just to be nice—we needed a drummer bad. He wasn't in our idiom at all, but that was just because he'd never had any real hot-jazz schooling, and he was so eager to learn he could hardly sit still. I made it my business to stick with him as much as possible; the two of us ate, drank and breathed South Side jazz twenty-four hours a day. Dave Tough had made me promise never to show jazz drumming secrets to another living soul, but I still felt hot about the way he left me when he cut out for Paris, so I started to show Gene everything I knew.

There were still some great colored drummers of the old school to be heard around town: Tubby Hall was at the Sunset then with Louis Armstrong; Ollie Powell was with Jimmy Noone at the Nest; and Zutty Singleton was at Ethel Waters' cabaret, the Café de Paris (called the Lincoln Gardens in the days when Joe Oliver played there, and after that the Royal Gardens). Gene and Herman Foster and me made up a trio of walking delegates, touring the South Side spots every night. Gene ate it up, and so did Herman.

The South Side drummers gave Gene an entirely new slant on his instrument and showed him what a wide range of effects you could get with it. He was so loaded with inspiration, he set up his drums in the parlor of his house and began studying day and night. Once, when we were staying out kind of late, I asked him what would his mother think about his keeping such hours and he said, "Oh, it'll be all right, Milton, as long as I'm with you. Momma thinks you're a genius and anything I do with you is O.K." That struck me funny because I'd never met Mrs. Krupa, although I'd talked with her over the phone and Gene had told me she was a schoolteacher and what a wonderful person she was. Gene explained, "You see, Milton, ever since I've been going around with you I've been practising all day and all night—I'm really serious about the music and I'm with it all the time, and Momma thinks it's all your influence." That was the first time anybody's mother ever figured I was any other kind of influence but the kind you throw in the county jail. I sure wished my own mother appreciated me half as much.

The two of us practically crawled inside Gene's drums to study all their fine points. One important thing we worked out was the difference between starting a roll or a sequence of beats with the left hand or the right hand, how the tone and inflection changed entirely when you shifted hands. We'd sit for hours in my car while I pounded on the steering wheel, starting first with one hand and then with the other, trying to figure out the subtle differences in the effect. Then we went to work on the tomtoms, trying to get them in tune and studying the right times to use them; we kept punching holes in them with an icepick until they were pitched just right. (These were the old-style Chinese tomtoms with no tuning device.) Next, remembering more of the things I'd learned from Zutty and Baby Dodds, I showed Gene how to keep the bass and the snare drum in tune, and to get cymbals that rung in tune and were pitched in certain keys. After that we got to the cowbell and the woodblock, messing with them until we got them pitched in tune with the right keys. The way we sweated over that set of drums, you would have thought we were a couple of engineers tuning up a delicate aviation motor.

All the time we had our heads together, puzzling over the tricky points of the hide-beating art, we looked at the drums, not as just instruments to pound a monotone beat out of, but as having a broad range of tonal variations, so they could be played to fit into a harmonic pattern as well as a rhythmic one. To this day, Gene has kept some of that feeling about the drums with him, and that's why he can get effects that are much richer and more meaningful musically than a lot of these pounders in commercial bands, who sound like they got their musical schooling with a pneumatic drill on some asphalt pavement. Gene's mother was so tickled with the progress he was making that when I suggested it to her she bought him a set of kettle drums, gold tympanies that were tuned by a foot pedal, and a chromium-plated set of electric vibraphones. When Gene got enthroned behind all these trimmings he looked like a one-man band, and almost sounded like it too.

Gene lived way out on the far end of the South Side, and it took him more than an hour to get home by the streetcar or the El. His mother wanted him to stick with us as much as possible, and she bought him a car so we could get together easier. Night after night, after a visit to one of the South Side cabarets, we'd drive under the viaduct of Wacker Drive along the Chicago River and sit there talking until the squares began to come to their before-Abes. The subject that we kept coming back to, over and over, was this—How in hell could people be so stupid that they overlooked the wonderful things the Negro had to offer us? The same thing was happening inside Gene's head that happened inside mine years before. He'd started out being thunderstruck by the genius the colored people had for music. But when he got to thinking about it, he began to see that their music was only an expression of something that ran much deeper. Their wonderful music just reflected their whole make-up, their refreshing outlook and philosophy of living. You start out with just a technical interest in their music-making, but soon as you begin analyzing it you wind up trying to dig how they live and think and feel.

Everything the Negro did, we agreed, had a swing to it; he talked in rhythm, his tonal expression had a pleasing lilt to the ear, his movements were graceful. Was it this quality in him that made the white Southerners resent him so much, and was this why they kept him oppressed? Were they afraid that if the Negro was really set free he would make us all look sick with his genius for relaxed, high-spirited, unburdened living? We wondered about that. We could see that every move he made was as easy and neatly timed as anything Mother Nature had put down on this earth. His laughter was real and from way down inside. His whole manner and bearing was simple and natural. He could out-dance and out-sing anybody, in sports he could out-fight and out-run most all the competition, and when it comes to basketball don't say a word, just listen.

"You sure are right, Milton," Gene told me. "The colored guys really get out in front and set the pace when they're given half a chance. Why, look at how every white performer that ever aped the Negro became a headliner. Look at Sophie Tucker, Al Jolson, Eddie Cantor and the rest—where'd they be without their blackface routines and corny coonshouting and mammy numbers? And in our own field too, it's the musicians that tried to grasp a little of the Negro jazz idiom who've gotten to be famous."

More than anything, it was the Negro's sense of time and rhythm that fascinated us. I would sit there with Gene for hours, just beating out the rhythms of Zutty Singleton or Johnny Wells until my hands were swole double. I'd show him the secret that Dave Tough had dug, that there was a tonal pattern of harmony to be followed and that what seemed like a steady beat was really a sequence of different sounds accented at the right intervals, with just the correct amount of vibrations coming from the snare and the bass so that the other musicians who were improvising got the foundation to carry on and be more inventive.

Gene's head kept nodding like he had the palsy—he agreed with everything I said about the music and the Negroes who made it up. The eagerness that shone in his eyes when I played the different rhythms for him made me feel so good that I stayed with him. He kept telling me how he'd always remember our studies in the South Side and our all-night sessions afterwards. "Don't think I'll ever forget what you taught me about the colored race, Milton," he said later, "and some day I'll prove it to you."

Gene was a good kid, flowing over with talent. He had plenty on the ball, and he was destined to go places. But some of the places he traveled to were far away. He did forget.

Late in '27 sometime, Bix suddenly fell into town. He was playing at the Chicago Theater with Paul Whiteman's orchestra, and soon as we got the news, Eddie Condon and I shot over to knock him some skin. He came out backstage with Bing Crosby (Bing was singing in Whiteman's trio, The Rhythm Boys, with Harry Barris and Al Rinker). The first thing he said when he dug us was, "Come on, let's go get a drink." Down through the Loop he led us, along State Street, until just off of Lake Street we met up with a blackened-up old store that looked like it had been condemned before the Chicago fire. A peephole slid open, an eye appeared in the hole and gunned Bix; then the door swung open like a switch-blade. I guess the mug of that bottle-baby was known to every peephole attendant in the western hemisphere.

From then on this fillmill became the hangout for all of Chicago's hot men, and the home of the first jam sessions ever held in this country. The address was 222 North State Street, and after we hung out there awhile we named it the Three Deuces, parodying the name of the Four Deuces, one of the biggest syndicate whorehouses in town. Whenever we musicians wanted to get together with each other we'd say "Meet you at The Deuces tonight." Years later, after prohibition was repealed, the name was officially adopted and hung up on a sign outside, and the spot turned into a legit hot-music center.

It all started that night, after we had a few drinks and began to coax Bix to bring his horn with him after he finished up at the theater that night, so the boys could hear him play. "Where the hell we going to play?" Bix asked. Eddie said to just bring that horn around and we'd take care of the rest. We flew all around the town to hip the cats to what was going down, and finally we rounded up Tesch, Gene, Bud, Joe and Herman. Tesch's eyes almost jumped out of his head when we laid the news on him, and he kept on saying, "Yeah, yeah, that's the nuts," as though he couldn't believe it. He was crazy about Bix.

By midnight The Deuces was jumping. We were busy as a tout on Derby Day, buzzing in each other's ears, shaking hands and slapping backs, when all of a sudden Bud jumped up, eyes all shining like they were chromium-plated. "Milton," he yelled, "come on, there's a piano downstairs!" The colored porter in the place, digging our spiel about finding some place where we could play without having the cops on our necks, had gotten the okay from the bossman and tipped Bud off to the piano in the cellar. We all tore out for it, lugging our instruments with us, and in no time at all one of history's greatest jam sessions was under way. Bing had the spirit too. He beat time all night with his hands, like he was at a Holy Rollers meeting. Under Bix's spell, everybody was a genius that night.

I think the term "jam session" originated right in that cellar. Long before that, of course, the colored boys used to get together and play for kicks, but those were mostly private sessions, strictly for professional musicians, and the idea was usually to try and cut each other, each one trying to outdo the others and prove himself best. Those impromptu concerts of theirs were generally known as "cuttin' contests." Our idea, when we got going at The Deuces, was to play together, to make our improvisation really collective, using an organ background behind the one taking a solo, to see could we fit together and arrive at a climax all at once. Down in that basement concert hall, somebody was always yelling over to me, "Hey Jelly, what you gonna do?"—they gave me that nickname, or sometimes called me Roll, because I always wanted to play Clarence Williams' classic, *Jelly Roll*—and almost every time I'd cap them with, "Jelly's gonna jam some now," just as a kind of play on words. We always used the word "session" a lot, and I think the expression "jam session" grew up out of this playful yelling back and forth. At least I don't rightly remember ever hearing it before those sessions at The Deuces.

It was good kicks for us—about the last real spurt of collective improvisation the Chicagoans were to have before they were scattered all over the map. It was the hot swan-song of Chicago jazz that we busted out with, night after night, surrounded by cobwebs and flaky whitewash. The bosses, being an enterprising bunch of guys, soon put some tables and chairs down in the cellar, and before we knew it a small cabaret was going full blast. We started holding our first jam sessions for the public here. Everybody came around. Ben Pollack was sometimes on hand to beat the drums, and Jimmy Mac-Partland and Bix often played trumpet, while Tesch took off on his clarinet. As often as not, Bix would knock himself out on the piano when he wasn't taking a chorus on his horn. Jimmy was working with Ben Pollack's band at the Southmore Hotel then, along with Benny Goodman and Glenn Miller, and a few times he brought both those guys with him. Gene Krupa became a fixture in the place, always with his drums, and Eddie Condon was never without his banjo. I usually acted as master of ceremonies and I guess I made out all right because the audience never threw anything at me. What a time we had. We were always real gay.

It was at The Deuces that Red McKenzie first caught up with us. Red was a stocky, bowlegged cat, with a mop of danger-signal hair that would have made a bull with the rheumatiz begin pawing and prancing; he'd started out as a jockey but he fell off a horse and got hurt, so he quit riding. How he got into the music field is a funny story. He'd been working as a bellhop in the Claridge Hotel in St. Louis, and across the street, in a joint where a guy named Dick Slevin worked, there was a phonograph going all the time and a little colored shoeshine boy used to beat time on the shoes. Red liked the rhythm the kid made, and he used to join in by blowing into a comb that had a sheet of tissue paper wrapped around it. Slevin played a kazoo, because he had a ticklish mouth and the vibrations from the paper on the comb were too fuzzy. Well, one day Slevin ran into a guy named Jack Bland, who owned a banjo. They started playing together, and then got hold of Red. So there was a trio:

comb, kazoo, and banjo. The name they took for themselves was the Mound City Blue Blowers, and later on it became a foursome when they added Eddie Lang on guitar. In 1924 they were brought into the Friars Inn in Chicago, and Isham Jones, who was around at the time, arranged a recording date at Brunswick for them. The two records they made then, *Arkansas Blues* and *Blue Blues*, sold way over a million copies. Soon after that they played the Palace in New York, then made a European tour on which they played for the Prince of Wales, and finally Red showed up in Chicago again. That was when we got to know him.

Red wasn't really in our idiom at all, although he kind of went for New Orleans music when he heard it. The reason his early Blue Blowers records swept the country was that they were such a novelty, and in those crazy Twenties the sensation-hungry public was ready for a new fad every twenty-four hours.

It's the same story with Red as it was with The Original Dixieland Jazz Band that opened in New York at Reisenweber's in 1917 and immediately became a sensation on two continents. They were really a corny outfit, and if they ever had a touch of New Orleans it was frail as a nail and twice as pale, strictly a white-man's version. But they were fast and energetic and they had a gang of novelty effects that the public went wild about—jangling cowbells, honking automobile horns, barnyard imitations, noises that sounded like everything but music. (Remember, when I was just a kid, in Pontiac Reformatory, I was hit hard by the Dixieland Jazz Band's recording of *Livery Stable Blues*, but what really got me was the tricky clarinet playing of Larry Shields, and Nick LaRocca's trumpet that sounded kind of interesting but wasn't as good as the playing of our cellmate, the colored boy Yellow.) The public didn't know this wasn't the real jazz; and they didn't care. Pretty soon the Dixieland Jazz Band was the rage of the East, and of Europe as well, and "dixieland style" became the password of a lot of corny musicians, as it still is today.

Well, the Mound City Blue Blowers had the same kind of overnight success. They really didn't play much music, but their toy instruments and novelty effects hit the public's fancy and put them over. Red had a solid streak in him, and if he had sat down and mastered a professional instrument and spent a lot of time studying New Orleans music he could have come out all right. But the quick success put him in a commercial vein. Instead of woodshedding, he went out after the big money with the primitive equipment he had when he started. That's the way it always goes: somebody blows his guts out creating a new and authentic art form, then the unhip boys with shrewd commercial instincts come along and begin exploiting it, without bothering to learn it first. The result is that the public hears only the bastard version and goes crazy about it, figuring it's the real thing.

Red was very tough and guttural, always talking out of the corner of his mouth, giving you a kind of Southern-gangster impression because he tried to use Negro colloquialisms. He drank quite a lot, but he was a strict Catholic and was dead against the muta. He and Eddie Condon both had a smart business slant; they were practical, good managers and organizers, and they were always on the lookout for commercial possibilities. The rest of us, we were the artists, the boys with their heads in the clouds, scornful of keeping books and negotiating deals and adding up the give-and-take. It took somebody like Red or Eddie to make sure there was some money coming in at the end of the week. We really needed a business manager. But the history of our music might have been changed some if Red, who stepped in and took over the job, had been closer to the spirit of the music that obsessed us all.

Eddie Condon brought McKenzie around to The Deuces one night, and things began to happen fast. Red had it in mind to organize some recording dates for the Chicago boys, and he went to work hiring the musicians that very night. For that first date (four sides were made for Okeh, reissued later by Columbia), organized under the title of "McKenzie and Condon's Chicagoans," the line-up was: Jimmy MacPartland, cornet; Frank Teschemacher, clarinet; Bud Freeman, tenor sax; Joe Sullivan, piano; Eddie Condon, banjo; Jim Lannigan, bass and tuba; Gene Krupa, drums. Red seemed to sense that I was one of the charter members of the Chicago group, and didn't feel so good about my being left out, because he called me aside and said, "Look, Mezzrow, we're gonna take these kids and make some records, but we'll have to leave you out on the date because Tesch plays clarinet and Bud plays tenor and we're only gonna use seven men. I want you to know that I'm comin' back in the Spring to make some more records and we'll sure give you a break on the next dates." I guess Red saw how Gene and some of the others were kind of under my wing, and he didn't want me to feel bad about it. He asked me to come around to the studio anyhow and help supervise the recordings.

Before the date Tesch came over to my house and we wrote the introductions together, using some of Eddie Condon's ideas and figuring out the right voicing by playing clarinet duets until it sounded good to us. There was a week to go, so Tesch, Gene and I stuck close together, going out in my car every night and jamming. Then the day before the recording Eddie made me promise again that I would show up at the studio. That was right after we had closed at the Rendezvous, so my gold was getting scarce again, and when I went to check up on my assets I found I had $1.50 to my name. "Hell," said Eddie, "you take a cab to the studio with that dough and I'll pay you back." So when the big day rolled around I spent my last chips on a taxi.

During this period recording had taken a big step ahead, from the old acoustical method to the electrical system. In the old days the musicians had to blow into big wooden loudspeakers, but now they were beginning to use microphones and the engineers in the control room wore earphones so they could hear what was going on and signal to the players to correct things that were going wrong. There was plenty of trouble that day. This was one of the first dates where a drummer was allowed to use a full set of drums on a recording, because the bass drum had a tendency to knock the needle right out of the groove or make it dig too deep a cut. We began to fool around with all kinds of experiments to muffle Gene's big drum. The first thing we tried was to hang the bass drum cover over the front of the drum, but this wasn't enough, so we finally wound up with all of our overcoats wrapped around it. That drum looked like a dead ringer for Admiral Byrd at the South Pole, but it finally recorded right. Then we found the cymbals weren't coming through very clearly, so when we got ready to make a master I held the cymbals close to the mike and Gene reached over his bass drum to bang them.

Four sides were made that day: *Nobody's Sweetheart*, *China Boy*, *Sugar* and *Liza*. Those records made history. When they were released, along with the ones we made a couple months later, and fell into the hands of jazz experts, especially in Europe, they caused a lot of comment and controversy, and before the critics were through yelling their praises a new term was born—"Chicago style." These were the records that first defined that style.*

I sure didn't have much right to be uppity in those days, but I guess I was, because I told the boys I liked some things about the records but all in all they weren't so much to me. Tesch had a terrible hard reed that day, and Jimmy dragged pretty bad, and I had the feeling that nobody showed that old punch of Louis Armstrong's. The guys got kind of sore at me for being so critical, because they all thought they outdid themselves. What I was trying to say, even though I didn't have the right words for it and my ideas weren't too straight yet, was this—they were coming along fine, they were latching on to the classic New Orleans style, but they still had a long way to go, we all did, and there was no use our patting ourselves on the back. We weren't in the same class with the Armstrongs and the Bechets, the Noones and the Olivers, and we might as well admit it and keep on studying.

The boys weren't all of one mind about that. Some of them were beginning to wonder if we could ever get in that A-1 class. Others were beginning to ask themselves if it was even worth trying. Maybe Chicago style was good enough—in a class by itself, worth sticking with and to hell with backgrounds and origins. My instincts kept telling me that Chicago style wasn't a new school that could stand on its own two feet but only the style of a bunch of white youngsters with plenty of talent who were beginning to absorb the New Orleans idiom but hadn't finished their schooling by a long shot. It was just an imperfect reflection, like you get in a distorting mirror,

* See Appendix 1 for further discussion.

of the only real jazz, the colored man's music. We couldn't rest on our laurels, even if the unhip critics thought we had exploded with a brand-new kind of music. We had to recognize where we derived from, and try all the time to be more authentic, purer, closer to the source. That worked up some friction between us.

Oh, I want to remind Eddie Condon of a little debt he still has got on his books—he never did pay me back that $1.50. But I guess I'm still ahead because he loaned me fifty bucks towards a note on the car I lost in Kansas City. Hell, I should never have brought the subject up. Looks like I owe the guy $48.50.

Somewhere under the surface, deep down, there was a disagreement, some kind of split in perspectives, between me and some of the other Chicago cats. It never came completely out in the open, and we couldn't put our finger on any one thing and say that was it. We didn't know enough about ourselves or our music in those days to figure it out. But it was there, and it was beginning to weigh on all our minds—the way we couldn't see eye-to-eye about those recordings was just an example of it. That friction sure brought me down. Sometimes I'd even begin to wonder if there wasn't something screwy about me, because I was almost in a minority of one.

Not long after we left the Rendezvous, Herman Foster got himself a job in a roadhouse outside Chicago, and one night Gene, Bud and I drove out to see him. I felt like jamming some that night, so when they asked me I climbed up and sat in with the band on tenor sax. I really got worked up in that session. I guess I was a little on the defensive, after all our arguing about the records, so I practically blew my windpipe inside out trying to play a strictly New Orleans, Armstrong-Noone-Oliver style. Every note I forced out was an answer to the rest of the Chicago boys in the running argument we were having about the music. Every time I blew a riff down into the faces of my buddies, it meant "See? This is what I mean! This is where we got to go, and keep on going!" I didn't know exactly what was going on myself, but I sure knew I was trying to prove something that night.

Right in the middle of a hot passage, when we were all knocking ourselves out, the colored chef came running out of the kitchen, togged in full cook's regalia, fancy cupcake headgear and all. He came running right up to the stand and stood in front of me while I kept blowing away. His hands were on his hips and his feet were planted wide apart and his mouth was as open as it could get without surgery. Then suddenly he pointed at me, slapped the floor with his foot, and yelled in my face, "Boy, you is the saxophonest blowinest man I ever heard in all my born days. Where'd you come from poppa?"

Bud almost died, he was so delighted, and it sent a thrill through me like a high-powered electric current. I don't know why, but it was just like I'd been in the toughest fight of my life, where everything I had and believed in was at stake, and doggone if I didn't come out the winner. I felt fine the rest of the night.

In the beginning of 1928 I took a band into the Purple Grackle, a beautiful modernistic Spanish-patio kind of roadhouse, lousy with heavy purple plush drapes all over the joint. It was about thirty miles out of Chicago on the road to Joliet, between Aurora and Elgin. There was a big sign out in front, reading "Milton Mezzrow and his Purple Grackle Orchestra," and it puzzles me to this day because I still don't know what in hell a purple or any other color grackle is. The job lasted for about three months, and it was the last job I ever did have around the Windy City. In the band were: Freddy Goodman (Benny's brother) on trumpet, Floyd O'Brien on trombone, Pete Viera on piano, Herman Foster on guitar, Gene Krupa on drums, and myself on clarinet. The guy who ran the Grackle, a hot-jazz fan named Val, who was the first real record collector I ever knew, was crazy about Johnny Dodds and spent all his money going to Kelly's Stables to hear his band and buying all his records. He recognized right away that Floyd and Gene and Herman and I had absorbed the Negro idiom, and that was why he hired us and gave us so much encouragement. His appreciation amazed us all, because all the café owners we ever knew were more familiar with machine guns than they were with music.

Those first months of '28, when we were at the Grackle, were important to us because we made a gang of records then, the first ones I ever played on. Here's how our three dates went:

First date: I Found a New Baby, There'll Be Some Changes Made, and *Baby Won't You Please Come Home* (this one wasn't released until 1945), plus a fourth side that was never released. McKenzie and Condon got this date with Brunswick, and the records were made under the name of the "Chicago Rhythm Kings." By this time Bud Freeman and Jimmy MacPartland had joined Ben Pollack in New York, so they used Muggsie Spanier on cornet and me on tenor sax; the rest of the band was the same as on that earlier Okeh date. I had to make these sides with a strange sax that I borrowed somewhere because my own was in hock, and I had about as much lip for a tenor as a condemned man does for the judge that handed down the sentence. I'd been playing clarinet all the time at the Grackle, and the embouchure is entirely different on the two horns.

Second date: Friars Point Shuffle and *Darktown Strutters Ball,* with the same personnel as on the first date, except for George Wettling on drums instead of Gene, and McKenzie making the mistake of trying a vocal. These sides were made for Paramount under the name of "The Jungle Kings."

Third date: Just one side, *Jazz Me Blues,* under the name of "Frank Teschemacher's Chicagoans." This recording, done for Paramount, wasn't released until 1938 when Hugues Panassié, the French jazz critic, came over from Paris and convinced Milt Gabler, owner of the Commodore Record Shop in New York, to release it under the UHCA label (the letters stand for the United Hot Clubs of America). For this session we used two saxes and a clarinet in the front line, with four rhythm instruments, so the full personnel was: Tesch on clarinet, the late Rod Cless on alto sax, myself on tenor, Sullivan on piano, Condon on banjo, Lannigan on tuba, and Krupa on drums.

With these records, Chicago style was defined for all time, for better and for worse. A gang of myths has sprung up around them, but the one thing they really prove is that we were a plenty uneven and erratic bunch of performers even at the height of our Chicago careers, and that's the truth—guys with a lot of talent, maybe, but not by a long shot a well-established and independent group. Our music was *derived*, that's what these records show: we took some things over from the colored musicians (the flare-up, the explosion, shuffle rhythm, the break) and sometimes did them good; we drifted away from their pattern in places and fell down. The Chicago School was a turning-point along the line of march, a betwixt-and-between affair; it was a halfway-house. Play these records with some Armstrongs and Noones and Bechets, and see for yourself.*

Well, the Chicago School no sooner got its name than school was over; all the star pupils scrambled out of the classroom and went truant. Our break-up was in the cards. Influences from the outside kept slamming at the Austin High boys every whichaway and knocked them off the track. Tesch was a prize example: while he was working up a style that sometimes came kind of close to the Armstrong-Noone school, he was huddled up more and more at his phonograph at home, listening to all kinds of symphonic razzmatazz like Holst's *The Planets* and Stravinsky and Ravel. That poor guy was so confused about where he was going, he'd play his own records over a few times and then grab hold of them and slam them down over his knee like a madman, breaking them into a thousand pieces. And don't forget that Bix, who was a bitch-on-wheels to Tesch and all kinds of a virtuoso, was tugging hard at these kids too, needling some of them with his skullbusting classical jive. New Orleans had put her grabbers on them like a powerful magnet; but there were plenty of other magnets yanking at them too. Half the time they didn't know whether they were coming on or going tangent. Confusion had the day.

When I first met the Austin High Gang, they'd damn near splintered their toupees over the way I kept trying to stick to a straight Negro style. But it wasn't all a honeymoon kick for us; after a while some of them started to get a little lecture-shy and bit-chomping when I kept yapping at them every time they drifted off one inch from the pure style. The way they dug me, I was dogmatic as a preacher-man at a revival meeting, narrow-minded

* See Appendix 1.

as a Georgia cracker; I kept sounding off like I had a real fixation or obsession, saying Yeah, you played that real good, it sounded just Louis or Baby Dodds, or No, you ain't got that just right, Jimmy Noone wouldn't of played it that way. They had a comeback: So what? And I didn't have enough wig-trigs to explain why you had to sound like Louis and Jimmy Noone. The trouble was, I was still fumbling around some in the dark myself. I had plenty of instincts and a powerful feeling about the music. But I didn't have any worked-out philosophy or musical theory to back them up. Half the time I wasn't clear on what I was getting at myself, although I sure worked up plenty of steam on the way. I was long on criticism, short on ideas. They couldn't help but bristle up sometimes at my spiels.

Besides, the pure hot man was beginning to run into a gang of cold shoulders; the big name-bands were going places and not coming back, but we were finding it plenty tough to get our vittles unless we catered to the tastes of the unhip general public and watered our music down to a thin, sad gravy with no more body to it than some tired dishwater. When Red McKenzie showed up with his hardheaded practical slant and gave the boys a peep at how much big money was to be made, they figured they already had the secret of the music and were gone with it. It wasn't just the fancy dough that set their minds to buzzing, although that was a part of it. What Red was offering them was a short cut out of their musical dilemma too. Red didn't mean no wrong. He just wasn't steeped in the real colored man's idiom, like some of us had started out to be.

Finally, one motherferyer day, all the guys decided to cut out of Chicago, under Red's and Eddie's leadership, and head for the bright lights of New York. And there wasn't any place for me in the set-up. They had a practical reason for not taking me along, the same reason I was left off of the first records: Tesch played clarinet and Bud tenor sax, so there wasn't any opening for me unless the band was made bigger. But there was another reason too. In Chicago, at least you had a real Basin Street tradition built up, and some of the great colored jazzmen, the founders of our school, were still around playing their wonderful music. But New York was Tin Pan Alley, flooded with commercialism. They'd hardly even heard any jazz up there; the best they got all through the early Twenties was the barnyard imitations of the Original Dixieland Jazz Band, plus sticky-sweet show music played by groggy pit orchestras during musical comedies. The guys didn't want a monomaniac tagging along on this trip. They'd always kidded me about how I ran with the colored boys so much, till I was talking like them as well as trying to play like them. And I didn't give much promise of changing any. I wasn't budging much more than a hincty mule in those days, though I couldn't give a good reason why. A guy like me wouldn't be very good company in New York.

On their last night in town, when they already had their train-tickets bought and their luggage packed up, we all got together for a farewell party at the Nest. That had become our hangout, when we weren't jamming at The Deuces, because Jimmy Noone had his band there and we couldn't get enough of that guy. The management had set aside a special table just for us, in a corner alongside the bandstand, and night after night we'd been hugging that spot, lamping the band and shaking our heads because it was too much. Jimmy usually started out early in the evening by playing arrangements of popular tunes of the day, and how he played them; but when we eased in and began shooting our requests at him, he'd always shift over to the blues for us, beaming down at our table and asking what we wanted next, so it was real lowdown New Orleans gutbucket all night long for us. Jimmy was our boy.

That night the guys were a little embarrassed and red-in-the face, and they sat around kind of stiff and awkward. Gene Krupa was going along with them on their treasure-hunt in The Big Apple, and they all knew that Gene was my protégé, that I'd wised him up to everything I knew about the colored man's drum technique, including things I'd got from Zutty Singleton and Baby Dodds that I'd promised Dave Tough I'd never show to anybody else on this earth. And I'd spent a lot of time coaching Joe Sullivan too, giving him little hints I'd picked up from Tony Jackson, Earl

Hines and all the other great Negroes who had ever grabbed a handful of keys. I sure don't want to give the impression that I was Poppa Jazz, surrounded by a flock of know-nothing disciples who were rising up in revolt against the master. No, that's not the story. It was just that I was a few years older than most of these kids, and I'd enrolled in the New Orleans school earlier than any of them did. I still had a long and wearisome way to go myself, no mistake about that. But I'd had more schooling than them, and I shared whatever I knew with them all.

This evil dim, as we sat around our table at the Nest, I was still as a hoot-owl, sad and sick at heart. We'd come up a long, painful road together, the gang of us, and now we were going off in opposite directions. Maybe we'd never meet again. Maybe, if we did join up in later years, we'd be strangers to each other. The future was a study in midnight black. Buddy, I had the sulks' whole family.

All night long we kept asking Jimmy Noone to play the blues for us, and he kept saying sure, glad to, but all night he played only some arrangements of show tunes that were in his repertoire. It began to dawn on us that we hadn't heard not one of the blues, in spite of all our requests. Now that was bothersome, because Jimmy and the boys liked us, knew we were crazy about their music, and they usually turned the place over to us whenever we showed up. And this was a special occasion, with all the guys leaving—you'd think this time, for sure, Jimmy would be extra nice to them all. But the blues kept on not being played. It made us kind of uneasy to be politely igged this way, and that put still another wet blanket on the party, which was sopping already. Weep City was just around the turn, and we were traveling on the express.

Finally it got late. The wake began to break up. We stood up, shaking hands all around mumbling our good-byes, trying to smile at each other but looking like a bunch of professional mourners who didn't get paid. I was froze in my tracks—it hit me all of a sudden that when those guys walked through the door it would be for the last time. From now on this table was going to be reserved in my name alone. Weight was really on me. I'm not too proud to admit that there were more tears in my eyes than I could see through.

The boys threaded their way through the joint, and then they pulled up at the exit and turned around for one last look. Just at that moment, with split-second timing, the band struck up a gut-clenching blues that was like one big sob breaking over the room, a terrible moanful "preachin' blues."

For hours the band had steered clear of every blues number we asked for, lightly and politely. Now, when everybody was leaving, here it came, a carload of moans and wails. I began to realize that there was some point to this. It didn't just happen like that. The boys knew something was up too, because they stopped dead, their faces all wrinkled up with questions, and stood facing the band.

In a minute the second chorus came on. Goddamn if old Doc Poston, who played alto sax and clarinet in the band, didn't raise up from his seat and begin to preach. I couldn't believe it was happening. To dig the issue, you got to know that in all the time we'd been haunting the Nest, not one preaching blues did the band ever play. Preaching blues was strictly race music, played by colored musicians for their own kind. It was private between-us stuff, made for private consumption. Of all the different kinds of blues, it was about the only one us white musicians never got to take over at all. And now here it came at us. While the band played a stop time behind him, Doc Poston stood and in his husky moanful voice he started to preach. He was the preachinest man I ever did hear. And what he was preaching that night was a homemade hard-cutting psychoanalysis of every man standing up there in the doorway.

Red McKenzie was first in line; Eddie Condon stood next to him, Joe Sullivan next, and Gene Krupa brought up the rear. Doc took them in the same order, reading from left to right. He sang:

There stands Red McKenzie right over there,
He's goin' to New York with his mop of red hair,
He'll be back pretty soon I do declare,
Cause the stuff he's puttin' down really ain't nowhere.

Condon's standin' side him and he's all red in the face,
Leavin' Mezz behind him, thinks he's really goin' some place,
But if he knew like I do he would make a change of pace
Cause he ain't goin' nowhere but on a wild goose chase.

Sullivan's goin' with them an' I don't understan'
Why he'd travel with that runt an' that red-headed man,
He'll be writin' home for help but he won't have the stamps,
The only thing he'll have will be the miss-meal cramps.

Gene was next on the list, but before Doc could take up his
case he came tearing across the floor and sat down again with me.
The other guys stood still as icicles, trying to smile but looking
like they'd been chewing on some alum. Then they all turned and
bolted for the lobby. They couldn't get out of the place fast enough.
Gene sat with me the rest of the night, till he had to cut out to
catch the train for New York.

I can't tell you how I felt. What Jimmy Noone and Doc Poston
did that night was just about the most powerful experience I have
ever had in my whole life. It was like I was going down for the
third time and all of a sudden somebody I didn't even know was
a close friend to me threw out a life-saver. Jack, I was saved that
night, and in the nick of time. There was still no word spoken
between the band and me, but now they struck up the blues and
stayed with them right until closing, playing every number they
knew was a favorite of mine. I didn't try to put my feeling into
words, and they didn't expect me to. If I'd opened my mouth
then, I would have turned on the weeps.

Right there is a trait of the race that always hits me more than
any other in this world. They hardly ever discuss anything, chew
up a topic until it's as limp and tore-up as an old dishrag. Hell,
there's no time for discussion; besides, gumbeating is just a waste
of energy, because words were mostly invented to lock up the
truth and sneak it out of sight, not to get it across. Those guys
understand what goes on, and expect everybody else to understand,
through looks and unspoken attitudes, little gestures and subtle

hints and the things swimming deep in a man's eyes, just out of the whole atmosphere, by a kind of mental telepathy. They dug what the score was with us that night. I never spoke to them about the other guys leaving, but they'd heard about this gravy-train excursion to New York and they knew what was behind it. What they'd been saying all evening long—first by not playing their real music when the guys asked for it, then by blasting them with the preaching blues—was that in their eyes I was trying to be true to the spirit of their music, no matter how I fumbled and fussed, and the other cats weren't saying good-bye to me as much as to the good, solid, honest and a-romping jazz world, where your emotions are clean and straight and you pour them out in a right and heartfelt way.

Doc's words didn't mean that Red and the others were mean or anything like that. No, as a matter of fact they were all good guys, and Doc knew it. But if they went tangent to the real jazz music and kept kidding themselves that they were still steering straight, they wouldn't be nowhere, and at the end of their rainbow in New York they'd find a can of mouldy beans instead of that pot of gold. Doc was saying to hell with the money and the fame, just fly right, hew to the line, stick with it. We got us a fine new music here, he was saying, and let's keep on making it as honest and good as we know how, and, if we don't hit the headlines and cop the gold, the hell with it, we'll know we always did our best and we'll be straight with ourselves. That's what Doc was preaching. And to emphasize it still more, the band refused to give their music to these guys, then hit them with the real race music when they all went to leave.

Gene and I were their guests for the rest of the night. When they had a break they all came off the stand and walked over to our table with real friendly, paternal smiles, patting me on the shoulder and acting so nice and warm I couldn't hardly speak. They understood about things, those guys did. It was just another case of the smile that speaks volumes and the real deep sympathy that I have got from the race every time I felt lonely and forgotten and the misery was heavy on me. If I managed to live through that sorrowful night at all, I have Jimmy Noone and his band to thank for it.

Gene didn't say a word about what happened, and I didn't either. I don't think we've spoken of it to this day. But he sure must have gotten the point, and so did I.

As soon as all our buddies broomed off to Tin-Pan-Alleyland, Chicago turned from a frolic-pad into a mortician's icebox. A fraughty issue, Jim, really sad. Now that our brotherhood of music studs was bust up and scattered to the four footloose winds, Josh Billings and I moped all around town like a pair of alleycats, poking our noses in creepy cellars and the quiet ones off the main drag to find some sign of life. No luck.

"This old burg just laid down and died on us," Josh moaned, "only it refuses to close its eyes. Some killjoy bastard with a big rubber hose sneaked in here and syphoned all the goddamned life out of it, every last drop. We're lost in a morgue, surrounded by two million corpses."

He wasn't telling no lie either. That town was sad as a map and twice as flat to us. King Jazz had packed his trunk and made his get-away, taking all his monkey-glands and hypodermic needles with him. There wasn't a shot of adrenalin left to make this droopy town sit up and take notice again.

Josh really went to Beef City. "The hell with it Josh," I sighed, singing the blues for real. "The hell with everything. Let's you and me go over to Pasquale's and light up for a while."

That was how we always wound up. At the Mexican's we could at least get loaded on good hay and forget our misery for a couple of chimes. The nights were coming to be long shimmying chains of muggles for us, reaching from nowhere all the way to nothing-doing, each one longer and knottier than the last. The weed was the only thing that kept us going, no jive.

Pasquale lived in a tired-looking excuse for a house over in a gloomy industrial section of the West Side, a lopsided cubby of tarpaper and slats held together with a string and a prayer. Inside, the scene was always the same: around the only real hunk of furniture in the room, a big hollowed-out tree stump that squatted in the middle of the slanting floor, sat Pasquale and his friends, rocking on their heels, so high they were about to fly, with wide-brimmed hats big as beach umbrellas stuck way back on their heads. It was a weird picture, lifted straight out of some jungle in the Sierra Madres, lit up by nervous gas-lights that threw snaky India-rubber shadows over the room and across the dark oily faces of Pasquale and his *compañeros*. In one corner was a wooden box, over which they'd shake the muta on a newspaper until all the seeds dropped out and rolled down. Then this seeded muta—real golden-leaf, smuggled across from south of the Rio Grande—was dumped into the carved-out tree stump, and these guys would crouch around their pile of shredded joy and roll muggles on a twenty-four-hour shift, jabbering away in spic and smoking up all the profits. A couple of them always took time out to strum their guitars and wail songs like *La Cucaracha*. Pasquale, a swarthy matchstick of a squirt with hollow cheeks, no bigger than a blink, always gay and full of laughs, was bossman of this dive; while he waggled his fingers, rolling with a more expert touch than any piecework slave on the assembly line, he kept chuckling, cursing, yelling crazy Mexican songs and sucking on a stick of gauge like it was a hunk of peppermint candy. "*Chingando cabrones!*" he'd shout. "Sonumabitch, make quick, *oiga!* Meelton is here, *verdad,* roll 'em *cabrones*, roll 'em fat, *amigos mios!*" Little Pasquale used to sell his muggles six for a dollar but he gave us a cut-rate price, a tobacco tin full-up with muta for two dollars, or a Diamond matchbox full for four or five. It was real mellow too, purer than Ivory Soap and guaranteed to keep you afloat twice as long.

This night they were beating up their chops like mad, popping at each other like their lungs were filled with soda water, and they looked like they had just seen a whole battalion of ghosts, they were so scared. Their eyes were rounder than cannonballs, and exclamation marks hopped off their tongues like fidgety frogs. Seemed like they were having some kind of hot argument, passing a Mexican newspaper around the circle while they slung high-speed peon jive at each other.

"Hey," Josh said, holding up his hand to stop the tongue-wagging traffic, "what's a matter, you got trouble, Pasquale?"

For an answer the little guy grabbed the paper out of somebody's hand and shoved it right under Josh's nose. "*HOY—FIN DEL MUNDO!*" was what the banner headline screamed, or something like that. It didn't mean a thing to unspic us. "Is all finish!" Pasquale bellowed. "*Finito*, yessir! It say here, make one hell of big noise tonight, boom, whole *chingando* world blow up like Fourth July! Is not long, *mira*—one-two hour more, when clock make twelve, world come to end!"

Josh and I busted out with the giggles, once the screwy idea sank in. I felt pretty smug because, no matter how unhip I was to all the Blue-Broadway jive, at least I knew the Old Fireball was going to come ballooning up in the East tomorrow morning. When all these Calamity Joes crowded around us to dig what we knew about the good Lord's timetable, we waved them off, explaining that we weren't at liberty to give out any inside information. Then we eased out and sat down on the rickety little porch to light up. After all, we had our own troubles.

We must have been out there for quite a while, just gunning the ground and not cracking our jaws once, getting more and more wrapped up in our dark-brown thoughts. My frame sopped up that muta like a blotter does ink, and I felt the glow creep all through me, but I still couldn't shake off my drugg feelings and neither could Josh—we were as lonely as a couple of longshoremen in the middle of the Sahara. Then all of a sudden I looked up and, poppa, it was on. I'll be a motherferyer if that old sky, black as an undertaker's shroud a minute before, wasn't all lit up with crazy jitterbugging shafts of light, all of them different colors, restless and jumpy and quivering like some wet puppies on ice. Looked like Mother Earth was blowing her top for real. The rainbow was on a spree up there, a-hopping and a-skipping from one clump of driftsmoke to another, zooming around like a frantic cat with a tin can tied to its tail. I'd never seen anything like that in my whole life—big dancing ribbons of color that shimmied from horizon to horizon, like somebody had struck a match and set fire to the air way up to the stratosphere. At first I thought the muta was making me see things, but I shook my head till it rattled like a penny-bank and rubbed my eyes till they were ironed flat, and when I looked up again some practical joker was still tossing those neon javelins around Saint Peter's dommy.

Daddy, them was fireworks! I began to know how insignificant and puny I was, along with the funking little whirling pingpong ball of an earth I was squatting on. Those great big technicolor tongues kept shooting out, lapping at the sky, twisting and squirming like the arms of an octopus about to snatch up the earth and squeeze it into a spray of dust and tears—and then, goddamn, those words popped into my head again: "*HOY—FIN DEL MUNDO!*" *Hoy,* it said. Oi-oi, I said. Lordy, that scrawny little Mexican paper must really have been in the know, after all. That four-page hot-tamale sheet had gone and scooped the A.P., the U.P., and the I.N.S., along with Reuters and Tass and all the other globe-circling know-it-all newshawks. This was it! Another minute now, just time for another quick drag on my muta, and there'd be one hell of a blow-up, Chicago would go avalanching into Lake Michigan and the whole Western Hemisphere would begin boiling and fizzing, the earth would crack open and turn inside-out like a punctured old tennis ball and all of us strutting little fly-specks, Josh and me and Pasquale and all the guitar players, we'd all go tumbling into space head over heels, in a shower of boulders and gravel from the Rocky Mountains, with maybe a little extra débris from Fujiyama. . . .

"Ooooo-*oo!*" Josh yelled. I'd been too scared to open my yap and point it out to him, but he had just looked up and got a load of it for himself. "Well, what do you know!" he said, like he was seeing something in a dream. "It's the Aurora Borealis, Milton, that's what it is, the Aurora Borealis! You don't get to see that very often. Isn't it wonderful?"

"What, what in the hell is that?" I said, in the closest thing to a human voice I could produce on such short notice.

"Why, it's the Northern Lights, you dope," Josh said. He went on to talk about magnetic fields and the laws of reflection and refraction and a whole lot of electrical jive, because he was a bug on amazing-stories magazines and he was really up on all that Jules Verne stuff. I didn't pay him no mind after that—I was too busy learning how to breathe again.

All the weight was off me, finally; I wiped my face dry and then I thought of the Mexicans inside. "Hey," I said, "let's go get those guys out here, Josh. They've got this idea about the world coming to an end and they'll really pass out when they see *this*." I felt so foolish about having been so shaky, I guess I wanted to see somebody else throw a fit too.

We banged on the door and slipped inside again. "Pasquale," I said, "you and your boys come on out pronto, we're gonna show you something." They all scraped themselves off the floor and trucked out behind us.

Brother, you should have seen their maps when they took one peep at those strutting searchlights up above. There was death-and-taxes writ all over their poor frantic mugs. "*Chinga!*" Pasquale howled, The Reaper doing a Charleston round and round his saucer-eyes. "*A la mierda!* Oh, *Jesu Cristu, madre mia*, world is come to end, my paper she is right! Is come, is time now, is all finish!" The whole gang of them dropped to their knees and began crossing themselves as fast as if they were slapping mosquitoes, yelping and yapping like madmen. Then came the pay-off. "*Amigos!*" Pasquale yelled out, "Hey, *vamo'nos*, come quick, we get ready!" Into the house they flew, those greyhound peons, and no sooner did they get inside than there was a mad scramble for all the rosaries, holy medals, sombreros and guitars that they could lay their hands on. Then they lit out for the street.

All of a sudden Pasquale stopped them short with one hysterical yell. "*Grefa!*" he screamed. "*Grefa, grefa!*" You should have seen them put on the breaks; it was like a call-to-arms, a rallying cry. Zip! About they faced and back into the house they tore, like a school of meteors on drill.

To prepare for the long, long journey, every last man began scooping up great handfuls of rolled and loose grefa, cramming it in their kicks, shoving it down inside their raggedy shirts, stuffing it into their big sombreros. They weren't going to be caught short, no matter how they wound up; not these hombres. Don't expect any hay in the Blue Broadway, so carry it with you, that's the play.

I could have hugged those peons then, one and all, if they would only of stood still long enough—guess I got a soft spot for any guy who'll go out to meet Judgment Day packed up with a battered old git-box and as much hay as he can carry. The last we saw of them they were flying down a dark alley, screaming bloody murder and bulging like a load of overstuffed potato sacks, their guitars swatting the air and muta coming out of their ears.

Things went from bad to worse, and kept right on traveling. I was dead beat, troubled with the shorts; not penny one did I have, and I prowled around town in the only suit I had to my name, a beat-up old tuxedo with holes in the pants where I sat, and my hair grew so long that Louis Armstrong got the impression I was a violin player. I was living in a scrimy moth-eaten dump of a furnished room with my wife and stepson, and if the rent got paid I never knew about it. Bonnie worked a little as a hat designer to scrape up some eating money, but just about then her season wound up, so beg-borrow-or-steal was the play and I was too nervous to steal. The blues had me, Jack. I was melancholy, morbid and miseryful, and I felt bad too. I was really bad off, the forgottenest man in town; my smiles all got born upside down, and when somebody cracked a joke my eyes would wet up with tears. All night long I would sit around with Josh, getting loaded and playing my records (until my landlady wound up with most of them for the back rent). Josh was no vacation for anybody either. He had the dismals too.

The way it happened, we were sprawled out one night in a friend's car, carving up the gloom with our fingernails. Mike, the guy who owned this buggy, was a saxophone player and a hell of a regular cat, and he was working and sticking, but he was singing the blues too. He was a close pal of Gene Krupa's, and two weeks had limped by with no word from young Gene.

"Mike," I said, "tell me one thing, have you got this car of yours insured?" The answer was yes, and I began to talk very fast, putting down a righteous spiel. "Look, Mike, I got a proposition to make and it'll be a life-saver for us if you're game. Josh and me have got to clear out of this town before they start padding up a couple of cells around us. What do you say you fill up your car with gas and oil and let us drive it to New York? Just give us about twenty-four hours, see, then report to the police that your car's stolen. As soon as we hit The Big Apple we'll ditch the buggy, and when the New York cops find it your insurance company will have to pick it up and ship it back to you. How about it, Mike, what do you say?" I would have been down on my knees if that car was a little roomier.

The idea was solid—we scuffled with it from all angles but we couldn't find any slip-ups. Good old Mike! He agreed right away, without a second's hesitation, on one condition, that we would send for him if we ever got a job in New York. We said sure. Then, to top it off, he dug into his poke and laid fifty bucks on us for pocket money. If we didn't kiss him it was only because we were parked in a congested area at the time, and people might not have understood.

Buster, Jim; this was soft as cotton and twice as fuzzy. We scooted home and got together a few belongings—some records, my horns, a portable record player and a good supply of muta. Then, just so's I'd be sure to have enough fuel to hold me up, I made a stop on the South Side and bought me twenty capsules of cocaine, to help me keep awake on our no-stop drive to the East. Some of us had taken to sniffing snow not long before; we liked it because it makes your mind very alert, you do some high-jive thinking and talk up a breeze. Many was the night we sniffed and philosophized, philosophized and sniffed, until the early bright was upon us.

Then, finally, we were all set. So long, warden! Bye-bye Chicago, you old rockpile of a town! Plant you now and dig you later. Off we shot in a cloud of dust, hitting the road like a couple of cons making a get-away.

170

That car must have come with an automatic pilot installed in it, because we sure didn't pay much attention to driving it. When we weren't inhaling snow we were sipping tea, and most of the time we hardly knew whether we were scraping the big drink in a submarine or clipping the cloud-tips in a plane. We couldn't wait to get with the gang in New York; we kept telling ourselves how it was going to be when we busted in on them, how we'd all jump with joy and play the records we brought along and smoke up all the grefa. Time bulleted by that way, and all of a sudden we found ourselves way up on some mountain, riding smack in the middle of a cloud. It must have been in Pennsylvania, somewhere in the Alleghenies, near as I could figure out afterwards. Man, the fog was so thick you couldn't see for looking. Visibility hit zero and kept sinking. We were up near the Head Knock's territory, messing with his jive that makes it drip, and we were scared. Talk about Bix's mist—right quick the sky was filled with a mixture of shaving lather, beer suds, woolpack and Pacific surf. *In a Mist*, hell. If Bix could have dug this mess he would have written a number called *In the Pea-Soup*.

I was plenty jumpy and I didn't want Josh to leave me, but it had to be done. While I stayed glued to the wheel, he got out and walked a foot or two ahead of the bumpers; he'd yell out "Okay!" and I'd shoot ahead another inch or two. My spirit was dropping fast, because even with my messy mathematics I could see that the way we were going, we'd hit the big city somewhere in 1970, and we only had a few more hours before Mike sounded the alarm about his car being stolen. There was little time to go before I'd be a hot musician in a hot car, and I didn't much like the idea of playing tag with John Law no-way. "Okay!" Josh bellowed. I swam another yard through the moo-juice.

Then Josh up and disappeared: I squinted and strained, but not one trace of him could I spot up ahead. I got panicky. "Josh!" I shouted. "Hey Josh, where are you! Come back, hear?" I began to get a queer, unreal feeling, like the whole world was dissolving in a dirty gray spray and I was drifting along in the middle of all the swirling muck, ten million miles from nowhere, just me and my little coupé, lost in space. I sure felt lonely. A flagpole sitter on top of Mount Everest would have thought he was surrounded, compared to how I felt just then. I didn't care if Josh came back with green hair, one eye in the middle of his forehead, and six thumbs on each hand, as long as he came back. "Hey Jo-osh, can you hear me?" No answer. I wished we had gotten more cocaine. My hands were trembling.

Then I saw something—it was just a wavering vague blob of a shadow at first, rising up out of the fog, and then it began to take on some outline. Whew! Josh was there after all. What a relief! Only there was something funny, it didn't look just right, it sure as hell was a face but. . . . The face kept getting bigger and bigger, and clearer and clearer, and I kept on liking it less and less. Because the head was too goddamned big, that was the trouble, and the eyes were heavy-lidded and twice the size they should of been, and the lips were thick and loose and sliding over each other while saliva kept dripping down from them, and there were funny pointed ears that stood straight up, and a neck as big around as a tree-trunk. Oh Lord, I thought, we're in some other world where they've gone and changed Josh into something like a cow. Oh Lord, I whispered, make Josh stop being a cow and I promise, I'll never sniff any more cocaine or smoke any more grefa, word of honor. . . .

My prayer was answered; all of a sudden Josh was back in his own frame, standing beside the car and leaning over towards me. "Guess what," he groaned. "We're caught in the middle of a herd of goddamned cows, so help me." And that's exactly how it was. Pretty soon I saw another maniac cow-face blinking stupidly at me, then another, then a whole gang of them, all around me. It was a herd of cows, all right, and the farmer leading them couldn't do a thing about it—he tried to clear a way for us but those dumb animals kept falling back into formation and blocking the road again, so it took us two hours just to get over the summit of that mountain, moving one foot at a time. Finally the cows turned off into a pasture, and we drove on until the fog was out of our face. I never did tell Josh about my fear that he had turned into a heifer; I just giggled a little too frantically every time I heard his voice, and let it go at that. For a while, though, I really thought seriously about laying off the dope. I never wanted to see Josh gunning me with that vacant idiot stare again, chewing his cud.

Well, we made it finally. Mike was supposed to give us a twenty-four-hour head start, and it had taken us thirty hours for the trip, so the Chicago police must have flashed a lookout about the stolen car hours ago. I was plenty jittery by the time we shot through the Holland Tunnel, and so was Josh. The minute we hit Canal Street in good old Manhattan, Apple of apples, we parked the car, gathered up our belongings, and started to do a Houdini out of the neighborhood. But we'd only gone a couple of blocks when Josh stopped short and let out a yell. "Hey!" he said. "This is terrible, we went and left two full cans of muta in the car!" I was all for leaving the stuff—for all we knew there was a squad of cops swarming all over the car by this time, and I wanted to be in another precinct entirely. I needed a brush with the law just then like a toad needs sidepockets. But try knocking some sense into that thick skull of Josh's. He couldn't stand to lose his supply. Back he went, while I waited with the luggage, and in a few minutes he showed up again, both pockets of his jacket loaded with the tin cans.

We rushed into a phone booth and called the Cumberland Hotel, at 54th and Broadway, where we knew the whole gang was flopping. I could hardly sit still while I waited for the switchboard to connect me. Finally there was a voice at the other end, Eddie Condon's voice, big as life! "Where are you Roll!" he shouted. It was sweet music to my ears, to hear that old nickname again. I could hear a loud gasp when I told him nonchalantly that I was down on Canal Street and Josh was with me. I guess he must have fainted.

There was a silence for a minute, and then Tesch's voice came rolling over the wires. He didn't waste any time on formalities. "Hey Milton," he said, "did you bring any muta?" Then I knew I was home again, back among my own people. Solid. Oh, good deal.

Josh and I shot down the street as fast as our shaky legs would carry us, headed for a subway and the old gang again. I rubbernecked around some as we streaked along the avenue: there were all the skyscrapers, just like you read about them, and the crowds bustling around, and the home-stretch tension and the faster-faster excitement. It was like seeing a fairy-tale come true. We had really made it, at last. Nothing could hold us back now. King Jazz was moving in, heading up his whole army of horn-tooters and skin-beaters, and I was right in there with them, ready to cover all spots.

There was The Big Apple dangling right in front of my nose, shiny red and round and juicy. I surer than hell was going to get me a taste of it. New York, look out! Here we is and we's gwine took over. Gonna grab you by the knockers and never let go, hear? Goin' to rock them bright lights till Broadway does the mess-around.

Made it, man. Oo-*wee*!

Book 3 (1928–1935)

The Big Apple

Praise Allah! Wiggle, wiggle, wiggle,
Praise Allah! Wiggle and dance. . . .

Everybody's doin' fine
All you folks that ain't in line
Come on out and rise and shine,
BIG APPLE! *(Have a bite. . . .)*

BIG APPLE

10

IF YOU CAN'T MAKE MONEY

I'd rather drink muddy water, Lord,
  sleep in a hollow log,
I'd rather drink muddy water, Lord,
  sleep in a hollow log,
Than to be up here in New York,
  treated like a dirty dog.

JACK TEAGARDEN sang that lament on a record of ours called *Makin'
Friends*, and it should have been the theme-song of the Chicagoans.
The panic was on. When we bust in on our pals we found them
all kipping in one scraggy room, practically sleeping in layers. They
should of had the SRO sign up. Eddie Condon was out scooting
around town with Red McKenzie, trying to scare up some work.
There wasn't a gas-meter between them all, and they couldn't remember when they'd greased their chops last. "Wait'll you get a
load of this burg—don't lose it," Tesch mumbled in his signifying
way, cocking his sorrowful eyes over those hornrimmed cheeters.

They'd had a job all lined up when they first breezed in, but
when they made the audition the boss got one earful of Chicago
music and yelled "Get those bums out of here!" That was how
jazz hit the tin ears of Tin Pan Alley. After one week at the Palace,
where they played slink-and-slump music behind a team of ballroom dancers, they all holed up in this cubby, singing those miss-
meal blues like Doc Poston had predicted. They picked up on some
vittles once today and then again the day after tomorrow.

Well, we all laid around in that fleabag-with-room-service for a couple of gripy weeks, and then, through a fiddle-stroker who was crazy about hot music, I landed a job in a roadhouse called the Castilian Gardens, out in Valley Stream, Long Island. Gene, Eddie, Sullivan and Billings made a beeline for the suburbs with me. Soon Gene left for Chicago. Then we eased our guitar player out and moved in Eddie with his long-necked banjo; next the piano player quit, by request, and Sullivan took over his place; finally our tenor sax player said, "Milton, Tesch needs to be in this band, and I can go with a straight dance band, so I'll gladly leave if only you'll teach me how to play jazz," so in a few days we began to sound like something. Talk about infiltration tactics—we just surrounded that band from within. The trumpet player quit soon after because he didn't know a single tune we played, as we kept reminding him, and right after that our leader got a bigtime offer somewhere, so he turned the whole band over to me. The boss wouldn't hire Tesch, and I couldn't get Gene and Bud back from Chicago, but still, out of seven men we were left with four and three of them were Chicagoans, so the band didn't sound so bad.

One night Jack "Legs" Diamond fell into the joint with scumpteen of his henchmen and ordered the doors closed, and Jim, it was on. Our music hit Legs' girl friend so hard, she jumped out on the dance floor and began rolling her hips like she was fresh in from Waikiki, with ball-bearings where her pelvis should of been; then she pulled up her dress till it was more off than on, showing her pretty linens or what she had of them. I nearly swallowed my horn, gunning Legs to see how he felt about it. I was all set to stop the band as soon as he batted an eye. The boss almost shook his wig off giving me the office from behind a post—he knew Legs wasn't so well liked in the underworld, and the last time this gang was in they almost wrecked the place. But the moment the music stopped this grave-bait ran pouting to her daddy, and Legs motioned to us to keep on playing. Before his finger stopped wagging we were halfway through the second chorus.

We were at the Castilian Gardens for about three months, right through the summer season. While we were out there Tesch left to go with Sam Lannin's orchestra, and I never did get to see him again before he got killed in 1932. Then, one night after Labor Day, when we all came to work togged in our tuxedos to open the fall season, we found a brand-new padlock on the slammer and we couldn't get in. The boss showed up and sighed, "Well boys, this is it—I couldn't pay the rent so the landlord closed me up, and just when I got an icebox full of ducks for the week-end dinner crowd." He was so bad off he couldn't even get up our back pay, which was a bringdown to me because my wife and her son had just come in from Chicago. Well, we broke open a side window and climbed in to get our horns, and at the boss' suggestion we trucked into the refrigerator and loaded ourselves with all the fowl we could carry, and that's how we wound up at Valley Stream getting paid off in ducks instead of dollars. "We ask for our salary and get the bird," said Joe Sullivan, but nobody even cracked a smile.

Walking down Broadway one afternoon, minding my own business, I was surprised to find the sidewalk heaving up into my face and the buildings beginning to jig and teeter, getting ready to crash-land on my skull. All mush behind the eyeballs and my muscles turned to jelly, I grabbed a lamppost and hung on. Sweat squirted from my face; my stomach was practising sailor's knots, there was a pain big as a baseball buried in the nape of my neck, and my scalp stretched so tight I was afraid it would split right down the middle. I held on, frantic, while The Apple melted down to churning applesauce and I bobbed in and through it all. My prayerbones played knock-knock. Jack, I was bad off. One look at me just then would have scared Doc Freud right back into the pill business.

I watched the people fly by. The men all had snap-brim Capone hats pulled down low over their eyes, their coat collars were all turned up, they had their shoulders hunched and their hands buried deep in their overcoat pockets. I could tell that every one of them had a handful of Colt .45. From the way they eyed me, I knew they all meant to get me, now or five minutes from now. That was the reason behind all their scampering and scurrying around; they were laying their plans, getting ready to ambush me. I saw clear that they were one big race of torpedoes, plug-uglies, and murder merchants. They had me surrounded and they were closing in. Any minute now all those automatics would start barking from all those overcoat pockets—in my direction. My stomach started to do flip-flops.

I knew I was more complexy than the whole Bellevue psycho-pathic ward, and that my nervous system had been building up to this breakdown for a long time. I first began switching to the psycho kick when I landed a job out at the Woodmansten Inn, on Pelham Parkway in the East Bronx. That's where my neuroses started sprouting neuroses. A drummer named Johnny Powell was leader of the band out there, and Eddie Condon and Joe Sullivan were playing alongside me, in addition to a fiddle player. It was early Fall by the time we went to work but the weather was still balmy, so we played in a very large screened-in open-air café, loaded up with the usual palm trees and Chinese lanterns.

Now you couldn't ask for a sweeter guy than Johnny Powell— a tall spry French-Canadian, with one of them twirl-away mous-taches. He worshipped the ground we Chicagoans walked on, and he was dying to learn the jazz technique on the drums because he knew that Gene Krupa had come up under our tutelage. But we were allergic to him. For one thing, he drove us crazy with his habit of always using the word "interpolate." "How can I interpolate that beat?" he would ask, and we all winced. "Do you guys think we ought to interpolate now or later," he wanted to know. Johnny was a very studious guy, all wrapped up in his drums, but he just didn't have it in him, interpolate or expectorate, and we suffered the agonies of the damned because his foot was so heavy and he dragged time till it drove me and Joe out of our minds. It was his gimpy tempo that first brought on my nervous indigestion.

The violin player got on our nerves too. He played sweet, with a full round tone, and he had plenty of technique, but there was that inevitable pulling back of the time again. Way back there, Bix and I used to talk about the dragging violins. We often won-dered if maybe it wasn't the large number of them in the symphony that made them lag behind, but here we were playing with only one violin and still we kept getting tangled up in its strings. That violin, added to the straggling drums, began to give us nightmares. Joe would take drink after drink and almost break his fingers on the keyboard, and I would blow until I was blue in the face, trying to get those slow-motion artists in step, but we might as well have tried to budge a couple of hungry mules. It was worse than the Chinese water torture, where they tie you up and let water trickle on your forehead drop by drop. Guys go howling mad and make a meal of their tongues, waiting for the next drop, and that's just what happened to us every time Johnny debated with himself whether he should interpolate now or later. In that fraction of a second while we waited for those two guys to catch up with our chord, I would sweat a bucket of blood and my ticker just gave up and quit altogether. It was like waiting for the accentuated beat of your heart when you're on a reefer jag, and you wait and you wait and the beat doesn't come and you think you've stopped living. I swear, after a few weeks I began to wonder if Johnny Powell wasn't using my head for a gong, conking me with delayed-action sledgehammers, while the violinist bowed across all my raw nerves with a hunk of jaggedy glass. It was an effort to keep from screaming, It's all right, beat me to a pulp, cut me to ribbons, only keep time, for Christ's sake, *just keep in time*.

With that waxed soup-strainer of his and that slick hair, Johnny took on some grotesque features in my hot mind. I'd look and look at him and begin to see him as Dirty Dan Desmond himself, cool and suave on the outside but with a heart full of evil and larceny. Sometimes I got to thinking that he was deliberately, cold-bloodedly trying to wear me down, make me blow my top. There was a conspiracy in Manhattan, headed by him, to give all Windy City musicians the heebies until they were ready to be bugged.

He was the kindest, gentlest, most considerate guy alive, was Johnny Powell, and I was beginning to despise him. All day long I shook like I had the palsy, dreading the hour of doom when I would have to face him again. I guess I was a little on the sensitive side just then. It came from being all bottled-up musically, and from seeing the Chicagoans getting lost in the stampede of the squares. I saw nothing ahead for us but yawning oblivion, and Johnny was greasing the way for us with that better-late-than-never beat of his.

To keep one jump ahead of the straitjacket squad, we used to drive down to Harlem after work on the hunt for some decent music, but it was nowhere to be had, even in the world's greatest Negro community. I missed the South Side plenty; New Orleans-Chicago jazz hadn't hit New York yet, so in Harlem too we were starved for our musical daily bread, cut off from the source of life and spirit. I felt like an alien here, an outsider who just came along for the ride, because I was advocating and signifying in an idiom that hadn't yet caught on in these parts. It was a feeling I never got on the South Side, and it didn't help my morale none. Harlem wasn't any nerve-tonic for mc. What made me feel even more like a foreigner was that most of the Harlem spots we hit were controlled by white hoodlums. The whole area was overrun with fay gangsters who got fat on the profits they raked in from the big nightclubs and speakeasies and from the numbers racket. I began to feel that the conspiracy against us, the white man's conspiracy, had reached up into Harlem too.

I'd had a bellyful of gangsters and muscle men by that time. They'd always been luring me on, trying to win me away from the music to their loutish way of life—all of them, from the gamblers and pimps in the Chicago syndicate to Frank Hitchcock's boys at Burnham and the hophead mugs over in Detroit. Our whole jazz music was, in a way, practically the theme-song of the underworld because, thanks to prohibition, about the only places we could play like we wanted were illegal dives. The gangsters had their dirty grabbers on our music too, just like they kept a death grip on everything else in this booby-hatch of a country. If I resisted their come-on even a little, it was only because of my obsession with the music. Every time I got in trouble, it was because I strayed away from the music. Whenever I latched on solid to the music, I flew right. I was beginning to sense a heap of moral in all this, but my hot instincts to stick with the music and keep straight were all frustrated now. I saw these white gangsters ruling the roost in Harlem, so I blamed them for it. I kept sinking lower and lower. Every night I would wind up in Harlem with nothing to do but wolf down a mess of barbequed ribs smothered in red-hot tabasco sauce and swill terrible rotgut by the barrel. That didn't soothe my jumpy stomach much either. At first my digestion was just nervous; pretty soon it stopped altogether.

I even made myself lose that Woodmansten Inn job, along with Eddie Condon and Sullivan, but still the jitters wouldn't quit me. The last night there I was blowing real hard, really reciting out in front of the band, when suddenly I went all shatter-brained. A bunch of ugly-looking gangsters had taken the joint over for a big party, and they were all wobbling around the floor with their floozies, so drunk they could hardly stand. One of these mugs danced right up under the bandstand and just stood there, staring at me. When I swayed, he swayed. When I stomped, he stomped. Suddenly I began to shake so bad I could hardly hold my clarinet. I had just remembered something that froze my spine. Joe E. Lewis had been working in a Chicago nightclub run by some gangsters, and one night he mentioned to his bosses that he was thinking about changing jobs because he had got a much better offer. Those hoodlums didn't argue with him. They didn't bargain. They just smiled, and paid him a visit and slit his throat from ear to ear. It happened in his hotel, just around the corner from where I was living.

I watched that yegg while my clarinet weaved a spell around him, and I thought, Jesus, this music sure has got a hold of him. Suppose he owns some club and likes my playing so much he wants me to go to work for him? Maybe he's thinking it over right now, while he's casing me. If I have to work for him I'll really be under his thumb, and if I try to make a move they'll just cut me open like they did poor Joe E. Lewis. . . . Right quick I changed the phrasing and meter of my improvisation, fading all the way into the background. The audience felt the let-down and yelled, "Come on, get hot," but I didn't feel like reciting any more—I'd lost all voice for it.

That same night I quit the job and rushed home. I sprinted all the way from the bus stop to my house, and took those stairs three at a time. I heard footsteps dogging me all the way, right up the stairs and into the house. They were slow and dragging, in gimp-time. They sounded like Johnny Powell's drums.

My mind was a cistern, clogged with maggoty memories. I remembered that just before I left Chicago, in the same apartment house where Tesch and I lived, right over my head, some dame had been strangled with a lamp cord. Then came the Saint Valentine's Day massacre, when a bunch of Capone's gangsters got dressed up like cops and drove up in a police wagon and lined another mob against the wall and mowed them down with machine guns, leaving the mangled bodies all crumpled up on the floor like some soggy lumber. Then, right after I hit New York, Arnold Rothstein the gambler was strolling down the stairs at the Park Central and came somersaulting down with a load of lead in his hide. And there was that subway train that got derailed at Times Square, leaving over two hundred bodies of dead and near-dead piled up ready for the dustbins. All that came flooding up in my mind, and plenty more. I remembered the way Legs Diamond wrecked the Castilian Gardens just for kicks one night, and the nightmares I had after that other party of his. I remembered Frank Hitchcock piled in a ditch, and Capone's wife masquarading out at the Martinique, and Bow Gistensohn on a cold marble slab and Emil Burbacher in Joliet, the frightened girls trying to run away from the syndicate whorehouses and their pimps coming after them, the opium-smoking bigshots of the Purple Gang whose pictures were beginning to pop up in the papers because, one by one, they were being wheeled into the morgue icebox. Ten solid years of murder and riot. Ten years of a bloody showerbath. They kept unwinding in my head.

It looked to me like the whole continent was being drowned in a bath of blood, from coast to coast. The nation was committing mass suicide—it was like a slimy snake blowing its top, writhing and wriggling with the fits, beginning to chew up its own tail. Sure,

I was surrounded by a race of gangsters running amuck, a hundred million blowtops, born with icecubes for hearts and the appetites of a cannibal. "They devour one another, and cannot even digest themselves." Nietzsche said that. "See them clamber, these nimble apes! They clamber over one another, and thus scuffle into the mud and the abyss." They were sure clambering some in the U.S. of A. Nobody was safe in this funky jungle. It was all one great big underworld, and they'd put their dirty grabbers on the one good thing left on earth, our music, and sucked it down into the mud with them.

I found I was getting so sensitive to odors, any strong smell was a torture. Almost any kind of heavy odor would make me dizzy and send me reeling down the street, my stomach quaking in shuffle rhythm. The worst ordeal of all, one I really dreaded, was to take the Seventh Avenue subway uptown, to get to where I was living with my family just then, on Park Avenue just below Fordham Road. There's a long stretch from 96th Street to 110th, where the train passes under Central Park, heading into Harlem, and I used to go out of my mind there because of the extra strong odor of scorched steel. It reminded me of the burnt-rags stench of the ether they doused me with back in The Band House when they took my appendix out, and I couldn't stand it. I used to sit huddled up on my seat, shrinking into a corner, my head shoved down between my knees and my arms wrapped tight around it, to keep from screaming.

One day, just as the train pulled into 110th Street, I felt a gentle tap on my shoulder, and when I worked up enough courage to raise my head, there was a nice-looking old colored man with a thick crop of snow-white hair, looking down at me with the kindest, most sympathetic expression I ever saw. "Son," he said to me real soft, "if you can't make money, make friends," and with that he stepped out on the platform and drifted away. He saved my life that day. Of course, it wasn't money I was worrying about, it was that metallic odor that reminded me of jail and burnt powder and all the scowling evil in the gangster world I knew. But that old man had the answer anyway: fall in with some

185

regular guys and you're saved. I had such a tender feeling for that man that when I was on a record date a little later I remembered his words, and that's how we got the title for those blues Jack Teagarden sang, *Makin' Friends*.

"Ten times must thou laugh during the day, and be cheerful; otherwise thy stomach, the father of affliction, will disturb thee in the night." That's what the wise man said to Zarathustra. I thought about those lines a lot—I sure had forgotten how to laugh, and my stomach was on the blink too, and maybe there was some connection. Well, the doctors couldn't give me any prescription for breaking out in smiles, but they at least might be able to set my stomach straight.

Tommy Dorsey sent me around to see his physician, Dr. Irving Grad, and he wanted to pump my stomach, but I couldn't see that at all. "Well," he told me, "you've got to get your system cleaned out somehow, so if you don't want to use a pump why don't you take an ocean trip? In your condition you're bound to get seasick, and Nature will do the job for you." I couldn't think of anywhere to go, that was the trouble. I didn't feel like taking one of them ocean jaunts; I just wanted to dig a hole in the ground and crawl way down into it and pull it in after me. I told him I would think it over.

The doc told me to take long walks and get as much fresh air as I could, so every day I would totter over to the Bronx Zoo, which was a little ways down Fordham Road from where I lived. Once I stopped by the seal pond and stood there for a long time, watching a big black glistening seal go jack-knifing through his tricks. It got me in a trance. All of a sudden it hit me that this high-spirited animal, that was so graceful it made me want to cry, really had the secret, and nobody suspected it. "And to me also, who appreciate life," said Nietzsche, "the butterflies, and soapbubbles, and whatever is like them amongst us, seem most to enjoy happiness." With those moustaches and that bright, clear-eyed look of his, this seal struck me as being a gentle and wise old man, digging the whole world and at peace with it. He belonged to the world of butterflies and soapbubbles. While all us two-legged ounce-brains jittered around real frantic outside his bars, cutting our throats and bumping each other off, he just kept diving and leapfrogging through the water with that heartbreaking ease and sureness, one tight beautiful unit from head to tail—sunning himself, knowing his natural strength and his ability to use it, taking a gang of delight in his sleek supple body, just coasting along without tension or nerve-knotting worry. That fine animal never suffered from nervous indigestion a day in his life; thy stomach, the father of affliction, never broke up his solid sleep. He laughed ten times a day every day at us strutting simps. It became very important to me to study every flick and ripple of his body, to try and dig his marvelous control, the secret of his ease.

Goddamn if that animal wasn't so anxious to help me out, he started romping around just for my benefit. He would dive and then go through his wriggles slow-motion, right at the surface of the pond so I could follow him. Then he would climb right up in front of me and look straight in my eyes and I knew he was saying to me, Well brother, you see how it's done, watch close now—all you got to do is relax and take it easy and use yourself the way Nature intended you to, and then you'll be happy just like all us seals, you'll live forever and you'll never need a Seidlitz powder. He was pointing his wise old snout straight at the millennium, and wanted me to follow him there. We understood each other so perfectly, I got self-conscious. Pretty soon I hurried away because other people were drifting near and I didn't want any square outsiders standing around while that seal and I spoke to each other. They wouldn't have understood.

Well, on January 23rd, 1929, I got a cablegram from Dave Tough in Paris saying, HAVE GOOD JOB COME AT ONCE BRING RECORDS AND MUSIC WIRE IMMEDIATELY. Right away I thought of Doc Grad's advice about a sea voyage. Here was the answer, dropped right in my lap.

Now all I had to do was raise money for my passage. As luck would have it, Gil Rodin, who was playing with Ben Pollack's band just then at the Park Central Grille, was going to have his tonsils out and asked would I take his place for a couple of weeks. So I played there, alongside Benny Goodman and his brother Harry, Jimmy MacPartland, Glenn Miller, Jack Teagarden and Ray Bauduc. Even though we played all show tunes and dreamy dance music, things sometimes began to happen when Jack Teagarden, taking his trombone apart and playing with just the slide and a water glass like the colored boys sometimes did, would start off the blues in a major key, then change to the minor, same as he does on *Makin' Friends*. Jack could really get in the jazz idiom, and he did a lot to make this job bearable to me.

During this period I sat in on a recording date with the Pollack band, just a couple hours after I'd had a gang of teeth yanked, because my biters were going bad along with all my other parts. It turned out that the piano player had had a tooth pulled that morning too, so we sat with a spittoon between us and took turns spitting blood between choruses. Then there was another date, under the title of "Eddie Condon And His Foot Warmers," where a band made up mostly of Chicagoans recorded *Makin' Friends* and *I'm Sorry I Made You Cry* for Okeh. Then we got together for Victor, under the title of "Eddie Condon's Hot Shots," and made two more sides, *I'm Gonna Stomp Mr. Henry Lee* and *That's a Mighty Serious Thing*. (On this date we had one of the first mixed groups that ever recorded—besides three colored boys from Harlem, there were Teagarden, Sullivan, Condon, and me.) Jimmy Dorsey asked me to substitute for him for a couple of weeks in the pit orchestra at the "Rain and Shine" show. Finally I had enough loot for the trip.

I wrote home for a birth certificate, which I needed to get my passport, and my dad sent it to me along with a note. "Go anywhere you wish son," he wrote, "but always remember, *sei a mensch*." That's the Yiddish for "be a human being." Then I booked passage for a second-class stateroom on the *Île de France*. Nobody knew I was leaving except my wife. Close to midnight on March the 2nd, 1929, I drove down to Pier 54, Bonnie coming along with me because I was so hopped-up she didn't dare let me go alone. All the taxis honking and the porters yelling drove me near crazy; I had to chew on my tongue to keep from screaming. Until the whistle tooted its last phlegmy good-bye and the boat started to creep down the Hudson I was in steady fear. I couldn't stop shaking.

Weaving from side to side like a lushhead, I groped my way to my stateroom. My stomach was churning worse than a volcano. I felt like I wouldn't live through the night. I crawled into my cubby and found I had a roommate, no butterfly or soapbubble exactly, but a suave and oily continental guy, who was counting a tremendous roll of hundred-dollar bills. He informed me cheerfully that he had strangled one man in Europe for raping his sister, stabbed another to death in a gambling fracas, and was now beating it from the States because of a third murder rap.

11

VO-DO-DE-O AND A MINSKY PIZZICATO

POPPA NEPTUNE was having himself an epileptic fit—for six days and nights he kept foaming at the mouth. We tossed in a sea of nausea until our faces were green as go-signs, and the traffic was all one way, outward bound. Not one mouthful of food did I swallow that whole trip. My dreambox kept spinning in circles, my stomach practised the loop-the-loop. I was one miserable cat. In my nightmares the throbbing ship, the whirlpool waves and the belching skies all began to look like parts of a diabolic machine, one hell of a big stomach pump. . . . Somewhere along in mid-ocean I heard a rasping bellow, far-off, like Jupiter was bowing a gutbucket bass fiddle to announce the Second Flood. I was delirious, but I started to crawl on all fours, and when I made the porthole and looked out I saw the lights of a ship in the distance, heading for the States. Dave Tough was on it.

We inched and wabbled our way into Le Havre ten hours late, where they let us know we'd had one of the worst voyages in twenty-five years. The *Île de France* was laid up for two weeks after, for repairs, with her stern bashed in about eight feet. Nobody thought to measure how deep my gut was bashed in.

When the train pulled into the Paris station I tangled with a walrus parading as a porter—I kept handing him fifteen cents, all the change I had, and he kept throwing it on the ground and snorting *"Merde alors"* while the handlebars of his moustache beat up a breeze. Finally a Thomas Cook guide took pity on me and led me, more dead than alive, to a pleasant little pension, and when I tottered into the small vestibule and saw a little gray-haired lady standing there, smiling and greeting me in French, I knew I was a safe man. My stomach started to unwind. In English that was not only broken but mashed too, the landlady told me she knew all about the terrible crossing we had, and she made me sit down while she scooted off to fetch some brandy. I was scared about touching the stuff—I remembered too well how all the buildings in Manhattan got the shakes every time I downed a shot. But she handed me some three-star Martell's, and when I sipped that wonderful gut-warming manna all my insides began to purr. I tingled all over. Damn if I didn't break out with a smile. I tried it on again, for size, and it fitted. I laughed. Then I knew I was cured—Doc Grad sure knew what he was talking about when he told me my stomach would be straightened out by Old Lady Nature, and not spelled backwards either, or even sideways. To this day I have never been troubled with nervous indigestion any more. Thy stomach never fathered another lick of affliction in me.

After sleeping like King Tut, I woke up frisky and frolicsome as a two-year-old, lined my flue with some fine chocolate and brioche dished out by this gay old lady, and flew down to American Express to find Dave. No trace of that cat. Well, where could I locate any American musicians in town? The man at the window figured there was a fellow countryman of mine downstairs who might straighten me out. Down the stairs I went, and before I reached the landing I heard the rhythmic slapping of a shoeshine rag just like it was talking to me. It was sweet music to my ears, that ragtime—I knew who must be behind it because I'd listened to many a concert like that on the South Side. "Do it poppa!" I shouted. The colored boy's head shot around, and his face beamed a welcome to me. "Where in the hell did you come from?" he asked.

Poppa-stoppa, his friendly relaxed voice, and the easygoing lilt to his words, just gassed me. Soon as you leave the South Side or Harlem the pulse speeds up, gets jumpy and staccato, and the velvet harmony gives way to jangling discord, but you just coast along, drugged, and not till something like this goes down do you realize how wonderful it was to be lolling around with your friends back in those good old spots. Somebody lays a gentle, mellow phrase on you and it's like your memory crooking its finger—all of a sudden you're whisked back to that other life where you were always doused in a shower bath of warm bubbling emotions, where your nerves could stop vibrating and snap back in place.

We were strangers, yet we felt like we had known each other for years, and he was as glad to see me as I was to see him. We talked and smiled at each other for a while. Finally I asked did he know anything about Dave Tough. His eyes lit up. "You mean that little bit of something or other that beats all that hide? Do I know him? Does your maw know her children? Just go over to the Maison du Jazz in the Montmarte, on Rue Victor Massé, and they'll tell you where he's at." At this Maison, a music store and hangout for jazz-men, I found out about Dave's sailing for the States on that boat I'd passed—I'd forgotten to answer his cable, so he figured I wasn't coming. But at least I was able to track down Jack O'Brien, the piano player who'd been working with Dave, and he no sooner got a look at me than he asked "Did you bring your horn?" That same afternoon, after checking in at Jack's dommy, the Hotel Victor Massé, I started work at Le Grand Hermitage Muscovite, 24 Rue Coumartime (Opéra), a café run by some White Russians who posed around like they were still having a ball in the Czar's court.

What a staff they had: a jazz-loving Russian general's son named Mischa Levendovsky was our *chef d'orchestre*, the headwaiter had been an admiral in the Czar's navy, our waiters and bartenders were all counts or dukes, and the cab drivers squatting on the curb had once had the pick of Europe's royal chicks for their mistresses. Even the lavatory attendants looked bored enough to have noble blood in them—they handed you a towel with such an elegant air you felt like you ought to salaam three times or at least curtsy. That Hermitage lobby was always loaded up with slick-haired gigolos who pranced the tango and the Charleston with American dowagers and collected their fees after each whirl like they'd just turned in an honest day's work. On a typical night in that vodka pad you'd find titled Frenchmen rubbing elbows with Russians who still sported their well-polished Czarist decorations, all mixed up with Chinese, Swahili, turbanned Hindus, ramrod-spined Englishmen balancing monocles, swarthy cattlemen from the Argentine, sugar planters from Batavia, sabre-scarred Prussian officers, bullfighters from Madrid, college kids with crew haircuts from Wilkes-Barre and Des Moines, and a fair sprinkling of plain ordinary bums whose nationalities had been rubbed off, leaving them just citizens of the world or anyway the underworld. Our five-piece jazz band, which supplemented a *gipsy orchestre* under R. Volodarsky, a bunch of warblers called the *Unique Quatour de Boyards*, and a gang of other entertainers with jaw-busting names, caused a riot every time we came on. *Royal Garden*, *Jelly Roll* and all the old standbys made up our repertoire, and the crowd ate it up even more than they did *Oche Chornia*.

That gypsy orchestra really sent me. It was made up of five solo first-chair strings from the Paris Symphony Orchestra, and the real jazz got their curiosity jumping because of its soulful phrases and the harmony patterns with quarter-tones at the most interesting places. We all got to be good friends. It wasn't long before I was giving alto-sax lessons to Francis Lucas, *contrabasse solo de l'Orchestre de Paris*, because he was wild about the blues and meant to learn them. Then there were two other cats whose genius knocked me out—Nitza Codolban, the world's greatest gypsy cymbalist, and the pianist Constantinoff, a nineteen-year-old kid who played with the Symphony and had also gotten several compositions accepted by that longhair crowd. Nitza had been offered some fabulous sum to join up with Paul Whiteman but he loved Paris so much he wouldn't budge. It was from these two great artists that I first heard collective improvisation in the classical world, because they would start fooling around while they were tuning up and then Nitza would knock out a rich chord progression and Constantinoff would pick it up quick and get off some riffs that always ended up on the note that was out of tune, and they were gone. What kicks I got when I loaned Constantinoff my records of Louis Armstrong's *West End Blues* and Bix's *In a Mist*, and in a few days he came back and played Earl

193

Hines' *West End Blues* piano solo note for note, of course with a slight European accent but still with perfect mastery, and that's a plenty tough solo to play. About Bix's number he said, "That shows talent and a liking for Ravel and Debussy, but this Earl Hines of yours, he is the one with tremendous inventive genius." I felt like busting out all over—here was a genius in his own right, one of the real masters of the classical school, telling me exactly what I was coming to believe myself about the merits of the real authentic jazz. Louis Armstrong, this deep-digging kid told me, was without a doubt the greatest genius of them all.

Besides those two records I loaned Constantinoff, I also had with me Bessie Smith's *Empty Bed Blues*, Joe Oliver's *Dipper Mouth*, Louis' *Heebie Jeebies*, and Ethel Waters' *Dinah*, and they turned out to be my real passport to Paris, because they led to another fine friendship. One afternoon a studious young chap, all eyes and ears for our music, animated as a Disney cartoon, dropped in, and after digging the band for a while he came up and said, "I am very much interested in jazz, Monsieur Mezzrow, and I wonder if you could find time to show me some things on the saxophone?" His name was Hugues Panassié, and he came from a family that once owned a mess of radium mines in Russia, and his brother-in-law was something called *Fondé de pouvoirs de la Direction-genérale de la Banque-Chinoise pour la Commerce et l'Industrie*. I don't rightly know what all that jive signifies but it sure brought on some bowing and scraping when I flashed a letter from him to help me get my work permit.

I liked this kid's enthusiasm, so I went over to see him one day, lugging my records and horns along. I found him living in a great big house where he had a special study lined with shelves and shelves of records. When he got straight on my version of *My Blue Heaven* I played the second harmony sax part along with him, and that got him steamed up some. Then I let him hear those records, and all excited, he ran into the foyer and shouted for his whole family to come down and listen. The question he asked made me ashamed to admit that I came from the good old U.S.A. "Why, Milton," he wanted to know, "haven't I ever heard any of these terrific records before? I never saw them in any of the record companies' pamphlets." That was when I realized how the record companies in those days were keeping this wonderful music from the world. The records of the great colored jazz artists were always listed under a separate heading, as "race records." To a naïve guy like a Frenchman, who isn't color-conscious because he didn't grow up with Jim Crow, and a dark skin doesn't make the word "race" jump up in his mind, that listing might have suggested horse races or auto races— almost anything but jazz.

I gave Hugues all those records because he loved them so much. His sincere, right-from-the-heart enthusiasm made me feel good. All inspired, he went to work rounding up a lot of other records, "race" and otherwise, and the lessons I gave him on the saxophone tickled his appetite for the music still more. After developing into the world's most fanatic record collector, he started to get his musical ideas in shape and put them down on paper, and that was how he became the first real scholar and critic of jazz, outside of Robert Goffin in Belgium. That youngster sure kept himself busy in the years that followed—writing a book called *Le Jazz Hot*, starting a monthly jazz review in Paris by the same name (it soon had dozens of rivals, in almost as many languages, all through Europe), and launching the Hot Clubs of France, which got to be a world-wide movement; then he supervised jazz recordings on both sides of the Atlantic, ran jazz programs on the radio, and wrote a second book that was published in this country as *The Real Jazz*. Practically every jazz critic that I know about today—Timmy Rosenkrantz, Harry Lim, Roger Kaye, Nesuhi Ertegun, John Hammond, Charles Edward Smith, Frederic Ramsey, Charles Delaunay, Walter Schaap, and even Leonard Feather—was discovered, or helped along, or in some way influenced by Hugues. Even the German occupation of France didn't stop him any: he managed to keep a jazz radio program going in spite of the Germans' hatred for "decadent" American music. When the German censor came hawkshawing around to see what Hugues was doing on his program, he was shown a record labeled *La Tristesse de St. Louis*, and Hugues explained helpfully that it was a sad song written about poor Louie the Fourteenth, lousy with that old French tradition. What that Kultur-hound didn't know was that underneath the phony label was a genuine Victor one, giving Louis Armstrong as the recording artist and stating the real name of the number—*St. Louis Blues*. And all during those bad years Hugues kept on writing his books and articles in private—they're just now being published. Ever since that cat latched on to jazz, he's been a one-man mass movement.

What knocked me out, as I followed this kid's career, was to see how his ideas about the music kept pushing in the same direction as mine did, fighting their way back to the real jazz. At first he couldn't lay his hands on many of the original Negro records, few as they were anyhow, so naturally he heard a lot more Chicago-style white jazz than he did genuine New Orleans. That's why in his first book he kind of went off the deep end about the white jazzmen grouped around the Chicagoans. I did that myself, as I was growing up in Chicago. A lot of guys have gotten that far in their education, at the halfway mark, and then closed their minds up and stopped growing altogether. But not Hugues. The more he heard of the authentic colored man's music, the more it grew on him, and his eyes were opened to the difference between the original and the derived, between the solid sturdy trunk and the feeble, crooked, stunted branches. So he reversed himself in his second book, this time giving the Negro his full due.

Some simps gave him the horse laugh when his trend of thought shifted like that, but for my dough it took plenty of guts, and he was more honest than these muddle-headed critics who talk up all this commercial slop as "real art" and rake in plenty of profits for doing it. All on his ownsome, separated by an ocean from the battlefield of jazz, he punched his way straight back to the good and solid source, just like I was trying to do in my playing and preaching. In some of the dark hours that fell on me later, the only thing that kept me going was to remember how this fine friend across the Atlantic was struggling to find the right answers, beating his way against the whole "modern" and "progressive" current to get where he had to go. Today too many pencil-pushers, who find the artistic score in a bankbook, put their stamp of approval on any music that's fashionable and flashy; but Hugues built up a tradition in the field of jazz criticism of always looking for lasting merit instead of frantic fads. He always listened hard, with real historical perspective, instead of eyeballing the box-office to decide whether somebody's music was good or bad.

The millennium that he was reaching for, it was the same place I had to find too. We finally got there, each traveling his own way. I made a real friend in young Hugues Panassié.

Rue Auber; fly little chick gets stranglehold on my lapel, tries to cruise me up to her apartment, me mumbling all the time, "No, no, no comprenez, baby." Down she reaches and yanks my pants open and yells, "Now you unnerstan', eh?" Gotcha. Cop across the street, instead of making his pinch, holds onto his big fat belly and roars. . . . Creaky old two-wheel wine cart clattering down Rue Pigalle, sideswipes shiny new Renault sedan. Jabber jabber: big crowd gathers, gang of babbling and hands start flying. Hell of a traffic jam. Along comes traffic cop, muscling his way in. Crowd hauls him up and dumps him right back in the middle of the crossing, where he belongs. Three things a Frenchman hates: clergyman, soldier, and copper. . . . Tearing along through Latin Quarter, big hurry, appointment to keep. Cab driver eases over to curb and pulls a fade-out; I wait and wait, gunning him while he polishes off a couple of *fines* in a bistro. Back he comes, smacking his chops and grunting, drives off again without a word. . . . In the café where we swill Martell's and Courvoisier all night long after work, chicks from dance-hall next to Hotel Victor Massé drooping around tables, one of them sets her peepers on me. Stumble into my dommy one night and there she is, stretched out on the framer in a long black lace negligée, bottle of cognac within easy reaching distance on side-table. Can't speak a word of English; smiles. I thumb through my conversational phrase-book with the jive about *ouvrez la fenêtre* and *quelle heure est-il madame*, then I throw it away and slide out my muta and we light up. Discover we got a common language, after all. . . . House of All Nations, looks like picture gallery and dicty embassy combined, but it's a brothel. Madame Fifi makes chicks parade around in fine silk kimonos, waltzing in samples from the four corners of the globe till you decide what corner you want to hang out on tonight. Twenty francs, no cover charge. . . . Pigall's Tabac —wonderful breakfasts for the price of a cup of java, bleary-eyed dames who keep whining, "You pay me drink, pay me leedle drink?" . . . Lady attendant in men's room at the Hermitage, bored, handing out towels; nothing to see there she ain't seen before, and better. Wonderful feasts with Rigikoff, the boss; mountains of *cotelettes Kievsky* and *blinis pirojskis* and sweet-and-sour *bortche cacha* and *chachlik Caucasien* and *gourievskaia cacha*, served up in gleaming gold-lined silver platters and washed down with 1926 vintage of Mumm's or some fifty-year-old Napoleon brandy. Wonderful smells everywhere. No burnt rags, no scorched steel. Bouquets of rich savory sauces. Fine aroma of even the ordinary soaps. Walking down the street, glimming the cute kittens trilling along, head snapping from side to side while your sniffer sucks in the perfumes. Easygoing relaxed faces all around, everything fine and mellow. Musicians considered artists, treated like royalty—separate Artists' Room at the Hermitage, full of plush-covered sofas, and when your friends come around asking for you they don't get thrown out by the bouncer for not spending enough loot but they're ushered into this private room and told to take it easy, monsieur. Nobody carves up your Adam's apple. . . . Your insides stop galloping in that town, slow down to a lazy stroll. Everybody taking it easy, doing no more work than they need to get by, laughing ten times every hour and soothing thy breadbasket, affliction's old man, with fine brandies and saucy dishes and a gang of living. Everybody living hard, and sleeping easy. . . .

Man, how I loved that town; it just grabbed a hold of my fancy and never let go. But now that I was patched up I had to get with my music again, and it wasn't to be found around here. The guys I wanted to play with and listen to were all on the other side of the drink. Time to get moving. Some bigtime impresario offered me a fine deal, heading a band to tour all through Africa and the Near East, so I thought maybe I'd fly back home and see couldn't I round up the gang to come back with me. I took one last fond look around, inhaled one last lungful of those fine Paris smells, got smacked on both cheeks by Panassié, shook hands with Madame Fifi and the symphony first-strings and the uncrowned heads and the shoeshine boy, and hopped on the *Aquitania* just before it sailed in April. No seasickness this trip. My stomach cooed and chirped all the way over, and at every meal I scoffed back double helpings and yelled for more.

Ten minutes after I made home-sweet-home and laid some Chanel Number Five and some fine handmade underwear on my old lady, I mushed her and cut out for the Riverside Towers, on the West Side overlooking the Hudson, where the gang dommied. They were all cooking up some jive with Red Nichols just then—it being prom-time, they were going to tour the Eastern colleges under Red's neurotic baton, and there was a spot for me in the band. This was almost the last time any real group of Chicagoans were together, and it was frantic.... Dig you later, Paris old gal. Keep on wriggling your saucy duster and smelling sweet. We were off to Dartmouth, Brown, Harvard, Cornell and the White Mountains, on the Vo-de-o-do Special. Get hot. Yeah man. Swing it, right from the rafters.

That was a bunch of wild men Red Nichols got together; besides a couple of foreigners from California on trumpet and trombone, there was a sax section of Pee Wee Russell, Bud Freeman and me; Dave Tough on drums, Eddie Condon on banjo, Joe Sullivan on piano, and little Max Kaminsky on the cornet. We had always thought Nichols stunk, with or without his corny Dixieland Five Pennies, but the boys had got an overdose of being troubled with the shorts and they figured to clean up some money fast with this good old college try and have a good time.

Our bass player, a little sixteen-year-old named Sammy, practically had to stand on tiptoe to reach the bridge of his instrument, but he was supposed to be a genius, and Red saw a commercial angle in his age and size, so along he came. Well, we set up headquarters in Boston and took off to rock New England, traveling around in two seven-passenger touring cars, and little Sammy just came along for the ride because he sure never got to play that bass much. We tried tying the big fiddle to the roof of a car but it kept sliding around so much, poking its nose down into the window every few minutes, that we decided to ship it by American Express. Now American Express, in its own quiet way, is a real friend to hot jazz. Regular as clockwork, that bass showed up in each town on our itinerary the morning after we left, dogging us round just one day late. Little Sammy fiddled with his tie and plucked his suspenders.

Red loved that old limelight. He would hardly ever give little Maxie Kaminsky a chorus until the college kids swarmed around one night and yelled right in his face, "Hey, put your horn down, we want to hear the kid play." Red's face got brighter than his hair, but he had to give it to Maxie after being mobbed like that. Maxie's richer tone and intelligent phrasing inspired Dave Tough so much that the drums sounded entirely different, and so did the whole band, without Nichols on their necks. Red figured we were framing him. From then on he was an evil cat.

One stormy night only a few couples came, and they must have arrived by boat. Red told Maxie to take charge, and as soon as he was out of sight I yelled "Let's jam some." Everybody was for it, and when we got going on *Sweet Sue* it was such a relief to shake Red's arrangements out of our hair that we got in a pretty good groove. Just as we finished and laid back feeling happy, Red came tearing into the hall and jumped up on the stand. "The whole god-damned band's fired," he barked. "You're all on two weeks' notice."

Finally the remaining dates were cancelled. Back to New York we rolled, unemployed once more and no meal-ticket in sight. Sammy's bass fiddle showed up in town about three weeks later, after it made the rounds slow and steady, just one day behind schedule, playing all the cancelled engagements by itself.

Seems like a guy has to try everything once—next thing I knew I was sitting in the pit of a burlesque house. This was Minsky's original look-but-don't-grab emporium, the famous National Winter Garden on the sixth floor at the corner of Houston Street and Second Avenue. It was the Summer of 1929. Jack Levy was directing the pit orchestra then, and I was hired to play tenor sax and clarinet because Jack went for the hot style of playing. This band was nowhere, except in my hair. I never did hear the piano or the bass fiddle because they were a block away, on the other side of the pit, but with the other pieces I wasn't so lucky. All the guys were wonderful to me, just like Johnny Powell had been, but they couldn't play the note before note one. Every time I broke into a hot chorus Jack would bend way over his fiddle till his back was humped, plucking a pizzicato afterbeat on his strings that sounded like he was clopping behind me on a pogo stick, and the drummer got so inspired he started another afterbeat going on the cymbal, gaining time with his fidgety foot on the bass-drum pedal. We'd have two tempos gimping along at the same time, and then, to top it off, the trumpet would play a muted razzmatazz, but it wasn't muted enough because I could still hear him. I would sit there in the pit chain-smoking reefers, but I couldn't make myself drop dead. I began to wonder why, in this mechano-land where they dreamed up noiseless typewriters and engine mufflers and Maxim silencers, some friend of man didn't invent a set of noiseless musical instruments for pit orchestras.

The Minsky brothers, being specialists in sucker-bait, set up a loudspeaker under the marquee outside the theater, and they kept playing some corny phonograph records over the P.A. system. That gave me a wig-trig. There was a wonderful colored boy named Columbus Covington running one of the elevators in the theater, and when I told him we ought to play some hot records instead of those sweet-and-sour concoctions, he put it right up to the Minskys and they were game. Columbus had never heard my favorite musicians, but when that loudspeaker introduced him to Louis' *West End Blues* and *When You're Smiling* and also his record of Fats Waller's *Ain't Misbehavin'*, he jumped for joy. Man, those records caused a traffic jam for blocks around. All day long the lobby was packed tight with little old bearded grandpas in long black pongee frock-coats and cupcake-shaped yomelkehs, rubbing their hands behind their backs and shaking their heads sadly at Louis' moans, like they understood everything he had to say. "Boy, where'd you get them records?" Columbus said all in one breath. "Gee, that Armstrong guy can really blow that horn, and when he starts to sing, well, it's just too much." I felt as proud as if I had made those records myself. Columbus and I became great friends.

Here was that phenomenon of jazz again. No matter who I played those records for—the Paris symphony or the Minsky house band, the turned-up noses in Park Avenue drawing rooms or the turned-down ones in the ghetto, the intelligentsia or the people who couldn't even read—I got the same response. "Wonderful!" they all shouted, knocked out by the beauty of this music, its pulse, its romance and soulfulness. "Genius!" said the symphony. "Who in the hell is that?" said the layman unbelievingly. It taught me that all in all, what we got here is a real people's music, that rings the bell in every walk of life where there's any life left. It was a music that came out of the cellar, from the mangy bottomdogs, but its truth was so naked and it packed such a punch that it stunned even the pampered pedigreed poodles in the penthouses. I got my kicks from the way the Lower East Side took the colored man's music to its heart, especially the blues. Guess it proves the language of the oppressed is universal, and hops right across those boundaries of nationality. But the biggest thrill of all was to see Columbus Covington tremble with emotion when Louis sang or played. He was almost in tears. More than anybody else, he knew what Louis was saying.

Columbus and I started to hang out together. Nights, after the last show, we'd trail up to Harlem to hang around for hours at the great crossroads, the corner of 131st Street and Seventh Avenue. Between shows we'd ease across Second Avenue to the famous Moskowitz & Lupowitz restaurant and kill ourselves with two-inch steaks served on wooden platters. Columbus was so wrapped up in the music that I started to bring Eddie Condon, Joe Sullivan, Gene Krupa and Dave Tough down to meet him and dig the funky extravaganzas Minsky was putting on. The gang would line up in the front row during the show, and we'd giggle at how the audience ate up the corny Joe Miller routines. Often we'd sneak into one of the lodge halls in the building (Columbus had all the keys) and play the blues on the piano. Columbus had a little blues of his own that he played for us, and it was real pretty. Some day soon I'm going to write those fine blues down and make a record of them, and I'll call them *Lum's Blues* because Lum was Columbus' nickname.

For weeks I sulked in that pit, keeping alive on muta, staring up fuzzy-eyed at the stage while the chorus lumbered around like a herd of asthmatic cows. It made me feel bad to see any human beings trudge and dog-trot around so gawky, without a sign of the natural grace they should show to justify ever being put down on this earth. It was embarrassing to see humans clatter around like so many hunks of board; you don't deserve to have a body unless you can use it with easy-flowing rhythms and smooth pleasing glides, like you were proud of it and treated it right. Night after night I sat there swathed in gloom, watching them shuffle and slump through their mechanical routines, and it grew on me that out of that whole chorus line there were only two girls whose spirits weren't tied up in straitjackets. These two kids were just too much—every step they made breathed life and spirit; they took their breaks with real joy in the rhythmic use of their whole bodies, tapped delicately and with real animation where the others stumbled around heavy and listless as robots. Then it hit me. Goddamn, those girls were too good—they must be colored kids passing for white! I told Columbus about it right away, and he almost died. "Man," he said, "how in the hell did you dig that? I been suspicioning the same thing myself."

These two fly chicks got up on their high-horse when we quizzed them about it—one insisted she was pure Spanish, and sported a crucifix right over the breastworks to prove it, and the other, who let us know she was a Hebrew with some kind of Arabian blood, had a star of David strung around her neck just as big. Columbus and I cooked up a plot between us, and one night, after wising up all the boys on 131st Street, we cruised these two chicks up to Harlem for some ribs. We sat in that rib joint all night, and our friends strolled in one by one and joined us, and the hype that was laid down that night was really a killer. Talking in a perfectly normal, casual way, as though they were just passing the time, all these cats slipped subtle hip phrases into the conversation, and added sly little innuendos in their special lingo, and these girls laughed in all the right places and dug little side-issues like no white girl could have done because this hipster's language, a kind of a linguistic short-hand, is full of oblique and tangent cues never even heard by a white girl. That was a dead give-away to us. Finally the kids had to break down and confess, and when we came to take them home damn if they didn't live right in Harlem, on 109th Street.

The night wound up with them accusing *me* of trying to pass for white, because they couldn't believe that any white man could be as hip to the jive as I was! They told me they'd been suspecting me all along, as they watched me in the pit at Minsky's. That twist gave Columbus double kicks. He kept on saying, "Man, why don't you come clean, don't nobody fault you for makin' out you's ofaginzy," talking as though he was on the girls' side and knew I was really colored. To this day those girls probably believe that I was passing. "If you ain't one of us," they argued, "how in hell could you play that horn the way you do?" How I wished they were right.

Minsky's was sure getting me down. The star strip-teaser would come out on the runway, unwrap her enamel, and then begin grinding the ozone while the hysterical short-histe audience shrieked "More! More! More!" I never could see what the hell they wanted more for. She was well-built and voluptuous, all right, but she didn't do a thing with her body that an elephant couldn't do. Those simps just had to see a free-wheeling pelvis throw a couple of bumps and grinds their way, and their tongues were hanging out. They got their kicks from watching a headless and soulless sex-machine, or a reasonable facsimile of one, jogging for a while—it never occurred to them that this chick couldn't dance step one and didn't have an ounce of talent in her body. If it was violent and brutal and set their nerves jumping, it was art to them.

I couldn't help thinking about how different it was in Harlem. When you passed over 110th Street it was like zooming off to an-other planet where they didn't build any brick walls between want-ing and doing, the urge and the act. People up there, even the kids, led full and functioning lives, no matter how heavy a ball of oppression they carried around their necks, so they weren't walking skinfuls of repressions and they didn't mope around having sex flashes every hour on the hour. They never had to sneak like emotional pickpockets into shows and movie-houses to get their erotic kicks second-hand.

I felt like I wanted to take all the "clean living" people, Brother Sanctimonious and Sister Full-Bosom and their whole congregation of paralytics, down to Minsky's to get a good look at those rows of heated-up faces and frustrated maniac grins and bulging eyeballs every time the strip-teaser heaved her middle. Then let them tell me that their kind of "morality" produced a race of healthy human beings. People of "culture" couldn't live loose and carefree like my Harlem friends? Sure, you got culture, plenty of it. A culture where all your dreams dangle from a G-string. Take a good look around Minsky's. In our "culture," between the urge and the act come the footlights, or anyhow a movie projector. It's culture, maybe, a culture of masturbators. . . . Up in Harlem a dancer had to have real talent, make wonderful graceful steps with her feet and do delicate things with her body, really express something, before anybody applauded. Tongues didn't hang out at the sight of a torso with the palsy.

I gave the Minskys my notice. That was the last ofay job I ever held in my life, the last time I was ever connected with anything white and awkward, ugly and soul-starved. In the Fall of 1929 my soul moved across 110th Street, straight into Harlem, with me toddling along right behind it. The two of us have been living there ever since. I've never again been inside a burlesque house.

Some people think that I run out on my own kind, scampered away like a scared rabbit. Sometimes I'm told that I was a turncoat, a renegade to my "own" flesh-and-blood. Well, like that T. S. Eliot says,

> In a world of fugitives
> The person taking the opposite direction
> Will appear to run away.

That's the stuff you got to watch.

12

TELL A GREEN MAN SOMETHING

WAY back there the music grabbed me by the stringpost and yanked me off The Corner on Chicago's Northwest Side. Now the same music parked me right smack on another corner, this time in the heart of Harlem where 131st Street breezes across Seventh Avenue.

This wasn't just one more of them busy street crossings, with a poolroom for a hangout. Uh, uh. This corner was a whole atlas by itself—the crossroads of the universe, meeting-place of the hipsters' fraternal order. In this block-long beehive life was close-packed and teeming, a-bubble with novelty, and in its many crannies you could find all the many kicks and capers your heart yenned after. Back on Chicago's street-corner haunts you tangled with gamblers and racketeers and poolroom sharks, and all day long your tongue wagged its way from money to horses to women and back again. There your outlook was plenty hemmed-in, squeezed down to one dimension. But on The Corner in Harlem you stood with your jaws swinging wide open while all there is to this crazy world, the whole frantic works, strutted by. Life was full and jumping in that fantastic place, covered all spots and invaded all dimensions, including the fourth.

Anything you had a yen for—that's no lie. You couldn't see for looking, there were so many things to dig on The Stroll between 131st and 132nd. Dramas and tragedies in your face all the livelong day, till there were more lumps in your throat than you'd find in drugstore mashed potatoes. Happiness and ease too, in such big doses that fine-and-mellow was the play day in and day out. All the emotions, all the time, simmering in one big bubbling cauldron that covered a city block. Most all the great musicians, performers and entertainers the race produced used to congregate on The Corner, drawn back there by a powerful magnet after traveling all over the world. This place was the central clearing-house for a global grapevine—you could stand under the Tree of Hope without budging from one year to the next and know what was going down all through the South, or in Hollywood and Chicago, or Paris and London and Berlin and Stockholm. Let any of our boys get in a scrape with the pecks down in Memphis or Little Rock, or let them panic the English in Albert Hall or send the Danes in the Tivalis Koncertsal, and the news buzzed back to us on Seventh Avenue quicker than right now.

When good old Buck, of Buck and Bubbles, was driving along down South in his big Cadillac and dared to challenge the supremacy of the white race by passing a couple of white trash in a dinky old rattletrap Ford, he spent the night in jail for his crime and we knew all about it almost before his cell door closed. When Fats Waller was touring the South and kept having his big Lincoln sedan wrecked, with sand poured into the crankcase and the tires slashed, he made his booking agent rent him a whole private Pullman car before he'd budge, and we heard about it before Fats boarded his special train. When a little white girl was out strolling with her mother along a Paris boulevard, and then spotted Louis Armstrong and ran up and threw her arms around him yelling "M'sieur Armstrong, M'sieur Armstrong, comme il est beau!" and Louis grinned with delight, we were in on it before he stopped grinning, damn near. We were planted at the race's switchboard there, the listening-post for the whole planet. We had our earphones on all the time.

You had your pick of hangouts on The Corner. Just on Seventh Avenue alone, going north from 131st Street, the line-up was: a barber-shop, a drugstore, the Performers and Entertainers Club and under it the dicty Connie's Inn, then the Lafayette Theater, then a candy store, the Hoofers' Club down in the basement, and finally, Big John's famous ginmill. Around on 132nd Street were Tabb's Restaurant, and next to it the Rhythm Club, where you could call any hour of the day or night and hire a musician. And back on 131st Street, soon as you turned into it you found a fine rib joint called the Barbeque, the entrance to a gang of upstairs halls where top bands like Armstrong's and Count Basie's and Jimmy Lunceford's and Cab Calloway's and Erskine Hawkins' used to rehearse, and a speakeasy and nightclub called the Bandbox. Most important of all, there was an areaway running all around the corner building there, a wide alley with entrances from both Seventh Avenue and 131st Street. This alley led to the Lafayette's backstage entrance and also to a special bar in the rear of the Bandbox, and here it was that most of our social life was spent. Louis Armstrong was heading the Connie's Inn show (it was "Hot Chocolates," written by Fats Waller and Andy Razaff and staged by Leonard Harper, and it was doubling at the Hudson Theater down on 46th Street) and all the cats from the show would come out in the alley and mingle with the other great performers of Harlem who were appearing at the Lafayette, and they would be joined by visitors from all over, including a lot of white musicians that I began to bring up from downtown. I dragged so many cats uptown, I got to be known as the "link between the races" after a while.

And, finally, out in front of the Connie's Inn marquee on Seventh Avenue there was the legendary Tree of Hope, Harlem's Blarney Stone, which the guys would hug and kiss half playfully when they prayed for their dreams to come true. Once a good friend of mine, a fine hoofer who was having trouble getting bookings, ran up to that tree, gave it a big smack, and yelled "Lawd please make me a pimp, any kind of a pimp, long as I'm pimpin'. I'm tired of scufflin' and my feet are too long outa work." Years later, when Seventh Avenue was widened, Bill Robinson had the Tree of Hope transplanted out to the strip of parkway that was built in the middle of the avenue, and there it still stands today.

This was my happy hunting ground. Right from the start I was surrounded by a lot of wonderful friends, the first gang of vipers in Harlem (who I didn't make vipers out of, no matter what anybody says, because they were buying their gauge from some Spanish boys over on Lenox Avenue before I ever came to Harlem). There were some other fine kids too, including Little Fats, who knew everybody and was the key to the grapevine, another youngster named Mark, an orphan boy named Travis, a dancer named George Morton, little Frankie Walker and his dancing partner Dooley, Oakie, Nappy, Brother Raymond of that famous dance trio, Tip, Tap & Toe, and two girls named Thelma and Myrtle. Most all of us were real poor, until some of us began pushing reefer, but we loved each other and we had our fun. We'd sit in the Barbeque, right over the bandstand in Connie's Inn, and wait to catch the first few notes from Louis' horn. Zutty used to really punish those tomtoms when Louise Cook was doing her Salome routine, and the whole building would bump and fishtail right along with her. Soon as we heard the finale we knew Louis was going to start playing for the dancers, so we'd tear out for the street and kneel down on the sidewalk at a small boarded-up window, where Louis came through loud and clear.

Then it got to be wintertime, and the sidewalk was covered with snow, so we'd race into the alleyway and huddle up in front of a huge exhaust fan that was built into a shed. You could hear Louis there too, if you didn't choke first on the smoke and funk that was pumped in your face. Warm air came out of the fan too, so things were groovy. Course, I could have gone downstairs in the Inn and stood backstage to hear Pops, but it wouldn't have been so good that way, with all my friends outside at the fan. I wanted to stick with the gang because those cats enjoyed every note Louis made, and their delight sent me even more. I couldn't sneak down and get those kicks by myself—that kind of selfish quality evaporated when it came to hearing Louis because you wanted the whole world to dig what he had to say on his horn. Roaches were passed round and round, and even though some of those vipers were plenty raggedy they loved Louis like nobody else. We spent most all the Winter of 1930 squoze together in front of that fan-shed.

Yes, it was my hunting ground, and it was solid happy. Course, my home wasn't exactly in Harlem—Bonnie wasn't with me all the way on that issue, and she had her son to think of, so I compromised by moving right next door to Harlem, just across the river in the Bronx, on the Grand Concourse. But it was just a quick ten-minute ride to The Corner from where we lived, and all my waking hours were passed down there. . . . My brain would never soak up all the jive my eyes and ears were drinking in. It was really too much.

On The Corner I was to become known as the Reefer King, the Link between the Races, the Philosopher, the Mezz, Poppa Mezz, Mother Mezz, Pop's Boy, the White Mayor of Harlem, the Man about Town, the Man that Hipped the World, the Man that Made History, the Man with the Righteous Bush, He who Diggeth the Digger, Father Neptune. I don't mean to boast; that's what the cats really called me, at different times. I did become a kind of link between the races there. My education was completed on The Stroll, and I became a Negro. The next ten years of my life were to be spent there, and in a cellar opium pad a few blocks away.

We vipers lived in the Barbeque, eating ribs five or six times a day and listening to one of the first juke boxes in Harlem. Little Frankie Walker was always at my side, even though we never lit him up on account of his age. Frankie was a hell of a bright kid, only about fourteen, and he loved me as much as I did him. He had razor legs, snaggle teeth and dribble lips, and many of my white friends were embarrassed when I first brought him in their company, but after Frankie sat down and cut a few steps for them everything was jam-up and they all took a liking to him. That kid would sit in a chair and lay more iron than a lot of the best dancers who stood up and beat the boards in Harlem. He was an orphan and lived with his partner, Dooley, and his mother. I sort of adopted Frankie and dressed him up, and wherever I went he went too and danced on all settings.

When I first hit The Stroll, Guy Lombardo was head man on the juke boxes—the girls liked him especially, because his sax section had such a lyrical quality and played the sentimental tunes so pretty. Well, one day I caught up with the man changing records in the Barbeque, and gave him the names of some of Louis' records. Pretty soon Frankie cornered me and told me he heard through the grapevine that the juke-box man was looking for me. I went to see this guy, and he gave me a big hello and bought me some drinks.

"Man," he said, "those records of Louis' are making me a young fortune on my machines." He begged me to give him some more suggestions, so I named Louis' *Ain't Misbehavin'*, *Black and Blue*, *Some of These Days*, *After You're Gone*, *St. Louis Blues*, *Rockin' Chair* and *Song of the Islands*. They all hit the juke boxes fast, and they rocked all Harlem. Everywhere we went we got the proprietor to install more boxes, and they all blared out Louis, Louis, and more Louis. The Armstrong craze spilled over from Harlem right after that, and before long there wasn't a juke box in the country that Louis wasn't scatting on. Around The Corner there was only one record we'd allow on the boxes with Louis, Bing Crosby's *When the Blue of the Night*. That was a concession to the sentimental chicks too, because they were starved for sweet romance and they sure didn't get much of it from Louis' recordings.

Louis had brought his private chauffeur to New York with him, a fellow we all knew from the Sunset and the Nest in Chicago. Anywhere you showed up on the South Side, there was Too Sweet on the scene, ready to act as a guide to the younger boys who came around. Now Too Sweet was about six-foot-two, with a massive body, his playground sticking out in front of him about two feet. With Louis getting so famous, he started to walk up and down The Avenue, posing back with a cane so you almost thought he was Mr. Armstrong himself. One day as little Frankie and I approached the corner, we saw a crowd out in front of Connie's Inn, and we made our way through to pick up on what was going down. It seemed as though Too Sweet couldn't stand Louis' getting all the glory in The Apple, because everywhere you turned the cats were buzzing about Pops, and Too Sweet couldn't get in the play. This night he decided he was going to get some note for himself, so there he stood on The Corner in a pair of bright purple shorts and a yellow top shirt, swinging a walking stick with a knob on it big as an oak tree stump, and on his shoulder was an honest-to-God monkey. Too Sweet stopped traffic that night, and he was happy. He even made the papers.

Louis and I were running together all the time, and we togged so sharp we got to be known as the Esquires of Harlem. Dig these outfits: oxford-gray double-breasted suits, white silk-broadcloth shirts (Louis wore Barrymore collars for comfort when he played, with great big knots in his ties), black double-breasted velvet-collared overcoats, formal white silk mufflers, French lisle hand-clocked socks, black custom-built London brogues, white silk handkerchiefs tucked in the breast pockets of our suits, a derby for Louis, a light gray felt for me with the brim turned down on one side, kind of debonair and rakish. Louis always held a handkerchief in his hand because he perspired so much, onstage and off, and that started a real fad—before long all the kids on The Avenue were running up to him with white handkerchiefs in their hands too, to show how much they loved him. Louis always stood with his hands clasped in front of him, in a kind of easy slouch. Pretty soon all the kids were lounging around The Corner with their hands locked in front of them, one foot a little in front of the other, and a white handkerchief always peeking out from between their fingers. All the raggedy kids, especially those who became vipers, were so inspired with self-respect after digging how neat and natty Louis was, they started to dress up real good, and took pride in it too, because if Louis did it it must be right. The slogan in our circle of vipers became, *Light up and be somebody*.

Every day, soon as I woke up about four in the P.M., I would jump up to Louis' apartment and most of the time catch him in the shower. That man really enjoyed his bath and shave. I would sit there watching him handle his razor, sliding it along with such rhythm and grace you could feel each individual hair being cut, and I'd think it was just like the way he fingered the valves on his horn, in fact, just like he did everything. When he slid his fingertips over the buttons, delicate as an embroiderer and still so masculine, the tones took wing as though they sprang from his fingers instead of his lips. The way he shaved put me in mind of the time Louis was blowing and I brushed up against him by accident, and goddamn if I didn't feel his whole body vibrating like one of those electric testing machines in the penny arcade that tell how many volts your frame can stand. Louis really blew with every dancing molecule in his body. He did everything like that, graceful and easy but still full of power and drive. He was a dynamo with a slight slouch.

He was kind of stout then—that was many years before Hollywood made him reduce for that picture he made with Bing Crosby —and he had the most magnetic personality I ever saw. Those sparkling teeth of his, white as a cotton ball, reminded me of the record where Bessie Smith sings "My man's got teeth shine like a lighthouse on the sea." What a warm, good-hearted, down-to-earth gem of a human being was Louis. With all the money and success that came to him, you could still talk behind him because he never said anything he didn't mean and didn't speak any foolishness. He always looked at the humorous side of life and if he saw anybody angry he'd look the situation over and say gently, "Well, he hasn't dug life yet but he's a good cat at heart." He never lowrated anybody, always believed the best about his fellow-man. A lot of people, mostly white, took plenty of advantage of Louis' good heart, but he never once came up evil about it. He was a prince. Hell, he was king of the tribe.

One of my friends, a fine musician, cornered me one day and we began to discuss our outcome with the tea. I wasn't selling it yet, and we tried to analyze the difference there was between gauge and whisky.

"Man, they can say what they want about us vipers," he said, "but you just dig them lushhounds with their old antique jive, always comin' up loud and wrong, whippin' their old ladies and wastin' up all their pay, and then the next day your head feels like all the hammers in the piano is beatin' out a tune on your brain. Just look at the difference between you and them other cats, that come uptown juiced to the gills, crackin' out of line and passin' out in anybody's hallway. Don't nobody come up thataway when he picks up on some good grass."

I sure knew what he was talking about. The very same thing, that contrast between the lushies and the vipers, had hit me hard way back in Chicago and Detroit, and I told him so.

"Yeah," he said, "and then for instance you take a lot of ofay liquor-heads, when they come up here and pass the jug around. Half of them will say they had enough 'cause some spade just took a drink out of it, and those that do take it will hem and haw, tryin' to rub the top off the bottle so's you can't see them, 'fore they put it to their chops. Now with vipers it's different. You don't have to pass a roach to a viper, he'll take it right out of your hand and go to puffin' on it not even thinkin' about who had it in his chops before. Them Indians must of had some gauge in that pipe of peace that they passed around, at least they had the right idea, ha ha! Now, far as hurtin' anybody is concerned, you know and I know that we can wake up the next day and go on about our business, marihuana or mary-don't-wanna, and that's that. It ain't against the law and you told me they couldn't put it under the Harrison Act because it wasn't habit-forming, so let's carry on from here. We'll both smoke it every day for about two or three months and then one of us'll quit for a while and find out for ourselves what happens."

That's exactly what we did. I was the first one to stop for a trial, and I have yet to find any bad after-effects, outside of a twenty-month jail sentence.

(Before I go any further I want to make one thing clear: I never advocated that anybody should use marihuana, and I sure don't mean to start now. Even during the years when I sold the stuff I never "pushed" it like a salesman pushes vacuum cleaners or Fuller brushes. I had it for anybody who came asking, if he was a friend of mine. I didn't promote it anywhere, and I never gave it to kids, not even to little Frankie Walker. I sold it to grown-up friends of mine who had got to using it on their own, just like I did; it was a family affair, not any high-pressure business. Sort of everybody to their own notion, that was the whole spirit. I laid off five years ago, and if anybody asks my advice today, I tell them straight to steer clear of it because it carries a rap. That's my final word to all the cats: today I know of one very bad thing the tea can do to you—it can put you in jail. 'Nuff said.)

Most of us were getting our tea from some Spanish boys, and one day they showed up with a guy who pushed the stuff in Detroit when I was there. He wasn't selling it any more, but he put us in touch with another cat who kept coming up from Mexico with real golden-leaf, the best that could be had. As soon as we got some of that Mexican bush we almost blew our tops. Poppa, you never smacked your chops on anything sweeter in all your days of viping. It had such a wonderful smell and the kick you got was really out of this world. Guys used to say it tasted like chocolate candy, a brand Hershey never even thought of. I laid it on the cats in the Barbeque, and pretty soon all Harlem was after me to light them up. I wasn't working then and didn't have much money left to gaycat with, but I couldn't refuse to light my friends up. Before I knew it I had to write to our connection for a large supply, because everybody I knew wanted some. "Man, you can be ridin' on rubber in no time with that stuff, and it ain't against the law neither," the cats told me. "Just think how many cats you can make happy," they kept saying. Before I knew it, I was standing on The Corner pushing gauge. Only I did no pushing. I just stood under the Tree of Hope, my pokes full up, and the cats came and went, and so did all my golden-leaf.

Overnight I was the most popular man in Harlem. New words came into being to meet the situation: *the mezz* and *the mighty mezz*, referring, I blush to say, to me and to the tea both; *mezzroll*, to describe the kind of fat, well-packed and clean cigarette I used to roll (this word later got corrupted to *meserole* and it's still used to mean a certain size and shape of reefer, which is different from the so-called panatella); *the hard-cuttin' mezz* and *the righteous bush*. Some of those phrases really found a permanent place in Harlemese, and even crept out to color American slang in general. I was knocked out the other day when I picked up a copy of Cab Calloway's *Hipster's Dictionary* and found *mezz* defined there as "anything supreme, genuine"; and in Dan Burley's *Original Handbook of Harlem Jive* the same word is defined as meaning "tops, sincere"!

Stuff Smith wrote a song, later recorded by Rosetta Howard for Decca under the name of *If You're a Viper*, that started out

> *Dreamed about a reefer five foot long*
> *The mighty mezz but not too strong,*

> *You'll be high but not for long*
> *If you're a viper.*

The words *lozies* and *lozeerose* were coined so guys could refer to my gauge without having anybody else dig it, and some of our musician pals used to stick these hip phrases into their songs when they broadcast over the radio, because they knew we'd be huddled around the radio in the Barbeque and that was their way of saying hello to me and all the vipers. That mellow Mexican leaf really started something in Harlem—a whole new language, almost a whole new culture. The hard-cuttin' mezz really cut a brand-new one in this old world, through no fault of mine.

I'm standing under the Tree of Hope, pushing my gauge. The vipers come up, one by one.*

FIRST CAT: Hey there Poppa Mezz, is you anywhere?

ME: Man I'm down with it, stickin' like a honky.

FIRST CAT: Lay a trey on me, ole man.

ME: Got to do it, slot. *(Pointing to a man standing in front of Big John's ginmill.)* Gun the snatcher on your left raise—the head mixer laid a bundle his ways, he's posin' back like crime sure pays.

FIRST CAT: Father grab him, I ain't payin' him no rabbit. Jim, this jive you got is a gasser, I'm goin' up to my dommy and dig that new mess Pops laid down for Okeh. I hear he riffed back on *Zackly*. Pick you up at The Track when the kitchen mechanics romp.

SECOND CAT: Hey Mezzie, lay some of that hard-cuttin' mess on me. I'm short a deuce of blips but I'll straighten you later.

ME: Righteous, gizz, you're a poor boy but a good boy—now don't come up crummy.

SECOND CAT: Never no crummy, chummy. I'm gonna lay a drape under the trey of knockers for Tenth Street and I'll be on the scene wearin' the green.

THIRD CAT *(Coming up with his chick)*: Baby this is that powerful man with that good grass that'll make you tip through the high-

* A translation of this passage is given in Appendix 2.

216

ways and byways like a Maltese kitten. Mezz, this is my new dinner and she's a solid viper.

GIRL: All the chicks is always talkin' 'bout you and Pops. Sure it ain't somethin' freakish goin' down 'tween you two? You sure got the ups on us pigeons, we been on a frantic kick tryin' to divide who's who. But everybody love Pops and we know just how your bloodstream's runnin'.

FOURTH CAT *(Coming up with a stranger)*: Mezz, this here is Sonny Thompson, he one of the regular cats on The Avenue and can lay some iron too. Sonny's hip from way back and solid can blow some gauge, so lay an ace on us and let us get gay. He and Pops been knowin' each other for years.

ME: Solid man, any stud that's all right with Pops must really be in there. Here, pick up Sonny, the climb's on me.

SONNY *(To his friend)*: Man, you know one thing? This cat should of been born J. B., he collars all jive and comes on like a spaginzy. *(Turning to me.)* Boy, is you sure it ain't some of us in your family way down the line? Boy you're too much, stay with it, you got to git it.

FIFTH CAT: Hey Poppa Mezz! Stickin'?

ME: Like the chinaberry trees in Aunt Hagar's backyard.

FIFTH CAT: Lay an ace on me so's I can elevate myself and I'll pick you up on the late watch.

SIXTH CAT *(Seeing me hand the reefers to Cat Number Five)*: Ow, I know I'm gonna get straight now, I know you gonna put me on.

FIFTH CAT: Back up boy, forty-five feet. Always lookin' for a freebie. Jim why don't you let up sometime, hawk's out here with his axe and me with this lead sheet on, tryin' to scuffle up those two's and fews for uncle so's I can bail out my full orchestration.

SIXTH CAT: Aw, come on and bust your vest, what you goin' to make out of sportin' life? You know you took the last chorus with me.

FIFTH CAT: Looks like he got me Mezz, but this cat wouldn't feed grass to a horse in a concrete pasture. He's so tight he wouldn't buy a pair of shorts for a flea. Man, just look at him, dig that vine all offtime and his strollers look like he's ready to jump. This cat's playin' ketch-up and I got to tighten his wig. Hold it down, Jim, and I'll come up with line two like I said. Come on Jack, let's final to my main stash.

SEVENTH CAT: Mash me a trey gate, so's I can go bust my conk. What is this hangin' out with you? (*Nodding towards Frankie Walker.*)

FRANKIE: Don't pay that razor-legged axe-handled slew-footed motherferyer no mind, Milton. He's a Jeff Davis from down under and ain't been up here a hot minute. Look at them cuckaburrs sittin' up there coverin' his fusebox that blew out long ago. If the drip ever hit him in his kitchen it would roll up like a window shade, you ole hankachief-head signifyin' half-hipped square from Delaware, you're just like Jack the Bear, ain't nowhere, and like his brother No Fu'ther. You snapped your cap long ago.

SEVENTH CAT: Your boy's too much, Mezz, but he better join the bird family else I'll get somethin' from him.

EIGHTH CAT (*Yelling to passing friend*): Hey rough, give it up tough, you've had it long enough.

HIS FRIEND: Hey, homey! Man, ain't nothin' to it, just here. Saw that dinner up the street guzzlin' foam in the drink den and the sharks was droppin' shucks like the Yellow Kid, tryin' to tighten her, and weavin' the four F's all 'round her.

EIGHTH CAT: Huh, I nixed her out long ago, man she's too sometimey, she will and she won't, she do and she don't, always on the fence and sleeps with her glasses on. Man she's faust to me, so skip it and fergit it. Knock me some of that righteous bush, Poppa Mezz, so we can get tall and have a ball. Hey buddy ghee, why don't you put it with me and we'll cop a deuceways, don't you see, and take some of this weight right off'n me.

HIS FRIEND: Solid ole man, pick up on this rock, and it didn't come from no mudkicker in the block—I had to bring time for it don't you see, so raise up Jack and let me be. How'm I doin' Poppa Mezz, am I rhymin' or am I rhymin'.

ME: You ain't climbin', you're really chimin', if you ain't timin' a hawk can't see. Came on like Little Children and went off like A-and-A.

EIGHTH CAT: Listen at ole Mezz, cappin' and on time. Jim you really in there, and fine as May wine. This hemp that you're pushin' is groovy studdy, so tell all the cats light up and be somebody. Well Jim, I'm goin' to knock a fade up the main stroll and see what's on the rail for the lizard.

NINTH CAT: Czaro! Whatcha puttin' out?

ME: Nothin' but my laundry.

NINTH CAT: And you gets it back starched and clean, solid ole man. You know one thing, I wrastled some shake-up last night with some unbooted wren, blowin' salt and pepper till my hair hurts. I ain't greased since the big bean collared a nod in the early black, and I gotta stretch my chippy's playground. I know I'm gonna call some hogs soon as I hit my roost, so pick up on this dime note and call it even-steven so's I can widen. I'm gonna lay dead till half past the unlucky comes on, and dig ole Satch when he goes upstairs.

TENTH CAT: The mighty Mezz, what you puttin' down poppa?

ME: Punks and skunks, and hey Jim, your main saw on the hitch just trailed down the cruncher about tick twenty and you better quit it 'cause they're talkin' about goin' to Slice City.

TENTH CAT: Well tell a green man somethin', Jack. I know they're briny 'cause they dug me with a brace of browns the other fish-black, coppin' a squat in my boy's rubber, and we sold out. They been raisin' sand ever since. I haven't even seen my dreamers in a deuce of brights and the other dim, when the Head Knock turned on the splash that was most anxious ole man, they were on that frantic tip again. I don't much runnin' into some un-glamorous action by that frompy queen, but if push comes to shove I'll bet I'll become a cage of apes to them. Nayo hoss, I ain't fer it. Lemme pick up on some of that hard-cuttin' jive 'cause all I got left is a roach no longer than a pretty chick's memory. I'm gonna breeze to my personal snatchpad and switch my dry goods while they're out on the turf, and thanks for pullin' my coat, ole man. See ya, hear. . . .

What weird kind of polyglot patois was this, that they slung around my head on The Corner? It was nothing but the "new poetry of the proletariat." Dan Burley, famous old Negro newspaperman and editor of Harlem's *Amsterdam News*, describes jive that way, and I got a feeling he's right. It's *the language of action*, says Dan, "which comes from the bars, the dancehalls, the prisons, honky-tonks, ginmills, etc., wherever people are busy living, loving, fighting, working or conniving to get the better of one another." But don't think that it's a kind of petty patter, reserved for small talk. Uh, uh. In it the cats discuss "politics, religion, science, war, dancing, business, love, economics, and the occult." Jive, I found out, is not only a strange linguistic mixture of dream and deed; it's a whole new attitude towards life.

In the snatches of viper conversation up above, and in the bits of jive scattered over some other pages of this story, you don't get the full flavor of this street-corner poetry. This lingo has to be *heard*, not seen, because its free-flowing rhythms and intonations and easy elisions, all following a kind of instinctive musical pattern just like Bessie Smith's mangling of the English language, can only hit the ear, not the eye. Besides, if I wrote the hip language straight, most everything I said would sound like plain gibberish. (The word *jive* probably comes from the old English word *jibe*, out of which came the words *jibberish* and *gibberish*, describing sounds without meaning, speech that isn't intelligible.) This jive is a private affair, a secret inner-circle code cooked up partly to mystify the outsiders, while it brings those in the know closer together because they alone have the key to the puzzle. The hipster's lingo is a private kind of folk-poetry, meant for the ears of the brethren alone.

How can any outsider latch on to the real flavor of a secret code in which *tick twenty* means ten o'clock and *line forty* means the price is twenty dollars; friends are addressed as *gate* or *slot*, verbal shorthand for *gatemouth* and *slotmouth*, which are inner-circle racial jokes to begin with; *they* or *them people* means, not two or more persons, but a man's wife or mistress; *Tenth Street* isn't a city thoroughfare but a ten-dollar bill; specific places are known by special nicknames—New York City as *The Apple*, Seventh Avenue as *The Stroll*, the Savoy Ballroom as *The Track*; doubletalk nonsense-syllables like *lozeerose*, that resemble no regular words in any regular language, are invented to refer to private matters like marihuana? Guys talk that way when they don't want to be spied on, resent eavesdroppers; when they're jealously guarding their private lives, which are lived under great pressure, and don't want the details known to outsiders—detectives, square ofay musicians, informers, rivals from white show business, thrill-hungry tourists who come slumming up to "savage" and "primitive" Harlem to eyeball and gape.

Another well-known author and journalist, Earl Conrad, talks about jive as a kind of caricatured twist the Negro gives to the language that was foisted on him. "White America perpetrated a new and foreign language on the Africans it enslaved. Slowly, over the generations, Negro America, living by and large in its own segregated world, with its own thoughts, found its own way of expression, found its own way of handling English, as it had to find its own way in handling many other aspects of a white, hostile world. Jive is one of the end-results. . . . Jive talk may have been originally a kind of 'pig Latin' that the slaves talked with each other, a code—when they were in the presence of whites. Take the word 'ofay.' Ninety million white Americans right now probably don't know that that means 'a white,' but Negroes know it. Negroes needed to have a word like that in their language, needed to create it in self-defense." *Ofay*, of course, is pig Latin for *foe*.

Conrad's right a hundred times over, but I think you have to make a big distinction between the Southern Negro's strictly cautious and defensive private lingo and the high-spirited, belligerent jive of the younger Northern Negroes. Down South, before the Civil War and for long decades after it, right up to today, the colored folks had to nurse their wounds in private, never show their hurts and resentments, and talk among themselves in conspiratorial whispers. The language was mostly a self-protective code to them, and so it wasn't very elaborate or full of bubbling energy and unshackled invention; it was the tongue of a *beaten* people. But once the big migration got under way and the more adventurous Negroes started trekking northward up the Mississippi, a lot of their pent-up feelings busted out and romped all over the place. They brought their New Orleans music with them, and it exploded over Chicago and the whole North with one hell of a roar. And their talk got more explosive too, more animated, filled with a little hope and spirit. That's when jive as we know it today really got going.

I heard the jive language in its early stages, when I was hanging around the South Side in Chicago. It was the first furious babbling of a people who suddenly woke up to find that their death-sentence had been revoked, or at least postponed, and they were stunned and dazzled at first, hardly able to believe it. Then came the full exuberant waking up, the full realization that the bossman, at least the peckerwood kind with a bullwhip in his hand, was gone. The music got wilder and wilder. The excited rush of talk on street-corners, and in poolrooms and ginmills, swelled up to a torrent. That was the first real jive—the lingo of prisoners with a temporary reprieve. When I got to Harlem I found it had spread to the East, and really come of age. These Harlem kids had decided they wouldn't be led back to jail nohow. They spieled a mile a minute, making that clear.

Jive, Dan Burley says, "is the same means of escape that brought into being the spirituals as sung by American slaves; the blues songs of protest that bubble in the breasts of black men and women believed by their fellow white countrymen to have been born to be menials, to be wards of a nation, even though they are tagged with a whimsical designation as belonging to the body politic. . . . Jive serves a definite need of the people the same as do the Knights of Pythias, the Elks, or the Sons and Daughters of I Do Arise, with their signs, passwords, handclasps, and so on."

Sure. But I think you've got to keep hammering away at the fact that it *is* a protest, and not so inarticulate at that. That's what makes it entirely unique, a different kind of language from the traditional Southern Negro's, which didn't challenge the white oppressor but only tried to escape from his eagle eye, and those of his watchdogs. Jive does knit together a kind of tight secret society—-but it's a society which resents and nourishes its resentment, and is readying to strike back. The hipsters' fraternal order isn't just an escape valve, a defense mechanism; it's a kind of drilling academy too, preparing for future battles.

Jive isn't just a reflection of a primitive state; not by a long shot. The Negro doesn't add action metaphors to abstractions, put movement into static phrases, throw warmth into frozen logical categories, just because he can't understand them any other way. That's open to question. What is sure is that he's got too much poetry and rhythmic feeling in him, still alive and kicking, to be expressed in the bookish accents of educated white speech. He's got to pep up that bedraggled lingo to hold his interest and give vent to his emotions.

It's sure true, as all the writers point out, that the heart of jive is action. That's the most important fact about it. That's why it's peculiarly and uniquely a *Northern* Negro's creation. The ground-down Southern Negroes didn't develop an *action* language anywhere near as rich as this, although they had their own rich folk-poetry, because they couldn't see any possibility of action. But these Northern kids I hung around with were so active they couldn't sit still. Life below the Mason-Dixon line was sluggish, sleepwalking; up above 110th Street it was hyperthyroid. Life meant constant move-ment to these youngsters. They even called each other *cats* approvingly because they wanted to be as alert and keen-sighted as an alley-cat, that slinks through the dark streets and back lanes all night long, never closing its eyes, gunning everything and ready for all comers. . . . Their language could hardly keep up with their restless, roving activities. It was the poetic expression of an immobilized people who, at last, see the day coming when all the action in the world will be open to them, and all things will become possible.

The young citified Northern Negroes I got to know, unlike a lot of the older colored folks down South, were plenty alert and attentive, keyed-up with the effort to see and hear everything all at once, because that's how bottomdogs got to be unless they want to get lost in the shuffle. And, from where they were standing —blasted at by the radio, drowned in newsprint, suffocated by Hollywood epics—it looked to them like the top-of-the-pile white man is a bulging bundle of words. That T. S. Eliot described us all as hollow men, stuffed with straw. To the colored boys, we were all stuffed with pages from Webster's Dictionary.

Back off a thousand miles and look for yourself—what's the mark of the upper-crust American, the lawyer, the doctor, the financier, the politician? It's his command of the King's English, the way he spouts his high-powered jive so glib and smooth. Colored kids up North, dead-set on bettering themselves, dig the fact that the ofays with the most education have the highest standing, the most money and power—and the first thing that hits you about these high-riding guys is a smooth kind of gab, full of long skullbusting words and cliquish doubletalk.

Well, if talk shows your worth in this world the colored kids never made, then they sure aim to talk some too—not because they believe in it, but just to show they can do it. That's the first step: to prove to others, *and to themselves*, that they're in the running, have got what it takes. You can't get by in the hard American scuffle just by shaking your weary old head and pulling your scraggly whiskers. You got to *talk*, man. If you're Negro, and don't want to stick in a spiritual gallion all your days, you got to talk twice as fast as anybody else. So these high-spirited hip kids I hung out with made up their own private tongue. Most of them didn't even finish grammar school; they were operating just with their own native mother-wit. And in some ways it turned out richer and more human than the ofay's. It was just as complicated and specialized, just as subtle and roundabout, as any lingo the whites ever thought of. And less artificial too, more down-to-earth, alive with a deep-felt poetic sense and a rich imagery born out of Nature, jammed with the profound wisdom of the streets.

And all the while, as I could guess from the oblique kind of humor in the language, from the comic nature of its symbols and images, there was a great bellylaugh hid away in it. The colored boys never stopped to bemoan their fate in this hip language of theirs; there's no time for self-pity in this scuffle. Maybe they *were* schooling themselves in a kind of eloquence they wouldn't aim for on their own; maybe they *were* playing the ofay game of making-with-the-words. But they were also mocking the game and the rule-makers too, and mocking the whole idea of eloquence, the idea that words are anything but hypes and camouflage. The hip cat plays the game with his tongue almost coming through his cheek.

Once and for all, these smart Northern kids meant to show that they're not the ounce-brained tongue-tied stuttering Sambos of the blackface vaudeville routines, the Lazybones' of the comic strips, the Old Mose's of the Southern plantations. Historically, the hip-ster's lingo reverses the whole Uncle Tom attitude of the beaten-down Southern Negro. Uncle Tom believes he's good-for-nothing, shiftless, sub-human, just like the white bossman says he is. Uncle Tom scrapes and bows before his ofay "superiors," kills off all his self-respect and manliness, agrees that he's downtrodden because he doesn't deserve any better. Well, the kids who grew up in Northern cities wouldn't have any more of that kneebending and kowtowing. They sure meant to stand up on their hind legs and let the world know they're as good as anybody else and won't take anybody's sass. They were smart, popping with talent, ready for any challenge. Some of them had creative abilities you could hardly match anywhere else. Once they tore off the soul-destroying strait-jacket of Uncle Tomism, those talents and creative energies just busted out all over. These kids weren't schooled to use their gifts in any regular way. So their artistry and spirit romped out into their language. They began out-lingoing the ofay linguists, talking up a specialized breeze that would blow right over the white man's head. It gave them more confidence in themselves.

Deny the Negro the culture of the land? O.K. He'll brew his own culture—on the street corner. Lock him out from the seats of higher learning? He pays it no nevermind—he'll dream up his own professional doubletalk, from the professions that *are* open to him, the professions of musician, entertainer, maid, butler, tap-dancer, handyman, reefer-pusher, gambler, counterman, porter, chauffeur, numbers racketeer, day laborer, pimp, stevedore. These boys I ran with at The Corner, breathing half-comic prayers at the Tree of Hope, they were the new sophisticates of the race, the jivers, the sweettalkers, the jawblockers. They spouted at each other like soldiers sharpening their bayonets—what they were sharpening, in all this verbal horseplay, was their wits, the only weapons they had. Their sophistication didn't come out of moldy books and dicty colleges. It came from opening their eyes wide and gunning the world hard. Soon as you stop bowing your head low and resting your timid, humble eyes on the ground, soon as you straighten your spine and look the world right in the eye, you dig plenty. . . . Their hipness, I could see, bubbled up out of the brute scramble and sweat of living. If it came out a little too raw and strong for your stomach, that's because you been used to a more refined diet. You didn't come of age on the welfare, snagging butts out of the gutter. You can afford the luxury of being a little delicate, friend.

You know who they were, all these fast-talking kids with their four-dimensional surrealist patter? I found out they were the cream of the race—the professionals of Harlem who never got within reaching distance of a white collar. They were the razor-witted doctors without M.D.'s, lawyers who never had a shingle to hang out, financiers without penny one in their pokes, political leaders without a party, diploma-less professors and scientists minus a laboratory. They held their office-hours and made their speeches on The Corner. There they wrote their prose poems, painted their word pictures. They were the genius of their people, always on their toes, never missing a trick, asking no favors and taking no guff, not looking for trouble but solid ready for it. Spawned in a social vacuum and hung up in mid-air, they were beginning to build their own culture. Their language was a declaration of independence.

I found some signifying clues to the hip lingo in the way it described traits and qualities the young Negro admires. The *cat* he looks up to is *hip*, like a guy who carries a bottle or a bankroll or, more likely, a gun on his hip—in other words, he sure is well-primed and can take care of himself in any situation; he's *solid*, which is short for *solid as the Rock of Gibraltar*, and describes a man who isn't going to be washed away so easy; he's *got his boots on and they're laced up all the way*, meaning that he's torn himself away from the insane-asylum of the South, where the poor beaten Uncle Toms plod around in the gallion barefoot, and only the white boss-man wears boots; he's *righteous*, in the Biblical sense of having justice on your side, and he's *ready*, like a boxer poised to take on all comers, and he's *really in there*, as a prizefighter wades into the thick of it instead of running away from his opponent; he really *comes on*, like a performer making his entrance on the stage, full of self-confidence and self-control, aware of his own talents and the ability to use them; or he really *gets off*, that is, is so capable of expressing himself fully that he gets the load of oppression off, the load that weighs down poor broken people who are miserable and can't do anything about it, can't even put it into words; and he's *groovy*, the way musicians are groovy when they pool their talents instead of competing with each other, work together and all slip into the same groove, heading in the same direction, co-operating all the way; and finally, he's a *solid sender*, he can send your spirit soaring and make you real happy, because no matter how heavy his burden is he still isn't brought down, he keeps his sense of humor and his joy in life, and uses them to make you feel good too.

Those are the qualities the young cats go for, the ones they've invented new phrases to describe. Fitted together, they form a portrait of Uncle Tom—in *reverse*, a negative print. They add up to something mighty impressive, a real man. As their new American lingo tells you, that's what these hip kids mean to become. I could see how hard they worked at it. A heap of them made it.

What struck me as a wonderful thing was that they never lost their perspective—the language lets you know that too. The hipster stays conscious of the fraud of language. Where many ofays will hold forth pompously, like they had The Word, the Negro mimics them sarcastically. As a final subtle touch, his language is also a parody, a satire on the conventional ofay's gift of gab and gibberish. A lot of it consists of flowery ofay phrases and puffed-up clichés that are purposely twisted around to show how corny and funky they are, like a man's features are twisted in a caricature to show how simpy he is inside. I never once saw those kids get dead serious and all swole up with pompous airs. It inspired me to realize that these hip cats were half-conscious comic artists, playing with words. Their lingo was more than a secret code; it was jammed with a fine sense of the ridiculous that had behind it some solid social criticism.

The feeling of brotherhood on The Corner never stopped astonishing me. Look: to most whites the ginmills of Harlem mean only one thing, the underworld. Well, there's a world of difference between the ofay underworld and the colored underworld. You see, all of Harlem—the whole colored race, in a sense—is one great big underworld, because practically all of these people are shoved to the bottom of the pile and kept there on account of the one thing they have in common, the pigmentation of their skin. The oppression that rules all their lives has caused a kind of fraternity to spring up among many of them that you almost never get among the whites in any very broad group. At the bottom of the pile, with all the weight of white society crushing you, there isn't much room for one group to back off and glare down their noses at another group. It happens, of course, like it does among all human beings, but not to anywhere near the same extent as among the whites, not with the same insane and frenzied competition, as though your whole life depended on outdoing your next-door neighbor. The housing situation down there at the bottom doesn't favor much backing off. It's much too crowded for such hincty antics. You're all in the same boat together, and most of you realize it— all in the same underworld. Instead of backing off, which is impossible anyway, pretty soon you put your arm around your neighbor to be more comfortable, and the two of you begin looking out for each other. No room for shooting contests in that boat.

Marihuana took Harlem by storm, and before long several colored boys started to peddle it. First they wanted to sell it for me, but I explained to them that I couldn't get enough of it to become a wholesaler, and besides I just wanted to spread it around in my own circle of friends, not make a real business out of it. So these boys, without any hard feelings, went off and made a connection with some Spanish guys down on Lenox Avenue, and began selling it on their own. They rolled it in a different sized paper, about half an inch longer than mine and much thinner, and they called their product a "panatella."

Now get a load of their sales-talk. "This may not be as good as the mezz," they'd tell their customers in front, "but it's pretty close to it. Ain't no more reefer after the mezz." Try to imagine Al Capone's mugs telling a saloonkeeper that their needled beer wasn't as good as the Purple Gang's because Louis the Wop had the best beer on the market! Why, white guys in the same situation would be shooting each other up all over the place, trying to move in on each other. There was never a breath of competition between us. We were all real good friends. To top it off, these very same cats, my "competitors," would come around to see me on The Corner and buy my gauge for their own personal use! Nobody once got taken for a ride.

During this same period, bootlegging and the numbers racket flourished in Harlem, but the boys didn't want no part of its leaders and trigger men. The way they handled the gangster situation amazed me. They admired guys who got by on their wits, without cutting the next fellow down, but muscle men, always acting loutish and clinching their arguments with machine guns, didn't command any respect from them. Any simp can handle a machine gun; that's not a brainy occupation. They always wanted to see the best man win, not the guy with the biggest arsenal.

One night I was standing at the bar in Big John's when some of Dutch Schultz's torpedoes came swaggering in, dressed like fashion plates and hats cocked every whichaway. Dutch was down in Connie's Inn having himself a ball, and these mugs, about five of them all told, had some time to kill. They ordered drinks for the house, and one of them ankled over to the juke box to play some records. As soon as the music started, one of the guys in our crowd yelled real loud, looking straight at this guy, "Man, that's a *killer!*" He could have been talking about the music, but everybody in that room knew different. Right quick another cat spoke up real loud, saying, "That's *murder* man, really murder," and his eyes were signifying too. All these gunmen began to shift from foot to foot, fixing their ties and scratching their noses, faces red and Adam's apples jumping. Before we knew it they had gulped their drinks and beat it out the door, saying good-bye to the bartender with their hats way down over their eyebrows and their eyes gunning the ground. That's what Harlem thought of the white underworld.

Within the brotherhood there was some lively competition too, sure. The idea right smack in the middle of every cat's mind all the time was this: he had to sharpen his wits every way he could, make himself smarter and keener, better able to handle himself, more *hip*. The hip language was one kind of verbal horseplay invented to do that. Lots of other games sprang up for the same reason: snagging, rhyming, the dirty dozens, cutting contests. On The Corner the idea of a kind of mutual needling held sway, each guy spurring the other guy on to think faster and be more nimble-witted.

Through all these friendly but lively competitions you could see the Negro's appreciation of real talent and merit, his demand for fair play, and his ardor for the best man wins and don't you come around here with no jive. Boasting doesn't cut any ice; if you think you've got something, don't waste time talking yourself up, go to work and prove it. If you have the stuff the other cats will recognize it frankly, with solid admiration. That's especially true in the field of music, which has a double importance to the Negro because that's where he really shines, where his inventiveness and artistry come through in full force. The colored boys prove their musical talents in those competitions called cutting contests, and there it really is the best man wins, because the Negro audience is extra critical when it comes to music and won't accept anything second-rate. These cutting contests are just a musical version of the verbal duels. They're staged to see which performer can snag and cap all the others *musically*. And by the way, these battles have helped to produce some of the race's greatest musicians.

The contests generally happened in the early morning, after the musicians came uptown from their various jobs. There was always some small private club or speakeasy that had a piano in it, and when some new musician came to town he was obliged to come up with his instrument and get off for the other musicians. If he didn't show, that proved he wasn't sure of himself in the fast company around Harlem. The one that rated best on his particular instrument was told, "Hey man, So-and-So's in town and he was looking for you at Such-and-Such's this morning." All the contenders for the title were worked up that way, each being told the others were looking for him because they wanted to cut him down—that is, prove they were the best in the field. Things really got stirred up that way, and before the night was over all the cats were in some smoky room, really blowing up a breeze. If it was a close call—say, for instance, Lester Young and Ben Webster and Don Byas were all blowing their saxes, and the people couldn't come to much decision about who was best—then somebody would sneak out and get Coleman Hawkins, and when he unwrapped his horn it settled all arguments and sent the boys back to practise some more.

These contests taught the musicians never to rest on their laurels, to keep on woodshedding and improving themselves. Dancers had the same kind of competitions, and so did most other kinds of entertainers. Many's the time some hoofer would be strutting his stuff in the alley outside the Lafayette Theater, with a crowd around him, and Bubbles would wander up and jump in the circle and lay some hot iron that lowrated the guy, then walk off saying, "Go on home and wrastle with that one, Jim." There wasn't any room for complacency. Bubbles wasn't just showing off. He was making that cat work harder.

One morning a sensational cutting contest took place, just between piano players. Fats Waller picked up a gang of us at some café—Eddie Condon, Jack Bland, me and a couple of other whites, and two other colored piano players, Willie "The Lion" Smith and Corky Williams—and we went up to his house about four A.M. Fats was a wonderful guy, one of the most jovial persons I have ever met, always bubbling with jokes so it was impossible to feel brought down in his company. He stood about six foot tall and weighed well over two hundred pounds, and his feet, that were a stylish size fifteen, he referred to as his "pedal extremities." He was always coming around to play for me and my friends down in the Riverside Towers (it was down there, after I'd been urging him to play the blues, that he wrote his famous *Ain't Misbehavin'*). He'd sit at the piano all night long, and sometimes part of the next day, without even getting up to see that man about that canine. We'd set up quart after quart of bathtub gin for him— one on top of the piano, so when he was playing treble he could reach up with his left hand, and another at his foot, so while he beat out the bass he could reach down and grab the jug with his right hand. . . . Well, this morning out came several quarts of liquor, and it was on.

Corky sat down and started to play *Tea for Two*, a number that Willie The Lion could give a fit. All of a sudden Willie jumped up and said to Corky, "Git up from there you no-piano-playin' son of a bitch, I got it," and with that he sat down next to Corky. As Corky slid over, Willie started to play just the treble, while Corky still kept up the bass, and then he picked up with his left hand too, the tempo not even wavering and without missing a beat. Willie played for a while and then Fats took over, sliding into the seat the same way Willie had done. He played for a while, looking up at Willie and signifying every time he made a new or tricky passage. It went on like that, the music more and more frantic, that piano not resting for even a fraction of a second, until finally Fats said "I'm goin' to settle this argument good." He went into a huddle with his chauffeur, who left and returned about an hour later, but not alone. Fats had telephoned to Jamaica, Long Island, and woke up James P. Johnson out of his bed. When the chauffeur brought Jimmy in he was still rubbing his eyes, but as soon as he sat down at the piano that was all. He played so much piano you didn't have to yell "Put out all the lights and call the law," because the law came up by request of the neighbors. "We been sittin' downstairs enjoying this music," the cops told us, "when we got a call from the station house to see who was disturbing the peace around here. Some people ain't got no appreciation for music at all. Fats, just close them windows and pour us a drink, and take up where you left off." So for the rest of the morning the contest went on, with these two coppers lolling around drinking our liquor and listening to our fine music. It was great.

13

ONCE MORE, AGAIN, AND
ANOTHER TIME

IT WAS a fine Spring night in 1931. We were jiving and thriving lightly; up above, the leaves on the Tree of Hope carried on their own rustling doubletalk. Up the tree trunk snaked the grapevine and plugged into my receivers. "Yeah man," it buzzed, "they got your boy all messed up down in Memphis."

Louis Armstrong, had swung down to New Orleans and then headed back up to Memphis. Mrs. Collins, his manager's wife, was in charge of their transportation, and she had chartered a big shiny new Greyhound bus so they could get through the Murder Belt without riding in dirty spine-cracking Jim-Crow coaches. She always sat up front with Mike McKendricks, the guitar player, who helped her with luggage and things like that.

When that bus pulled into Memphis the pecks all crowded around goggle-eyed, staring at the well-dressed colored boys in this streamlined buggy, and especially at the one colored boy up front who was, God forbid, sitting there actually talking to a white woman cool as pie, just like he was human. They couldn't let that go down. The stink they raised was so funky that the manager at the bus terminal tried to shift the whole party to a dirty creaky old crate. Naturally, the boys sat tight, refusing to budge off their dusters. Next thing they knew, the police were on their necks, carting them off to be fingerprinted and locked up like common thieves. They got out just in time to make their regular broadcast.

All us vipers rushed into the Barbeque that night to hear the program come over the radio. When they hit the air, Louis started off with some doubletalk, and right in the middle of it he greeted me with a happy "How-de-do Lozeerose." Halfway through the broadcast he announced that he wanted to dedicate his next number to the Chief of Police of Memphis, Tennessee. "Dig this, Mezzeerola," he warbled while the band played his intro. Then he started to sing *I'll Be Glad When You're Dead You Rascal You.*

With Louis gallivanting round the country, there was a hole in my life big as the Grand Canyon. Soon, though, I was hanging out with Zutty Singleton. Most every night, after he got through at Connie's Inn, we'd have a bite to eat and then make the rounds together. Zutty was well liked by everybody, and he had a cheery way of greeting people by referring to their face—like if you had on a new tie or a set of drapes he'd call you "Tie Face" or "Suit Face," and other times he'd come up with names like "Boat Face" and "Boot Nose" and "Gizzard." Later on everybody started using the expression "Face" as a greeting: you'd say "Watcha know, Face," and the answer would come back, "Nothin' to it, Face." Zutty and I were always going around visiting friends in Harlem, and no matter where we went we'd always find everybody, from grandpa to the two-year-olds, able to do his number. What kicks I used to get when we'd puff our way up to some crummy walk-up tenement flat and find a tot, hardly able to walk, getting up to do a lively time-step and then break. And from the old folks' shuffle to the Suzie-Q and Sand, wasn't none of them steps new to grandpa —just the names were different. Pops could tell you about cutting them same steps when he was a kid barefooted. Everybody danced.

Monday mornings, about five A.M., we'd shoot over to the Lenox Club on 144th Street for the weekly breakfast dance. Here we'd always find most of the performers and musicians, ready to have a ball after working all night, and if you got home by noon you were lucky. Almost every bigtime act that was in town would get up and do their number; week after week, on one bill there, you'd see some of the biggest headliners in show business. It wasn't unusual to see, all in one morning, the Berry Brothers (one of the greatest dance teams that ever hit the boards), Buck and Bubbles, Ada Brown, Bill "Bojangles" Robinson, the Whitman Sisters' show (out of which came some of the finest acts the race ever had), Nina Mae McKinney, Valaida Snow, Ethel Waters, Batie and Foster with some fine comedy and dancing, Louis Armstrong, Duke Ellington, Cab Calloway (he didn't have his own band yet, he was singing in "Hot Chocolates"), Earl "Snakehips" Tucker (originator of the snakehip dance), Freddie "Snakehips" Taylor, Bessie Dudley (one of the greatest women tap and snake dancers of the day), and Louise Cook. It really romped.

The midnight shows at the Lafayette Theater were another great institution that the boys from downtown will never forget. Every Friday night I'd reserve the whole first three or four rows, and most of the musicians I knew would come up with their friends to gape at the goings-on. Acres of marihuana went up in smoke at every show there—and man, many a time even the performers would come on the stage and do some comedy routine about vipers, and they'd light up too, right in front of everybody. The most interesting part of the show was the race's reaction to the movies that filled in between stage shows. The pretentious acting in those beat-up Hollywood epics, which had always kept me away from the movies (to me the flickers were just a mild Minsky's on celluloid), was the ridicule of all Harlem. When a dramatic scene hit the screen that dripped with phony dressed-up sentimentalism, showing some lushhead writer's soap-opera idea of life with a capital L, all the kids would begin laughing and hooting, yelling "Man, why don't they go 'head with that ole stuff," and when a man in some love scene fell for the jive some chick was putting down, you'd hear the kids calling out "Don't go home and try to put that stuff down baby, 'cause you'll get your head whipped." The audience would roar so loud the picture was all forgotten for a few minutes.

When Louis came out of Connie's Inn and went on the road, one of the greatest teams in jazz history was broken up. Connie had bought a set of tunable tomtoms for Zutty and raised his salary, so when Louis asked him to go along with the roadshow he said, "Well Pops, you know friendship is one thing and business is another." He was a great artist himself, and felt maybe he'd get further on his own, and some day have his own band, so he stayed in Connie's. Louis swore from that day on Zutty would never play with him again, even though he was the only drummer in the world that could hold him up every inch of the way. That split-up hurt me more than either one of them, because it was such a great loss to the music. To this day those two wonderful artists don't realize how important it is for them to be together.

After Louis started his road tour he sent me a letter telling me the whole story of his break with Zutty, and even though I loved Zutty I began to feel guilty about hanging out with him, because to me Pops was the greatest of them all. Buck was also a close friend of Louis', and he would rib Zutty now and then about leaving Louis, so that put me on a complex even more. Pretty soon I was running with Buck, and didn't see much of Zutty. The cats on the avenue were all aware of what took place, because we were all one big family around The Corner, and they sort of sanctioned my move and respected my loyalty to Louis. Buck had the cornet that Louis used to play back in Chicago in the Sunset, and almost every day he'd wake me by calling me on the phone and then, without saying a word, play some chorus that Louis had just recorded. Sometimes he would sound just like Pops, especially when he played muted. He had such a wonderful ear, he played all Louis' slurs and little subtle inflections that to this day nobody else has ever captured.

He had a funny way of beating on people that is still the talk of The Avenue. If somebody passed a remark that wasn't in line, he'd start singing and beating on the offtime cat, catching the explosions on his head and back and every other part of his anatomy. You couldn't get away from him either. He slapped you easy enough, but the steady beating, with all eyes on you, made you stand there and take it. "Shoot the liquor to him John *boy*," he'd sing (a phrase that later got famous on records), and then he'd scat some riffs like "Riboppity-bop-bam, riboppity-bop-bam, riboppity-zhiboppity, riboppity-bop-*face*"—like a drummer catching an explosion on a cymbal and on the last word he'd slap your face from some fancy angle. This went on for as long as he felt you deserved it, and you either ran out of the place hot as a pistol or laughed till the tears came, but one thing sure, you never forgot it and you never repeated the remark that brought on this punishment. What a down-to-earth guy Buck was. If he was headlining at Loew's State at three thousand per week, he'd still walk up to the corner stand and eat his hotdog. His partner Bubbles was a great cat too—he danced without any set routine, all improvisation, so you never knew when he was going to cut a new step that all the dancers in Harlem would be trying to imitate the next morning, if they were sharp enough.

In fact, they were all wonderful guys, the gang around The Corner and the Lafayette and the Breakfast Dances, and if I'd had any sense I would never have drifted one single inch away from them. Looks like I keep a yen for trouble. Listen at what happened to me now.

Remember that room back in the Detroit hotel, with a wet sheet hanging over the door? Well, this is where I walked back in there, never to leave for four long years. And this time, like I said, I had to crawl out on all fours, with my whiskers scraping the floor.

You might ask, why in hell did I have to go and get hooked on hop right then, and you'd have a right to ask, buddy. Wasn't I doing all right for myself, at last? Wasn't I home, after all those years of knocking around on foreign territory, living with the people I loved the best, having the kind of life I always dreamed of having ever since Pontiac reform school? Sure. But there were complications. They weren't Harlem's fault, that's one thing sure, and some of them weren't even my fault, or anybody's; but there sure were complications. Seems like the millennium is just another word in the dictionary after all, even though at a few great moments in your life you feel like you really get close to it. I was plenty happy in Harlem, really blowing my top for joy. But it wasn't the millennium yet. For one thing, I wasn't making any music.

How come I get myself right smack in the middle of the greatest Negro community in the world—and then lay away my horns?

It's like this. My mainstay had been Gene Krupa, and now he was tied up with that Red Nichols (along with Benny Goodman, who he went with later on when Goodman started out for himself). So Gene was away from me. Of my other oldtime friends, who'd at least been schooled in the same idiom as me, Condon and McKenzie were together with the squeak-and-gargle Blue Blowers, and Tesch and them had gone back to Chicago, and I couldn't blow note one with the corny white bands around New York. To me all the fay outfits that might hire me were just fancier versions of the Minsky pit band, and I wasn't having any more of that off-time jive.

Why didn't I play with the colored boys? Sounds like a reasonable question—the music I was hot for was strictly a Negro creation, and all the top colored artists were my personal friends. Well, the colored bands around New York had plenty of virtuoso musicians in them, but they didn't play the New Orleans music that I was crazy about; they had an entirely different pulse and flavor and I couldn't have chimed in worth a damn. New Orleans hadn't come East yet, that was the sad fact of the matter. Louis had had a big band with him, sure, and that right away was a departure from the strict New Orleans tradition, but still and all he had Zutty behind him to give the ensemble a New Orleans rock and drive, and although the band played written arrangements they still made organ effects with the reeds and brasses, not holding Louis back, helping to give depth and richness to Louis' soaring horn. And besides, Louis was a genius and could make great music with nothing behind him but a washboard and a kazoo. I was no Louis. I needed a friendlier musical environment.

And another thing—the race made me feel inferior, started me thinking that maybe I wasn't worth beans as a musician or any kind of artist, in spite of all my big ideas. The tremendous inventiveness, the spur-of-the-moment creativeness that I saw gushing out in all aspects of Harlem life, in the basketball games, the prizefights, the cutting contests, the fast and furious games of rhyming and snagging on The Corner—it all dazzled me, made me doubt if I was even in the running with these boys. Practically everybody

239

I knew was a virtuoso, popping with creative talents. Even though the musicians didn't play New Orleans style, yet and still they had so much on the ball, such brilliant technique and inventive inflections to brighten up even the dullest arrangements. I just said to myself, even if it isn't my kind of music I better listen close and learn some more about this, because no matter what they're doing they do it so *good*. I thought of the records I made with Condon and all the guys back in Chicago, and I was ashamed of how feeble and scrawny they were compared with what the colored boys in Harlem played every day in the week. I sure didn't want to go back to "Chicago style"—but I didn't know how to go forward either. Maybe, I thought, well Jesus, maybe after all I was cut out to be the philosopher, like Tiny Hunt had once named me, and not a musician at all. Some wise cat once said that those who can't, teach. Maybe I couldn't. Maybe I had to become the philosopher out of desperation.

I was sure suppressed on the creative side, but I didn't have the time to worry over it none. The action on The Avenue went down so fast that it was all I could do to strain my eyes and ears and follow it. Listen-and-learn was the play, all the way. And although I wasn't blowing my horn, I was sure advocating some, being the philosopher, and I got some kicks out of that. Wherever I went, in the cafés and theaters and dancehalls and ginmills, my say-so was respected. The bands always outplayed themselves trying to come on for me, because I'd talk all over town about the performers I liked, and my word was getting to mean something—now and then it led to other engagements, bigger bookings, and record dates. I was really, in a modest way but enough to make me feel good, acting as a kind of link between the races, hipping some of the whites to the genius of the most talented Negro boys, getting members of both groups closer together and beginning to appreciate each other more.

I could dig that there'd never be a way out for me without a mixed band—the most inspired whites and Negroes playing together. There'd maybe be room for me in such a set-up, sooner or later. But the mixed band was just a pipedream in those days (and still is, in any real sense of the term—one colored guy in a big white swing band isn't exactly a "mixture"). Louis and I used to talk about it all the time—it was our idea of the millennium. But Pops, with his great practical wisdom, figured that for a first step, it shouldn't be a colored band taking in a white man, but the other way around, because the privileged should make the first overtures of friendship towards the oppressed.

Anyhow, those talks with Louis did have one result: they led to the first important mixed-band recording dates that I know about. First Louis himself got together with Jack Teagarden, Eddie Lang, Joe Sullivan and some colored boys, and they made *Knockin' a Jug* and *Muggles* for Okeh, early in 1929. Chances are I would have been on that date, if I hadn't been on the high seas, bound for Paris. Then Fats Waller, who was solid for the idea too, got together a recording group for Victor that he called "Fats Waller and His Buddies." Under this name Fats played with Eddie Condon, Gene Krupa and Jack Teagarden, plus the colored boys, on *Lookin' Good and Feelin' Bad* and *I Need Someone Like You*; and then, using Eddie and Jack in the band, he made *Ridin' But Walkin', Won't You Get off It Please, Lookin' for Another Sweetie,* which was the original of the number that later got famous as *Confessin'*, and *When I'm Alone*. All these records were made in 1929 too, when we first began mulling the mixed-band idea over.

So there I was, advocating, signifying, being the link between the races, selling my reefer on The Corner—and not blowing a note. I never tried to make a real business out of the gauge, but the demand for it just sprang up by itself, and even after giving the other guys their cut I always had a couple of hundred bucks come the end of the week. I was able to take care of Bonnie and her kid real good, with some new furniture in the house, plenty of clothes, and everything else they needed. My name was getting around the country like wildfire. Cats would bust in from Texas or California and look me up, saying "Man, I heard about you and that good gauge way out on the coast." When Connie Immerman came out of his Inn and climbed into his great big Packard, the guys would say to me, "Mezz, you gonna be ridin' in one of them things some day too."

Maybe it should have set me up, all this success and easy money, but it didn't—it made me feel worse and worse. Even if muggles weren't illegal, they were still looked down on by the outside world, and what I was doing for a living was considered a racket. The last thing in the world I wanted to be was a racketeer. The last straw was when those East Side gangsters from downtown started coming around and making me fabulous offers to tie in with them and let them build up a real big racket out of the reefer. They were plenty bad guys. Not long before they had tried to rub Connie Immerman out, and I knew they would give the same treatment to anybody else who stood in their way. They hung around the gangster-owned saloons in Harlem and kept after me to get them big quantities of the weed wholesale. Soon I was getting visits from Dutch Schultz's boys and Vincent "Babyface" Coll's boys every day in the week. With each day they got less good-natured about it. Each day their voices got harder, and their demands more insistent.

Now I sure don't want to blame anybody for what happened to me next. People very seldom get themselves messed up unless they been asking for it some way, no matter how much of an innocent victim they look like from the outside. Here I was all bottled up musically, kind of deserted by the white musicians, and with my idol Louis gone too; all jammed up with inferiority feelings on account of not making music; worried over the prospect of peddling reefer the rest of my days; afraid that the gangsters would force me to become a racketeer, so I'd be trapped in a mess I couldn't ever fight my way out of again. You can see that I was ready for anything. . . . But the way it actually happened, I didn't go after the hop on my own. It was just about then that a couple of my old pals from downtown started to bother me about hop. They'd had it a couple of times back in Chicago and wanted to try it again just for a thrill, and they figured maybe I could make some connection in Harlem for them. Just to humor the guys along I told them I'd see what I could do, and then I put it out of my mind.

Back in Detroit the Purple Gang had put me on a complex about the stuff, so I wasn't hot for it.

Then one day, as I was coming out of the Rhythm Club, a cat stepped up and introduced himself as Frankie Ward the drummer, and said he wanted some gauge. We went into the alley to light up, and he said "You ever smoke hop Mezz? This don't compare to hop."

So I knew Frankie was a hophead. I thought no more about it until my friends began pestering me again about a hop connection. Then I ran into Frankie again and I asked him how about it. He took me by the arm and steered me over to "Beale Street," which is 133rd Street between Fifth and Lenox, the toughest block in Harlem, and there he introduced me to the guy who supplied him with opium, an old smoker by the name of Mike. Frankie told this man I was O.K. with Pops, and fixed it so I could get the stuff any time I wanted it.

During the next two months I went back to see Mike a couple of times, and picked up enough hop for my friends—my wife was out West visiting friends for a few weeks, so the boys came up to my house and there we smoked the stuff. Mike moved over to Eighth Avenue to take a job as superintendent in an old tenement house, and there I found him again. One night he invited me to lay down with him. I found out that Mike had started on hop when he was sixteen—in those days you could practically buy it in the corner candy store—and he'd been on the stuff for thirty-five solid years now.

How long did it take before you got the habit, I asked.

Oh, sixty days or less, he told me, depending on the strength of the stuff and how often you used it.

He agreed to let my friends come around and smoke with him once in a while. I went back myself, two, three, four times, I don't remember exactly how often. I told myself I would just watch it, not take too much, not go back too soon, and that way I'd be playing it safe. If you were smart, you wouldn't get the habit.

I went back once more, again, and another time. All the while I was taking care, playing it safe. Then, one fine morning, I woke up and pretty soon I found all my neuroses boiling up, and I was mean and evil all through. My mouth was dry as cotton and I couldn't stop yawning, and my stomach felt like it was caved in and my eyes were full up with water till I couldn't see. I wondered if I was coming down with pneumonia. I had a craving for something, I could hardly tell what; my hands were trembling something awful. I was one great miserable itching bundle of need. All my nerves were stretching their fingers out, begging for alms.

Then it hit me what the trouble was—I had a yen, a terrible terrible yen for hop. I had to have some right away, nothing could stop me. It was an obsession, it drove every other thought out of my head. I was going to get some hop fast, and if anybody stood in my way I'd cut his throat. Nothing else mattered. I was hooked.

14

TOUGH SCUFFLE, MEZZIE

FOR almost four years solid I laid around in The Bunk. Let me tell you about The Bunk. That was the name we gave to a little old six-foot-square coal bin down in the cellar of Mike's tenement that we cleaned out and converted into our hop-pad. In this kind of shed we set some heavy planks down on top of some beer boxes, then covered them up with some old Army horse blankets to make a big bed, and it was here that we stretched out for days on end and smoked and philosophized and smoked some more. We were a hophead triumvirate: in addition to Mike and me there was Mike's buddy Mackey, who lived with him and helped him out with the janitoring. Up on the brick wall of The Bunk was a big cowhide, hair and all, and the other walls were plastered with pictures of pretty chicks tore off some old calendars. We had an old beat-up gas heater to keep us warm, so things were pretty cozy. The days oozed by like a melted movie film, all run together.

Mike and Mackey were both along in their fifties, and they'd both grown up in the "Jungles" of San Juan Hill (the tough neighborhood on 10th Avenue along in the Sixties, just above Hell's Kitchen), so they had some stories to tell. We'd lay around there in a sunny haze and they'd tell me about how they were always fighting the Irish kids when they were young—how they had to battle their way to the grocery store and slug their way to school. About the only sport they remembered having was to sneak up on a roof somewhere and empty garbage cans loaded with bricks on the heads of the Irish cops on the beat. They'd grown up in that no-man's-land with James P. Johnson the fine piano player, and they still remembered him and loved him. When we laid down and began to cook, Mike's dog would smell the heavy fumes and bust right in. He had a bunk habit too, so he was evil in the morning, eyes watering and mouth gaping all the time, but as soon as he got a few whiffs of the smoke he'd settle down and go to sleep content, making soft little growls to show how he enjoyed his smoke.

Mackey, with a bellyful of hop and feeling all mellow and good, would sometimes jump up and say "Goddamn, it's eight o'clock and I ain't called my garbage yet." Then he'd rouse Mike and the two of them would go over to the dumbwaiter and start rounding up the garbage. They sure hated the idea of hauling that thing up and down, so they worked out a system to save wear and tear on their muscles. Soon as Mackey rang the dumbwaiter bell he yelled up the shaft "Garbage!" Then he'd put one hell of a big can in the shaft and not move it an inch from the basement, because the idea was for everybody to drop their garbage down the shaft, aiming for that can. Mackey'd yell up "Hey, never mind them pails baby, drop what you got in paper bags and you better not miss the can, hear!" As the bags thudded into the can, ka-plunk, ka-plop, he shouted "That's it! Your eye's pretty good today, baby! Hole in one!"

I was the handyman around there, and I helped out doing repairs and fixing sinks and toilets when they went bad, which they did all the time. That was some building. The rats were big as alleycats, and they ran up and down the dumbwaiter ropes just as bold, so when people hauled the dumbwaiter up they had to fight them monsters off with broomsticks. But when we got our big police dog he scared them away some. All the toilets in the building were out in the dark and narrow hallways, one to a floor, and the streetwalkers on the block would sneak inside with their customers and take them into the toilets, because they were always open. Whenever we'd be laying around late at night and we'd hear a toilet flush somewhere in the building, Mike would say "Uh, uh, there's one of them mudkickers again," and he'd run up and chase them out, yelling "G'wan, you didn't pay no room rent around here, scat!" What tenants we had there. On the second floor was a King Kong speakeasy, where you could get yourself five-cent and ten-cent shots of homebrewed corn, if you didn't care about dissolving the enamel on your teeth; then on the third floor there was another King Kong joint, only this one did nothing but a cash-and-carry package business; and up on the top floor, the fifth, some guys used an apartment to cook corn mash in a still, making King Kong. One thing, though, there weren't any whorehouses in the place. Mike figured they gave too much trouble and he was for having everything run smooth and respectable.

Mornings, when I came shuffling in full of quakes and quivers inside, a whole family of frantic bats in my stomach, I'd pass the fish store in front of the building and get walloped by the stink there, then I'd rush down through the basement and get slugged by the stench of the garbage cans lined up in rows. But as soon as I laid down and inhaled a few pills my guts relaxed and everything began to smell like Chanel Number Five to me. As we lolled around there, hour after wavery hour, we discussed everything under the sun and settled the problems of the world. We were a three-man town hall meeting, a real hophead forum. We analyzed Jim Crow, the numbers racket that was flourishing in Harlem, the white gangsters, the merits of different jails and penitentiaries, Uncle Tomism, how good all the different musicians and performers were, race psychology, war and peace and the international scene, which wasn't pretty. Mike would tell us how he was a pioneer in Harlem and knew Ethel Waters and Fats Waller when they first started, and we'd talk over the different shows at the Lafayette. I made Mike's apartment my headquarters for the gauge, and both Mike and Mackey helped me push it, so pretty soon a lot of the performers began dropping around to see us, and that gave us more to talk about.

With the money they began to make, and their new interest in life, these two wonderful guys began to crawl up out of their sunken life some. They got dressed up, ate porterhouse steaks most every night, started to move around to see different shows and nightclubs and various sights, and just woke up all around. We had a lot of talks about dope. They had a terrible contempt for the guys on the "white stuff"—heroin, morphine, and cocaine, all drugs that you took with a hypodermic needle—and they told me how when you got hooked on it you got afraid of water, let yourself get all dirty and would never wash or shave, and your clothes turned to rags and you just became a gutter-bum. Hopheads at least were clean and neat, and liked to tog sharp. It was funny: they shunned guys on the white stuff just like vipers shun liquor-heads.

Mike and Mackey were unschooled cats, illiterate and all, but still they were full of mother-wit, with a wonderful down-to-earth slant and practical wisdom. They sure didn't want me to get hooked, and they did their best to run me out of there. "Gate," Mike would tell me, so earnest his voice got the trembles, "you don't know what you're messin' with. If I could play that stick like you do I'd be out there runnin' with all them high-powered chicks in all the fine places, and you *white* too." There was an accusation in his words that upset me—he meant that, being white, I had all the advantages, and still I was so weak I let myself go just like he had. He at least had some excuse, he didn't have any other way to make himself feel good, he was a penniless beat black man and he was stuck. . . . He said to me, "What'll Louis say if he knows you're on this stuff, he ain't gonna like it. Boy, leave me tell you one thing, if you knew like we know, you'd leave this jive alone, but fast. . . ." They pleaded with me, like the wonderful friends they were. But I always consoled myself by saying I could break whenever I wanted to, I'd just go to a sanatorium and take the cure. Hop makes you feel so good when you've got a skinful that you just say to hell with everything, this is what I want, when I feel so fine there can't be anything bad about it. And then when you wake up next morning your whole nervous system is screaming, and you can't think about anything but getting some more, and fast. Then you get feeling hazy and mellow again, and nothing worries you. . . . So it's a vicious circle. I just whirled round and round it, kidding myself that I was always at the controls and could break whenever I wanted to. I never did tell Louis about it until years later, after I broke the habit, and then I didn't tell him the whole story.

That was the Summer of 1931, when I moved into The Bunk. All that season, and the following one too, I had part of a box reserved out at the Yankee Stadium, and when the sun was shining we'd get ourselves feeling fine, pack along some yen pox (opium pills that you eat), and go out there to the baseball game. A lot of our friends (*not* hopheads) would join us—Bill Robinson, Buck, Tommy Dorsey, and some cats from his band. I chewed on them pills like the other guys munched peanuts.

Mike lived in an apartment upstairs with Lil, his fine old lady, and she treated me so fine when I was there that everybody thought she was my wife. I installed a push-button under the sink in Lil's kitchen, and connected it to a buzzer down in The Bunk, and the idea was that Lil was to ring three times for me, twice for Mackey, once for Mike—and four times if the law showed its nose anywhere near. Well, it seems that one day some stoolie tipped off the cops that Lil was selling hop in her place, which was a lowdown dirty lie because it was only marihuana and I was selling it, not her. A whole squad of cops showed up, and that buzzer began to ring in four-four time. Mike and me grabbed our layout and out into the airshaft we climbed, till we finally got into the next building, and then we went up to the second floor and peeked out the window. There was Mackey out in front of the house just as unconcerned, sweeping the sidewalk with slow, easy strokes, while the cops swarmed all over the place. He was a busy man, and he just couldn't be bothered by such doings. Then he raised his head a little, and just out of the corner of his eye he spotted us two up in the window, holding our bellies to keep from collapsing with laughter. He didn't say anything; not even his eyebrow twitched. His expression was the same as before. Down went his head again, and this time he set to work sweeping that sidewalk like he was possessed, making that old broom fly so fast it was just a fuzzy blur. That was the only way he could show he was laughing with us, way inside. We three hopheads, we felt too good to be upset by a puny little police raid. It almost washed us away.

One day we were stretched out all together, wrapped in a dreamy fog, floating through the driftsmoke. All of a sudden there was a terrific booming explosion that made the whole house do a shimmy. Nobody said anything for a long while. Then Mike spoke up in heavy measured accents, like a judge, talking in slow motion. "I done tole you," he said to Mackey, "not to rent them goddamned rooms on the top floor to them Kong-cookin' hootchhead son-of-a-bitches. They done blew the roof off the building, and I don't need that much air."

We fell into silence again, huddled up with our weighty thoughts. An hour later it gradually penetrated my skull that he was talking about the guys up on the fifth floor who were always cooking King Kong in their still. What he meant was that the guy on duty had dozed off and the whole mess of corn mash had exploded. I gave it some serious thought, examining the idea from all angles. We laid there real philosophical, thinking it over. It wasn't something you accepted just like that. There were implications.

Pretty soon there was a hell of a clang-clang outside, like the whole New York fire department was tearing up. Mike kept cooking his hop, rolling the pill round and round, very slow and meditative.

Mackey stirred. He examined the ceiling for a long time, and finally he said, "Man, we oughta git up off our daniels and dig what's goin' on."

A deep silence again. "Juicy, lay down," Mike came back, after he had pondered it for a while. "That fire is way up on the fifth floor, see, and it'll be a long time 'fore it works its way down here to the basement, if it ever does. Can't ever tell about them things. Sometimes a house burns up, and sometimes it burns down, and could be this one's gonna burn up so the fire won't ever get near us. It ain't no hurry."

We passed the pipe around again. *Bam! Clunk!* Five-gallon tin cans full of flaming corn mash began crashing down the airshaft just outside The Bunk, and then the firemen on the roof turned their hoses down the shaft and it sounded like Niagara Falls outside the window. *Plop! Boff! Sssswish!* We passed the pipe around once more. *Ka-plunk!*

"The Giants are playin' tomorrow," Mackey said thoughtfully. *Wham!* "I been thinkin' if it's a nice sunny day we might go out there and see the game." *Crash! Pow!*

"It should be a good game," Mike said. *Clump!*

"Ain't nothin' I likes like a good baseball game," Mackey said. *Wallop! Fzzzz!*

Nobody looked out the window. We didn't get off that pad till way late next morning. We were feeling too good to let little things like fires, floods and earthquakes worry us any.

All that Winter I was lost in oblivion, stretched out in an opium stupor in The Bunk. Then, late in the Spring of '32, Louis played Philly, and I got the idea of going down there with Zutty. It was very important to me to try and bring those two guys together again. Maybe I couldn't help myself just then; maybe I was all washed up as a musician and a human being. But at least I could try to do something for the guys who stuck with it, who could make wonderful music and kept on making it. Louis had Tubby Hall beating drums for him now, and Tubby was in there too, but Zutty had some little extra touch that really sent Louis soaring on his horn.

Zutty wasn't doing so good after he left Louis, and me, I just wasn't doing, period. It was great to see Pops again. As soon as he went on, we ran down under the stage so we could listen to Louis just by ourselves.

After the opening, Louis began playing *Rockin' Chair*, his specialty. The great big wailing notes came shuddering down to us through the floor, each one a-tremble with strength and mastery. All those unbelievable little runs, strung out like diamond pendants by Louis' terrific artistry, full of sobs and bellylaughs, trickled down into our ears. Louis knew we were there, and he was adding his most magnificent touches just for us.

We listened, and the tears came to our eyes. Zutty leaned over to me and I leaned over towards him, his head on my shoulder and mine on his chest, and while we stood there hugging each other we just cried and cried. Our tears wouldn't stop coming. They were made up about fifty-fifty of pride and guilt.

Mike's wife used to turn on the radio in her apartment real loud, so we could hear it down the airshaft. One night the Mills Brothers came on, just before the Amos-and-Andy program that all Harlem listened to.

I'd never heard the Mills Brothers before. When that deep throbbing husky bass came vibrating into The Bunk, it electrified me. It sounded so much like the oldtime New Orleans blues guitar players, ones like Blind Lemon Jefferson and Johnny St. Cyr and them. All of a sudden I jerked upright on the bunk and began to shake all over. It roused me out of my stupor like a shot in the arm.

Mike and Mackey were tickled too. I'd been trying to explain to them just what New Orleans music was all about, so now I shouted "Goddamn, that's the bass I'm talkin' 'bout, it lifts you up and gives you wings, it sends you off like a rocket." I guess I got incoherent, babbling with excitement. The other guys agreed that it was solid, and we began to jabber back and forth. Pretty soon I was spieling some about what a wonderful piano player Earl Hines was, the greatest in the world. My mind was reeling back through the South Side, recapturing ten years of great music, and my tongue leapfrogged along after it, stumbling and tripping all the way. Mike came back with "Yeah, Earl Hines may be great, but what you gonna do 'bout Fats Waller," and I said he was great too but he wasn't like Tony Jackson and Teddy Weatherford and Earl Hines, he was more in the Eastern style and that wasn't up to New Orleans. Then Mike spoke up again: "Man, we got some records back there by a guy from the Jungles called James P. Johnson that'll make them all look sick." He jumped up and went into another bin, where he dragged out an old winding phonograph and a real old Victor piano recording of James P.'s, with *Bleedin' Hearted Blues* on one side and *You Can't Do What My Last Man Did* on the other. I started to quiver something awful when I heard that piano jump. James P. really did play something like Tony Jackson on those numbers, with a little Eastern inflection but still he had two fists full of piano and he was knocking out the real blues too. Every chord was a hammer-blow on my skull. My lips wouldn't stay put. I was on the verge of tears.

The Mills Brothers' bass, and then that record that was loaded with nostalgia in every groove, did something to me; my heart was jittering around inside my ribs like a blowtop frog. I couldn't sit still. For the first time in many months, jazz had jumped up in my face, and it was like a one-two punch that nearly floored me. I was hearing echoes from out of the South Side, all buzzing into my ear with a special message. The music was talking to me, taunting me, and I heard every word it was saying. I almost had a fit.

Down to Western Union I flew, to send Louis an SOS in California, telling him I needed a hundred and fifty dollars right away, my life depended on it. The money came by return wire, although Pops didn't know what it was for and to this day hasn't found out. Then I shot to a music store and bought me a brand-new clarinet (my old one had been stolen while I was at Minsky's). And then I went home and put myself to bed with my clarinet, and called the doctor and told him I was going to break my habit once and for all, any way and every way he said. He just laughed at me, real cynical, like he'd heard that story before. All he could give me was some nembutal tablets so I wouldn't blow my lid completely when the agony got too great.

I was frightened: after a few days without hop, when I picked up my clarinet I couldn't even blow into it, I was so weak, and my hands trembled so much that the horn just slipped from my nerveless fingers. It was like a death-sentence to me, when I looked at the clarinet lying on the floor. . . . I laid around in bed for a week, while somebody slashed at every nerve in my body with a razor, and I just couldn't make it. Well, I figured, this is it, this is what you read about in the books—I'm hooked for life, you just can't get off the stuff.

I called up Mike and pleaded with him to bring me the joint (the layout) and put me out of my misery. Instead he came up with

253

some medicine, a patent product called Wampoole's Mixture that was supposed to help you taper off the stuff. What you did was, you took a toy (a tin) of hop and shook it up with this medicine in a bottle and kept taking it every day. As the bottle got empty you kept filling it up again with more of the medicine, so the amount of hop kept going down and finally you were taking practically straight medicine. The second day I almost drank the whole bottle, I felt so bad. It pepped me up enough so's I could get out of bed and then I made a beeline for The Bunk again, and that was the end of my cure.

Right after that Buck found out about my being hooked, but he never said a word to me. He was working Loew's State on Broadway just then, and he invited me to come down to see him. When I got to his dressing room, there was Ruby Zwerling, the leader of the pit band, in there with him, and Buck introduced us, saying "Ruby, this is Mezzrow, the guy I was telling you about. I want you to put him in the band on the saxophone 'cause he's doin' something I don't want him to do." I lasted there for two weeks. The music was so corny that I couldn't even look at it, and it flew by me so fast that I was on one act while they were all turning the pages for the next one. I was in a fog all the time. That music, plus the dull acts, made me eat up more hop than ever. The final touch was the movie they had on at the time, *Dr. Jekyl and Mr. Hyde*. That's one picture they should never show to a hophead.

When I was on a get-off chorus, able to improvise a little, all the other guys got happy, but when we stuck to arrangements I tried to phrase my own way, to make it halfway bearable, and so I had to go. One day they politely asked me to leave. Back I went to Mike's cellar. From one pit to another. I still don't know which was worse.

December 19, 1932. Wire from Louis' manager: LOUIS RECORDING TOMORROW NIGHT CAMDEN AFTER SHOW BE THERE REGARDS JOHNNY COLLINS. (The show, a road edition of "Hot Chocolates," was playing at the Lincoln Theater in Philly, using Chick Webb's band.) I drove off right away, and found Louis getting ready to make some of the first recordings under his new contract with Victor. He had a terrible sore lip, in addition to being dogtired, and that day he had played five shows and made two broadcasts. We started off for the Camden recording studios at 1:30 in the morning. I didn't see how poor old Pops was going to blow note one.

In the dead of night we drove up to a large red brick church. I wondered if we were going to have a special prayer service to make sure Louis got through this grind, but when we went through the chapel door I saw it was a recording studio. "This is funny, ain't it, Mezza," Louis said, "jammin' in a ole church." I came back with "Where else should Gabriel blow?" and it tickled him.

Eli Oberstein, RCA-Victor's recording manager, took us on a guided tour, down through the chapel and into some gloomy rooms full of echoes, spookier than a mystery thriller, everything vague and the shadows running like molasses. Finally he switched on the lights in one room and we saw hundreds of gleaming pipes lined up there, ranging from five to fifteen or twenty feet in height, standing like so many soldiers all straight and erect in their gilt coats. "Man," Louis said, "can you beat this? Looks like the calliope on them Mississippi riverboats." These pipes belonged to one of the largest organs ever built in a church, and many an organ recording was made on it by Fats Waller and Jesse Crawford.

They wouldn't let Chick Webb use his bass drum on this date, mainly because Louis' lip was in such bad shape and without the bass he wouldn't be pushed so hard. The first number he recorded was *That's My Home*, and when the band played it through I noticed some bad notes in the tuba part and the piano bass. The wheels started to creak and wheeze way back in my head somewhere, but pretty soon they were humming, and ideas started to pop up. Without hardly realizing what I was doing, I began to advocate, knowing that Louis had called me down here to help out any way I could. I went into a huddle with some of the musicians, singing a few bars of a bass part for them to play that I figured would make Louis' lead stand out more and add a climax to the theme.

The atmosphere got tense. All the cats began looking our way with questions in their eyes, all sort of nervous because this was the first time they'd ever heard me sounding off about any arrangement, and while they were all in my corner they didn't know could I do anything with the music. Even Louis had never seen me put to any trial musically, because up to then we'd only talked about the music. But if he was worried he sure didn't show it—his easygoing grin never once left his face.

Soon as we finished our conference and got our head arrangement straight, Louis stomped off and started the band, this time for a test record. Not a word was spoken all through that studio. Nobody even looked at me, but I had a kind of telepathic feeling that all thoughts were centered on me. This really was a test record —a test for me. I was plenty shaky. What a thrill I got when that revised bass part came thumping out loud and forceful. The moment Louis finished playing his lead passage, he tore his horn away from his lips, came running over to me bubbling with joy, and exclaimed "From now on Mezz is my musical director!" The tension in that room snapped like an overstretched elastic band. Everybody was laughing and smiling approval at me. My blood rushed to my cheeks and I felt warm all over. I couldn't say a word. Don't forget, I'd been away from the music for a long time, and this proved I still had some grip on the one important thing in my life. Maybe I could get back to it somehow, if I tried hard enough. There was a little hope.

The next number was called *Hobo You Can't Ride This Train*, and it really taxed all of Louis' genius. Here he was handed a corny lyric he'd never heard nor seen and told to ad-lib it on a record. While the band played through the arrangement, Louis stood there trying to match the simpy words to the music. "Mezz, come here," he said. "Now what am I gonna do with this? I don't know nothin' 'bout no hoboes, any more'n this song-wroter did." That was where my hoboing stood me in good stead. I started to buzz fast in Louis' ear, telling him that A-Number-One was the greatest hobo who ever lived, hoboes ride the rods, blinds and tops of trains, it's the brakeman who throws freebie passengers off, and stuff like that. Then one of the musicians scraped a curtain rod across a washboard, imitating a steam engine starting up, and I rang a train bell, and Louis was off.

Man, what he did with those lyrics. With nothing but the phrases I breathed in his ear to go on, he let his inventive genius run wild and this is how he started off:

My my my my, listen at that rhythm train boy,
Boys I'll bet all them hoboes are all set under them rods,
Even A-Number-One and all them cats, ha ha, yeah man. . . .
All aboard for Pittsburgh, Harrisburg, oh all the burgs,
Hobo, oh hobo, you can't ride this train,
Now hobo, oh hobo, hobo you can't ride this train,
Now boy I'm the brakeman and I'm a tough man,
I ain't jokin', you can't ride this train. . . .

And on the last chorus he finished up with

Now listen here boy, you, you, you ain't so bad after all,
You all right with me son, I think I will let you ride, heh, heh, heh.

After five shows, two broadcasts, and a couple of hours of recording, Louis was still going strong. You just couldn't down old Pops.

The show moved on to Baltimore, and there I saw one of the most dramatic and pathetic scenes of Louis' career. His lip had been plenty sore when he played Philly; now it was so bad, all raw and swole up, that he just sat and looked at it all day in a mirror, all the time applying some lip salve for trumpet players that Vincent Bach had put on the market, so it wouldn't be agony for him every time he blew into his horn. To make things worse, he kept picking at the great sore with a needle. I couldn't stand to see it, every prick went all through me, I was so afraid he might infect himself and have to stop playing altogether. But when I told him to stop he just chuckled at me. "Oh, that's all right Mezz, I been doin' this for a long time you know, got to get them little pieces of dead skin out 'cause they plug up my mouthpiece. Now you just sit down and don't worry 'bout nothin'. That's my job. You let me do the worryin' 'round here. You supposed to be happy and have a good time, see, you my boy, so just leave all the worryin' to me, I know how to handle that, ha ha!" His lip looked like he had a big overgrown strawberry setting on it.

That night was New Year's Eve. When Louis went onstage to play his specialty number the wings were filled up with chorus girls and performers, who always gathered backstage all hushed and reverent to hear him play. Some of the performers had friends visiting them too, and the house out front was all sold out. It was a tense moment. I was standing in the opposite wing from where Louis made his entrance, so I could see him come on and he could see me and do some mugging at me. I always stood in the opposite wing because he would march onstage singing "Mezzeerola" or some phrase like that while going up to the microphone, in tune with the music the band was playing. It made us both feel good.

Well, that night he came on singing "Happy New Year Mezzeerola," and flashing a big grin at me, and I sang back "The sa-ame to you-ou" to finish the intro. Then Louis raised his horn to start blowing, while the band played the background for *Them There Eyes*, and it was so quiet backstage you could have heard a chinch sneeze. Everybody knew Louis' lip was worse than it had ever been, and they all thought sure he wasn't going to make this performance. This was the real drama of Louis' life, taking place before all those people who thought they were just seeing another good show.

He started to blow his chorus, tearing his heart out, and the tones that came vibrating out of those poor agonized lips of his sounded like a weary soul plodding down the lonesome road, the weight of the world's woe on his bent shoulders, crying for relief to all his people. He was fighting all the way, aiming to see it through and be understood by all, right down to the last heartrending wail of his plea. All the lament and heartache of life, of the colored man's life, came throbbing out through that horn. That wasn't any horn blowing this night. It was the conscience of the whole aching world, shouting damnation at the sins and evil. There were tears in all the eyes around me, tears for what Louis was preaching on that horn, tears for wonderful, overworked, sick and suffering Louis himself, the hero of his race. Everybody knew that each time that horn touched his lips, it was like a red-hot poker to him. Nobody said a word. The usual excited cries of "Yeah Louis" or "Play it poppa" weren't heard tonight. It would have been sacrilege to break the spell this night. Pops had the floor and he was holding it all alone. Out of that horn poured all the world's misery, torrents and torrents of it, flooding all through the theater and lapping at all of us. Then came the climax.

Louis was playing his last chorus and it seemed like he would never make it. He was using all the showmanship and great technique that only he had at his fingertips. The audience thought he was superb, sensing that some terrific drama was going on before their eyes, and they were all froze to the edges of their seats, their mouths open and eyes glued on him. Every time Louis slid slowly, oh so slowly up into one of those high-gliding wails, moaning his way along, all of us backstage shook with fear. Each time it sounded like he wasn't going to get up there. This time for sure he would fall, and break, and collapse with the strain. We heard the torture vibrating behind each searing note. The whole theater was petrified.

Suddenly Charlie "Big" Green, the trombone player, busted out in tears and ran off the stand in the middle of the chorus. I saw that the whole band was crying. All the performers and all the chorus girls had wet eyes. Big Green came and stood beside me and we cried like babies, holding each other's hand while we waited for those unbearable last few bars where Louis had to scramble up to the high F.

Chick Webb used all the masterful tactics he knew on the drums, trying to roll and punch out his feelings for Louis, giving him all the foundation he could, while the tears streamed down his face. The lights came down to red and blue, because the manager didn't want the audience to see how everybody was sobbing.

Then it happened. Louis began that torturous climb up to high F, the notes all agonized and strangled, each one dripping blood. He was like the prodigal son who finally sights his home, sick and weary of a lifetime of roaming, determined to get back there before his heart stops beating. He was fighting and sweating blood all the way, and what came out of his horn sounded less like music than like the terrible wild shrieking of the lost and damned. The band rode along up with him, trying to push him, giving him a crutch to lean on and telling him, Poppa we're with you, don't tear your heart out, we'll get you up there 'cause we all love you so.

And then, with the last breath of life left in him, like a man in death convulsions, heaving with his heart and soul and lacerated guts for the last time, Louis clutched and crawled and made that high F on his hands and knees, just barely made it, at the last nerve-slashing second.

A shock and a shiver ran through the theater. The whole house shuddered, then rocked with applause. Louis stood there holding his horn and panting, his mangled lip oozing blood that he licked away, and he managed to smile and bow and smile again, making pretty for the people.

I ran to his dressing room, and found him wiping the perspiration from his face. All his clothes were soaked through, wringing wet. Like some gallant warrior of old he grinned and said "Tough scuffle Mezzie, but that's all in life. Ha ha!" Then I slipped some yen pox into my mouth and we went out to enjoy New Year's Eve.

15

CRAWL 'FORE YOU CAN WALK

MANICURING some ribs at the Barbeque. Up jumps a stocky white man with football shoulders, togged in gabardine slacks, rubber-soled shoes, and a plaid jacket two shades louder than a checker-board, looking like he just hopped out of the Brooks Brothers win-dow. "Mezz!" he yells, grabbing my hand and crunching all the bones in it. "Why man, I've been wanting to meet you for the longest time! Say, you're really the king up here, aren't you? I want you to promise me one thing—drop around to my office real soon. I'm going to show you something that'll make your eyes pop out." I gave him the double-o after I lamped the engraved card he handed me. His name was Gerald X., one of the biggest radio booking agents in the business, who managed a lot of headliners and originated a gang of big network shows. My heart jumped.

A few days later, soon as I waded through a corps of secretaries and got to his movie-set hide-away, he reached into a drawer and came up with a funny contraption. "Now this is a petrographic microscope, Mezz," he explained. "You can examine rocks and other solid objects through it without slicing them up on slides, see? You look down into their pores and see them in three dimen-sions." Then he fished out a pile of little cardboard boxes and said, "You know what I've got here? I've collected about a dozen differ-ent species of marihuana, including yours, and now I'm going to prove to you scientifically that yours is the best on the market. . . ." I just barely made it to a chair before my legs gave out.

He planted me at the microscope. "Now here's one brand that I got from a Mexican in Chicago," he said. "Look how dark and musty it is, ugh. Then here's another kind I got from some Spanish boy—it's lighter in color but still it looks musty." He went through all his samples, groaning and shuddering over what was being put over on the unsuspecting public, and then he put some of my stuff under the scope, and the difference knocked me out. "The mezz" had all the colors of the rainbow, bright and sparkling, and each piece stood out separate and clean-looking, like some sculptor had carved it grain by grain. "Man, isn't that pretty!" Gerald said with real enthusiasm. "Why, it's like a beautiful sunset, just feast your eyes on it! You could frame that picture and hang it in the Metropolitan."

Then I found out what his story was. He was just showing me why everybody was so crazy about my stuff, was all. Hell, I had a million dollars right in the palm of my hand and didn't know it. He was going to show me how to get rich. All we do is, we get some smart attorney, form a corporation and push the stuff on a national scale, see, with branch offices from coast to coast, see. It's not illegal, and just suppose we sold a hundred pounds a week in each city of 25,000 or over, which is a cinch because there are way over a million vipers in the country this very minute. Why, with a national sales campaign, some smart promotion, in no time at all, etc. I'd have an income in seven figures. Gerald would put up the cash to back me. What did I say?

I was almost speechless. I began to shake all over. "Gerald," I finally managed to say, "I came up here to beg you to sponsor me with a mixed band, and here you want me to go deeper into something that I'm trying to break away from. I don't think your reefer syndicate would go because there's all this talk about the government clamping down sooner or later, habit-forming or no habit-forming. And don't forget they threw some musicians in the jug out in California for ten days, no matter what the federal law says. If they do brand this stuff as a narcotic, you'll be in organized crime, and that never pays off—look at this Dixie Davis-Jimmy Hines case that's been hitting the front pages lately. Besides, I couldn't get enough of the muta for a big deal like that. . . . I'm afraid it's no go. If you want to go into a new business, let me tell you I know some of the greatest musicians alive and they're out of work and I could get them for a band just by lifting the phone. Just think, Gerald, the first mixed band in history, the top colored and white boys playing together. With your radio and advertising connections you could launch us off to a career in no time. How about that, instead of the reefer?" I was pleading with him.

"Mezz," Gerald said, "you sure are a character, but maybe you've got something there. Let me have a day or two to think it over. I'll give you a ring."

Two days later I was back in his office, trying to steady my hand so I could sign a contract that mentioned net earnings over $40,000 a year and some other fantastic jive I couldn't even read, I was so excited. That was August 18, 1933. The scheme was to whip my band into shape, then get a big network to okay us for sustaining. The radio people didn't go for the mixed-band idea, but they at least agreed to let me have Alex Hill, a fine colored arranger, front the band, and also I could use a great colored act, the Five Spirits of Rhythm. It was an opening wedge, anyhow. Gerald said that later, if we went over, we could maybe write our own ticket about the personnel. Man, we were in. It had started with muta and ended with music.

I went right to work on the personnel, phoning like mad all over the country—to Joe Sullivan in Little Rock, Arkansas, Bud Freeman and Floyd O'Brien in Chicago, Max Kaminsky and Gene Krupa in Boston. They all agreed to come just for carfare. Eddie Condon and Pee Wee Russell were in New York, and they jumped at the idea. I rounded out the brass section with some good guys I picked up downtown, around Broadway and 48th Street, and we were set.

Now for arrangements. I cornered Fats Waller in Irving Berlin's one day, and when he heard my story he yelled for some manuscript paper and pencils, sat down at a piano and wrote two tunes out for me, *Walkin' the Floor* and *John Henry*. Alex Hill was all for me too. "Mezz," he told me, "just make sure you got enough money to keep me in gin and I'll knock out some of the finest arrangements that ever was put down on paper with you." With such good friends behind me, I felt I couldn't miss. I explained to Alex how I was fighting for a mixed band, but the man said to wait till I got some power, then I could do what I wanted. Why wait, I wanted to know. That's been going down for years, everybody waiting and nothing happening. "Mezz," Alex said, "I can appreciate how you feel, but everybody don't feel like you do and I think the man is right, whether we like it or not. You got to crawl 'fore you can walk, so take it easy, Jim, and we'll see what we can do."

By the time all the guys showed up (except Gene; he never did come), Alex and I had about fifteen arrangements finished; we sat up all night at my piano, turning them out at the rate of one a day. All the solos were spotted to keep the boys happy, and we hardly wrote in any first-alto solos for me at all, to keep peace in the family. . . . Well, the very first day we went into rehearsal, good old businessman Red McKenzie showed up and went wild about the Five Spirits of Rhythm. Next afternoon he went down and sold this act to the Famous Door on 52nd Street, and they went to work for this café, the first downtown swing club, and stayed there a long time. They were the first colored group on 52nd Street, and they practically made that block the swing center it's been ever since. I didn't mind losing them. There was loads of talent to be had from the race, and I was glad to see them working steady.

All the Chicago boys were tickled over Alex's arrangements—they were simple, in the best New Orleans tradition, yet they packed the punch needed to swing a big band. The music was written with saxophone figures behind the brass that helped keep the beat going instead of fighting it, and made rich organ backgrounds behind the solos. The last chorus usually came on with a heavy ensemble, the brass voiced in open harmony that gave a big round effect to the music and still kept us more in the New Orleans idiom than any big-band arrangers do nowadays. Flares were always in the right places, to help build up the pulse, and we always saw to it that the chords we called "bellychords" came in where they belonged. (You'll find some good examples of this effect in the record I made a little later, *Swingin' with Mezz,* where in one place an A seventh appears in the key of B-flat, making an abrupt change that hits you in the belly like a shot of good brandy.) In bands today you have the rhythm section fighting the brass and the brass fighting the saxophones; the piano and the bass and the drums all vie with each other to be heard, doing freakish and sensational things to attract attention instead of melting all together to build up a big beat so the guys out in front can blow better. Today's orchestrations are all overloaded, or over-arranged, and you'll find Shostakovitch and Delius and Ravel and Debussy sticking their noses out of every other bar—which may make them interesting to the streamlined concert-goer, but it sure isn't jazz. Alex Hill wrote arrangements that *were* jazz.

I was walking on clouds, and it wasn't just the hop that sent me. The music was so good, the boys were playing so fine, all my old friends were back with me, playing the music we loved, and the future looked plenty bright. And then we were breaking the ice so far as the race issue was concerned. We couldn't miss. . . . Then came our audition. For one half hour we sat in the studio, without any audience or commentator, just playing music that was piped into a conference room for the network board to hear. Alex Hill directed, and when we finished he came up to me wiping his forehead. "Mezz," he said, "whatever happens you know you broke down a barrier here today. I think I can truthfully say that I am the first Negro to direct an all-white band in these studios." Some of my dreams were beginning to come true at last. We were okayed for a sustaining program, and the network even gave us a letter of credit so we could get some uniforms for the band! We needed those uniforms because we already had our first job, substituting for Guy Lombardo in a Long Island café. Things were breaking all around, and not only precedents. I was even readying myself to break my habit—the hard way, without any Wampoole's Mixture.

We went over fine at that café. All the guys seemed happier than they'd been in years, playing the kind of music that meant some-

265

thing to them. Then, one day after rehearsal, I noticed all the boys were packing up in a great hurry, and I sensed something in the air. Finally Alex came up to me and said, "Mezz, I tried to keep from telling you this but I guess you might as well know what's going down right now as later. The boys are going to another rehearsal that Red McKenzie arranged with some politician's son named Cass Hagan who wants to be a band leader. Eddie Condon and Red asked me to make the arrangements for them but I stalled them off and they got Benny Carter instead."

I was ready to quit right there; I had no aim in life any more but to get up to The Bunk fast and fill myself full of hop. But Alex said no, we would fight it out and see who stayed. Next day the boys started out again for their private rehearsal. Max and Bud came back to me and said, "Milton, we've been rehearsing behind your back with Cass Hagan, but you needn't worry. The band stinks. They got Benny Carter to make the arrangements, and we've been rehearsing three days on the first eight bars of the first number, and we can't get it out yet. Benny sure is a friend of yours—he must have written it that way on purpose." That's the way with the race. Your friends give you a boost, and trip up the ones who aren't in your corner, and not a peep do you get out of them about it. Their actions tell the story.

Double trouble. Now comes a telephone call from Miss Lil, old Mike's wife. "Boy, you better come on down here right away," she said. "Don't ask me no questions, just meet me at 134th Street and Eighth Avenue at my sister's house. I got some talk for you." All I could think of was that the law had nailed Mike and Mackey in The Bunk. Well, I flew into my car and tore down Eighth Avenue, and when I got near 135th Street it looked like all the law in the country was holding a convention out in front of Mike's tenement; police cars were parked all over the street, stopping traffic on both sides, and I didn't hardly know whether to risk stopping or go on to rehearsal. But I pulled up to see Lil.

She came running down the stoop. "You know that juice joint up on the second floor?" she said. She was talking about the King-Kong pad in Mike's building. "Well, that new bouncer that they just brought up here from Carolina and Mackey had it last night, on account of that chick that's tendin' bar up there. You know Mackey and her were goin' together, and this bouncer man was kind of sweet on her too. Well, early this mornin' they was keepin' a lot of rumpus up there, and Mackey went up to keep them quiet. They doublebanked him and knocked him out with a piece of pipe, and Mackey came back in with his head bleedin' like a stuck pig. About an hour later the law came knockin' at our door and said he had to take Mike and Mackey to the station, 'cause the bouncer upstairs had been murdered. Somebody fired a shot right through the door, the one that's covered with a sheet of steel, and it hit him right square in the heart, many people as there was in there. God sure don't like ugly. They let Mike out but they held Mackey 'cause he had the fight with this guy before."

When Miss Lil finished her story I was no more good, and I went to rehearsal with my spirit dragging the floor. At rehearsal I found out Eddie Condon had gone to the Brunswick people and arranged for a recording date with the band, all on his own. Alex asked would I be angry if he made the arrangements—they were paying good money and he needed some then. I told him O.K. I knew he was solid for me and it wasn't his fault. Then I decided to throw in the sponge. Chalk up another victory for the entrepreneurs.

Mike and I hired a good lawyer for Mackey, and went down to see him in the Tombs. The poor old guy was scared to death, and we told him we were going to do everything we could for him. I asked him in front if he did it. He swore he didn't. "Mike can tell you that," he said. "After they hit me on the head with that pipe and a free-for-all got goin' on the joint, I crawled downstairs and Mike bathed my head for the longest time and I laid down to sleep. Now gate, you know you ain't never seen no pistol round the house and I don't know how to use one, but I'm goin' to plead guilty and take that time. You don't know what it feels like, waitin' in your cell to find out if you goin' to fry or not, and you know I ain't pink and I got two strikes against me now."

I believed Mackey's story all the way, and I still do. But he was plenty scared of the white man's court. He went up for a hearing and the judge appointed two more attorneys to the case, and these mouthpieces finally made a deal with the D.A. for Mackey to plead guilty to manslaughter or something like that, and Mackey was ready to do it because at least it meant he wouldn't burn. He was sent up to Sing Sing for seven-and-a-half to fifteen years, our old friend was, and without a single yen pox on him. By that time I was a man without a band again. I had plenty yen pox.

Gerald X.? His wind-up wasn't so good. I heard that he died a year or two later from the usual "overdose of sleeping pills," but some say it was heroin, or some kind of evil white stuff.

I went around to see Jack Kapp, recording manager at Brunswick, and told him my story, I was so mad. "If I give you a date, your records won't sound like Condon's, will they?" he wanted to know. I assured him they wouldn't, and got the date. Then I flew over to see Benny Carter. We only had a week to prepare our arrangements, so I sat down and wrote *Dissonance*, and also dug up one Alex and I had done called *Swingin' with Mezz*. Benny came up with two of his own, *Free Love* and *Love You're Not the One for Me*.

Then came the problem of men. Benny had just started his own band, and from it we took Teddy Wilson on piano, Johnny Russell on tenor, and Benny himself on sax, so with me on alto and clarinet that made four. I think this was Teddy's first date for Brunswick, and led to his getting a contract with them. For trumpets I got Ben Gusick, Max Kaminsky, and Freddie Goodman (Benny's brother), and Floyd O'Brien on trombone. Then there was Jack Sunshine on guitar, George "Pops" Foster on bass, Jack Maisel on drums. For one afternoon, at least, I had a real mixed band.

Teddy Wilson plays one of his finest solos on *Dissonance*, but it was Benny himself who gave me my biggest surprise. I had composed and arranged *Dissonance* long before, hoping to have Louis record it some day, and you get a pretty good idea of what Pops would have done to it from Benny's trumpet solo. I'd always known he was one hell of a sax man, but on this date he pulled out a trumpet and was gone, then topped it all by singing a chorus on the back of the record, and that was solid too. . . . Later, when the record was released in England, Louis was over there and he wrote: "Say Gate . . . how wonderful your records are. Everybody enjoys them very much. All of them are perfect. My favorite one is Love your not the one for me and the one where your trumpet player hits that F right square in the face Yea man. By the way who is that fellow? Who ever he is hes mess (Mezz) I aint no playin Hes perfect. . . ." That was Benny Pops was raving about.

I wandered back into the opium fog after that date, and didn't even try to break my habit again till the next year. In the Spring of 1934 RCA-Victor contacted me, saying Panassié had asked them to have me record and would I be interested in a date. That brought me out of my daze a little. Right away I got busy with Floyd O'Brien, who was living with me then, and together we arranged *35th and Calumet*. Then I wrote and arranged *Apologies,* and got out an arrangement of *Old Fashioned Love* by Alex Hill and me. The last number was a head arrangement I got together right in the studio, called *Sendin' the Vipers*. On this date we had no less than four colored orchestra leaders who were on their way to the top: Benny Carter on alto sax, Chick Webb on drums, John Kirby on bass, and Willie The Lion on piano. In fact, just about everybody on that session won the fame they deserved but Floyd O'Brien, who I consider studied harder and got closer to the New Orleans trombone style than any white man that ever lived. . . . So, once again, I was the mixed-band king for a day.

I tried again to break my habit, this time with Mike. Just couldn't make it; guess I didn't have enough incentive. My mind kept nagging me, telling me to go back to the music, but the craving was too deep under my skin, and the music too far away. . . . Mike saw how I suffered, and tried to console me by naming all the powerful men who had been hopheads at one time or another, but it didn't help. My mind wasn't eased even a little until Fats Waller came around and hired me for a recording date at Victor. I told him about Floyd, and he said sure, bring him along too. On this date we made six sides: *How Can You Face Me, Sweetie Pie,*

Mandy, You're Not the Only Oyster in the Stew, Let's Pretend That There's a Moon, and *Serenade to a Wealthy Widow*.

Just about then I got another lift. I'd been arguing with Louis for all of two years, trying to convince him he had a terrific future waiting for him if he toured England and Europe, and he'd been afraid of the idea, but finally he took my advice. When he went over there, first in 1932 and then later on a very long tour, he like to caused a riot wherever he went. He sent me a whole batch of clippings about the wild receptions he got, and they knocked me out. Best of all, he was an inspiration to Hugues Panassié, who went overboard for Pops and helped to arrange his concerts around Europe. Hearing Louis' great horn was such an eye-opener to Hugues that he sat right down and wrote his first book on jazz, which was a trail-blazer in lots of ways, even though he didn't have his perspectives at all straight yet. The book was *Le Jazz Hot*, and one day a copy of it arrived in the mails, with a little dedication written on the fly-leaf: "Dear Milton, if you had not come to France and taught me so many things I would never have been able to write this book."

Well, I figured, at least I had helped to spread the gospel around a little, and I'd done my modest bit to further the careers of two wonderful guys, Louis and Hugues. I might be finished, but they were just getting started. . . . I kept reading Hugues' inscription, and pasting Louis' press clippings in a scrapbook. It wasn't much consolation. I went on smoking my pills, and eating my yen pox, and feeling mighty bad.

You hear sometimes of these proud hermit guys who go forth into the wilderness, all alone under the twinklers, and have a great soul-shaking showdown with themselves, wrastling with that beast inside. In October of '34 I packed up with my family and moved out to Jackson Heights, Long Island, to fight it out in the wilderness of the Borough of Queens. No dice. I tried my damnedest, couldn't make it. . . . To ease my mind a little, every night I'd have Fats Waller, Teddy Wilson, Ben Webster, Floyd O'Brien, Max Kaminsky, Buck, and a gang of musicians come out, for a private jam session. Fats loved the Steinway grand in my living room, and Teddy too would sit there for hours playing. Down in the cellar I had an upright, so we could jam all night long without breaking up the neighborhood. When Gene Krupa first came out to visit me, he took a look at the layout and said, "Man, this looks like one of those Hollywood houses that you see in the movies." There was only one difference: this house had tins of opium stashed in every bureau.

I tried to stop selling the gauge, but when I'd fall out on The Avenue cats would say "Man, what you goin' to do with us, Mezz. If you don't want to push it no more, give the connection to somebody else, but don't let your people down like that." The Mexican who supplied me said that he would quit when I did, because he didn't want to do business with anybody else, but I couldn't tell the boys that—they would have thought I was jiving. I was really in the middle, what with the habit and the gauge and my rusty clarinet tugging at me from different directions. Day after day I'd go down in the cellar to practise, but the opium would make me fall asleep. One day I nodded and nodded till the clarinet fell right out of my hands. When that horn hit the floor, my blood froze. . . .

It got to be 1935, the days all clumping by on clubfeet. Then one fine day Louis popped up, just in from Europe, and moved out to my house. There was a Broadway agent who was mighty anxious to sign Pops up, because he had split up with Johnny Collins over in France, and this guy offered us a three-man corporation, me being the musical director and him the business manager. He offered me a thousand bucks if I could produce Louis in his office, and I brought him around there and the agent handed me his check for one grand. But when he showed us the corporation papers not a trace of my name could I spot anywhere; the guy was pulling a fast one, trying to tie Louis up all by himself. "Come on Mezz, let's go," Louis said, and dragged me out of the place. I took the check and tore it in a million pieces and strewed it all over the man's rug. . . . Back in my car I lost all control and began to cry like a baby. I tried to tell Pops that I had to get away from the tea racket because I wasn't happy, I needed to play music, that was where life began and ended for me. Now my chance to get with him was gone again. I couldn't bring myself to tell him about the habit, but it sure fed my weeps some too. "Mezz, stop cryin'," Louis said. He was about ready to bust out in tears himself. "Don't worry, I'll go back to Chi and rest my chops for a while, and you go to work on some arrangements for me and we'll start out together. Get that horn out and start workin' up your lip and you can get out in front of the band. I'll just come out and do my specialties, and then when your name gets big enough you can go and start your own band." I stopped crying then. It was on the tip of my tongue to tell him about the worst complication of all, but the words just wouldn't come.

When we got back home, Louis wrote out a note to Local 802 of the Associated Musicians of Greater New York, announcing to whom it may concern that Milton Mezzrow was his manager and musical director. Bad as I felt, I couldn't help smiling. I told him there wasn't any need for papers between the two of us. Then he pulled out his American Express traveler's checkbook and began to write. "Look Mezz," he said, "here's a thousand dollars, we're goin' to make plenty more and I'm stickin', I won't need it. You stop sellin' the gauge and pay up about six months' rent so's you can sit down and write some arrangements with a clear head, nobody knockin' at your door for the rent." I refused the money, so he tried to stash it away under the shirts in my bureau, and finally I compromised by taking five hundred of it. Then he left for Chicago, and soon he wrote to me (on March 12th), saying that his lips were getting better all the time, and he was knocking out a lot of new arrangements with Randolph, his second trumpet player. "You see 'Gate'" he wrote, "I figure with you and Randolph handling the Arrangement department I can't go wrong. Eh?"

It looked like I really was going to go with Louis, after all these years. There was the biggest chance of my life, dangling right in my face. I had to straighten myself out, right quick. I sat down and went to work on some arrangements for Louis, and I ran smack into that brick wall again—in two minutes I'd be nodding off, my eyes all fuzzy and my mind as alert as seaweed, and my elbows would slip off the piano and crash down on the keyboard. I couldn't keep my attention on the notes, couldn't even stay awake. I wasn't breaking the habit. It was breaking me.

Something sure got to go, I told myself—the hop or me. On April the 6th I called Doc Grad. "Doc," I said, punctuating my words with yawns, "you've got to promise to come out to the house every day from now on, because this time I'm going to cure myself or bust. I don't care if you chain me to the wall, or tie me up in a straitjacket, or stick me in a padded cell, you've got to help me keep away from the hop, you've got to." Then I dove into bed. I was asleep before I hit the pillow.

The doctor was blunt about it. "Milton," he said, "it's no use wasting your time and mine. You've tried several times before and it didn't work. There's one in a million that ever gets away from that stuff so there's no use kidding yourself."

"Oh yeah," I said. "Well doc, you can say it's two in a million now, because I'm breaking away right now."

"O.K.," he said wearily. "Have this prescription filled and stay in bed, and I'll be out again in the morning." The medicine was yellow nembutal capsules, to be taken as a sedative.

That night I slept pretty well, but I woke up in the morning wringing wet, my mind as soggy as the bedclothes. Pretty soon the doctor showed up and told me to double the dosage of nembutal, and then he took my wife aside. As I learned later, he gave her strict orders to disconnect the phone and allow me no visitors until he said so. I was to be treated like a prisoner, held incommunicado. That was to make sure that when the agony got too much I couldn't make any last-minute connection and start the merry-go-round whirling again.

I began to feel terrible weak. Along towards evening I started to throw up, and a sad case of dysentery took hold of me. I kept whipping around in the bed like an insomniac snake, my legs aching till I couldn't stand it, and I was dripping worse than a shower-bath. Then my head puffed up big as a dirigible and just floated off among the planets, somewhere beyond Saturn; I got delirious,

273

began to scream for the doctor, and swallowed almost all of those yellow capsules in one gulp. Bonnie and the doctor wound in and out of my feverish ravings, sponging me, taking my pulse, checking on my temperature, and most of the time I didn't know whether they were really there or was I just imagining them. I tossed and turned and screamed at the top of my lungs at everybody who was conspiring to do away with me. All of my nerves joined in the chorus, some bawling, some bellowing, some just whimpering, but none of them still for a moment. The doctor gave me some more medicine, much larger capsules this time and white instead of yellow. "Take one of these," he said, "and you'll go right to sleep," and he told Bonnie to give me one every time I woke up. They were some powerful kind of knockout powder; each one clunked me on the skull like a brickbat.

In the middle of the night I woke up yelling "Murder! Murder! They're killing me! You're a murderer!" and the neighbors heard me through the brick walls and called the cops. Legs Diamond and Babyface Coll and Dutch Schultz and Scarface and Louis the Wop, along with a gang of other mugs I couldn't quite recognize but still their murderous leers were sort of familiar, had been chasing me all over the Milky Way somewheres, and it was wet and slippery, gooey so I kept sinking and sliding, and they were all hugging enormous diamond-studded opium pipes close to their ribs like tommy guns, and they kept pelting me with hand grenades that thudded against my body with a sickening sticky softness because they weren't metal at all but great big overgrown yen pox, and I ran and ran, hearing a wailing weeping horn blasting away in my ears, and I knew if only I could find that horn Louis would be behind it and I would be saved but Louis wasn't anywhere, not behind any of the tremendous glistening diamonds that were planets, and when I got closer I saw that all those planets were diamonds and they were all set in tremendous opium pipes that stretched clear across the sky and out of sight, and behind each one was the evil leering face of Legs Diamond or Babyface Coll or Dutch Schultz. . . . I sure cussed up a breeze in my delirium. Bonnie gave me another knockout capsule and off to sleep I went, falling down and down, head over heels, into a big bottomless pit filled with blackness that was velvet-soft and yielding, gooey, suffocating. . . . In the morning I had the awfullest feeling of my whole life. I'd yawn for fully a minute, my mouth stretching wide open, and the hinges of my jaws hurt so bad I could hardly close my mouth again. Tears gushed out of my eyes and my nose ran like Niagara Falls, no blowing or nothing, just a steady stream down over my lips. The sheets were all soaked, and I couldn't control any of my functions. The muscles of my legs hurt so bad I just laid there kicking like a bike-racer on the seventh day. I screamed till poor Bonnie had a fit.

Then, just when I thought I couldn't take it any more, an idea hit me. Right away I got very oily and shrewd. I told Bonnie slyly to go down to the drugstore for some Sloane's Liniment to rub my aching muscles, figuring that while she was out I would sneak down to the cellar and find some empty tins of opium stashed away there and scrape enough together to eat and take this bad feeling off me. Soon as she left I tried to stand, and my knees caved in and I fell over backwards. When I opened my eyes, I found Bonnie standing over me with a wet towel, trying to raise me off the floor. I had conked myself on the radiator—my head was bleeding and I'd been out cold for half an hour. The doctor came again, and told me to take two of the white capsules instead of one. I did, and felt much better right away. . . . A little later, the doc confessed to me that those knockout capsules contained nothing but some real powerful powdered sugar.

Well, for about a week I couldn't stand to even smell food cooking, and the smoke from a cigarette made me nauseous. I lost about thirty pounds that first week, and it like to scared me to death. The second week I began to feel a little better, but my legs kept giving me a fit. It's funny: when you first take hop it goes right to your legs, and when you try to break away from it your legs go bad too. Coming or going, the hop aims straight for your pedal extremities. . . . Doc Grad kept telling me he never believed I'd do it, but now that I'd finally made it I had to stay in bed till he told me to get up. As if I could have moved even my little finger without a derrick. By the third week I could sit up for a few minutes at a time. With a little bit of arguing you could have convinced me I was alive.

Then something happened that almost sent me back to the hop. Just before I decided to break the habit, I traded my old car in for a new one. Now, just about when I was ready to get out of bed, a fellow from the finance company came out with some papers for me to sign. Bonnie showed him up to the bedroom, and he put the papers in my lap and handed me a fountain pen. When I tried to sign my name I couldn't write letter one.

If you ever want to feel that you're through for good, you should have that happen to you. I had no more control over my hands than a newborn babe. Now, I thought, I really know why they say you can never break a habit, and that you always go back to the stuff. That poor guy just looked at me with his mouth wide open. "Gee," he said, "you really must have been sick, don't bother signing now, I'll be back again sometime later." He grabbed his hat and coat and couldn't get out of the house fast enough. I just lay back and stared at my trembling hands. There was nothing in the world I craved just then but a tin of hop, a whole vat of it, so I could dive into it and never come up again. A guy who can't handle a fountain pen can't do much with a clarinet.

I grabbed the phone and told the doc about it. Laying back in the bed, all I could see was the opium layout dancing in front of my eyes. I thought of Louis waiting for some arrangements from me, and I started to sweat. Then I remembered Thomas De Quincey. Once before, when I went to break my habit, I'd bought a copy of *Confessions of an Opium Eater*, but that guy's experiences sounded so different from mine that I never bothered to finish it. Now I remembered that he spoke about all the pains and body troubles he had when he broke the habit, so I sent Bonnie downstairs to get the book, and this time I read it from top to bottom. The doc came in while I was studying it, and smiled when he saw what I was reading.

He sat down at the foot of the bed and said, "Milton, I know just what's on your mind, but don't worry. Why, just last night at a meeting we doctors hold once a month to discuss different cases of interest, I told them about your case and they would hardly believe it was true. So you can't let me down now. You see, you have to start life all over again—learn to walk, talk, write and everything else right from scratch, like a kid. You know it says in the Bible, 'and a little child shall lead them.' Well, think those words over, and when you're able to, you go out in the street and play with the little kids, those around seven or eight, get in their ball games and see through their eyes, and gradually everything will come back to you. The weather is nice now, and you can start to take little walks soon, after you've eaten for a while and gained some strength back. Then, pretty soon, all will be well again. You'll even start to play your clarinet, but not right away. First you've got to serve your apprenticeship out on the sandlot, and let those little children show you the way."

I couldn't understand everything he said, but it made me think of what Alex Hill once told me: You got to crawl before you can walk. Just then I couldn't even crawl; my legs were about as much use to me as a couple of India-rubber stilts, and I had so much trouble sleeping nights that the doc told Bonnie to massage my aching muscles with cocoa butter. I went back to De Quincey, but the best he could tell me was to drink some ammoniated tincture of valerian, which he took because he had such awful pains in his stomach. That cat had got himself a belly habit, which didn't apply to me. I thanked my lucky stars then that Mike and Mackey had warned me about the different habits, because while discussing opium in The Bunk one day they hipped me. "Gate," Mike said, "be sure you take a bottle of magnesia at least twice a week, 'cause if you don't you'll get a belly habit and that's the worst kind there is. Man, you double up with such cramps when your yen comes on, you can hardly draw on a pill." I was smart, for once. Instead of taking two bottles a week I took one every single night, before going to bed.

My spirits were jumpy, going into nosedives one minute, soaring high and hopeful the next. Sometimes I was afraid, and just huddled up in bed with the shakes, not daring to think ahead. Other times I was all rosy and glowing, sure of the future, confident I would make it. . . . I began to eat up a breeze, so I could get out of bed and into the street. Finally, one beautiful sunny afternoon in May, after thirty solid days in bed, I decided to take a walk.

When I went to put on my clothes I stared at them in amazement: the colors were dazzling and the textures were weird and exciting when I ran my hands over them, my socks felt funny, the shoes weighed a ton. I felt like a clown got up in polka-dot motley, with all the colors of the rainbow. It all hit me like a brand-new experience, and I was so tickled I wanted to shout for joy. The bathroom was some kind of fairyland, full of wonderful smooth snow-white playthings and crazy gleaming pipes that wound in and out—it was the sort of feeling you get when you're on the road a long, long time and then you wind up in some hotel room you never were in before, and it makes you a little dizzy. The water sounded so funny coming out of the faucet, when I heard it gurgling and splashing I thought it was laughing and I felt so good I wanted to laugh too. I could hardly wait to get out of doors, I was so sure the world out there, under the friendly bright sun, was jammed with wonders. I wouldn't have been surprised, just then, if I walked out into a land of peppermint-stick trees and roads paved with chocolate fudge.

When I got to the stairs I stopped, puzzled; I couldn't make up my mind which foot to use first. Finally I got out into the open air and took one deep breath and where did I do that before, I thought. The air was full of marvelous perfumes, it made my head swim. It was a new world, fresh out of its cellophane wrappings, all shiny and untarnished. The trees and houses were all mysterious, fantastic; I gaped around like I'd never seen such things in my life. I walked down to the corner, strolling on air, cushioned with love and joy, and I could hardly make it back upstairs again, I was so weak and overcome by all the sights and sounds and smells. I asked my wife to bring me my clarinet, and I put it together and wet the reed. When I tried to blow, the tone that came out was all wheezy and out of tune, and I could hardly hold enough air in it to produce a whole note. I put it away again, and fell into a coma.

The next few days caught me out on the street again, playing with kids who were all eight or nine years old. I coached them a little on big-league pitching form, and taught one promising youngster how to throw a curve. The sound of their excited high-pitched voices brought tears to my eyes. I was back on the sandlot on the Northwest Side, back in Humboldt Park, standing up at the plate all poised and tense while good old Sullivan smacked his big catcher's mitt behind me and Emil Burbacher jumped around at first and Bow Gistensohn was winding up in the pitcher's box, ready to heave a tricky curve at me. . . . Along about suppertime I began to listen to all the kid programs on the air, *Jack Armstrong*, *Dick Tracy* and all the rest. I got all wrought up when the get-away car skidded over the cliff and the desperadoes dug their tunnel right under the warden's office and the secret agent's plane ran out of fuel right over the highest range of the Andes, far above the weird lost city of the Incas that no white man had ever set eyes on before. Everything that happened was wonderful, full of mystery, telling me it was good to be alive in this strange world where all things were possible, your daydreams were acted out right before your eyes.

One night I was sitting there listening, and then I got up and took my clarinet and locked myself in my room. I put the horn together and looked at it for a long, long time. Then I raised it to my lips and blew. A beautiful, full, round and true note came vibrating out, a note with guts in it, with life and pounding strength. And then I started to cry.

I had cried plenty the last four years, but this time my tears were tears of pure joy. I was human. I was awake. I was 'live again.

BOOK 4 (1935–?)

BASIN STREET IS THE STREET

Oh, Basin Street is the street
Where black and white always meet,
In New Orleans, land of dreams,
You'll never know how sweet it seems
Or just how much it really means. . . .

Old version of BASIN STREET BLUES

16

GOD SURE DON'T LIKE UGLY

BUDDY, don't ever trot back from the grave—it only upsets people. After I opened my eyes, blinked a few times, and paddled frantically back across the River Styx, it took me five years and more to convince the world I was alive and kicking again. Seems like folks get right insulted that you won't stay properly dead and buried. The way some of them glared, I felt like I ought to scram back into my hole and zip the lawn shut above me. . . . Then there was my home life to get straight. Soon as I was back on my pins, I began running up to Harlem again, the only place where I felt I belonged at all. That was too much for Bonnie to take, and one day she upped and told me, "Milton, I stuck by you all through your sickness because I couldn't leave you alone then, but now we've got to face it—it just wasn't meant to work out between us two. You live in one world and I live in another, and we can't shut our eyes to it any longer." She was right, too. She'd taken plenty, sticking with me for so long, and I couldn't ask her to string along any more, especially when I didn't know where I was heading myself. We shook hands and parted the best of friends. . . . Then, to top it off, Louis Armstrong and I drifted apart for many a long year. As soon as I had strength enough to push the brake pedal down, I got in my car and rushed over to Washington in the hopes of getting with Pops finally, like he had said. The first words he spoke to me, sort of hurt and abrupt, were, "Where in the hell are those arrangements you promised me?" I had some with me, *Dissonance* and a few others, but I was so brought down I couldn't find words to explain. To make things worse, Louis had never received my special-delivery

283

answer to the last letter he'd sent me, so he thought I just never bothered to reply. In the end I had to ask him for some money to get back home, and he dug into his pocket and gave me half of what he found, three bucks. I managed to get across the George Washington Bridge all right, by coasting most of the way back; my car ran out of gas and stalled just as I hit 125th Street. Miss Lil was right: God sure don't like ugly. . . .

Then Irving Mills, manager for Duke Ellington and Cab Calloway, started some kind of "Cavalcade of Music" and he was sold on the idea of me having a band in it, so I signed contracts with him for a fourteen-piece orchestra. He blew up my picture and hung it between Cab's and the Duke's in his reception room, but the months stumbled by and no bookings did we see, and no recording dates, so finally I took my contract back and tore it up. . . . One night I was sitting in Big John's café up in Harlem when in walked a colored girl, tall and slender and with a warm smile on her face that had an aggravating question-mark in it, and when I looked at her I felt funny all over. Her name was Johnnie Mae, and she smiled when we were introduced and looked me straight in the eye and that was that. I wound up divorcing Bonnie, and in July of 1935 Johnnie Mae and I took that big step. Bonnie was as understanding about it as she was about most other things; her whole life was wrapped up in her fine son, and she'd always been satisfied because I looked out for him and treated him like my own, and the youngster and I were always great buddies. Bonnie came around to see Mae, and when our son Milton, Jr. was born, in May of 1936, she came up to see him too, and acted like a wonderful friend to us all. I moved up to Harlem with Johnnie Mae, and haven't left since.

Well, I really had to scuffle for a while, trying to make it in the music business and selling a little gauge on the side, because now I had two women to support, and pretty soon two kids too, and believe me the weight was dragging me. On June 6, 1936, good old Eli Oberstein ("O.B.") at Victor gave me a date to make some records under the Bluebird label, and when we showed up (the band was called "Mezz Mezzrow and His Swing Band") we didn't even know what tunes we were going to play until Eli came in the studio and handed them to me. They were mostly pop songs from moving pictures: *Lost, Melody from the Sky, Mutiny in the Parlor, The Panic Is On,* and Stuff Smith's *I'se A-Muggin'* (Parts One and Two). Originally I brought Henry "Red" Allen and Dave Nelson (trumpets), Sidney Bechet (soprano sax and clarinet), Willie The Lion Smith (piano), Albert Casey (guitar), Wellman Braud (bass), and George Stafford (drums). But while we were getting set I spotted Eli in the control room with John Hammond the jazz critic, and when they signalled for me to come inside I could see something was up. First off they told me I couldn't use Red Allen because he was under contract to some other company, and then Hammond sprang something else. "Mezz," he said earnestly, "you shouldn't have brought Bechet on this date, the two of you play so much alike that there won't be any contrast. Why don't you get somebody like Bud Freeman?" The remark about Bechet made me dummy up—here I'd been walking around with my head in the clouds because at last I was going to have a chance to get together with the one guy who, more than anybody else, spoke my language, the exact same idiom, so we'd be able to tear loose and romp around each other without friction. But I had to cancel the date that day on Hammond's say-so, and when we returned the next afternoon I had Frankie Newton on trumpet and Bud Freeman on sax. It was to be a long time yet before the critics and recording directors would let me get together with Bechet the way all my musical instincts yearned to.

I was practically locked out of the musical world for a whole year after that, except for occasional gigs and jam sessions, until on May 7th of 1937 I got another date from O.B., this time on the Victor label. We made four sides that day: *Blues in Disguise, That Is How I Feel Today, Hot Club Stomp,* and *The Swing Session's Called to Order.* The first three were arranged by Edgar Sampson and myself (Edgar was the guy who wrote the popular *Stompin' at the Savoy*), and the last one was an arrangement by Larry Clinton, whom O.B. was just beginning to build up as an orchestra leader. Here's the personnel on that date, under the title of the "Mezz Mezzrow Orchestra": Sy Oliver on trumpet (now Tommy Dorsey's ace arranger, who was then playing and arranging with Jimmy Lunceford's band), J. C. Higginbotham on trombone, Happy Cauldwell on tenor sax, Sonny White on piano, Bernard Addison on guitar, wonderful old Pops Foster on the bass, James Crawford on drums, and myself on clarinet.

And that was how it went, mostly coffee-an' stuff—until suddenly I woke up to find myself leading an all-star mixed band right on Broadway, the first one ever to hit Times Square, and bringing the house down every night too. The color line along the Great White Way wasn't broken, exactly, but it sure got dented some, during the weeks we blew our lumps down there.

"O.B.," I said, "I've got to start a mixed band, I've *got* to. You're the one guy in this business who understands what it's all about, and you've got to get me some backing." I was sitting in Eli Oberstein's office, pleading with him. The words weren't out of my mouth good before he was on the phone, making the wires hum, and a few hours later we were both sitting in a Broadway nightclub called the Harlem Uproar House (on 52nd Street, just off Broadway), huddled over a steak with the owner of the joint, Jay Faggin.

"Here's the idea," Eli said. "Mezz organizes a fifteen-piece all-star mixed band. We open it here at the Uproar House on November 20th. That's the same night we're inaugurating the RCA-Magic Key program on the air, so we spot the band on our radio show for a build-up. Recordings to follow. Promotion. My attorney will draw up corporation papers and we'll all be in business."

"Set," said Jay Faggin.

"I" I said in a low whisper. I choked on my drink.

When I came to, Jay and I discussed a new entertainment policy for the Uproar House. The joint wasn't doing so well right then, being in receivership and all, with Jay as the trustee appointed by his creditors, but we figured we had some drawing-cards that would pull the place out of the red. Instead of just killing time with the usual line of chorus girls, we'd get five teams of lindyhoppers from the Savoy Ballroom. Then for some acts: Hazel Scott was singing and playing at the little bar in the lobby, and we'd spot her in the floor show; Willie The Lion Smith would be hired for piano specialties; Lovey Lane, a very pretty soubrette, would do dance specialties; Flash Riley, an interpretive dancer, would be teamed up with Lovey Lane in a spectacular African dance routine; Dolly Armendra, a sensational colored female trumpeter from the old days of the South Side, would be featured with the band; Eli would get hold of the Casseras Brothers Trio to play between our sets. So far, so good. It was really shaping up.

I tore up to Zutty Singleton's place. "Zoot, I got it this time," I started to babble. "We're in the money, Jim, sit down and let me lay this jive on you poppa. My dream has finally come true."

Zutty thought I was feverish and tried to calm me down. "Take it easy Mezz," he said, "take it easy, what's this mess all about?"

"Man, I don't know where to start. Dig this, I went down to see Eli Oberstein today. . . ." I finally got the story out.

"Wow!" Zutty yelled. "This is it, ain't it gate! Man, we got to have a drink on that." As we were skipping down the avenue, he asked did I have a library, and I remembered all the old Alex Hill arrangements, but then we dropped over to see Count Basie at the Apollo, and he said "Great deal, man," as soon as we laid our racket on him, and slipped us some wonderful arrangements from his own library.

Now to get us a hunk of personnel. Eugene Cedric, clarinetist and tenor saxophonist, was with Fats Waller, but Fats was doing a single then and his band was laying off, so Cedric was tickled to come with us. Frankie Newton was playing trumpet with John Kirby on 52nd Street, but he gave his notice and joined. Sidney De Paris, the trumpet player, left Charlie Johnson to join. George Lugg the trombone player, whom I'd known in Chicago, joined. Vernon Brown, also on trombone (one of the St. Louis group of musicians from the old days), also joined. I sent Max Kaminsky train fare and he came down from Boston and joined. So there was my brass section. Then I hired Bernard Addison on guitar, Elmer James on bass and tuba, John Niccollini on piano, and three good guys on sax. With Zutty and me, that made fourteen—seven white, seven colored; and Dolly Armendra made fifteen. I found some more fine arrangements. There was a real excitement jumping in the air; it was a revolutionary thing, and all of us connected with it were so dazed we could hardly believe it was happening. But into rehearsal we went, and in a few days the band began to have a rock to it and it was solid. Musicians in other rooms at the rehearsal studios would bunch up outside our door listening—this was something new on old Broadway, and it started tongues wagging and ears to cocking up all over. Agents began to inquire if I wanted bookings, and guys stopped us in the corridors to compliment us on how terrific the band sounded through the closed doors. The millennium was on all of us. O.B. came through with some gold so Zutty could get some new drums and pay his back rent; arrangers worked for us on the cuff, Manny's supply house on West 48th Street furnished all the mutes, mute racks, metal hats and drum sticks, and wasn't in any hurry about the dough. Cy Devore togged us all in tuxedos. Oh, everything was greased for us.

The opening was a bang-up success. Benny Goodman was at one table with Gene Krupa, Teddy Wilson, Lionel Hampton and some of his other musicians; Tommy Dorsey and his band were at another. The house really came down—it looked like maybe a new day was dawning, at least in one small branch of the entertainment world, and everybody was filled with a festive spirit and joy took over. The hit of our floor show was the lindyhoppers' finale, when they came flying onstage to the tune of *Christopher Columbus*, played in a real frantic tempo. As soon as they hit the floor pandemonium broke loose in the place, because nothing like this had ever been seen on Broadway before. The dancers screamed at the band, and one little jumping-jack of a girl in particular, a cute chick named Ann, really had fits, yelling "Yeah Zutty, play it!" while others shouted "Ooowww!" and "Do it Poppa Mezz!" clapping their hands in time with the music and throwing their bodies about convulsively. How we enjoyed playing for them, and how the applause roared through the place when they finished. That routine closed the floor show like no other act I have ever seen in all the days of my life. It was phenomenal. Hearts beat a mile a minute, and from the waiters to the checkroom girls, from the spectators to the musicians, everybody was beaming, flushed, keyed-up and delighted.

The papers were wonderful to us, and what publicity we got. "MIXED BAND BOWS ON BROADWAY," a full-page headline in *Billboard* proclaimed—"Mezzrow Takes Sepia & Ofay Swingsters Out in the Open." The article went on to say: "Picking his personnel on the basis of good musicianship rather than skin coloration, Mezzrow makes his bid for a top position in the swing music heap. Not just a trio or quartet for the refreshing swing interludes as one gets it from [Benny] Goodman at the Hotel Pennsylvania. But a white leader fronting a bandstand that will show 15 musical swing stars culled from both the Caucasian and Negroid races. . . . Since music recognizes no language save its own and the swing motif knows no race but its own rhythm, since there is no color line in the playing of swing music and followers are representative of every race, Mezzrow has aptly christened his new combo the 'Disciples of Swing.'" And *The Orchestra World* shouted in its headlines: "OFAY-SEPIA 'DISCIPLES OF SWING' SHATTER BIG TOWN TRADITIONS." And John Hammond, in *Tempo*, wrote that the "news of the month" was "the formation of the first genuine black and white band in America, headed by the celebrated Mezz Mezzrow (Milton Mesirow to the ecstatic and worshipful French who consider him our greatest living clarinetist). In the band are some of the genuinely great American musicians. . . . The band is young and rough, but I can assure you that it has one of the best brass sections in the country and a vitality that the Casa Loma and Tommy Dorsey [bands] might do well to emulate. . . ." Our press was great everywhere. It looked good.

A couple of wonderful weeks trillied by, the house jammed every night, critics giving us rave notices, everybody in the show putting all his heart into it. Then one morning a messenger came to my house, sent by Jay Faggin. "You'd better come right down to the Uproar House," he said. "Something terrible has happened." He wouldn't say anything more, so I dressed and rushed downtown, my heart in my mouth.

It was worse than anything I could have dreamed up. When I got to the place there was a big crowd of cops and reporters, flash bulbs exploding all over and everybody looking tense and upset. The first thing I noticed was that a large framed display poster in the lobby, quoting *Billboard's* write-up, had been smeared with a hell of a big swastika in bright blue paint. I ran downstairs. There was a gang of people standing on the dance floor, looking at a great big swastika painted right across it. My library was strewn all over the place, all the chairs and tables were overturned, the place was a mess. Looked like somebody sure took offense at the idea of a mixed band. Jay was talking to a police captain and some detectives. "Ain't this a fine how-d'ya-do?" he said glumly. I couldn't speak.

That night the place was packed, partly on account of the publicity, I guess, and the boys all took it in their stride and put on a wonderful show, making the customers stomp and howl all over the place. It was like that on the following nights too. Until the night when we came to work and found the marquee lights out, and a sheriff at the padlocked door, and a poster tacked up informing whom it may concern that the creditors had gotten a court order and closed the place up. It seemed that the creditors had been wanting to appoint another trustee and ease Faggin out, but he'd put up a fight and this was the result.

Right away, naturally, some people who wanted it that way began to say I-told-you-so, it just proves the American public won't stand for a mixed band, etc. Well, for the sake of the record, let me say that band was one of the biggest successes Broadway has ever seen, and the creditors were so amazed at the business we were drawing that they were all set to invest plenty of thousands more in the joint, and I know because I'd had a meeting with them and they told me so. It was that legal squabble between Faggin and these other guys that closed the place down, in spite of the band's sensational success. And maybe those swastikas made the creditors a little jittery too; I don't know.

Well, the sheriff let us in to get our instruments and music, and downstairs we found Jay wandering around cussing out the creditors, looking like a drowned rat. For once, at least, we didn't get paid off in Long Island ducklings. No, indeedy. This time we carted off all the wine and whisky left in the liquor cellar. I guess that was progress. . . . The Disciples of Swing got booked, right after that, into the Savoy Ballroom, but in the meantime Artie Shaw, Benny

Goodman and Tommy Dorsey were dickering for some of the white guys in the band, and I began to lose my men to them, so we had to cancel that engagement and the disciples scattered to the four Jim-Crow winds again. . . .

Another year of swimming in dishwater: playing one-nighters now and then, pushing reefer, oblivion. Plenty of time to do some hard thinking about the jinx that seemed to dog me around in the music world. No doubt about it, it really looked like Old Lady Luck had crossed me off her list for good: no sooner do I fall in with a bunch of cats who go for my kind of music than they cut out from Chicago, leaving me behind; then when I get a radio-network band together, the guys do a disappearing act before we even get started; and now the Disciples of Swing begin doing their discipling for everybody but me. But when I put my mind on it I could see it wasn't anybody's fault in particular—not the fault of the musicians for sure.

One thing about musicians: they like to go where they can play music. Musicians follow their noses to where there's a job, where some eating money is to be had, and all the contracts and paper deals in the world won't stop them. The oldtime Negro jazzmen sometimes were funny in a way—they played just for the love of it, just for kicks, and when they didn't get a chance to play the one kind of music they craved, why, they just went to shining shoes or walloping crates on the dock, and that was that. The white boys are more used to eating regular, and so they'll traipse off to make music for Tommy Dorsey or Benny Goodman because the big bands are all the go and can provide them with their scoff. If I got a band together, plenty of my old pals would join it because they loved to play our brand of music. But when hard times fell on us, they had to scuffle in another alley. I knew that would always be happening to me, long as I tried to bust into the big-band field— a few miss-meal weeks and the band would be just a fond memory, because the musicians from our school were just too good and plenty offers from the top bands would get dangled in their chops fast.

It was the same old bout with economics, and I'd wind up on the losing end every time. A guy with my kind of monomania, who wouldn't load up his library with short-histe ballads and simpy show tunes, had two strikes against him in the popular-band field right from the start. Wasn't nobody to blame, except maybe the guy who invented the belly-cramp. . . .

It was a fraughty issue, Jack. But then came some wonderful news —Hugues Panassié writes in the Fall of 1938, saying he's dying to come over here and what do I think? Right quick I cabled him to come, and it didn't take long before he was galloping down the gangplank over in Hoboken, while Benny Carter, Zutty Singleton, my wife and me screamed hello to him. He rushed up to us and grabbed each one in turn, kissing us with great big smacks on both cheeks, which made me feel very queer because I never got that kind of affection from that direction before. Zutty and Benny fell out, and we dashed right over to Harlem. I moved into an apartment on 126th Street, Hugues came to live with me, and the house began to jump, so many things were going on. Hugues had brought a lot of money with him to record the musicians he liked, and we started to round them up. The first guy he asked about was Tommy Ladnier, a great New Orleans trumpet player who'd been completely lost from sight for years. It was a mad scramble, but we finally tracked him down in a two-bit cabaret somewhere outside of Buffalo, playing with a trio for coffee and cake.

Tommy, one of the greatest jazz musicians in the world, was a small and wiry cat, beginner brown in complexion, with sharp features and a very high forehead; a wonderful guy, philosophical and very sincere, and nobody understood him. He'd gotten so fed up playing corny commercial music in New York that he'd beat it to the sticks with this trio because he could play like he wanted up there. He saw eye to eye with us right away; we all agreed on the bad turn jazz had taken when it hit the East and fell into the hands of the promoters. He always wore a cap, cocked to one side, and it wasn't long before Hugues and I took up the fashion, so the three of us tramped around town like a trio of schoolkids and that's just the way we felt, it was so good to be together.

Tommy had wonderful stories to tell, because he'd traveled to all parts of the world and had stayed in Russia for a long time. In 1929 he and Bechet were with Noble Sissle's band in Europe, and when they got back to the States they formed their own band and called it the "New Orleans Feetwarmers," which played the Savoy Ballroom for a few weeks but didn't make much of a splash because the East had gone modern by then. During those weeks at the Savoy, though, the Feetwarmers had made some records for Victor—*I Want You Tonight, Lay Your Racket, Sweetie Dear, Maple Leaf Rag, I Found a New Baby,* and *Shag*—wonderful records that made Tommy's name, and Bechet's too, a password all around the globe wherever there are jazz lovers. Tommy had been born right outside of New Orleans in 1900 and had learned to play trumpet from Joe Oliver, and he was crazy about Bessie Smith and that other great singer, Lovey Austin, and used to run with both of them in Chicago. He was always lounging around at home smoking a pipe and listening to the oldtime blues singers on records. He had a wonderful sense of humor too, and was very relaxed. Tommy formed a club uptown that he called the Fish Club—he was the King Fish, I was Father Neptune, and Bechet was nicknamed the Flounder. Once I asked Bechet why Tommy called him that, and he said, "Well you see gate, all the rest of the fish swims kind of straight but I swims like this," and he zigzagged with his hand to show how a flounder swims. We had some great old times together. Best of all, under Hugues' auspices we rounded up some of the greatest musicians of them all, guys like Sidney Bechet and Tommy Ladnier and Pops Foster and Zutty Singleton and James P. Johnson, and we made a gang of records that soon caused a whole lot of stuff in the jazz world: *Comin' On with the Come On* (Parts One and Two), *Revolutionary Blues, Really the Blues, Jada, Weary Blues, When You and I Were Young Maggie, Everybody Loves My Baby, Ain't Gonna Give Nobody None of My Jelly Roll, Royal Garden Blues, If You See Me Comin', Gettin' Together.** I was really living again.

Panassié ran around like mad from the minute he hit the States, and he never stopped being amazed at Jim Crow, because he couldn't see how such a thing could happen to such a wonderful

* For further discussion of these records, see Appendix 3.

people. The faction in the music world that resented the Negro's leadership didn't like Hugues living in Harlem, and especially with me. "You'll lose all your prestige that way," they told him. "It won't do you any good sticking up in Harlem, and with that Mezzrow guy too. Why, Mezzrow's the reefer king up there; you don't want to be connected with him in any way." Hugues came home boiling mad. "What kind of funny people do you have over here?" he said, stomping up and down, he was so agitated. "*Merde alors*, they don't like Negroes!"

We were all invited to Jimmy Lunceford's opening at a new downtown club, and when we walked in with my wife, the whole place began to buzz—there wasn't another colored guest in the joint. They wouldn't let us near the ringside table that Jimmy had reserved for us, but stuck us way back near the door where we wouldn't be conspicuous. When the band finished playing their set they all came down to say hello, and we stood up to greet them, while the waiter served the drinks we had ordered. When we sat down again I happened to change seats with Johnnie Mae. Just before that I had noticed the waiter and the bartender and the owner putting their heads together over in the corner, but I paid it no mind.

Well, we drank up our drinks and told Jimmy we wouldn't stay because we didn't want to cause him any trouble on opening night, and on the way uptown in a cab Hugues and his secretary, Madeleine Gautier, began to rage about the treatment they gave our mixed party. "What nerve!" Madeleine said. "They make their money through the colored band they feature, and yet they don't want any colored people in the place, it doesn't make sense!" At just that moment, as we were cutting through Central Park, I suddenly got violently sick and all my insides started to erupt and I just fell flat on the floor of the cab, heaving. I finally realized, as I was turning inside out, that for the first time in my life I had met up with a great old American institution, the Mickey Finn. Of course, the drink had been meant for Johnnie Mae. "So this is the land of the free," Hugues murmured when they had carried me upstairs and put me to bed. I had no answer for him.

Right after the Frankie Newton date, Hugues took sick with a streptococcus infection of the throat, and he would have died if it hadn't been for the fast thinking of a fine colored doctor, Dr. Samuel C. McKinney, who lived in the same building with us. One morning he woke up gagging, unable to catch his breath, his throat was so clogged up, and I could see there wasn't any time to lose so I rushed him right downstairs to Doc McKinney's office, him making terrible rasping noises all the way. The doc took one look at Hugues and whispered to me, "Mezz, this is serious—stand by, I may need your help." While he was taking his coat off Hugues fell into a chair and started saying "Aaahhh," waving his arms wildly, to tell us he couldn't breathe. His face was turning purple, right before my eyes.

Well, the doc stuck his fingers down Hugues' throat and pulled out a thick string of phlegm that was as long as a footrule, I swear. When he yanked it out Hugues gave the biggest and longest gasp for air that I have ever heard; it sounded like he kept sucking in for five minutes. Then we got a cab and rushed him to the Harlem Eye & Ear Hospital, with the doctor holding all his scalpels and other surgical instruments ready in his lap and praying he wouldn't have to cut Hugues' throat open for a tracheotomy before we got there. We carried him in, and two white staff doctors took one gander down his throat and looked as scared as he did. Doc McKinney put in a hurry call to a friend of his, another colored specialist who had studied in Vienna, and he came and shook his head too after one quick look. Doc McKinney got all excited and angry when the others said how hopeless they all felt. "Don't worry, Mezz," he said to me, "I'll take care of this myself."

He shimmied out of his coat and dug in his bag, coming up with some pills. "This is a new drug called sulphanilimide, that I'm very much interested in," he explained. "The other doctors are afraid to use it and have declared themselves out, but I'm going to administer it by mouth on my own responsibility, because I've got a lot of confidence in it and I can't get the serum I need in New York. This might do the job until the serum arrives." We sat around for a whole week, watching Hugues' fever chart go up and down, our hearts jumping with it—and then one fine day it come down to about 100 and the danger was over, thanks to Doc McKinney.

Hugues stayed with us until the end of February, 1939, when, at the doctor's suggestion, he went back to his chateau in France for a long rest, because for a man as sensitive as him the pace over here was much too tough. Just before he climbed up the gangplank, he embraced me and said, "Mezz, I owe my life to a fine man and a superb and brilliant doctor whom a lot of your countrymen wouldn't allow at their dinner table because of the color of his skin. This is a strange, strange country."

All my luck disappeared up that gangplank with Hugues. His illness, and then his leaving, left me all tense and neurotic, and Johnnie Mae's nerves were on edge too, so we quarreled and she went home for a time to momma, down in Aiken, South Carolina, taking our son with her. Then there wasn't much doing in the music field, so I took a gamble and went into the music publishing game. But I didn't exactly make a fortune overnight out of the Gem Music Publishing Company, or even much eating money. And then Tommy Ladnier got to feeling so low about Hugues' going away that he went on a terrible King Kong kick, and I had my hands full trying to straighten him out. I made him move in with me, and he promised to stop drinking. We started to rehearse a small band (Zutty on drums, Pops Foster on bass, Happy Cauldwell on tenor sax, Cliff Jackson on piano, Tommy and me), and played a few gigs around town, but that's as far as we got because, as usual, swing had all the go. On May 28th we celebrated Tommy's thirty-ninth birthday. He boasted to me about how the doctors ten years ago had told him he wouldn't live five more years if he didn't give up playing.

A few nights later, on June the 4th, I came home from my office and found Tommy getting ready to go to a party some chicks were giving upstairs in our building. He was going with the super of the place, Harold, who was very friendly with us. I asked him to come over to the Savoy Ballroom with me to see Benny Carter, but he said he'd wait around for Harold and maybe turn in early because he felt kind of beat. Well, we sat around for a while playing records (he was crazy about some blues I had by Bumble Bee Slim and Big Bill), and then I cut out for the Savoy. I saw Benny Carter and got my business straight with him, but he insisted that I stay until two o'clock because he was trying out some trumpet players and wanted me to help him pick one. I hung around against my will. All the time something kept telling me to go home. It kept pulling at my mind.

Well, I kept trying to run out and Benny kept grabbing me by the sleeve, and it wasn't till near five in the morning before I finally dashed for a bus. Soon as I got in the house I found Tommy stretched out on the couch, window wide open and wind blowing in on him, billowing the curtains way up. "Hey Tommy," I said, "get up from there, you'll catch cold." He didn't budge. Oh, oh, I thought, Tommy's gone and got drunk again, up at that party. I walked over and picked up his arm and shook him. "Hey guy," I said, "get up off of there and get in the bed." Still not a peep out of him. I looked down at him and a funny feeling came over me. Hell, he didn't seem to be breathing. The idea flashed into my mind to get a mirror and hold it up to his lips, but then I thought of Doc McKinney, and I jumped in the elevator to go down to his apartment. I told myself I must be crazy, Tommy was all right, just drunk, and I'd be waking the doctor up for nothing. So instead I went on down to the basement, to the apartment of our friend Harold, the super.

Harold's wife opened the door, and I said, "Do you know whether Tommy went to a party with Harold last night and got drunk?"

"Why, no," she said, "Harold hasn't been out of the house all evening."

I almost fell to the floor. By this time Harold had come out of the bedroom, and he helped me over to a chair. "I don't know," I kept repeating, "I don't know, but I think Tommy's laying up there on the couch dead." Then I started to sob. "Give him some whisky!" Harold yelled to his wife, and flew out the door. Forty years later the door burst open, and through my tears I could see

Doc McKinney in his shirtsleeves. "Mezz," he screamed at me, "why didn't you call me? Tommy's still warm, maybe we could have saved him." I was no more good for a long time after that.

Then began a nightmare: cops, detectives, coroners all milling around, asking questions, accusing, grilling, threatening. Sitting there around Tommy's body, they wrangled and whispered among themselves, and kept shooting questions at me. You can imagine what ran, in their minds—a white man living alone with this colored man up in Harlem, and the white man doesn't know where the colored man was born or any of his people or even whether he was married. All the white man knows is that the colored man was the greatest trumpet player in the world, excusing Louis Armstrong. The grilling went on for hours. All through the ordeal Doc McKinney and his wife stood right in back of my chair, soothing and comforting me. Finally the doc said, "Gentlemen, this man is my patient and I think he's had enough, unless you want him to have a nervous breakdown." Just as he said that a colored policeman walked in, the first one I'd seen, and as soon as I looked at him I knew he would understand. I got some RCA-Victor pamphlets that had pictures of Hugues and Tommy and me in them, and the moment the colored cop saw that he said O.K., and the questioning let up.

Hours later I got some relief when Buck came in and saw us sitting with the police. He walked over to where Tommy's body was stretched out and said, "Come on slot, get up from there, I got some good gauge you can pick up on. . . . Oh, you don't want none? Well, I'll just light up with Mezz," and he pulled out a cigarette and puffed on it, imitating a cat pulling on some hemp. What a guy Buck was. He wasn't happy over Tommy's death, understand; just making the best of it, trying to keep on going and give me courage. . . . Finally the coroner was satisfied that I was telling the truth, and he had the body removed to the morgue for autopsy. Tommy was wrapped in a dirty canvas cover and stood up in a wicker basket with bloodstains all over it. "What'd I tell you Mezz," Buck said, "everybody goes when the wagon comes."

Now came a real headache: how to bury Tommy? I was broke as

a fish, and when I went down to the union I found out the guy had never paid up his initiation fee so there was no insurance to collect. I finally took up a collection among the musicians, and I want to mention right here and now that one record collector, a fellow named Frank Tack, contributed $35 towards the fund. On June 9th we buried Tommy in the Frederick Douglass Memorial Cemetery out on Staten Island, and I still owe the undertaker forty bucks which he refused to take because he thought some of the bigtime orchestra leaders should have come through for Tommy.

The police located a wife of Tommy's in Jackson, Michigan, and she wired me to call her collect. I did. The first and only thing she asked about Tommy was what had happened to his estate. "Tommy's estate is at the police station," I told her. "It consists of one pair of soiled socks, one torn shirt, and a set of raggedy underwear." That was the list of Tommy's worldly goods. He was one of the more prosperous New Orleans musicians.

17

Out of the Gallion

Gay New Orleans! And not a levee, crib, red light, barrelhouse or honky-tonk in sight. Oh, not the Gay New Orleans on the Mississippi delta. The streamlined one out on Flushing Meadows, Long Island, that Mike Todd opened up at the World's Fair for the summer tourists. That's where the law nabbed me again. . . . Mike Durso, a guy I knew, had the band out there. Being the sociable sort, and having bushels of time on my hands, I used to drop out there to gumbeat with the musicians and chorus girls. This evilest of evil days, little Frankie Walker scared up sixty cents from his landlady, so I'd have carfare and the price of admission to the fair grounds, and off I trotted.

It was August, 1940; a mellow, smiling, sun-drenched day. I headed straight for the backstage entrance at the Gay New Orleans, and all of a sudden a burly guy in shirtsleeves was frisking me, running his expert fingers over all my pockets. He was the law, prowling around after some dope peddler who'd been working in the neighborhood, but all he could find was me with my pockets full of reefer. He had to make some kind of pinch to keep his batting average up; it was a dull day. He run me in.

Down to the station house we went, and then he and another detective piled me into a cab and rode me up to Harlem, to check on where I was living. It floored them to find Johnnie Mae there, and little Milton, Jr., and on our way back they began to pop questions at me. Was I colored? No, Russian Jew, American-born. How in hell did I come to be living with a "spade"? Well, I had this screwy idea that when you loved a girl you married her, without consulting a color chart. What in Christ's name did my poor mother and father think about this cross they had to bear? "What in hell should they think?" I shouted, plenty worked up. "They're funny people—it makes them feel good to see their son married and happy." Those two representatives of New York's finest stared at me as though I had two heads. "Listen to this son-of-a-bitch," one said, in a voice full of wonder. "The jerk's a nigger-lover. Let's send him to the Island." He meant the city jail, out on Riker's Island; *he* knew where the enemies of society belonged. If they let *him* write the laws of the land, you'd get the electric chair for color-blindness.

Back in the Long Island City precinct house. They thumb through the books, digging hard, and find that possession of marihuana is a misdemeanor, violating some city ordinance. A pleasant gray-haired lieutenant books me, examining the pile of reefers they took off me and putting me down as a "suspected vendor." "That's interesting stuff," he says. "I've been hearing about it for the longest time." A lot of people on the city payroll must have thought it was interesting stuff: I had way over sixty cigarettes on me when I was picked up, and when my trial came up over four months later, less than forty were introduced for evidence. Too bad the trial wasn't postponed a little longer; all the evidence would have gone up in smoke. . . . "Watch out for this jerk," my pal the detective warns the lieutenant. "He lies every time he opens his trap." The lieutenant, soft-spoken and polite, looks at him. "I can see he's a low character and you're a very distinguished high-class gentleman," he says. "You know, I've noticed a strange coincidence here—officer and prisoner are wearing the same identical shirts." We looked, and it was true—our silk shirts must have come out of the same box at Sulka's. I busted out laughing. The gumshoe turned purple.

They locked me in a ratty shoebox of a cell, small enough to give a chinch claustrophobia, and not a wink did I sleep because the Long Island Railroad tracks were right outside my window and the freight trains switched back and forth all night long. I paced up and down, up and down, two steps each way, fidgety as a tiger in a thimble. I was one drugg cat. . . . In a way, I was almost glad the law caught up with me. For a long time now, my wife had been after me to get another band together, but I just couldn't round up the musicians, and bookings were not to be had, and economic conditions put the pinch on me so hard I was forced back to pushing the grass. For years I'd been bosom pals with oblivion. Now, at least, I was out of the racket for good. For two or three years solid I'd be able to practise—no rent to pay, no meal-ticket to scuffle for. When I came out I'd be ready. In some way I couldn't understand exactly, I had a vague feeling that I was guilty of something, not of what they booked me for because that was no crime in my eyes, but of something that went way deeper—of being untrue to myself, a traitor to the spirit in me, running out on my real vocation and destiny. It didn't make any difference that obstacles outside of my control, that I didn't build myself, had shunted me off; I was still guilty. My guilt came from the fact that I had given up fighting, quit cold, thrown in the sponge. My crime was to lose hope. It would be a kind of relief, almost, to pay for my sins, the sins that weren't on the books, the ones the city never passed any ordinances about. I would make up for everything by perfecting myself as a musician, and when I came out I would never stray away from my real calling again, never go tangent.

But three years in a hole like this would make me blow my top. I kept pacing, trying to quiet my nerves, and the chugging of the freight trains began to drill into my head, and then my fingers began to twitch. A tune, a weary aching gutbucket blues of a tune, crawling on all fours from one lament to the next, was beginning to percolate through my brain, and just automatically my hands started to pick it out on an imaginary clarinet. Oh, it was a low-down blues, and it had the woe of the jailbird in it, the lead-heavy steps of the con shuffling back and forth in his cubicle, the lone-liness of those nostalgic train whistles, the deadweight uneasy darkness of the cell I was locked in, the jangling misery of a man who forgot to do what he had to do with himself to justify his being alive. I felt like I was deserted, forgotten, abandoned. I had abandoned myself. Everything had gone away from me. Walking up and down, I began to moan those blues to myself, just the way the colored boys used to chant their heartache out long ago in the Pontiac reform school. Suddenly a name for those blues popped into my head: *Gone Away Blues*.

Yeah, sure; that was what I would call them. Right away I felt better. Some day, I told myself, I would have to record that tune, to get it out of my system—sure, with Sidney Bechet, playing those haunting moaning duets like we did on *Really the Blues*. I could work on it while I was in jail, getting ready to record it as soon as I was sprung. It was something to aim at. It cheered me up a lot.

Clark Monroe, a dancer who used to hang out with me at the Barbeque, had himself a cabaret in Harlem now called the Uptown House, and he put the joint up to stand bail for me. Soon as I hit Harlem again, I got a royal reception—everywhere I went the girls and fellows, many I didn't even know, would run up and hug and kiss me, going out of their way to show their affection and how they stood behind me. "Don't worry Mezz," they all told me, "everything's going to be all right, you got good friends everywhere and they won't ever forget you." It was an unplanned surge of solidarity, that sprang up the moment one of their boys was in trouble. It was heartfelt and sincere, and it was meant to show me that what was mine was theirs—not only the good things but the evil ones too. How fine they made me feel. . . .

The following January I came up for trial in Special Sessions Court, and a lieutenant from the narcotics squad turned up and tried every way he could to make me stool on other guys who peddled reefer in Harlem. I told him to prove to me that marihuana was a narcotic, or did anything bad to people, and then maybe I'd talk to him. When I was called in for sentence, this lieutenant asked for permission to address the court, and he stood up there and said, "I want the court to know that, according to my informers, this man was responsible for introducing marihuana to Harlem twelve years ago." My lawyer jumped up and bellowed, "You must be a most remarkable detective, and your narcotics squad must be the pride of the force. Here you've been on duty in Harlem for twelve years, knowing all about this fiend and monster, and never once were you able to so much as arrest him for his nefarious activities." All the bickering flew over my head; I was bored, and wished they'd get this foolishness over quick, so I could get settled in jail and go to work on my clarinet. The judge sentenced me to Riker's Island for an indefinite sentence of one to three years. My card was stamped "D.A.," which is short for dope addict. They were a little late with that one.

In the receiving room at Riker's we had to strip off all our clothes, and I got a real close-up view of New York's derelicts. Practically all the men with me were white, either lushheads or junkies, and this morning they all had the shakes and rattles real bad, whether from hootch or some kind of white stuff. The stench made my nose curl up. Everywhere I looked I saw running noses, bloodshot rheumy eyes, trembling matchstick legs, clattering teeth, sunken cheeks, faces etched with grime, matted hair, rotted flesh, and dirt-crusted skin. All the faces around me were grooved and stony, hunks of crumbling granite, like tombstones with the epitaphs left off. They were an obscene caricature of the life I'd escaped, the dying white-man's world seen in a distorting mirror. . . . We stood around naked, in miserable little clumps, scrofulous skinfuls of human wreckage, while an inmate with a spray gun squirted disinfectant over a man who had louse pockets all over his hide as big as silver dollars. Two other bored inmates twisted his arms behind him to hold him quiet, while he writhed and screamed with pain. I stopped thinking about the music.

While I was struggling into the funky clothes they handed me, I whispered to a colored inmate, asking if a pal of mine from Harlem, a guy named Roy, wasn't doing a bit on the Island. "Yeah," was the answer, "Roy's the clerk in Block Six, but that's for colored only and I doubt if you'll ever get to see him." I took one more good look around at the human junk-heaps in the room, at all the walking dead. I knew that colored cons were different; almost any colored guy can land in jail, not just the soulless zombies who have already shriveled up and died inside and are just postponing their date with the undertaker's icebox. Some of the finest, most high-spirited guys of the race landed in jail because of their conditions of life, not because they were rotted and maggot-eaten inside. I knew all that from past experience. I made up my mind to do something drastic.

Just as we were having our pictures took for the rogues' gallery, along came Mr. Slattery the deputy, and I nailed him and began to talk fast. "Mr. Slattery," I said, "I'm colored, even if I don't look it, and I don't think I'd get along in the white blocks, and besides, there might be some friends of mine in Block Six and they'd keep me out of trouble." Mr. Slattery jumped back, astounded, and studied my features real hard. He seemed a little relieved when he saw my nappy head. "I guess we can arrange that," he said. "Well, well, so you're Mezzrow. I read about you in the papers long ago and I've been wondering when you'd get out here. We need a good leader for our band and I think you're just the man for the job." He slipped me a card with "Block Six" written on it. I felt like I had gotten a reprieve.

The new inmates were lined up according to the cell blocks they were assigned to, and I fell in the Block Six line behind three real dark colored boys. They looked a little uncomfortable, shifting from one foot to another and exchanging uneasy glances. The silent system prevailed in the hall, so we couldn't say a word to each other. Then, as luck would have it, all the colored boys who lined up behind me were dark too, and I must have looked like a ghost standing there between them all. I began to pray for those interviews to be over, so we could get to the block.

When we hit Block Six the colored guard there, a guy named Harrison, assigned us to our cells, then called me aside. "Mezzrow," he said, "I heard a lot about you from Roy and you look like an intelligent fellow and I think you'll make it here. There's only one thing I insist on in this block and that is cleanliness. We pride ourselves in here for having the cleanest block on the Island, just to show that people can be civilized even if they come from Harlem. We've got several of the musicians from the band locking in here, and as soon as there's a vacant cell near them I'll put you up on their tier. I hope you do something with this band of ours because it's really sad." What a relief—here was a keeper who talked my language. I was ready to scrub that cell with my tongue for a guy as regular as that.

At lunch in the huge dining hall, all eyes were on me again. The keepers standing in the aisles thought they were seeing things when I marched in, and they kept gunning me, so I made sure to get seated between two of the darkest boys in the block, guys who worked on the coal gang. I sensed the tension in all these fay keepers, but they couldn't say a word. They struck me so funny the way they stood there, each one trying to look tougher and nastier than the next. That's the psychology that's been put down on the Island ever since the Welfare Island scandal (when they found out that Johnny Rao, the gangster, was running the whole jail out there, having porterhouse steaks and fancy liquors and everything sent in, running big card games and bossing the officials around). There's no talking in the dining room, even among the keepers. Their idea of "rehabilitation" is to make you feel you're living in a morgue, surrounded by scowling corpses with holsters on their hips. We were served on trays, cafeteria style, and you could hardly pick up your silverware, it was so greasy. When you took a piece of bread and tried to rub some of the grease off your knife and fork, the bread turned black because all the plating was rubbed off the cheap metal.

After lunch another bringdown: I was transferred to a white cell because I looked too "conspicuous" in the mess hall. Mr. Harrison was furious and told me not to worry, he'd have me back real quick. I was led to Block Five, just across the way, and began to feel like an alien right away. There I could hardly listen to the talk of my cellmates, their language and mannerisms and gestures were so coarse and brutal, they spoke with their lips all twisted up, in harsh accents that jarred on my nerves. I realized again how well off I'd been these last few years, being able to live far away from all this grimy, grating white underworld, up in Harlem where people were real and earthy. My cell stunk and had dust all over it, and the tough clerk with his brutish ofay prison vernacular made me sick to my stomach. I started to clean up the cell, trying to console myself by thinking about the band I was going to lead. I couldn't wait to get my hands on a horn.

This place was better than The Band House in one way, anyhow: the cells at least had brand-new stools, and the walls were of steel, painted a sort of battleship gray—in fact, the whole block reminded you of a big ship. There was a washbowl with ice-cold running water that was sure to wake you up in the morning, and the bed was a killer. It was a solid sheet of steel, with a little molding running all around it, and it had been designed to hold a rubber mattress, the kind that's blown up with air. Those rubber mattresses somehow never arrived, so they gave us some ordinary ones stuffed with cotton batting, about two inches thick, which was just enough padding to keep your vertebrae from cracking.

Just as I finished making up my bed, the clerk called out my name. "Get your things together," he said, "you're going back to Block Six." It looked like I was becoming quite a football in the little Jim-Crow skirmishes that they had out on this island, but this time, at least, we could chalk up one for our side. What a welcome I got from Mr. Harrison and all the cats. When I left them, they'd all congregated around in front of the block, with long faces that told me, What a drag Mezz, but carry on, you'll make it. Now they were all beaming. I was sure glad to be home again, and they were glad to have me back.

There was a sort of feud going on in this joint, under the surface. One faction was made up of the keepers and their henchmen, and on the other side were most of the civilian employees on the prison staff. Now the civilians, being more or less interested in educating the inmates and rehabilitating them, treated us sometimes like half-way human beings, but the keeper faction had never even heard of the word rehabilitation and thought those civilians were too soft and sentimental with us, "coddling" instead of waving a club. Mr. Costello, the civilian band master, a very old and pleasant gentleman who'd once been a symphony clarinetist, was one of the "soft" guys, but he knew nothing about jazz and didn't much care for it.

He gave me some saxophones and clarinets that were from the Year of One, and they leaked so bad you couldn't get a sound out of them with a high-pressure air pump. I took several days out and patched up some of them. . . .

One thing I'll grant those scowling mugs of the keeper faction: they were sick of Mr. Costello's corny music, and they all seemed glad to see me take over the popular-music activities of the band. Life in the prison wasn't any picnic for them either, having to stand around looking nasty all day long, afraid to relax and going more neurotic by the minute. . . . Well, for two weeks we sweated and slaved, getting ready for our first concert, and even though we had some very poor musicians to work with, the band came on just the same. For the second time in my life I had a mixed band, and this time I didn't have to worry about Tommy Dorsey or Benny Goodman or Artie Shaw stealing any of my men. . . .

One of the musicians was a real old colored man named Pop Baxter, who played solid tailgate trombone. He'd worked in the old minstrel shows and barnstormed around the country with circus bands, and all the young kids were ridiculing his old antique style when I first arrived, but I soon cured them of that. Here was a gem hidden away behind the walls of Riker's Island, and I promised myself that when I got out of jail I was going to use Pop on the first recording date I could arrange, maybe even to record *Gone Away Blues* with Sidney Bechet and me. I'll never forget how that fine old man made his mellow glissandos, greasing the way so all the younger guys could just slip into the groove and go gliding along after him. Pop left the Island before I did, after doing thirty months, and he got killed some way the second week out. They brought his body back to the Island to be dumped out in Potters Field. We all mourned for him, and when the cemetery gang dropped his body into a big hole with a lot of other unclaimed paupers' corpses, I asked them to make a little mound over the spot, so his grave would have some kind of mark.

One night I was listening to the radio in our cell block, and a recording of Count Basie's *One O'Clock Jump* started to rock over the air. A fit of depression grabbed me and tears began to roll from my eyes. What a difference there was between those full booming tones that vibrated out of the loudspeaker and the music our amateur musicians played; it hit me hard. Then I remembered that I knew Jack Bregman, of Bregman, Vocco and Conn, publishers of Count Basie's numbers, so right quick I sat down and wrote him a letter, asking him to save my life by sending me the arrangements of *One O'Clock Jump, Jumping at the Woodside,* and everything else in the Basie series. Next day they called me into the recreation department and told me the city wasn't allowed to accept charity, but they'd spend thirty dollars a month to buy music for the band if only I'd order some of the popular tunes on the Hit Parade too. I settled for sandwiching *Frénesie* and a couple other pop tunes into our repertoire, and got all the Basie arrangements I wanted.

That first concert was really something. The colored boys were sitting in their section of the auditorium, up front and to the right of the band pit, looking all tense and keyed-up, as though their reputation was at stake and they didn't know whether we were going to let them down or not. Old Mr. Costello took the stick first and directed us through some light overture, and then I stepped up and we swung into the first few bars of *One O'Clock Jump* and the house came down. A ripple of shock and joy went through the colored section like a high wind through a wheat field, and you could see that all the boys wanted to shout out loud but they just sat there patting their feet and bouncing up and down, with glee written all over their faces. Finally, when one of the trumpet players got up to take a solo, the guys couldn't hold back any longer. "*Ooooowwwww!*" one of them screamed, and the house rocked. I got scared to death, but when I shot a quick look at the deputy he just smiled approvingly, encouraging me to keep going. What a change swept over all the keepers; it was like somebody unlocked the frozen machinery of their faces and let them go into some human action again. When the number was finished, all the keepers, deputies and captains joined the twenty-five hundred inmates in the clapping and stomping and howling, making the walls shake, and was Block Six proud. I felt as great as if I'd just played a smash-hit concert in Carnegie Hall. Mr. Harrison stood there chesty as a peacock, and from then on the relationship between keepers and inmates became a little more human.

I sat up nights in my cell, making arrangements of *Swingin' with Mezz* and *Gone Away Blues*, and doing little paste jobs on some parts of the published orchestrations that were too hard for our boys. The work became such an obsession with me, I could hardly sleep a wink; I'd sit up humming chords to myself and writing like mad, till there were spots before my eyes and all of them were blue notes. This was the first time I ever tried arranging without a piano, and it gave me a terrific lift to find out I could do it all in my head. . . . We got a surprise at our next concert. Word was all over the Island about our band, and when we trooped in this Sunday who should be sitting on the aisle but the warden himself, Mr. Ashworth, with his wife and a party of about fifteen special guests. We romped again that afternoon, and the weight was off the Island. Things began to take on a more human aspect all around, and inmates and keepers both looked forward to those Sunday afternoons of ours, and once in a while we'd even run across a keeper who was so confused that he forgot his professional dignity and, glory be, actually smiled at us. Yes, we rehabilitated a keeper so much, we made him smile.

Sitting in Roy's cell one night after dinner, playing Chinese checkers, I began to cough, and when I spit in the bowl I saw a big lump of blood. I sucked on all of my teeth to see if maybe one of them had gone bad and was bleeding, but all I got was saliva. Oh, oh, I thought, this is it, I really got the con; for once I won't have to fake TB. I reported at the hospital for a TB work-up, and the report was negative but they made me lay around there for six weeks, doing the kind of easy bit a jailbird always dreams about.

I wasn't happy; the band couldn't play those orchestrations without my first-sax part, and I missed the music plenty. And besides, I longed to be back with my buddies in Block Six, where I didn't come in contact with any white guys unless they were musicians. The doc thought I was nuts—here was a con beefing about being in the TB ward where you got the best of everything, soft bed, bath any time you wanted it, visitors right alongside your bed so you could kiss them instead of eyeballing them through a small glass window. He told me I ought to get myself shifted to another branch of the city prison, further up the East River on Hart's Island. "You'll be able to get out in the air," he told me, "and they have a band up there too." I finally decided to take the trip, after we figured out that the lousy hot-air ventilation in our cell blocks was what made me cough up that blood. Only one thing worried me: all the junkies were sent up there to Hart's and I sure didn't want to be classed as a junkie, no matter how many "D.A.'s" they stamped on my card.

I noticed the difference in the atmosphere as soon as we hit the road to the receiving room. The inmates working on the docks shouted greetings to their buddies among the newcomers, right in front of the keepers, and some of them were even chatting with the keepers, as though they never heard of the silent system. Then I was assigned to the band, and things began to look much brighter for me. Off we marched to our respective divisions (that was what they called the dormitories we bunked in; they didn't have any private cells here) and luck was really with me. When I met some of the guys from the band who locked in this dormitory, who should turn out to be the first trumpet player but good old Travis Roberts (one of my old pals from The Corner), and of all people, the drummer was Frankie Ward (the guy who introduced me to my hop connection). It was one hell of a reunion we had. They told me all about how the inmates practically ran this Island, sort of self-governing themselves, with their own inmate captains and clerks in each division. We slept on rows of beds with springs in them, and each inmate had a private locker with a key to it, where he could keep his belongings safe. It was more like a military academy than a pen.

Travis fixed it so I got a bed next to his, and as soon as he got me alone he said, "Jim, I don't dig you, you must want the tough side of life. What's your story? I heard of many a cat passin' for white, but this is the first time I ever heard of a white man passin' for colored, and in jail too. You'll have to get me straight on that issue." I tried to explain how I had felt about Block Six on Riker's, and he understood a little. Then he went over the music situation on Hart's for me, telling me about the German professor who was in charge of the band. "Marches are that cat's specialty," he told me, "and we play Wagner too, and then some more Wagner, and after that a whole gang of Wagner. The weather is gettin' nice now, and pretty soon he'll have us marchin' all over the Island, playin' *Our Director* and stuff like that. See if you can't get him to let us play some swing around here."

Next day we went into a huddle with Herr Professor Mr. Fritz Frosch, and we told him that swing was the colored man's music and we didn't see why we shouldn't be allowed to play it. We were playing German, French and Italian pieces, and the marches of John Philip Sousa, so why shouldn't we play the music of Count Basie and Duke Ellington? He agreed to let me take charge of the swing band, and soon I got hold of another set of Basie arrangements and was even allowed to send for my clarinet, which was in the pawnshop. Before long we had the Island really jumping on Sunday afternoons, out on the ball field. Up here they didn't show any movies, but the band played marches as the divisions paraded onto the field, and then there was a ball game, sometimes with a visiting team from the outside, and while they played we had our jam session. The inmates would crowd around the stand, listening to all the Basie numbers, and some of my own, and then Duke Ellington's arrangement of *Solitude*, after Sidney Mills the publisher sent it to me. Lucky Tin Pan Alley didn't catch wind of the musical craze that shook our little penal colony, or there would have been a stampede of songpluggers on the East River ferry, scrambling to get over to Hart's Island. Songpluggers go everywhere, like termites and earthworms.

Seventeen months gandydanced by; months that were like galloping minutes, flashing past before I could draw my breath, like in a muta dream. I was so absorbed in the music, my whole being so wrapped up in sheet music and orchestrations, that I took no notice. Only random little snatches of events, plucked out of the grabbag with my eyes blindfolded, flickered into my attention. Something tremendous, jam-up, was jumping inside of me, all my groggy nerves were sitting up and yawning and then opening their eyes big as saucers and springing to attention, wide awake. Weird meandering canyons, mist-filled caverns, all kinds of crazy gopherholes began to open up in me, deeper than I ever expected I went, and I began feeling my way into them, exploring, not sure what I would find. I didn't have much mind for the parade outside my skull. . . .

I remember Dan Leary, though; tough thin-lipped Danny, ringleader of the white faction in the band, in it only for a soft touch. Danny's a two-fisted con from way back, his record's as long as a Modern Library Giant. Then one day he hears some of us colored boys running over some new Basie orchestrations—sticks his nose in the door, says sort of shyly, "Hey, don't you need a bass for this music?" We tell him yes, sure, to get his bass and join in. The walking-bass part knocks him out. "Jesus," he says over and over, with little-kid delight, "this here's what you call a real bass, it's like I sing in the quartet, hell, I can read the goddamned thing at sight. *Bum-bum-bum-bum,* oh man, the way it goes up and down the chords." Asks if maybe he couldn't learn this music from us and get a job playing bass in some dance band, so he'd have something to occupy his mind and keep him from landing in jail again. We beg the professor to buy a string bass for Danny to practise on; seventeen months go by but no bass fiddle do we ever see. . . . Fashion note: colored kids working in the tailor shop tired of corny prison outfits, go to work on their dungarees, pegging the legs till they're real sharp and zooty. Warden spots them parading through the halls, begins to roar, makes them all take off their pants and continue on in their underwear. . . . December 7th, 1941: we're listening to some hot records over the radio, news flash comes through telling about Pearl Harbor. Frenzy runs all through the division, white guys put their heads together down at their end, begin to buzz, all agitated; us colored guys slump together at opposite end, quiet, tense, worried. White guys around Danny Leary

agitating about how maybe they'll get out of here now, all join up
in the Air Corps and become heroes and bump off fifty, a hundred,
a thousand Japs, come back famous and chests loaded with decorations. Nobody in our group talks much about becoming a hero.
Terrible deep worry on all the faces at our end—one big unspoken
question between us, the Japanese are a colored race, that old color
issue is right smack in our face again. . . . Letter from Madeleine
Gautier, Panassié's secretary, dated December 7th. "Dear Milton,
we finally succeeded in having your address, and I hurry up writing to you, for you must feel very sad with your worries. You don't
know how much we have been upset, Hugues and I with those
rotten news concerning you. We do hope that you are not too low
down, and you must be sure that in the bad as in the good, we are
still your friends. . . . They all know you in Switzerland, and now
that Hugues and I spent a month in Zürich last September, they
like you still more, for you know how Hugues is clever to make
love the things and people he loves himself. We feel very sad to
think that you are in troubles, you who gave so much joy to so
many with your beautiful music. . . . You know how much our
heart is near yours. Where is the great time when we all lived together! . . . How long will you stay in that funny place? We both
love you very much. . . ." I'm a lucky guy, I think, to have friends
like that. . . .

Great lumbering Big John McDonnell, the warden, an overgrown
good-natured hulk of an Irishman. Some mean hack of a keeper
nabs a colored boy on the coal gang for snitching a loaf of bread.
Big John screams at him, "Huh, some cop you arre, pinchin' a man
with a loaf of bread, and what in the hell did you think he was
goin' to do with it but eat it, and what arre you going to do with
it now, surre and you won't eat it since he's had his hands on it.
If ever I catch yez throwin' one slice of bread in the garrbage can
and wastin' the city's money, surre and I'll suspend you for thirrty
days. This boy wasn't sittin' on his arse all day like you, he's been
shovelin' coal all day and he's hungry, now git out beforre I lose
me temper and pinch yez for disturrbin' the peace." After that two
extra loaves of bread go every day to the Seventh Division, where

the colored coal gang is housed. . . . Mrs. McDonnell one day passes the bing (cramped little cell where guys are stuck in solitary confinement, as punishment), finds somebody locked up there and runs to Big John screaming: "Now you go and turn that poor child loose! How would you like to have your son locked up in an old dungeon like that for fightin' with some boy in school! You go and let him out this very minute!" Bing's closed from then on, guys get switched to the cemetery gang for punishment. . . . Big John wandering through mess hall, peering at the portions in our plates, snorting "Uh *huh*, I thought so." Flies through the kitchen door, comes back with big bucket full of food and walks up and down the aisles ladling out second helpings and mumbling, "That dirrty bastard in there must want to make somebody's hogs fat. . . ."

Gang of WPA workers running sewer pipe from City Island through Hart's; among them some Spanish boys with some fine bush. We buy enough sticks from them to stay high a week, light up in rehearsal hall and the music begins to sound wonderful to us, Travis playing passages that Louis once taught him, real soulful, the whole band rocking. Evenings we sprawl out in the dormitory, hazy and mellow, sipping our tea, and the keeper sniffs the smoke and thinks somebody's blanket is burning. . . . Danny Leary dogging us colored musicians around, in spite of ridicule from other white inmates in his gang. He gets a tipple ukelele, one of the colored boys gets a guitar, and in the evenings we hold jam sessions, crowding in a corner of the dormitory with most all the inmates ganged around us. Corner used to be monopolized by Danny's group of bigshot ofays who ran the division; whole dormitory was divided into two parts, whites on one side and colored boys, including me, segregated on the other. But now we all sit on Danny's bed, colored and white, and his friends get used to the idea and accept us. Pretty soon we're moving colored boys in between white ones in the rows of cots, scrambling them up, and the dividing line gets more and more blurred, finally disappears. Jim Crow scrambles out of the window, drowns himself in the East River. . . .

Big John tickled about how the band's doing; decides to branch out with more musical activities, starts a choir in the Catholic church on the Island, with Danny Leary directing. Along come the Jewish holidays and with them a weird situation. The Jewish boys, not to be outdone by the Catholics, organize their own choir and ask me, a colored guy, wouldn't I care to lead it. I find out once more how music of different oppressed peoples blends together. Jewish or Hebrew religious music mostly minor, in a simple form, full of wailing and lament. When I add Negro inflections to it they fit so perfect, it thrills me. I add dominant sevenths to minor chords, sometimes the ninth too; effect colorful and stirring as a bellychord. I just sing "Oh, oh, oh," over and over with the choir because I don't know the Hebrew chants, but I give it a weepy blues inflection and the guys are all happy about it. They can't understand how come a colored guy digs the spirit of their music so good. . . .

Cemetery squad gives the guys the willies. Regular shipments of bodies from the city morgues, guys have to unload the crates at the pier and cart them up to Potters Field and dump them in the holes, fifteen or twenty corpses piled up in one big grave. Those big rough wooden boxes keep arriving, some of them packed solid with nothing but legs, or arms, or torsos, or heads, or sometimes just fingers, nothing but fingers, like they were scraps from some slaughterhouse. Once Travis gets stuck on the graveyard squad, has to help unload a shipment of bodies. While he's struggling with a big pine box the end falls out and a stiff slides halfway out, conking him on the skull. In nothing flat he's down to the end of the pier and in the East River, clothes and all, scrubbing himself like mad, never once stopping to think that there's a strict rule against inmates going swimming. . . . Sometimes people show up a year after the burial to claim some body long since lost in the shuffle. Then the gang has to go and dig up the whole works, sorting through the pile of rotted corpses to find the one whose relatives suddenly discovered a great family affection for him. The stink that hung over the Island on those grave-robbing days was terrific. We dreaded those scavenger hunts. . . . Guys who handle the stiffs aren't licked at all, come out way ahead because they strike gold in those graves. All you need is a pair of pliers and a hammer, and you're a prospector—all the 24-carat crowns and silver bridge-work in Potters Field are yours for the asking, or anyhow the digging. Many a Bull Durham sack bulging out of a con's hip pocket, filled with this loot, literally worth its weight in gold. . . .

Often on Sunday afternoons, after our band concerts, I would wander by myself across the old cemetery and get to thinking of all those thousands of society's cast-offs, the despised paupers who were expelled from life; there was civilization's dung-heap, the guys who had worshipped at the altar of the almighty hand-out, laying there under my feet flat on their backs, staring up vacantly at me. I got a funny feeling, sometimes, that they all had their right hands stretched out to me, and that they were all chanting, in a whining sing-song, "Buddy, can you spare a nickel. . . ." It made me uneasy, like I was guilty of something. I wondered how many Bow Gistensohns and Mitter Foleys, and other guys like my friends of earlier days, were sandwiched in there, hugging the sod. There, I told myself, there, but for the grace of Bessie Smith, lay I. Sweet dreams, all you flophouse grads, I said to myself. R.I.P., you stumblebums. At least they'll never charge you an-other quarter for a night's lodging in a flea-bag; you'll never toss and turn again in a Bowery scratchpad, digging the lice and chinches out of your hide. Rest easy, boys, the scuffle's over. Relax, laugh ten times every eon or so. Plant you now, dig you later. . . .

I noticed something funny—a lot of guys on Hart's Island were quietly disappearing, sometimes for weeks at a time, only to turn up again with a big grin on their faces, looking smug and mighty pleased with themselves. I tuned in on the grapevine, and learned that inmates from both Hart's and Riker's were being shipped over to King's County Hospital, where they were used as guinea-pigs by some city doctors to find out what the score was with mari-huana. They stayed over in that hospital smoking all the reefer they wanted at the city's expense, playing records, eating good, and talking up a breeze, while the doctors made all kinds of tests. As the guys came drifting back they told me those doctors had gone over them from stem to stern, not missing a square inch, and hadn't been able to find one harmful effect, or prove that reefer was in any way habit-forming. I began to feel plenty sore, doing a twenty-month stretch (that's the bit the parole board finally dished out to me) for being in possession of some stuff the city's own doctors couldn't prove was any more harmful than some cornsilk cigarettes.

Just about then I spied an interesting story in the papers. A certain Justice in the Bronx Supreme Court had spoken up in protest over the city's system for punishing misdemeanors, and his whole attack was quoted. This guy said the law was in a strange condition, when on one side of the street in Westchester County you'd get one year for a certain misdemeanor, and on the other side you might get three years for the exact same thing. He went on to criticize the whole rehabilitation program, because rehabilitation was supposed to take from one to three years, but the guys sent to Riker's and Hart's, supposedly for rehabilitation, might get two or three consecutive bits for the same misdemeanor, so sometimes they'd serve as much as nine years in one stretch.

Goddamn, I thought, here's one judge who makes a lot of sense. The other cons thought so too; right quick there was a wild rush for writs of habeas corpus, so they could come up on appeal before this Justice. I saw this mad scramble and figured I might as well join it. I got myself a writ, and appeared before this same Justice.

"Your Honor," I said, "I don't know much about pleading a case in legal language, but I think it's sure funny that I should be doing all this time for possessing marihuana when the city's doctors themselves can't find out anything bad about the stuff."

"How about its effect on children?" the Judge asked. "Do you advocate its use by everyone, even minors?"

"I never advocated anything, Your Honor," I said. "I just smoked the stuff and liked it, and so did my friends, and the only thing you'd ever have to watch about it is its effect as an aphrodisiac. Naturally, kids shouldn't have that kind of stimulus handy, any more'n they should have liquor. But you take a guy thirty, forty, fifty years old, if he needs some Nature he sure can get it from marihuana, and no harm done."

"You know, don't you," said the Judge, "that the state has the right to put you away and take care of you? Are you aware of that?"

"Sure, Judge," I said. "But I been put away for something your best scientists can't prove is bad, no matter how many 'D.A's' they stamp on my record. And if the state really wants to take care of somebody, how about taking care of my wife and child while I'm stuck away in Hart's Island and can't earn a living for them?"

When he heard me mention my family, the Judge looked over the papers on my case, studying them real carefully. And then he must have come to the line about the prisoner's race, because he looked like somebody suddenly hit him in the face. When he raised his eyes again there was an entirely different expression in them. "Young man," he said, "the only trouble is, if I let you go you'll get right out with all the rest of your people and re-elect Roosevelt." He may have been joking, but it was getting on to election time, the Summer of 1942. The whole court kyaw-kyawed, and back to the Island I went. And to think that I never voted in my life.

One afternoon things came to a head for me; in ten frantic minutes the formless mush of my life bubbled and seethed and then jelled, in a shape I could finally recognize. Fireworks busted loose in my skull with a great woosh and crackle, and all of a sudden the tangled threads of my past life were pulled together and wove into a pattern that made sense, and it was the climax of all my born days—I was a man who was finally knit together in one piece again, a little tattered on the edges, maybe, with a couple of the patches still showing, but still in one piece. It happened in a matter of minutes. It may not sound like much, frozen in cold type, but it's been with me every day of my life since then, and it'll stay locked in my conkhouse till the day I die. . . .

Powerful forces had been working away inside of me, ever since the day of my arrest: that was the turning-point. I was alert and keyed-up, my mind like a muddy pool that's slowly clearing up as the scum settles to the bottom, flooding out wider all the time, sucking up new things, lapping into new places. Sitting in rehearsals

319

with the band, I'd get the strange feeling that I was on the brink of some great new discovery—my soggy brain would begin to churn and foam, wild thoughts burbling through it, and I'd go dizzy and limp. The music did that to me, mostly. Don't forget, this was the first time in twelve years, the first time since I left Chicago, that I was free to concentrate on the music with all my being. I was getting born again, going through violent growing-pains, but I kind of felt something great would burst over me one of these days and then in a flash I'd be grown-up, come to full size, a complete and functioning man, one tight seal-like unit from head to foot. The music was giving my spirit back to me. Sitting there playing, I'd feel that my life was taking on some purpose again—I was heading in the right direction, straight and true. It wasn't just by accident that I had crossed the color line; that I was holed up with my boys Travis and Frankie Ward; that I had a mixed band again, and could write my own kind of music for it. Most all the things I'd been scrambling after for so many years were coming my way now, out in the Hart's Island jail. It couldn't be an accident. There was some deep design to it. It had to lead somewhere.

There was a terrific new drive and striving in my music. Travis' melodious Armstrong runs on his horn roused something way deep inside me, Frankie's rollicking rolls and rumbles on the drums set my skin to tingling—I got the feeling that they were talking to me, saying something that would change my whole life, and I had to talk back, give them the right answers or the great thing wouldn't happen. I blew harder and harder into my clarinet, as though my life depended on it. I was on edge, taut, expectant all the time. After each rehearsal I was so worked up that my knees would buckle and I was sweating all over and there was a hollow feeling in the pit of my stomach. It was all leading up to something, something that would crack wide open with one hell of an explosion. We got frantic during those rehearsals, straining and stretching, trying to grab hold of that promising thing that dangled just out of reach. Frankie and Travis felt it too. Those rehearsals left them screwed up to a fever pitch of excitement. We could hardly talk to each other afterwards, our tongues wagged so fast and furious. Something big was in the air.

And then, on one sunny afternoon, the blow-up came. It won't sound like anything much—we were just marching along in the band, playing the same old corny *Our Director*, and the professor stopped to talk with the warden but we continued on across the Island. I was captain of the band by this time, so I took over. Then we drew close to the powerhouse, where the all-colored Ninth Division was working, and all the guys came running out to hear us, like they always did.

It always gave us more incentive to see our buddies there; we played louder and brighter for them, trying to hype up the music with a touch of the lively rhythm and spirit that they liked. It made me feel sort of foolish to be parading past all these big husky sweaty guys with nothing but a little bit of a clarinet in my hand —these boys were all holding shovels and were soaked through from using them, and I had a lot of respect for them. Just the thought of marching around all afternoon while they sweated their asses off made me feel sort of inferior, a gold-bricking weakling, and I had to justify myself somehow, so I watched every step I took, making sure it was as rhythmic and graceful as I could make it but never pretentious or flashy. I thought that if I could at least strut by them graceful and smooth in my movements, feeling every beat of the drum and showing that I felt it, it would get across something to these powerhouse guys, because they were always so sensitive to a person handling his body with ease, no matter where they saw it. That would excuse my being in this silly goddamned parade just a little.

Well, as I stepped along, the rhythm of the march made me feel exhilarated and lightheaded, and when we got near to the powerhouse and I saw all our friends there, I decided to break all the chains off me and let myself go. I was so excited and tense, all of a sudden, you would of thought I was about to rob a bank. I started to improvise the march on my clarinet, forgetting all the written music we'd rehearsed with the professor. And then, Jesus, I fell into a queer dreamy state, a kind of trance, where it seemed

321

like I wasn't in control of myself any more, my body was running through its easy relaxed motions and my fingers were flying over the keys without any push or effort from me—somebody else had taken over and was directing all my moves, with me just drifting right along with it, feeling it was all fitting and good and proper. I got that serene, crazy kind of exaltation that you hear religious people sometimes talking about and think they're cracked. And it was exactly, down to a T, the same serene exaltation I'd sensed in New Orleans music as a kid, and that had haunted me all my life, that I'd always wanted to recapture for myself and couldn't. Frankie Ward was just behind me, and the spirit caught hold of him too and he fell right in, playing drums that suddenly weren't talking the beat-up language of Sousa but the ageless language of New Orleans, thumping it out loud and forceful. Right away the whole band stiffened up and began to sparkle, like they'd all got a heavy shot of thyroid extract. Travis, who was playing the lead on his horn, got carried away in the flood too and he began to swing out with a sudden husky vibrant tone, taking his breath at the natural intervals just where he felt them, and the whole band was suddenly marching and swaying to a new rhythm. And every beat Frankie pounded on his drums was in perfect time with every variation somebody picked out on my clarinet, and my clarinet and the trumpet melted together in one gigantic harmonic orgasm, and my fingers ran every whichaway, and the fellows in the Ninth Division began to grin and stomp and shout. "Blow it Mezz!" they yelled. "Yeah, I hear you!" "Get away, poppa!" "Put me in the alley!"

And all of a sudden, you know who I was? I was Jimmy Noone and Johnny Dodds and Sidney Bechet, swinging down Rampart Street and Basin Street and Perdido Street, down through Storyville, stepping high and handsome, blowing all the joy and bounce of life through my clarinet. While the guy on those powerful drums behind me was Tubby Hall and Baby Dodds and Zutty Singleton, all rolled up in one, and the boy on the trumpet that was playing melodious hide-and-seek with my clarinet was King Oliver and Tommy Ladnier, and yes, Louis too, the one and only Pops, the greatest of them all. And it was Mardi Gras time, and we were strutting on down at the head of the gay parade, blowing *High Society* and *Didn't He Ramble* and *Moose March* and *Dusty Rag* and *Muskrat Ramble* and *Milneburg Joys* and *When the Saints Go Marching In* and *We Shall Walk Through the Streets of the City*, back in the great days when jazz was born, back at the throbbing root and source of all jazz, making it all fresh and new. All of a sudden we were right smack in Gay New Orleans. Not the one out on Flushing Meadows, Long Island, the mecca of the summer tourists—the one down on the Mississippi delta, full of levees and cribs and red lights and barrelhouse joints and honkytonks, where the greatest music in the world first trembled and soared into being. I had been wandering for twenty years, looking for this fine fabled place, and suddenly I made it, I was home. I was solid home.

For the very first time in my life, you see, I had fallen all the way into the groove and I was playing real authentic jazz, and it was *right*—not Chicago, not Dixieland, not swing or jump or Debussy or Ravel, but *jazz*, primitive, solid, rocking and weaving. All my life I'd been yearning to play this way, and all my life I'd been so scared I couldn't do it (even during those Panassié recordings) that I'd kept running off into sidestreets and detours to avoid trying and failing—and all my misery and frustration and going tangent came from that fear and that running away. Now I was no more afraid. All the rambling years behind suddenly began to make sense, fitted into the picture: the prison days, the miss-meal blues, the hophead oblivion, the jangled nerves, the reefer flights, the underworld meemies. They were all part of my education, had gone into my make-up until I was battered and bruised enough to stumble into the New Orleans idiom and have something to say in it. Those twenty years of striving and failing had all gone down into my fingertips, so that now, all of a sudden, I could tickle the clarinet keys and squeeze out the only language in the whole wide world that would let me speak my piece.

And you know what my piece was? A very simple story: *Life is good, it's great to be alive!* No matter how many times you go hungry, how many times you get a boot in your backside and a club over your head—no matter how tough the scuffle is, it's great to be alive, brother! I had to get my knocks, plenty of them, before I could understand that. The colored people, fresh up out of three hundred years of slavery, still the despised pariahs of the country in spite of their "liberation," had understood it all along, and finally, forty, fifty years ago, had roared out a revolutionary new music to shout that message to the world. That was what New Orleans was really saying—it was a celebration of life, of breathing, of muscle-flexing, of eye-blinking, of licking-the-chops, in spite of everything the world might do to you. It was a defiance of the undertaker. It was a refusal to go under, a stubborn hanging on, a shout of praise to the circulatory system, hosannas for the sweat-glands, hymns to the guts that ache when they're hollow. Glory be, brother! Hallelujah, the sun's shining! Praise be the almighty pulse! Ain't nobody going to wash us away. We here, and we going to stay put—don't recognize no eviction notices from the good green earth. Spirit's still in us, and it sure must got to jump. We going to tell 'bout all that in this fine music of ours. . . . I knew exactly what there was to say on my horn now; knew all the words in the New Orleans idiom, and how to express them. Jimmy Noone and Johnny Dodds and Sidney Bechet, they'd known all along, and now they were inside my skin, making my fingers work right so I could speak my piece.

Yes, right then and there I busted out of my spiritual gallion and came home, and my burden melted away. The rest of my life spread out in front of me smooth and serene, because I not only knew what I had to do, I knew I could do it. *I could do it.* I was with it Jim, really with it. The millennium was on me—a small-size, strictly one-man millennium, but still a millennium. It told this green man something.

Once, not long before they sprung me, I was lolling around in the dormitory, listening to the radio. We had a record program tuned on, and they began to play a recording of Sidney Bechet's, *The Blues of Bechet,* and then they turned it over and played the other side, *The Sheik of Araby.* I had never heard those two re-

cordings before—they must have been made while I was in jail—
and I sat there trembling all over, unable to believe my ears.

There are six instruments used on both sides: clarinet, soprano
sax, tenor sax, piano, bass, and drums. *And all six are played by
Bechet!* It was an engineering stunt, of course: he'd record one
instrument, then add another while the previous disc was played
back, until he built up a complete six-piece band. But if you think
it was just a gag and not wonderful music-making, better than
almost any group of five musicians could have done with Bechet,
listen to what the critics said later in *The Jazz Record Book*:
"Demonstrating the versatility of this self-taught genius, this disc
is also an interesting experiment in unity of style. It produces an
amazing and uncanny sensation when one hears all the parts
played with the intonation and intense vibrato characteristic of
Bechet."

Unity of style is right, brother. I sat there full of flutters and
quakes over that unity of style. Those two unbelievable records
are two of the greatest New Orleans jazz performances ever recorded,
with a perfect blend and balance between all six pieces, and it had
to be done by Bechet single-handed! That was the final and most
eloquent comment on the level to which our jazz had sunk, in this
mechanical swing-band age of jump, organ-grinder riffs, mop-mop
and rip-bop; there were so few musicians left around who were
still inspired with that New Orleans love of rich melodious invention, spirited teamwork, and weaving counterpoint, that when
Bechet wanted a full harmonic and rhythmic background for his
preaching, why, he had to supply it himself. Every jazz musician
alive ought to hang his head in shame, I thought, to see the great
genius of Bechet so isolated that it has to provide its own musical
environment, its own lush context.

I thought a lot about Bechet that night, especially about the thrill
I got when I recorded with him and Tommy Ladnier. I started to
pace up and down that dormitory, dreaming up musical ideas that
we could work up together once I got out of this place. I wanted
to play and record with him so much, at that moment, the need
was gnawing away in my guts like an ache. He and I were striving

for the same thing, the same rich and meaningful patterns, the same soul-satisfying blends; we would have to get together again, I knew it, and this time I would do better. Then I remembered my *Gone Away Blues*. There, right off the bat, was one thing we could do together—we'd record those blues of mine with never a solo, never a trace of musical egotism from either one of us, moaning our way through it in perfect teamwork! It was a natural for us—I was more convinced of it than ever. I got all excited, thinking about it. Old Sidney Bechet was my natural musical mate, if only he would have me.

I remembered a story Sidney had once told me, about the time he was playing with a band in Paris. He had been fighting with the other guys for weeks, trying to get them to work up one big beat and make vibrant organ chords in the background so he wouldn't be alone in his playing, there'd be a real collective spirit. That was the deepest need of his whole being, a musical collectivity; he kept screaming for it, it was an obsession with him. And one night the argument got so violent, one of the guys whom Sidney had been yelling at went and got a gun and came back and took some potshots at him, missing him but winging some innocent bystanders. Both guys were shoved in the Bastille for that, and stayed there for eleven months; Sidney's hair turned completely white in that dungeon. . . .

The story began to mean a hell of a lot to me, as I thought about it now. Teamwork, collective spirit, rich blending harmony—that was Sidney Bechet's whole life. He had to fight for it if it killed him. He needed it so bad, that as an act of desperation and a gesture to show his own integrity, he finally sat down and did it all by himself, on those two incredible records. What a terrific moral was buried in that virtuoso exhibition! It meant: Life gets neurotic and bestial when people can't be at peace with each other, say amen to each other, chime in with each other's feeling and personality; and if discord is going to rule the world, with each guy at the next guy's throat, all harmony gone—why, the only thing for a man to do, if he wants to survive, if he won't get evil like all the other beasts in the jungle, is to make that harmony inside himself, be at peace with himself, unify his own insides while the snarling world gets pulverized. If the harmonic environment was gone, well, Sidney could still manage. He carried his own environment around inside him, for emergencies. It was kind of a parable for the world.

There was the great secret of Sidney's genius, and of all our music, in one concentrated capsule. Sidney was the supreme example of a man at peace with himself, all his parts in harmony —in three-part harmony, to be exact, with the pulse of his heart and guts and nervous system bouncing along underneath to provide a three-piece rhythm section for it. That was how you had to be if you wanted to play this great music. Let yourself get blown into a thousand jagged fragments, like the world around you, and you can't pour harmonious New Orleans music out of your soul—that serene exaltation is gone. If you let yourself get all split up and pulverized inside, maybe you can make "modern" music, the music of tics, the swing and jump and rip-bop. That's the musical mania of the blowtops, the running-amuck music of guys wrastling with themselves, rolling around on the ground and having fits while their broken-up souls carry on a war inside them. Modern swing and jump is frantic, savage, frenzied, berserk—it's the agony of the split, hacked-up personality. It's got nothing at all in common with New Orleans, which by contrast is dignified, balanced, deeply harmonious, high-spirited but pervaded all through with a mysterious calm and placidity—the music of a personality that hasn't exploded like a fragmentation bomb.

Yes, you had to be integrated and harmonized yourself, all your parts running along side by side, never tripping each other up, locking arms and keeping in step all the way. Because that was the whole spirit of our music, of collective improvisation, and you had to have it in you, in every molecule, before you could blow it into a horn or beat it out on a drum. *Get together* is the slogan for our music. *Get yourself together* is the personal slogan for all the guys who want to make this great music. New Orleans, first and foremost, is nothing but fellowship in music, fraternity, brotherhood, mutual aid. Get unified yourself, and then you can work with the other guys. And then, if you don't find the other guys to work with, you can even do it all on your own—like the great Louis Armstrong adding runs on the end of his phrases to fill out the harmony missing in his background, like the great Sidney Bechet making a whole goddamned band out of his great harmonious soul.

I'll never forget the night I heard those two records. It was another terrific moment of revelation. It put the final touches to my education, in music and a whole gang of other things.

September 28th, 1942: they bring me into an office where there's a guy from a New York Local Draft Board. It's the day before my release. He asks me some questions, then hands me my draft card: "Milton Mezzrow; Height, 5′ 10″; Weight, 165; Race, Negro. . . ." Next day I climbed on board the ferry, waved good-bye to all the guys on the dock, and sailed across the river to Manhattan. No doubts or hesitations this trip; Poppa Hamlet had been dispossessed from my skull for good. Straight back into Harlem I headed, said hello to all the boys and girls, and settled down and unpacked my clarinet. Talk about rehabilitation. I was rehabilitated so good that for months the taste of real butter nauseated me, and one whiff of perfume made my stomach rise up like a balloon. . . .

I did some more work on *Gone Away Blues*; I wrote *Out of the Gallion*, and a gang of blues and other numbers. Right away I started to play—in pick-up bands, on one-night gigs, in jam sessions on 52nd Street and down in Greenwich Village, in little nightclubs and dancehalls. I travelled to Harvard, up to Montreal and Toronto, to Philly, to Washington, all over; I played for the Turkish Ambassador's son in his fancy embassy, at the National Press Club in Washington, for a fraternity house in Cambridge, for Newspaper Guild parties, in high-school auditoriums during assemblies, for everybody, everywhere. Mostly I played with colored guys from Harlem, sometimes with white guys close to the New Orleans idiom. If I made a lot of money, all right—but there were times when I was flat broke, and that was all right too, I wasn't brought down. If you can't make money, make friends. I made friends.

I found that I was making friends everywhere, thanks to my earlier records mostly, especially the Panassié ones. Wherever I went, merchant seamen, soldiers and sailors from many different countries, and writers and critics and artists and students and fellow musicians too, would drop around to say hello, tell me they'd picked up some of those records I made with Bechet and Tommy Ladnier in some far corner of the earth, let me know how much they liked them. How I wished that Tommy could have been with me now, to enjoy the little fame that he deserved so much and was just now beginning to get. . . . The Thirties hadn't been a great big blank in my life after all; I'd tried to pull myself together a few times during those years, at least to make some records, and the effort was beginning to pay dividends. I got many friendly letters from different countries—from Australia, from England, from South Africa and Java and Morocco and the Belgian Congo, from jazz enthusiasts in the underground in France and Belgium and Holland and Norway. They'd started to trickle in even before the war. "Dear Mezz!" one guy had written from Zürich back in '39, "All the Hot Club of Zürich has been out of this world by hearing this afternoon at a great record session the first time your two wonderful records which you have recorded for 'Swing.' We all are hoping, if Hitler and Mussolini will not loose their nerves and destroy in a beastical way our good old Europa, that we can make coming also the other fourteen sides, made under your leadership, from Paris to us. . . . A great fan of good jazz, like Armstrong, Bechet and you do it, sends you his most sincerely greetings and wishes. . . ." All these kids kept up their interest in the music, and their letters began to arrive more and more often, partly, I guess, on account of Panassié and Madeleine Gautier getting them to write so I wouldn't be too blue after my months in prison. "Dear Milton," a nineteen-year-old British student wrote from Switzerland while I was still in jail, "I just got your 'new address' from Hugues and thought I might write to you just to let you know that the greatest white musician of all time hasn't been forgotten in spite of everything. . . ." Then I got a whole gang of letters from other guys in Hot Clubs all over the world, like the one which said:

"From my dear friend, Hugues Panassié, I've learned your address, and I'm anxious to tell you all the admiration I have for you. Most of your records are my strongest favourites and I don't think there was ever a white musician who is able to play the right kind of jazz (before all, the blues) with such sincerity and inspiration as you do. . . ." The letters kept on coming. I knew their praise for me was much much too lavish, but I appreciated their gestures of friendship. I began to get a picture of the hot-jazz fraternity as a kind of global network, a real one-world organization without manifestos or declarations of principle, and there was a place for me in it, a satisfying place, where I could play and be in touch with a gang of regular guys, guys who talked my language. All in all, I felt good.

Finally I went into Jimmy Ryan's on 52nd Street and stayed there for almost a full year, playing with a little trio. And one night a tall skinny young blond guy came in, and sat there for hours quietly, just listening to the music. I thought he might be some jazz-loving visitor from Harvard or Yale, but when we got to talking he told me his name was John van Beuren and he wasn't a college kid at all but an electronics engineer specializing in radar and stuff like that, and he owned some kind of electronics manufacturing plant out in Jersey where he made radar measuring equipment for the government. He had all the records I made with Ladnier and Bechet too, and he said he thought they were fine and that I ought to record some more with guys like that.

We talked for a long time. He was a rare bird, one of those scientists who can see way beyond a test tube. He told me he had a theory that you get the same kind of excitement and satisfaction from jazz, real collectively improvised jazz, that you do from solving a tough problem in mathematics, and it made sense the way he put it. "When you take off on a number, it sounds as though you never know where you're going to come out, you just go flying off into musical space," he said. "Then, almost by a miracle, you finally all come together and the tension is resolved. I imagine it's the same kind of good feeling a mathematician gets when he digs into a problem, working blind, groping his way along, and then suddenly the right formula clicks and the whole thing resolves itself, and all the pieces fit together." I had flunked algebra in high school so I couldn't go very deep into the subject with him, but I liked this guy's enthusiasm and his serious approach to the music. I began to see a lot of him and his wife Jane, visited their house often, gabbed all night long about what is jazz and what isn't.

And then, one night, he upped and said, "Mezz, you and I have the same ideas about this music—how about getting together with me and my partner Harry Houck and going into the record business? There's a real need for a recording company that will concentrate on the best blues and New Orleans music, while the great oldtimers are still around to play it. . . ." Things began to happen in a dizzy whirl, after that; I remember saying "Yeah, sure," and before I knew it I was sitting behind a desk in a midtown office, trying to look like an executive. Executive, hell: I was president of the corporation, and I had to be damned careful about not wearing socks with holes where they showed. King Jazz, Inc.; Milton Mezzrow, Prezz. I've got business cards to prove it, and I'll be glad to let you have one if I can find any without fingerprint smudges on them. Why, I even got office hours. I hold auditions, I hire people. The Morris Plan thinks I'm so solid and substantial, they want to make me a loan. Pretty soon I'm going to be a home-owner, and I'll be paying taxes like all solid citizens. I only hope they spell my name right in *Who's Who*, and get the dates of my prison record straight, and don't forget to say "Race, Negro."

We began to record like mad: during the first months of 1945 alone, we made over fifty sides. And who do you think I recorded with? A lot of wonderful guys who used to knock me out on the South Side of Chicago in the great days—Big Sid Catlett on drums, and Kaiser Marshall on drums too; and wonderful old Pops Foster on bass, the same guy I'd worshipped when he was in King Oliver's historic band. Then we got Pappa Snow White on trumpet, and Jimmy Blythe, Jr., and Fitz Weston on piano, all solid musicians in the New Orleans idiom. And on soprano sax—Sidney Bechet!

Sidney the one-man band, in person! One of the numbers I recorded with Bechet and the others was *Gone Away Blues*; then we did *Out of the Gallion*, and a gang of others that had terrific personal meaning for me. I was the only white man in the crowd. I walked on clouds all through those recording sessions. . . . We got hold of a great old vaudeville team, Sox Wilson and his wife Coot Grant, marvelous oldtime blues singers and composers who'd worked with Louis Armstrong and Sidney Bechet and Ma Rainy on the South Side, and they wrote some up-from-the-guts blues for us, and we got hold of Pleasant Joe, a blues singer three months out of New Orleans, to do the vocals for us, and it was good. The music we played together, not a note of it on paper, all of it welling up out of our enthusiasm and our warm feeling for each other, was New Orleans, some forty or fifty years old and always new. And that's what we're going to go on making and recording, for as long as we've still got a breath of wind left in our bodies and a solid beat left in our hearts.

Ernest Borneman, the anthropologist and musicologist, got around to reviewing these records in *The Record Changer*, and it knocked me out when he said that the blues I recorded with Bechet, the same ones I thought up during my jail bit, went "back beyond Louis and beyond Bunk Johnson and beyond Buddy Bolden, to the very roots of the music, to the cane fields and the rice and the indigo and the worksongs and the slave ships and the dance music of the inland Ashanti and the canoe songs of the Wolof and Mandingo along the Senegal River." That was plenty good enough for me. I had spent my whole life digging for those roots. Maybe I had found some of them at last, even though I didn't know their names. Maybe, at last, I was a real jazz musician. . . . Sometimes now, when I play those records over and close my eyes and let those weary wails go through me, the tears start coming and I think to myself, Jack, maybe I got it, maybe I solid got it. I keep thinking, some day good old Pops, wonderful old Louis Armstrong, is going to hear this way-back music we made and he'll understand how I kept fighting to get with him all these years and we'll get back in the same old groove we were in long ago. I hope he digs these records some day, and reads this book too. They'll tell him all the things I just couldn't get my lips to say because I didn't know the words then.

When I wash away, don't nobody mourn for me, and don't nobody cart me out to Potters Field to dump me all in a heap with the other scorned and forgotten castaways. I don't aim to have my fillings and bridgework picked out, to fatten the Bull Durham sack in some junkie's or lushhead's pocket. Uh, uh. Just take my body and shove it in one of them blast furnaces, and when I'm melted down good, scrape out the dust and mix it up with some shellac and press it into a record with a King Jazz label on it. Don't stamp any "D.A." on the label. Just mark down, "Here lies Mezz the Prezz, home at last." And on one side press *Gone Away Blues*, and on the other *Out of the Gallion*, and then take it up to Harlem and give it to some raggedy kid on The Corner who hasn't got the price of admission to see the stage show at the Apollo or a deuce of blips to buy himself a glass of foam. Let him play that record until it cracks or wears out, or until he gets tired of it, and then let him throw it away and that's that. Just do that, and you'll know I'll be happy. That's memorial enough for me.

I'm playing in a jam session in a Village basement joint when in wanders this young white fellow who tells me he don't know much about music, he's a writer, but he likes my records fine—they're a kind of jazz you don't get much of any more. He's figuring on maybe doing some kind of magazine article about me and what do I think of the idea? Right away he begins to pop more questions than a D.A.; and pretty soon I'm blabbing away like crazy, running my mouth for hours at a time, and him drinking it all in. I'm beginning to remember all the things that ever happened to me, and it kind of scares me, but under this guy's cross-examination it all comes flooding out. Never saw a guy who got his ears bent so much without saying boo. Hell, he even seemed to like it. He must of been on one of them masochism kicks that are all the go today.

He begins hanging around up in Harlem with me. Finally one night he comes out with it. "Listen Mezz," he says, and I know there's a hype coming. "You know you've got a pretty interesting story to tell—nobody could do justice to it in one lousy article, and besides, if we told the truth, no magazine in the country would dare to print it, they'd be so scared of corrupting the morals of the young. It needs a book, a hell of a long book, and you've got to write it. It's more important than you think."

"Me write a book?" I say. "Hell, that's like asking a bricklayer to take up embroidery for a hobby. Why man, the King's English would never recover from the shock. I better keep on telling my story on my horn, and let it go at that."

But this guy is persistent; he's always talking to me about writers I never heard of, André Gide, B. Traven, Céline, Henry Miller and guys like that, and reading parts of their books to me. He says, "Mezz, you've got a story to tell just like those writers did, and it deserves to get down on paper. Look: you've been lying flat on your back for a quarter of a century, almost, watching the screwy kaleidoscope of American life jiggle and squirm over your head. Not very many people have gotten a good look at their country from that bottom-of-the-pit angle before, seen the slimy underside of the rock—at least, they haven't put it down for other people to read. It's a chunk of Americana, as they say, and it should get written. It's a real American success story, upside down: Horatio Alger standing on his head. Of course, it's not the cute kind of folk-lore that hammy poets write sloganizing verse plays out of, not one of those epic, synthetic, soap-opera fantasies about the land of the free, down-to-earth with a thump by the sound-effects man. It couldn't be intoned over the radio on patriotic occasions, for the edification of the young citizenry. Maybe it would even be too raw to sell very well as a book, so you couldn't count on much of a com-mercial success. You can't quite picture the book clubs dishing it out to the middle classes for week-end titillation in a hammock."

He's always drifting off like that, using tongue-twisting words at the drop of a hat, this literary pal of mine.

"But," he goes on, soon as he gets his wind back, "your story would have this virtue: it's true, authentic. Things happen, in this country especially, the way you've told them to me, not the way they're pictured in the soap-operas and the flag-waving verse plays for narrator and star-spangled chorus. In a real sense, Mezz, your story is the plight of the creative artist in the U.S.A.—to borrow a phrase from Henry Miller, that writer I told you about. It's the odyssey of an individualist, through a land where the population is manufactured by the system of interchangeable parts. It's the saga of a guy who wanted to make friends, in a jungle where everybody was too busy making money and dodging his own shadow. It's that, and plenty of other things, and if you don't write it yourself you've got to sit down and write it with me."

I sure never suspected I was living a saga and an odyssey, during all those frantic years. I thought I was just trying to keep my head above water, and feed my breadbasket now and then, and maybe chase a butterfly and a soapbubble or two. Now it turns out I was *significant!* Man oh man, it looks like you got to watch every move you make; you can't be too careful. If I'd known I was being significant, instead of just hungry and beat, I sure would have changed my ways.

I wasn't convinced, but this guy was such a gab-artist, damn if he didn't talk me into it. We put our heads together hard, with a crack that jolted both of us right down to our socks, and we kept them together for two solid years, and we finally wrote that book, losing several tons of weight and a few decades of sleep in the process. This is the book. If it got in your mouth, don't fault me. Like I said, it's a story that happened in the U.S. of A.

APPENDICES

New Orleans and Chicago: the Root and the Branch

WHAT IS "Chicago style"?

The whole Chicago school was an offshoot from New Orleans. Now, the typical New Orleans jazz band had six or seven pieces in it: a rocking rhythm section in the background, made up of piano sometimes, banjo, bass fiddle or tuba, and drums, with two or three wind instruments romping out in front, weaving together around the melody, the trumpet or cornet, the clarinet, and the trombone. The rhythm instruments just provided a solid, steady beat, never trying to fight their way into the lead as solo instruments. The trumpet played a kind of lead on a harmony part, paving the way and setting the pace, laying down the basic riffs of the *improvised* melody. The trombone played more of a bass part, or, say, a bass and a sort of baritone mixed, which gave a solid foundation for the clarinet to keep weaving in and out, contrapuntally filling in the gaps. The banjo was strummed in a steady four-four, sometimes accentuating the afterbeat and in some cases using an afterbeat by itself, and the bass, drums and piano kept right in step. Those oldtime colored musicians who played the piano or banjo followed common harmony sequences with the correct inversions, using triads of the chords and adding the dominant seventh at the right time, so the various instrumentalists were given freedom to invent as they wanted.

It was chamber music, Basin Street style, and it was good. The jazz band was made up out of the main instruments in the street bands, and they worked up ideas taken over from the blues and worksongs of the colored folks, plus the fast-stepping music of the marching societies. Into their improvisation, not thinking about it, just letting all the stored-up music in their skulls percolate around some, they wove the stomps and joys and hollers, the shouts and laments, the gavottes and quadrilles, all the different kinds of music that came from Creole string trios and Storyville whorehouse pianos, and from the levee and the riverboat and the picnicgrounds and the burial-grounds too. And the players had it seared into their bones how their people used to moan and wail their sorrows when they had the blues, and how they bubbled with laughter, and so they tried to get the same heartfelt sounds on their instruments when they played. They never had much training in the classical European school of music, so they weren't taught to get a "pure" and untainted tone out of each instrument. Their wind instruments played the way that was most natural to them; grunted and growled, sobbed and laughed too, like human voices. They *spoke* on their horns. They got sounds out of those horns that the classical musicians said you never could get, because it was their souls speaking out full and frank. And all the time the rhythm section paced the way in the background, with a pulse that made it all rock. The horns played muted a whole lot, and the trumpet got different tonal effects by using plungers and other homemade devices. And they all played together, doing little or no solo work, strictly ensemble, each one adding another brick to the simple and sturdy structure of the music. They all came out of the same world and had the same story to tell, so they had a real collective brotherly feeling. They kept on speaking all together and bolstering each other. Some New Orleans trumpet players, in fact, took over the inflections of the preacher and actually "preached" on their horns to each other. Joe Oliver and Bubber Miley were famous for this effect. One trumpet player even got the nickname of "Preacher."

That's how it was with New Orleans music. With each player trying to give the others a richer and fuller accompaniment, no musician ever had to accompany himself in taking a chorus like a lot of players do today, to fill out the harmony background. Listen to Louis Armstrong playing in front of a big band. His style is built solidly on New Orleans, but when he plays with a written accompaniment he gets the feeling that certain notes or sequences of notes are missing in the mechanical harmony. So when hé finishes a melodic run he will wind up the phrase by adding a beautiful note or series of notes that belong to the harmony. He's just accompanying himself, making up for the lacks in the arrangement and the composer's ear. That's how some of his most famous riffs got born—not as flourishes to dress up a melody, but to make the harmony fuller and add the most colorful sequences. That never happened in a real good New Orleans band. They gave you the needed background, rhythmically and harmonically; a real hard-packed foundation, without the sophistication that gets mechanical. It's a funny thing, but the New Orleans drum patterns, the core of the band's rhythm, were closest to "legitimate" music, because they came right out of the military beat of the march. *Muskrat Ramble*, like many New Orleans classics, is based entirely on the march idiom. Even in a New Orleans military band, a colored drummer would send you because each beat of his drum was clear; he just used a snare and he really got a tone out of his drums to fit in with the music being played, so when he laid down the rhythm all the other instruments just naturally fell in with him. And the harmonic color and flavor of the whole band came from the blues idiom and the spirituals, added to the marches. The major and the minor were combined: they gave you a dominant seventh with a minor third above it, producing the wailing moan that is characteristic of the blues and so vital to all New Orleans jazz.

Now, about the Chicagoans. When they first started to play, what they followed mostly was the music of the white New Orleans Rhythm Kings and of Bix and the Wolverines, and they did what the Wolverines had done—they dropped the New Orleans tailgate trombone in favoɪ of the tenor sax. So now, when the cornet or trumpet played the lead, the clarinet was voiced above it, stuck up near the musical ceiling, and the tenor sax played under it instead of a trombone. They lost a lot there. Now they got a different voicing and flavoring; the original thick sauce was watered down. With this changed harmony structure, the tenor sax couldn't add anything but a third part harmony, couldn't get bass effects as well as a lyrical quality like the trombone did, and the clarinet had to jump to that voicing always above the trumpet, instead of being free to use the unanchored arpeggio style, running over all the registers, for which the clarinet is best suited. Right here is one of the main reasons why Tesch didn't sound so good on his Brunswick recordings.* (This is another point where New Orleans agreed with the classical teachings. Symphony clarinetists, and composers too, know that the instrument works out best with the arpeggio style of playing. I'll bet ten dollars Johnny Dodds and Jimmy Noone never had to woodshed in any conservatory of music to learn that secret.) So, to begin with, the lack of that real deep, masculine, tailgate New Orleans trombone in the cellar threw the boys way off.

Chicago style is an innocent style. It's the playing of talented youngsters just learning their musical ABC's, and New Orleans was its source, but you can't expect any derivative to be as good as the source. New Orleans was simple, but not innocent. It vibrated with deep musical understanding; it showed a real grounding in fundamentals, an instinctive urge to fit together the right way. Art in its simplest form is always the most beautiful, and that's why New Orleans was great. But in their innocence, wanting to outdo their elders and kind of show off how precocious they were, the Chicagoans lost their simplicity, the *rightness* of musical pattern. Trying to show how good they were, they got too fancy, sometimes, too ornate and over-elaborate, full of uncalled-for frills and ruffles. When they took over a lot of New Orleans effects, they sometimes used them mechanically, not building up to them so solidly that you felt they were needed by the whole logic of the music, but just reeling them off and pronouncing them too much. They got a lot of flash, musical fireworks; but the *rightness* wasn't always there. New Orleans stayed close to fundamentals, relying on strong steady rhythm and real soulful interpretation

* See pages 346-349.

by wind instruments, on rich tonal effects, to give it power, instead of on a lot of complicated chords and fancy musical patterns.

The Chicagoans had trouble. They didn't trust themselves to be inventive from start to finish, like the New Orleans musicians who started off with nothing but a beat from the drummer and made it up from then on, the leader not even tipping them off as to what key they were going to play in. (King Oliver always said, "Man, you're a musician, ain't you—what you got to know the key for?") Feeling kind of uncertain, these youngsters needed some kind of musical anchor that would hold them all together, something they could all tie a lifeline to; and a musical spring-board too, to get them started. So they usually picked on some published number they all knew, and followed the melody through, playing around it but never deserting it entirely in favor of their own melodic ideas. When I first met them all, they never played the blues at all, except for Muggsy Spanier. Maybe they were worried that if they didn't have some known tune to guide them, their musical instincts wouldn't be strong enough to lead them all into the right harmony patterns. The way Tesch sometimes drops back to the written melody when his invention falters, like a flier taxiing into the airfield again when his fuel gets low and his engine begins to sputter, is an example of this lack of assurance. They needed some signpost that would be in everybody's sight all through. It was collective improvisation with them, maybe, but it was limited by the laid-down melody.

They did take over a lot of New Orleans effects, but they were sometimes too self-conscious about their use, instead of letting them always build up naturally. They got a lot of Negroid touches; some of them were good, some too pronounced. Some of these derived tricks later came to be identified with the Chicago school. Here are the main ones:

The flare-up: At the first ending of a chorus, the band holds a chord and the Chicago drummer makes a break and hits his cymbal. This was a call to all the wandering sheep to come back to the fold, the signal for a musical reunion. A big chord and rhythm are built up at the same time; this is a meeting-place for all the instruments; they've been romping around and now they're back together again, before they set out on their travels once more. It's like a runway for a rocket ship to take off. This came straight from New Orleans (except that in New Orleans the trumpet alone usually holds the note), but it was sometimes a little artificial because there wasn't enough running wild before it. In New Orleans, the flare's punch comes from the fact that the improvising musicians have been tearing loose for real, so their coming together is spectacular—it's kind of a bunching-up before a wild leap into the unknown again. But the Chicago boys, sticking with a written melody the way they did, couldn't stray too far off, and so the flare-up doesn't develop naturally all the time; there's not always enough build-up for it. They laid back waiting for it and made it too pronounced. The funny thing is that Tin Pan Alley's arrangers picked this trick up and still use it.

The explosion: This comes either at the end of the first eight bars of a 32-bar number, where the harmony has a tendency to modulate itself back to the beginning of the number; or at the end of the 16th bar of a 32-bar number where there is no release; or at the end of the release. The drum makes a cymbal crash and a heavy bass-drum beat on the fourth beat of the measure, giving the musicians a chance to catch their breath and get ready to start their collective improvisation again. They're all poised now, ready to shove off into the next eight bars. With New Orleans, the explosion was an incidental cymbal and bass-drum beat accented behind whoever was speaking his piece on his horn—sort of an amen from the congregation. New Orleans drummers used this effect with faultless taste, just where it belonged; Chicago players sometimes just stuck it in because it was a thing to do, not because a musical progression, paced by a masterful drummer like Baby Dodds or Zutty Singleton, cried out for it, to keep the pulse going and call everybody home.

The shuffle rhythm: Born out of doubling tempo, this beat is a lost art today. What novelty bands call shuffle rhythm nowadays doesn't have anything in common with what the Chicagoans did. We played a more staccato style on the release, keeping it steady, without strong accents, except for the drums pointing the beat up; it was like the regular time-step of a good fast dancer. We got that rhythm from Baby Dodds and Jimmy Noone, and it was Dave Tough who hipped us to it. It came from Baby Dodds playing on the woodblock or the rims of his bass drums (when he couldn't play the drums in the regular way during recordings) and from lower-register variations of Jimmy Noone. Dave and Bud Freeman used to walk around singing this rhythm to each other, and this more than anything else came to identify Chicago style. What makes the beat sound like it's accented and syncopated is that when it's played on the drum you play the first three beats from left hand to right hand or right to left as a pick-up to the bar, and then one beat with the left hand and two more with the right hand, continuing for the rest of the measures until the explosion is reached, sort of a waltz beat against four-four time. As a matter of fact, we coined the term *explosion* first to describe the climax the shuffle rhythm builds up to.

The break: This is a spot where the whole band lays back for two or four bars, and one musician steps forward to speak for himself. It was sort of a novelty effect invented by the colored boys to show off the versatility of the different instrumentalists, who never had to play the same thing twice. Sometimes the break even happened in a solo, with the harmony dropping away so the player is all by himself. The Chicagoans used this trick pretty well too, just as they did the shuffle rhythm, but they couldn't often get off like the colored boys to take full advantage of the breaks—they weren't usually as forceful, rich and novel in their inventions.

Those are the main elements of Chicago style. The only thing we can claim to have developed at all was the shuffle rhythm. Everything else was taken pretty much as is right out of New Orleans. And our total effect was uneven. Of the whole gang, you'll find that only three instruments, the drums, trombone, and cornet, were really near the Negro idiom. Gene and Floyd O'Brien and Muggsy came closer to the source than anyone else, including myself, on a couple of those early records. To this day Muggsy plays nearer to Louis Armstrong than any white cornet player, although he lacks Louis' drive and inventive genius. And, as you can hear on the old records, Gene played some things on his snare and bass drum that few drummers, including the colored ones today, have captured. They're a direct challenge to Gene's own style today. More than any other white Floyd O'Brien mastered the real solid tailgate style of Kid Ory, and the plunger and growl of Tricky Sam Nanton, greatest trombone player who ever lived. Herman Foster played good blues guitar. Dave Tough and Whettling played drums like Baby Dodds and Tubby Hall, and Joe Sullivan's chordal inflections on the piano (he played correct inversions, with his left hand beating out tenths and keeping the bass moving) showed he was catching the New Orleans spirit, especially Earl Hines'. As for Tesch, he was going tangent to the colored man's idiom more and more, thanks to his obsession with the modern-classical composers.

The best way to bring this discussion down to earth is to take a good listen at some of the prize examples of Chicago style that have been preserved in wax. Let's try to rip some of them open and look at their insides:

I Found a New Baby, a straight 32-bar number with a release (or middle part), opens up without any introduction. The first chorus is ensemble and a little unorganized—Tesch has trouble finding a harmony pattern to weave and gets completely lost in the 23rd and 24th bars. The second chorus is a typical Tesch clarinet solo—he plays more of a fiddle style (the fiddle was his original instrument), and when he does use arpeggios as the colored clarinetists did they're based on a melodic line without enough contrapuntal awareness to make it New Orleans. At the end of the release in his solo there's a South Side inflection in the *explosion*. Right after Tesch's chorus, in the first ending leading into Sullivan's piano solo, Muggsy uses one of Louis Armstrong's two-bar *flares*. Sullivan's piano chorus defines his character at the time—he was a studious but timid musician, but he had two hands full of piano compared with the other white piano players of the day. At the end of the piano chorus, in the last two bars, Muggsy uses another *flare* in which only the last bar is Armstrong's riff, the first being his own touch. The next chorus is mine; I open up with a rhythmic riff and go into a *shuffle rhythm* in the release, finishing with a typical Negroid inflection in the last two bars, before the first ending. This chorus is more in the blues than the jazz idiom, on account of my absorption of the blues in Pontiac and from Bessie Smith's records; I hadn't fully soaked up the New Orleans style of Jimmy Noone and Johnny Dodds. There's another typical Armstrong *flare* by Muggsy at the end of my chorus, and we go into the fifth chorus, ensemble again. Here, in the eighth bar, I play what is known as a *blue note*, which demands an explosion, and Gene catches me with a hard bass-drum beat to accent it. (This is a good example of how important the drums are to this music, and how alert a drummer must be.) We go into another explosion at the end of the release, and we end the number with a two-bar *break* on the tenor sax, followed by a Charleston beat on the cowbell which I got from Armstrong. But this part was unfinished: there should have been two more bars to this break, but the fellows didn't want to take the time to figure out the harmony parts, so they let it go at that.

There'll Be Some Changes Made is a 32-bar number with a four-bar tag (a repeat of the last four bars), and no release, which is very characteristic of Clarence Williams' song structure. (There's no release in the blues pattern either.) It opens with a four-bar introduction with Tesch playing the lead, the bass drum making two beats in typical New Orleans fashion, and then it goes into the first chorus, collectively improvised, with Muggsy playing the lead kind of like Armstrong. There's no flare at the wind-up, and Tesch is having trouble again in orienting himself harmonically; it's a weak first ending but Muggsy plays a typical Armstrong riff in the 27th and 28th bars, full of vigor, one of Louis' beautiful trademarks. For the second chorus McKenzie sings all out of time, in his St. Louis racetrack inflection without a trace of New Orleans spirit—and at that his vocal is better than most white singers of the day could do. At the end of the vocal there's another Armstrong riff and *flare* by Muggsy. Then Tesch takes his solo, and here you'll see him jumping back to the melody a few times because his ear and technique weren't trained well enough in the

New Orleans idiom, so he has trouble weaving through the chordal progressions. It's this falling back on the melody, and dropping the roving New Orleans arpeggio style, that has led naïve critics to call Tesch's style an economic, "few notes" one. The few notes come from a failure, not a special gift. At the end of this chorus there's another Armstrong *flare* by Muggsy, which leads into the last ensemble chorus. Here again there's a typical work-up into an *explosion* at the end of the 16th bar. In the 29th bar Tesch comes in on one of those rare occasions when he uses a real Jimmy Noone riff, but it's out of place here because Jimmy always used it to end a number. This misplaced New Orleans inflection drives Muggsy mad, because it derails him. Muggsy is so disgusted he doesn't even finish his last two bars—he just stops blowing altogether. He was so hot when we ended that his face was real red and he ran over to the window and tried to throw his horn out, through the glass and all. Muggsy knew the New Orleans music better than anybody else, including myself, and it knocked him way off to find that Noone riff used so mechanically, in such a stereotyped fashion. The reason he stopped blowing was not what the myth says, that he "missed" his notes, but because he was consoling himself with the thought that this was just too sad and we would have to make the whole record over. When he saw that everybody was happy about the way the record went down, and the engineers signalling "okay" from the control room, that was when his disgust got too much for him and he went for the window. So if any more ladies want to write novels about jazz musicians where they make legends out of real incidents, let them get the facts straight first.

Baby Won't You Please Come Home, a 16-bar tune with a tag (another New Orleans pattern), is an abortion that deserves to be famous for its failures. It's like a musical primer on what-not-to-do. In the introduction Condon "takes the window"—he comes in with a banjo-on-my-knee, strictly minstrel style, playing a loud riff that sounds like he's stroking a tin can, and hitting the strings so hard with his pick it's like he's saying, "This is my date and I aim to be heard." We do something pretty rare here, playing the verse of the number as well as the chorus (a New Orleans habit), and Muggsy plays it pretty nice. In the last part of the first chorus, where Muggsy is playing good, Tesch goes off again on some real bad harmony which like to ruined the lead. The same thing happens in the ensemble beginning of the second chorus. The third chorus is Eddie Condon's vocal monstrosity, probably the worst singing effort in the whole history of recorded jazz. This miscarriage led Brunswick's own critic, when he was writing the notes for a Tesch album in 1945, to say that this recording is "notable for one of the worst vocal choruses in the history of recording . . . [ending] with a fanciful flourish that is strictly out of a happily vanished era." That is an understatement. In the next ensemble there's a mechanical *explosion*, stuck in without any build-up—the number's too slow to justify using it. The ending has one of Eddie's corny Dixieland inflections: two notes rounding out the last bar that have no life at all and just sound like the victrola is running down. Tesch gets lost again near the ending. This is not a good record.

Jazz Me Blues is by far Tesch's best recording job: it shows him off to best advantage as a clarinet player and an orchestrator both. I helped him some with the voicing and phrasing, but most of the ideas were his. The number opens without an introduction, going right into the verse; then the first chorus on alto sax is by Tesch, and it reminds me of the way he used to play in the Midway Gardens with Muggsy and Jess Stacy—you can hear him groping for an idiom on the sax, patterning his style a little after his clarinet playing, doing an awful lot of tonguing. Tesch always used a stiff reed and got a peculiar tone because he had to force it, it was late coming out and had no resonance or flexibility. After the alto solo comes a four-bar piano *break*, then we go back to the verse ensemble. Next comes an interlude leading into the piano solo which is characteristic of the style and the idiom that Tesch loved— a definitely set melody with three-part harmony, pretty and with a lot of sentimental quality. During Sullivan's piano solo, Gene uses a heavy press roll on the snare drum and accents the second beat with the foot pedal on the bass drum, a characteristic beat of Zutty Singleton's. Tesch invented the four-bar *break* which follows his clarinet solo, opening with a duet by Rod and me and continuing with Rod alone for the last two bars, as a lead-in to his alto solo. Tesch comes in on the first ending, and we all go into the last chorus ensemble, with a heavy riff by the saxes that was taken from New Orleans. There's another four-bar *break* in this last chorus, split four ways: Tesch takes the first bar, Rod the second, myself the third, and Eddie the last. This was Tesch's idea too, adapted from the South Side bands. Tesch's clarinet playing on this record was his very best.

A whole lot more could be said about these records, but that's plenty for now. The reason for all this analysis is that these were some of the trail-blazing records: they defined the Chicago School, so-called. There have been so many myths grown up around them and the guys who made them that I wanted to help, as much as I could, to get the story straight.

Many years later Bud Freeman showed an unusually solid understanding of the confused perspectives and derivative quality of Chicago style. In an interview in *Down Beat* (December 1, 1942), he said: "In our youth . . . we were schooled on the New Orleans Rhythm Kings (a white band). They brought a new kind of music to us. It was something that we had never heard or felt before. We didn't know what it was . . . didn't even realize that it was to any extent Negroid. . . . That was in the very early days when the Negro bands hadn't really begun to develop out of New Orleans and Memphis. There were some colored bands who had come up the river and migrated to Chicago, that's true, but they weren't developed, organized bands then. And another thing, they were playing in places that we weren't supposed to go as kids." He goes on to tell how Dave Tough one day went to the Lincoln Gardens to hear Joe Oliver's band with Louis Armstrong in it, and how Dave went crazy over this new music. "At first we didn't understand the music. We didn't know if we liked it or not. It was a more vigorous music than the Rhythm Kings and it was really quite a lot different. Although we were at first confused by Joe Oliver's band, we soon decided that it was the thing so we took up their style and dropped that of the Rhythm Kings. When

Louis left Joe and started playing on his own at the Sunset with Earl Hines, we followed him. . . . Then about that time, just to confuse things more, Bix Beiderbecke came along with a still different style to exert the greatest influence that any white man had on us. Take, if you can, a composite of, first, the New Orleans Rhythm Kings who planted the seed, and then Joe Oliver, Louis Armstrong, Bix, Jimmy Noone . . . and Bessie Smith. Our style, 'Chicago style,' came from all of that."

Bud went on to say some very nice things about me: "I think that our style and our success individually depended as much upon a fellow by the name of Mezz Mezzrow, as it did upon all of the musicians put together. Mezz never spent enough time on his instrument to make the splash that he could have, but he understood what we were doing and what we wanted and he gave us more inspiration and influenced us more than it seemed any single man could ever do. . . . He used to drive us hundreds of miles to see a band or a new musician. It's funny how much his encouragement and interest did to give us confidence in ourselves and our style. . . . [That] style was a driving style, more on the beat than others. It was as typical of the Negroes as we could make it. That was what we were striving for." Bud's words are kind, but it wasn't thanks to any remarkable qualities in me that I was able to influence the Chicagoans a little. It was only because I was trying to fight my way upstream, straight back to the source, and ignoring the side eddies and tangent ripples like Bix and modern classicism. It was because of my monomania; there was some kind of method in my madness, though I sure as hell couldn't claim credit for putting it there.

The Chicagoans, all in all, were learning fast. They were alert, and they were talented. If we had all stuck together we would have made it, we would have captured the New Orleans idiom almost completely. We'd reached the point where we played collectively, but the melodic line we followed was still a white-man's conception, a mixture of New Orleans, ragtime and white jazz. We still had plenty to learn about solid rhythm and soulful interpretation.

It was prejudice and aloofness of mind, plus some inferiority complex way down, that kept the Chicagoans from finishing what they had begun. A few of them, even though they took the Negro's music, were biased against the Negro, and wouldn't get close enough to him to learn at first-hand. When they latched on to a few riffs and played them over among themselves, without a colored audience, they got all excited and thought they had something great. That's how they acted when they recorded *Nobody's Sweetheart*. But when colored musicians listened they saw a lot was lacking. Then these kids, instead of trying to learn more, got antagonistic and shied away—maybe because they were over-sensitive and got hurt too easy, maybe, too, because they weren't sure they could do better.

Bud and Dave used to ridicule me all the time, saying nobody could ever touch the Negro race, nobody could ever play as good as them, it had to be born in you. They were in a world by themselves, you could just get close but not close enough. Bud's conclusion was that you might as well go commercial, join up with the big bands and make money. They kept saying I would never make it, I'd just break my heart trying, and wind up a tea-man, and that was that. Some of them thought that three thousand years of prejudice towering up between the races was too high a fence to hurdle. And besides, some of them figured that we'd come up with a music that didn't have to be just a shadow of New Orleans because it was good enough by itself. We really had it so to hell with any more working at it.

It was easy for them to kid themselves along like that. The general public isn't hip enough to separate what's authentic and what's phony. Even today, a white musician can go along doing his own little things, being kind of mechanical and repetitious, and then he'll suddenly play a riff taken from Noone or Armstrong or Bechet, just one—and the kids hear it and recognize it and immediately put this guy on the same level as Noone, Armstrong and Bechet, regardless of the corn that preceded and followed this one authentic touch, regardless of how that one copied riff sticks out like a sore thumb. You can coast along like that, if you want to. You don't have to work too hard at this business.

I never believed that you had to practise and study a hell of a lot to play real New Orleans. The secret is more mental than technical. If you want to play real jazz, go live close to the Negro, see through his eyes, laugh and cry with him, soak up his spirit. That's the best way to prepare for a recording; it's what I always do. If you're not prepared to do that, then okay, play your own music but don't pretend that it has anything to do with jazz. Make up a new name for what you're doing, just to keep the record straight. But if you're humble enough, and strip off all the prejudices that are a barrier between you and the source, you'll make it. It takes a lot of living and loving, among the right people. The rest comes easy.

It's taken me thirty years, but I think maybe I've finally made it. That's the road I followed. All my life I've been striving for those weaving patterns that Jimmy Noone and Johnny Dodds and Sidney Bechet left imbedded in my skull, and I think I've finally gotten pretty close to them. If I have, it's only because I spent my life fighting to get back to the source. It wasn't any special talent in me; I didn't have any more gifts than a lot of those Chicago boys. It was only a mental attitude, an instinct that steered me right. I never wanted to take up permanent lodging in the halfway-house that has gone down in history as the Chicago School.

Translation of the Jive Section

(pp. 216-219)

I'M STANDING under the Tree of Hope, selling my marihuana. The customers come up, one by one.

FIRST CAT: Hello Mezz, have you got any marihuana?

ME: Plenty, old man, my pockets are full as a factory hand's on payday.

FIRST CAT: Let me have three cigarettes [fifty cents' worth].

ME: I sure will, slotmouth. [A private inner-racial joke, suggesting a mouth as big and as avaricious as the coin slot in a vending machine, always looking for something to put in it.] (*Pointing to a man standing in front of Big John's ginmill.*) Look at the detective on your left—the head bartender slipped him some hush money, and he's swaggering around as if crime *does* pay.

FIRST CAT: I hope he croaks, I'm not paying him even a tiny bit of mind. [Literally, *father grab him* suggests that the Lord ought to snatch the man and haul him away; and when you *don't pay a man no rabbit*, you're not paying him any more attention than would a rabbit's butt as it disappears hurriedly over the fence.] Friend, this marihuana of yours is terrific, I'm going home and listen to that new record Louis Armstrong made for the Okeh company. I hear he did some wonderful playing and singing on the number *Exactly Like You.* See you at the Savoy ballroom on Thursday. [That is, the maids' night off, when all the domestic workers will be dancing there.]

SECOND CAT: Hello Mezz, give me some of that marihuana that makes all the others look silly. I'm short ten cents but I'll pay you later.

ME: O.K., gizzard, you're poor but you're honest—now don't disappoint me. [*Gizzard* has a subtle overtone here: a gizzard is stuffed, and *stuff* means jive or kidding in hip talk, so the implication is: *don't come up with no stuff,* in other words, *don't kid me, make sure that you pay me.*]

SECOND CAT: I never lie, friend. I'm going to bring a suit to the pawnshop to raise ten dollars, and I'll show up with some money.

THIRD CAT (*Coming up with his girl*): Baby, this is that fine man who has the good marihuana that will make you walk through life as unburdened as a blueblood kitten. Mezz, this is my new girl friend and she's regular, she smokes marihuana.

GIRL: All the girls are always talking about you and Louis. Are you sure there isn't something funny between you two? You've sure got the upper hand on us young girls, we've been going crazy trying to decide which of you is the wife and which the husband. But everybody loves him and we know how he must have gone right to your heart.

FOURTH CAT (*Coming up with a stranger*): Mezz, this is Sonny Thompson, he's one of the regular guys on Seventh Avenue and he's a fine dancer too. Sonny has known what it's all about since he was a kid, and he smokes a lot of marihuana, so give us a dollar's worth and let us get happy. He and Louis have been friends for years.

ME: Any guy Louis thinks is all right must really be O.K. Here, have a smoke, Sonny, you're going to get high on me this time.

SONNY (*To his friend*): Do you want to know something? This guy should have been born jet black, he understands all our subtleties and talks like a Negro. (*Turning to me.*) Boy, are you sure there isn't some colored blood in your family tree? Boy, you're too much to cope with, you keep plugging, you're bound to be successful in life.

FIFTH CAT: Hello Mezz! Got any marihuana?

ME: I'm as loaded as the chinaberry trees in Aunt Hagar's backyard. [Aunt Hagar is a kind of generic name for the old colored mammy, immortalized in the famous old blues, *Aunt*

Hagar's Blues. The name summons up the picture of an old colored woman living in a ramshackle little hut in the gallion, with elderberry trees growing in the yard.]

FIFTH CAT: Give me a dollar's worth so I can get high and I'll come back and pay you late tonight. [The *late watch* is about three or four in the morning, when the musicians and entertainers get through work, and when the streetwalkers begin parading the streets with less fear of the law.]

SIXTH CAT (*Seeing me hand the cigarettes to Cat Number Five*): Wow, I know I'm going to be straightened out now, I know you're going to let me smoke some of that marihuana.

FIFTH CAT: Get away from me boy, far away. You're always looking for a handout, why don't you cut it out for once, the winter's here and the icy wind is blowing and here I am with this topcoat on, trying to raise a few bucks for the pawnbroker so I can get my overcoat out of hock. [*Two's and fews:* prostitutes try to collect the standard two dollars for their services, but often they have to take whatever they can get—in other words, *two's* when they can get them, *fews* when they can't. The term has come to have a meaning less limited occupationally: a little money, whatever you can raise, the most you can scare up. As for *lead sheet*, it's only one sheet of music out of a whole orchestration, with only the melody line on it, and hence thin enough to mean *topcoat*; whereas the *full orchestration* is, by contrast, thick and bulky, and could only mean a heavy *overcoat*.]

SIXTH CAT: Oh, come on and be big for once, don't spoil our fun and make life so grim. You know I treated you last time.

FIFTH CAT: Looks like he has me cornered, Mezz, but this guy is so selfish he would turn his back on a completely helpless animal. He's as tight as they come. Just look at him, and get a load of that old-fashioned suit, and his trousers are so baggy at the knees that it looks like he's crouching, ready to jump. This guy's trying to catch up with me [even the score, because he treated last time], and I've got to get him high. Stay on the corner, Mezz, and I'll bring you the dollar as I promised I would. [*Line two* means the

356

price is a dollar; prices, like times of the day, are often doubled so that outsiders won't understand the details.] Come on friend, let's go over to my home. [*Main stash* is home, where you and your wife or steady girlfriend live, as distinguished from other secondary "homes" you might have, where other women friends of yours live. In the same sense, your wife is the *main saw on the hitch*; you may have other *saws* to cut your wood, and you might say that you were hitched to them too, but not in such a basic way.]

SEVENTH CAT: Give me three cigarettes, gatemouth [another private inner-racial joke, suggesting a mouth whose lower lip swings like a gate], so I can go and make myself feel good. What kind of object is this keeping you company? (*Nodding towards Frankie Walker.*)

FRANKIE: Don't pay any attention to that razor-legged, axe-handled, slew-footed obscenity, Milton. [The hyphenated epithets here are all inner-racial jokes too, referring to the shape of the knee and shinbone, and to the flat-footed, toes-out manner of walking. *Motherferyer* is an incestuous obscenity which has its counterpart in every language in the world.] He's an antiquated guy from down South who hasn't been up North long enough to learn what the score is. His hair is as knotty as if he had acorns sticking to his scalp, up on top of that brain which hasn't been working for a long time. If the rain ever struck the back of your neck, that hair [which has been smoothed down with hair-grease] would roll up again like a windowshade, you conceited, un-enlightened dope from down South, you look like an old Southern mammy with a handkerchief over her head, you don't amount to anything. You went crazy long ago. [Obviously, when you're *like Jack the Bear, you ain't nowhere*, because for a good part of the year a bear is just huddled snugly in a hole, oblivious to the world. *His brother, No Fu'ther,* is in the same sorry predicament, far from alert.]

SEVENTH CAT: Your friend is too smart, Mezz, but he'd better grow wings and fly away, or else I'll cut a piece out of his hide.

EIGHTH CAT (*Yelling to passing friend*): Hey, you look like you're making plenty of money, so don't treat me so rough and tough, tell me the secret of your success because you've been keeping it to yourself long enough.

HIS FRIEND: Hey, hometown boy [friend from down home]! There's nothing to my apparent prosperity, I don't own anything besides the one good outfit that you see on me now. I saw that girl up the street, drinking beer in a saloon, and the smart boys were conning her like the Yellow Kid [a famous con-man], trying to catch her on their line [as they would catch a fish] and win her. [*To weave the four F's* around a girl means a lot more than just winning her; actually, as nearly as it can be translated in public, it means to *find her, fool her, frig her, and forget her.*]

EIGHTH CAT: Hm, I gave her up long ago [to *nix out* has about the same meaning as *cross off your list*], she's subject to too many changing moods; one minute she says yes and the next minute she says no, she never commits herself and she's too snooty. [It's the last word in ritzy behavior, obviously, to keep your glasses, or lorgnette, on when you go to bed.] Friend, she looks like the devil himself to me, so don't give her another thought. Give me some of your good marihuana, Mezz, so we can get high and have a good time. Hey buddy [*buddy ghee* really means *guy who is my buddy*, the word *guy* being pronounced in the prison vernacular, as *ghee*], why don't you and I go fifty-fifty and we'll buy two dollars' worth of marihuana, so I won't have to carry the burden all by myself.

HIS FRIEND: O.K., take this dollar, but it didn't come from a street-walker on the avenue. I had to put in time working for it, so don't try to get any more out of me. [The idea is: I'm no pimp, I work for a living, and my money is hard come by.] How am I doing, Mezz, am I playing the rhyming game expertly or not?

ME: You were doing nothing else but, you're really ringing true, if you're not coming in on time a hawk can't see. You started as smoothly as Horn-&-Hardart's famous amateur radio show, and you wound up with as much of a bang as Amos-and-Andy. [Such references to popular radio shows, movies, and comic strips are common in this language. Another good example is the phrase,

358

you came on like gangbusters, a reference to the well-known radio program. The phrase implies that you're as strong as the law on that program, since the law always wins. When this expression got too popular and the whites began to use it, it was changed to read, *you came on like Buster's gang,* and finally, just the word *buster* was retained, as in the succinct phrases, *that's a buster, Jack,* or just *Buster, Jack,* which state your hearty approval or appreciation of something.]

EIGHTH CAT: Listen to old Mezz, feeding us the comebacks and right on schedule too. Friend, you really know what the score is, and you're a fine fellow. This marihuana you're selling is wonderful, pal, everybody ought to smoke it and wake up. [The expression, *light up and be somebody,* implies that some Negroes are so down-and-out and beat that they don't care about anything, but when they smoke marihuana it stirs their spirits and gives them ambition to amount to something.] Well, I'm going to disappear up Seventh Avenue and see if there's anything interesting waiting for me. [In other words, he's going to stroll along the street like a lizard crawling along the railroad tracks, to see what he can find.]

NINTH CAT: Hello, czar! What are you giving away?

ME: I don't give anything away except in the manner that I give away my laundry. [That is, I'm going to give this man some marihuana, but I expect something in return; no handouts.]

NINTH CAT: That's right, old man, you give it away but you get it back, just like your laundry. You want to know something, I drank some cheap corn whisky mixed with wine with some dumb girl last night, smoking cheap marihuana till even my hair hurt. I haven't eaten since sunset, and I have to fill my stomach. I know I'm going to start snoring as soon as I get into bed, so take this ten-dollar bill and give me ten dollars' worth of marihuana, so I can leave. [To *widen* means to widen the gap between you and the other person—in other words, to leave.] I'm going to stay home until midnight on Friday, and then I'll go over to see the midnight show at the Lafayette Theater, and hear Louis Armstrong when he begins to play those high notes.

TENTH CAT: Hello Mezz, what are you getting rid of? [The sense being, do you have any news for the grapevine?]

ME: Nothing much. [*Punks* and *skunks* are unclean, unpleasant people; in other words, there's nothing very exciting to report.] But look, friend, your wife just walked down the sidewalk about ten o'clock and you'd better beat it because she was talking about cutting you up.

TENTH CAT: Well, tip me off buddy, I didn't know that. I know she's sore at me because she saw me sitting with a couple of colored girls in a friend's car last Friday night, and we drove away fast. She's been raising the dickens ever since. I haven't seen the sheets on my bed in two days, and the other night, when it rained so hard, she was on the warpath again. I don't look forward to any unpleasant moves from that ugly female, but if my back's to the wall I guarantee that I'll fight her like a cage full of apes. No indeed, old man, I don't relish a fight with her. Let me smoke some of that fine marihuana you pass out because I've just got a tiny butt of one left. I'm going to go over to my house and change my clothes while my wife is still out on the street, and thanks for tipping me off, old man. I'll be seeing you. . . . [*Unglamorous action* is the kind of act that is most unbecoming—especially in a woman, from whom you're supposed to expect only glamorous things, as any Hollywood opus teaches you. An example of some *unglamorous action* from a queen, frompy or otherwise, would be when she hits you over the head with a beer bottle. As for the phrase *pulling my coat*, it refers to what a man does when he grabs your coat-tail and tugs it two or three times, as a warning or hint or cue when he can't speak up directly; the sort of thing someone might do when you're in a group of people and he wants to call your attention to something; a variation on the nudge. Quite naturally, in the language of action which is jive, *pulling somebody's coat* has come to be the more graphic description of what correct English, in more abstract ways, refers to as *informing* or *enlightening* someone.]

A Note on the Panassié Recordings

During the two months that Hugues Panassié was over here, he organized and supervised four recording dates. The records that came out of those sessions started a lot of hot air circulating in the music world. Now that the critics have had their say about them I'd like to put down what really happened.

Hugues, Tommy and I put our heads together and doped out the personnel for our first date: James P. Johnson (piano), Zutty Singleton (drums), Elmer James (bass), Teddy Bunn (guitar), Sidney De Paris (trumpet), besides Tommy and me. On November 21st, 1938 we recorded three sides down at the Victor studio: *Revolutionary Blues* and *Comin' on with the Come On* (Parts One and Two).

For years I had been struck by the fact that whenever we played the authentic blues in a café or dancehall, no matter how good we played, the reaction was the same: very mild and cool. It kept worrying me. This was the music I really loved and could play the best, but very few people warmed up to it. Sometimes I used to think that this was our punishment for stealing a great music from its rightful creators and owners, but later I got some perspective on it. This blues music was born of terrible oppression, and the moment the colored people were released just the least little bit, after the Civil War, and got into New Orleans and started to march in Mardi Gras parades and organize their street bands so they could strut their stuff a little, why, some of the weight was off them and their music perked up, took on a happier and breezier spirit. So out of the blues and the worksongs, that went right back to the days of Simon Legree, came New Orleans jazz, and pretty soon it traveled up the

Mississippi to Chicago and points east. It enjoyed success everywhere it hit, but on its travels it picked up a lot of trimmings. Later on when people were first introduced to it all they saw to it was those trimmings, which often smothered the whole soul of the original music—the backgrounds were lost entirely.

What were the things that made it go tangent? Well, aside from all the social and economic forces at work, first of all it picked up the piano on its travels, and the piano is one of the most selfish instruments known to mankind. It can be tolerated in New Orleans music only when it sticks to a rhythmic function, with either a four-four tempo or strictly comp. (The kind of accompaniment where there's a bass beat in the left hand, then the correct inversion of the chord in triad or diminished or augmented form. Lil Armstrong's piano playing on Louis' Hot Five records is a pretty good example of what I mean.) Now don't misunderstand me, I think the piano is a wonderful instrument, but the real jazz was born from march time and the piano can only fit into it as a rhythm instrument; you've got to get somebody to play it who has a very congenial nature, won't hog the spotlight all to himself but devotes himself to helping all the other artists to express themselves. When I tried to give Joe Sullivan some hints about how to play the blues on the piano, and dug into harmony a little, I found out all about this and readily understood why the symphony doesn't use the piano.

After that, the modern symphonic-jazz composers got hold of this music and stuffed their version of jazz with Ravel and Debussy and Delius and them, adding ninths, thirteenths and what they call sixteenths to it. They completely changed the progressions with these "symphonic" chords; you see, certain chords, like the ones the modernists use, leave you at a dead-end in jazz, no sequence to lead into, so you have to make stereotyped and mechanical passages, play one feeble run over and over because there's no way out of the trap. (Did you ever hear a horn player in a big modern swing band blast one note over and over, in a monotone riff? That's because he's got no place to go, harmonically speaking; he's stuck on that tonal plateau because there are no chords to use as stepladders in climbing up or down.) When you're caught in a blind-alley like that, you have no alternative: you have o grope your way back to the beginning and build up again. Whatever gifts for improvisation you may have are squelched. The modern inflection has done all this to jazz.

And then, to make things worse, along came an invention called the sock cymbal or highhat cymbal, and that was the end. This cymbal is played by the drummer with his left foot, as though he didn't already have enough to do, what with his bass and snare drums and the cowbell and the woodblock and the rachet and the two or three Chinese and Turkish cymbals that real jazz drummers use. The result is a sort of topheavy effect, um-*ching*, um-*ching*, um-*ching* for a beat instead of the steady tempo of the New Orleans drummers, and that strangles the rhythm so necessary to jazz. Now the tendency for the swing drummer is to play cymbal solos all the way through, fighting all the other musicians instead of helping to build them up. An offbeat ring comes out of his sock cymbal because the human body just isn't constructed to do so many things all together—and that delayed *ching* makes all the horn players fall into a kind of hesitation style, waiting for the drummer's lagging cymbal beat before they can come up with their own notes. And they have to overblow their instruments, fighting to be heard above the drummer's loud metallic hum; trumpets and clarinets go way up into their upper registers and become shrill and squealing, losing the rounded soulful tone of New Orleans music. Your improvisation, if you're allowed any, isn't built from a rich harmonic pattern any more, but centers around that clanging cymbal beat. Arrangers have to keep the sock cymbal in mind, and they build their orchestrations around it instead of using free chordal progressions, and all the New Orleans color is lost. When people with sensitive ears get apoplexy over the terrible din of so much modern swing and jump, they ought to remember that it's not jazz they're so horrified at. It's the corruption of jazz that was brought about by the wrong, egocentric use of the piano, the individualistic sock cymbal, the modern-classical influence, and the terrible mechanization of today's arrangements.

Now, for all these years, whenever I went back to the good old-time blues, the vibrant source of all our jazz, it sounded so foreign to modern ears that I got no reaction. No one cared to hear our story —people saw only the modern trimmings and identified them with jazz, they didn't know about roots and sources. That made me so mad, one night when we were playing in the Castilian Gardens out on Long Island, that I decided to try and pick up the tempo of the blues, like it had been picked up in the happier New Orleans jazz. We had just finished a real slow blues and didn't get applause once, so I told the band to hold it, we were going to play the same thing only in a brighter tempo, and I stomped it out. Then we sailed into it again and I worked it up to such a pitch that I finally succeeded in reaching that audience with my message, and they screamed for ten minutes. We had been giving them a lesson in musical history —going from the lowdown blues of the gallion slave to the high-spirited strutting music of New Orleans, and it was infectious, it caught hold of the whole crowd. All the musicians jumped up in their excitement, faces flushed, and I'll never forget the expression of joy on Eddie Condon's face as he looked at me.

Well, I remembered this experience, so when we got to the Victor studio that day I told Hugues about this trick of picking up the blues tempo, and he got all enthusiastic over the idea. We got the engineers together and told them we wanted to try something new, if they'd give us a hand: we wanted to have two turntables ready with masters on them, and we'd start out for the first record playing a traditionally slow blues, and at the end of the first record they were to drop the needle on the second master. While they shifted to the other master I would knock out four beats, so they'd have enough time and there'd be silence to start the second record, and then we'd sail into a real bright tempo with the same tune. And that's how we came to make *Comin' on With the Come On* in two parts, and to name it as we did. In a sense, that record is an attempt to give a capsule history of the birth of New Orleans music, and to entice people that way into an appreciation of the blues. But it didn't quite work.

When we hit upon Sidney De Paris for the second trumpet on this date, I noticed Tommy Ladnier screw his face up and frown, because he was afraid Sidney played in a too modern idiom. I told him I would talk to Sidney and explain what we were doing, so there wouldn't be any friction. To this day I regret that I didn't heed Tommy's warning, because Sidney is one hell of a talented guy but the modern style had taken deeper roots in him than I'd realized. "Sidney," I said, "we're going to try and capture Joe Oliver's idea with this band in the way we use the two trumpets, and I want you to play second or third harmony to Tommy's part, depending on what he leads into, and then in some choruses you'll play the first or second part, whichever fits at the time. If you guys weave together we should have some fine records that'll be an eye-opener to all the kids." Sidney agreed, and I came to the studio with a clear mind, but on Side Two, where the tempo is picked up, the fireworks came.

Things had gone along fair for about the first nine choruses, but then Sidney's suppressed "modern" instincts got the better of him and he got evil and began to growl on his horn. The riff he growled was a discordant one that went way tangent to the whole spirit of the music, and it made Tommy furious. Then Sidney wound up the first ending of the tenth chorus with a real modern swing riff that's a terrible cliché. That made Tommy say "*Merde!*" real loud on his horn, and it scared everybody in the band so bad that we didn't have our bearings to start the eleventh chorus. After Tommy's blast Sidney shut up almost entirely, and hardly played note one from then on. By the time the twelfth chorus came up, Zutty was the only one really in there trotting. But now Tommy was completely disgusted, hearing the band fall to pieces all around him, and he was hardly playing at all.

Zutty played the most wonderful drums I have ever heard on records on this side, really in the New Orleans idiom, but it sounds sort of out of place when he hits the beat on his cowbell, because he's not in a real New Orleans atmosphere. It just proved all over again that the modern riffs which took the music world by storm are all against the rhythmic and harmonic patterns of the real jazz. For those who don't read music I'll try to put it down in words: the riff I'm talking about is just a steady *duh-duh-dum*, *duh-duh-dum*, *duh-duh-dum*, *duh-duh-dum*, all hitting on one note, the tonic of the key being played in. That's what Sidney De Paris did on the recording. We had started out to show how the blues led into New Orleans, but what came out was really a history of how New Orleans got corrupted into modern swing and jump. That riff will be self-explanatory to you if you're acquainted with the harmonic progressions to a first ending in our music—in fact, if you're familiar with any music that resolves to the tonic, where a dominant seventh for two beats, or an augmented chord, brings you back to the key signature in common harmony sequence.

On the same date we made *Revolutionary Blues*, a type of blues that comes from the real old school and has been almost completely forgotten. It has thirty-two bars, but differs from the standard thirty-two bar chorus that Tin Pan Alley uses, because it isn't divided into first eight bars, second eight bars, then the release for eight, and then back to the first eight. It starts with sixteen bars, then resolves back to them with no release, and the last eight bars have a definite resolution that was invented by the real New Orleans jazz school. Feeling that all the hip musicians would play these blues as soon as they heard them, and hoping that they might revolutionize the standard blues sequence that most musicians played because they never heard any others, I named this record *Revolutionary Blues*. I'm afraid not many people got the point.

Well, we never did get to finish our fourth side on this date, although we started one. Tommy and James P. Johnson were so fed up with the way things were going, and Tommy resented Sidney's modern style so much, that both he and James P. got real juiced. In the middle of the next record Tommy yelled "*Vive la France!*" and James P. fell off the piano stool. They both wobbled out of the studio and we tried to make a side with just the five of us, but it didn't work.

In one short and frantic afternoon, we'd relived the bloody musical battles of a full quarter of a century. It was a history lesson, and it taught us plenty. The best remark I ever heard about these records was made by Bubbles, of Buck and Bubbles, when he first listened to the test pressings at my house. "I hear what you're tryin' to do on them records Mezz," he said. "You're tryin' to call them all home but it's a tough scuffle."

On our next date, November 28th, 1938, under the title of "Tommy Ladnier and His Orchestra," we left Sidney De Paris out, replacing him with Sidney Bechet, and we used Cliff Jackson on piano and Manzie Johnson on drums. I got one of the biggest thrills of my life that day, because at last I was playing with wonderful old Sidney Bechet, in spite of John Hammond's warning. How easy it was falling in with Bechet—what an instinctive mastery of harmony he has, and how marvelously delicate his ear is! We fitted together like pieces of a jigsaw puzzle. Before I go any further I want to go on record and say that of all the living New Orleans musicians he is the greatest, along with Zutty Singleton and Louis Armstrong and Tommy Ladnier, a truly remarkable genius.

On this date we made *Really the Blues*, which I named the moment I heard it played back after the recording, because it brought tears to my eyes and I felt we had caught the real spirit of the old blues more than any other record I knew of. Bechet played such a wonderful second part to my second chorus; I was ashamed of not being better than I was, to give him the support he deserved and the inspiration too. That tune had come to me one night in a back-room joint in Harlem where I used to sit in with Manzie Johnson's trio most every evening, and Bechet had never heard it before we started to make this record, but he stepped right in with his clarinet and wove through the harmony like he'd been practising it all his life. Then, to top it off, he picked up his soprano sax after Tommy's fine chorus and played two of the greatest choruses I have ever heard on that tough instrument, ending the record with a spectacular display of brilliance that left me all trembling inside.

We made three more sides that day, *Jada*, *Weary Blues*, and *When You and I Were Young Maggie*. *Weary Blues* is a wonderful record, and in the closing chorus we work up to a pitch closer to that of King Oliver's original Lincoln Garden band than any other recorded music I know about. Bechet plays terrific clarinet all the way through, and Tommy's trumpet eats right into your soul. As I listen to that record today his tone makes me limp all over—its deeply sorrowful accents, full of haunting overtones, were already hinting that he wasn't long for this world.

On *Jada* I played tenor sax, because Panassié had a nostalgia for my sax playing, and Teddy Bunn and Tommy both show their genius. Teddy is one of the greatest guitar players of the day; even though he has gone modern to some extent now he can still come on, and those records prove it. (On this date, by the way, Bechet had to use the pseudonym of Pops King because he was under contract to another company.)

There was a third date on December 19th, 1938, this time under the title of the "Mezzrow-Ladnier Quintet." We decided not to use any piano, so our line-up was: Tommy, Teddy Bunn, Pops Foster, Manzie Johnson, and myself. The five sides we recorded that day were: *Everybody Loves My Baby, Ain't Gonna Give Nobody None of My Jelly Roll, Royal Garden Blues, If You See Me Comin'*, and *Gettin' Together*. When we started on *If You See Me Comin'* I just asked Teddy to make an introduction on his guitar, and goddamn if he didn't bust out with a vocal on the first chorus, followed by a guitar solo, one of the very few such solos to be played without a pick since the early Twenties. Teddy always played the guitar with his fingers. I followed him in a lower register solo which I still don't think very much of, but then Tommy came on for the next two choruses with some beautiful arpeggios and changes that you can hardly equal anywhere. On *Royal Garden* Tommy and I play together like we'd been bosom pals for years. I swear, this was the first time, right during those Panassié sessions, that I've ever played with either him or Bechet and it really bolstered up my ego and improved my morale, because then I really knew that, no matter how uneven my performance might be, my musical convictions were right. How I wished I could have been up in their class in tone, in inventiveness, in sheer mastery of my instrument. I felt and believed everything those guys did, now more than ever. If only I could play like them!

After the quintet date Hugues decided that he wanted to record some of the modern musicians, so on January 13th, 1939, there was a fourth session during which, under the title of "Frankie Newton and His Orchestra," we made *Rosetta, The World Is Waiting for the Sunrise, Minor Jive, Rompin' at Victor, Blues My Baby Gave to Me*, and *Who*. These records are made up almost entirely of individual solos, without very much of the New Orleans collective spirit of teamwork. The personnel consisted of Frankie Newton (trumpet), Pete Brown (alto sax), Albert Casey (guitar), John Kirby (bass), James P. Johnson (piano), Cozy Cole (drums), and myself on clarinet. Two of the numbers, *Minor Jive* and *Blues My Baby Gave to Me*, were compositions of mine.

So much for Panassié's history-making recordings. There's one thing I want to say to you youngsters who hear our music for the first time, in this age of swing and jump, and are puzzled by it, even though you sense its great pulse and vitality. You may be discouraged at some of the things you hear on our records, and they may lead you away from New Orleans. You may say to yourself, "Hell, I don't know, there seems to be something missing—the polish, the suaveness, the finished quality. Listen to that gutty tone Bechet gets, or Mezzrow's clinkers on the clarinet. It doesn't sound good. There's something rough and crude about it." You've hit on something there; you're partly right in bringing those questions up. But what you have to keep in mind is that any unfinished quality in our music is no reflection on New Orleans style—and that goes especially for the unevenness you may find in my own performances. I will tell you where the roughness, the jagged edges, come from. We never practise. When we're not working, which is only too often, we forget about our horns, which is wrong but it's understandable. Don't forget that all of us have to keep on eating, and when we can't make a living out of our music we have to scramble for our doughnuts at something else, and that means that months and even years may go by without our touching our horns. Remember that New Orleans musicians, even the greatest, haven't had an easy time of it: many of them have spent long years, during the total eclipse of New Orleans music, working as stevedores, truckdrivers, janitors, farmhands, and whatnot.

And then, maybe after years of oblivion, suddenly a chance to play for a while, or make a few records, comes along, and we all grab it like a drowning man grabs at a straw. What comes out, naturally, isn't always smooth and polished. But still, there's the old throbbing pulse, the old ensemble spirit, the good old lively, breezy, racy quality, and that in itself is enough to mark off our music, for all its rawness, from the dead mechanical big-band music of today. I prostituted my music for many a year, and then had the nerve to record with the great men in the field, but don't think I regret it, especially when I hear the records. I wish I could have played better—there's so much room for improvement, I grit my teeth as I play them over and ache for a chance to do it again. Still and all, what we did together stands up; it's a great, almost-dead American music being revived, a music that has no equal anywhere else, and its unique flavor should be recaptured and preserved, as it is on those records.

The clarinet, of all the instruments, requires the most constant practice, it's so sensitive that you've got to have a real embouchure. If you don't have any "lip" you can't control your breathing perfectly, and that's just what happened to me on those records. I was running arpeggios in the New Orleans idiom, and they take a lot of breath, and with no embouchure the air just escapes through the corners of your mouth, and as a result the shortage of breath may make you fade out on a pretty run before you reach the end, or prevent you from even trying it.

But still, as I say, I'm not sorry I made those records. They are landmarks in the history of New Orleans. The flavor, the tang of the unbeatable oldtime stuff is there. It's up to the kids to absorb it fully, work at it hard, and make it better than our generation, for a lot of reasons, was able to. When this music comes back in all its glory, as it's bound to, as it's already beginning to, it'll be the kids who recapture it fully and lead it back to green pastures again.

Glossary

Ace: *dollar's worth, dollar, one, first-rate*

Advocate: *help to build and perfect*

Anywhere: *State of possession* (is you anywhere?=do you have any?)

Back: *adverb used for emphasis* (scoffed back=ate very heartily)

Ball: *n., a good time; v., enjoy yourself*

Barrelhouse: *n., low, boisterous dive; adj., the original style of playing jazz, once associated with such low dives*

Beat: *exhausted, broke*

Beat the boards: *tapdance*

Beat up your chops: *talk a lot*

Before-Abe: *job* (the implication being that a Negro's employment is slavery, of the type that existed before Abe Lincoln)

Beginner Brown: *Negro with light brown skin-tone*

Bellychord: *a pleasing, abrupt musical chord that hits the listener hard*

Belly habit: *an opium habit that, unlike the head type, affects the addict in the stomach*

The Big Apple: *New York City*

Big bean: *Sun*

Biggity: *swaggering, putting on airs*

Bing: *jail cell for solitary confinement*

Bit: *jail sentence*

Biters: *teeth*

Blip: *nickel*

Blinds: *spaces between tender and baggage car in any train*

Blow: *smoke marihuana*

Blowtop: *a crazy or violent person*

Blow your fuse: *go crazy*

Blow your lid: *go crazy*

Blow your lump: *find a full outlet for your emotions*

Blow your top: *go crazy*

Blue Broadway: *the sky*

Boogie-woogie: *a happier style of music which grew out of the blues; also, a style of dancing*

Boogity-boogity: *pell-mell*

Bottle babies: *drunks*

Breadbasket: *stomach*

Break: *a brief ensemble pause by a jazz band so that one player can extemporize a solo for a few measures*

Break it up: *bring the house down*

Break time: *get out of tempo*

Breeze: *go*

Bright: *morning*

Bring down: *depress*

Bringdown: *a depressing thing, a disappointment*

Bring time: *punch a time-clock, work*

Briny: *unpleasant, hostile*

Broom off: *go away*

Brown: *Negro with brown skin-tone*

Buddy ghee: *pal*

Bug: *put in the insane asylum*

Bundle: *bankroll*

Bunk habit: *practice of lounging around while others smoke opium, and inhaling the fumes*

Bust: *arrest*

Bust your conk: *become extremely happy and carefree*

Bust your vest: *be big, magnanimous*

Buster: *something extremely good*

Buzz: *tell, whisper*

Buzz tone: *a trumpet or trombone tone similar to that of a kazoo*

Bloodhound tip: *snooping behavior of a policeman (see tip)*

Café sunburn: *pallor*

Call some hogs: *snore*

Canhouse: *whorehouse*

Can't see for looking: *to stare so intently, usually with hostility, that your vision is blurred; to have your perspective distorted due to anger or jealousy*

Cap: *have the last word, go one better, outdo*

Carry: *escort*

Case: *study carefully*

Cat: *regular fellow, guy*

Cathouse: *whorehouse*

Chances go around: *everybody gets his turn, the wheel of chance keeps spinning*

Change: *money*

Chesty: *conceited*

Chick: *young girl*

Chicken dinner: *pretty young girl*

Chimes: *hours*

Chinch: *bedbug*

Chippy's playground: *stomach*

Chips: *money*

Chops: *lips*

Claws: *fingers*

Climb's on somebody: *marihuana smokers get high; when somebody treats them to the marihuana, the climb's on him*

C-notes: *hundred-dollar bills*

Clinker: *bad musical note*

Collar: *understand, get hold of*

Collar all jive: *understand all the subtleties*

Coin gold: *make a lot of money*

Collar a nod: *get some sleep*

Come on: *give a terrific performance, be superb*

Comp: *accompaniment*

Complexy: *neurotic*

Con: *convict; also, consumption*

Conk: n., *head*; v., *hit on the head*

Conkhouse: *head*

Connection: *contact-man who supplies you with drugs, etc.*

Coonshout: *corny imitation of oldtime Negro style of singing*

Cop a deuceways: *buy two dollars' worth*

Cop a slave: *get a job*

Cop a squat: *sit down*

Corn: *anything hackneyed, cliché*

Cover all spots: *cope with all situations*

Crack your jaw: *talk*

Craunch: *grind*

Creep pad: *a whorehouse where the girls are pickpockets*

Crib: *type of one-room whorehouse in old New Orleans*

Croaker: *doctor*

Cruise: *entice*

Crummy: *obnoxious*

Cruncher: *sidewalk*

Crunchers: *feet*

Cubby: *home, apartment, room*

Cuckaburr: *acorn*

Cut: *outdo, out-perform*

Cut a brand-new one: *affect very powerfully, bowl over, pierce to the vitals*

Cut out: *leave*

Cut some rug: *dance*

Cut some steps: *dance*

Cutting contest: *competitive get-together of performers*

Dance on all setting: *crash the gates everywhere*

Daniel: *buttocks*

Deuce: *a couple*

Deuceways: *two dollars' worth*

Dicty: *snooty, high-class*

Dig: *understand, appreciate, listen to, follow, grasp, get*

Dim: *night*

Dime note: *ten-dollar bill*

Dinner: *pretty young girl*

Dirty dozens: *elaborate game in which participants insult each other's ancestors*

Do a Houdini: *disappear*

Dog around: *follow*

Dommy: *home, domicile*

Don't lose it: *sarcastic expression which really means it's no good, get rid of it.*

Doodlely-squat: *nothing, no more than the product of a child who squats to do his duty*

Dotey: *old, senile*

Doublebank: *gang up on*

Double-o: *studious look*

Downbeat: *conductor's signal for the band to begin playing*

Down under: *below the Mason-Dixon line*

Down with it: *top-notch, superlative*

Drape: *suit of clothes*

Dreambox: *head*

Dreamers: *blankets*

Driftsmoke: *clouds*

Drink: *ocean*

Drink den: *saloon*

Drip: *rain*

Drugg: *brought down, depressed*

Dry goods: *clothes*

Dummy up: *shut up, refuse to talk*

Duster: *buttocks*

Early black: *early evening*

Eat up a breeze: *eat a lot*

Enamel: *skin*

Evil: *unpleasant, obnoxious, hostile, neurotic*

Excusing: *except for*

Eyeball: *look, stare*

Face: *a form of greeting*

Fall in: *arrive on the scene*

Fall out: *be tickled to death*

Father grab somebody: *May the Lord take him away, to hell with him*

Fault: *blame*

Faust: *ugly (as the devil)*

Fay: n., *white person;* adj., *white*

Feds: *Federal agents*

Fer it: *in favor of it*

Fillmill: *saloon*

Final: *go*

Fish: *new inmates in a jail, fresh caught*

Fishblack: *Friday night*

Fishtail: *weaving motion of the buttocks during a dance*

Fix to: *intend to*

Flickers: *movies*

Fly: *smart, sophisticated, in the know, alert*

Fly right: *behave*

Foam: *beer*

For kicks: *for pleasure's sake*

Foxy: *sly, clever, good*

Fracture your toupee: *go crazy*

Fracture your wig: *go crazy with joy*

Frame: *body*

Framer: *bed*

Frantic: *wild, nervous, unusually good*

Fraughty issue: *unhappy state of affairs*

Freakish: *homosexual, perverted, weird*

Freebie: *handout, something gratis*

Frolic-pad: *place where you have a good time*

Frompy: *unattractive*

Fruit: *romance playfully*

Full orchestration: *overcoat*

Funk: *stench*

Funky: *smelly, obnoxious*

Fusebox: *head*

Gallion: *slave quarters, Jim-Crow section*

Gangbuster: *anything especially powerful*

Gas-meter: *a quarter*

Gasser: *something terrific that takes your breath away*

Gate: *form of greeting*

Gauge: *marihuana*

Gaycat: *have a good time*

Geechee: *Southerner from Georgia*

Get in your mouth: *disturb you, repel you*

Get off: *express yourself, render a good performance*

Get-off chorus: *improvised solo for one chorus*

Get straight: *reach an understanding, pay a debt*

Gig: *single engagement, club date*

Gimpy: *lame*

Git-box: *guitar*

Give the office to somebody: *to signal surreptitiously*

Gizz: *short for gizzard*

Gizzard: *form of greeting*

Glim: *look at*

Glimmer: *electric light*

Go down: *happen*

God sure don't like ugly: *you get what's coming to you*

Going to Slice City: *going to cut somebody up*

Golden-leaf: *the best marihuana*

Gone: *out of this world, superlative*

Gone with it: *really inspired, completely in control of the situation*

Grabbers: *hands*

Grass: *marihuana*

Grease: *eat*

Grease your chops: *eat*

Grefa: *marihuana*

Grimy: *Sour, unpleasant*

Groovy: *really good, in the groove, enjoyable*

Gully-low: *lowdown, unhappy*

Gumbeat: *talk*

Gun: *look, stare*

Gunboats: *large shoes*

Gunja: *marihuana*

Gutbucket: *earthy style of music*

Hack: *keeper in a jail*

Half-hipped: *not very enlightened or sophisticated*

Half past the unlucky: *midnight on Friday*

Hankachief-head: *old Southern mammy*

Hamfat: *ham performer, a nobody*

Hard-cutting: *powerful, very good*

Hard-cutting mezz: *the best brand of marihuana; anything that's tops*

Have a ball: *have a good time*

Have your hair fried: *have your hair treated with hot irons*

Hawk: *winter*

Hawk's out with his axe: *it's freezing weather*

Hay: *marihuana*

Head arrangement: *a musical arrangement by ear, without written music*

Head Knock: *God*

Heeb: *Jewish person*

Heebies: *jitters*

Hemp: *marihuana*

High: *intoxicated, or strongly affected by marihuana or other drugs*

High-jive: *intellectual patter, the smoothest and most elaborate line*

Highjiver: *smooth character with a very fancy and intellectual line of talk*

Hincty: *snobbish, stuck-up, full of airs; also, suspicious*

Hip: *in the know, worldly-wise, clever, enlightened, sophisticated*

Hipster: *man who's in the know, grasps everything, is alert*

Hit the jug: *drink heavily, often from the bottle; have a drink*

Homey: *form of greeting between people from the same place*

Honeymoon kick: *a situation of great intimacy, close friendship (see kick)*

Honky: *factory hand*

Hooked: *addicted*

Hop: *opium*

Hopdog: *insatiable opium addict*

Hophead: *opium addict*

Hot: *angry*

Hot for: *enthusiastic about, in favor of*

Hot minute: *brief moment (implying great hurry)*

House of many slammers: *jail*

Hustler: *prostitute; also, anybody who makes a living by hook or crook*

Hype: *v., to deliver a phony but convincing line, to build up a sucker for the kill, to lay the groundwork for a scheme; n., a build-up, a phony story*

Hype up: *build up (with ulterior motive)*

Ice: *diamonds*

If push comes to shove: *if a showdown comes, if things come to a head*

Igg: *ignore*

In front: *in advance, ahead of time*

In there: *very good, sincere, masterful, likeable*

Intro: *introduction to a musical piece*

Issue: *a questionable or serious case or situation*

Jag: *a state of extreme stimulation, produced by marihuana or some other stimulant*

Jam: *to play collectively improvised music*

Jam session: *a musical get-together in which all the playing is collectively improvised*

Jam-up: *very good, most pleasing*

Jawblock: *to engage in small talk*

J. B.: *jet black, a very dark Negro*

Jeff Davis: *an unenlightened person, a hick from down South; sometimes shortened to jeff*

Jim Crow: *the symbol of anti-Negro discrimination and segregation*

Jim-jam-jumping: *extremely lively, vivacious*

Jive: *v., to kid, to talk insincerely or without meaning, to use an elaborate and misleading line; n., confusing doubletalk, pretentious conversation, anything false or phony*

Jive that makes it drip: *clouds that produce rain*

John: *customer in a whorehouse*

Joint: *set of instruments used in smoking opium*

Joybox: *piano*

Juice: *n., liquor; v., to drink a lot*

Juiced: *drunk*

Jump: *turn, become (ex.: jump salty= turn sour or hostile)*

Jump: *modern corruption of jazz in which short cliché riffs are repeated over and over mechanically and the loud, ringing sock symbol sets the pace*

Jump stink: *turn sour and hostile*

Jungle bum: *a hobo who cooks out in the open*

Jungles: *San Juan Hill section of Manhattan, around Tenth Ave. in the Sixties*

Junkie: *dope fiend*

Keep a lot of rumpus: *act boisterously, make a lot of noise*

Kick: *good feeling, something that gives a lot of pleasure*

Killer: *anything very powerful, fine*

King Kong: *cheap moonshine, corn whisky*

Kip: *sleep (from camp)*

Kisser: *mouth or face*

Kitchen: *back of the head, the hair just above the nape of the neck*

Kitchen mechanics: *domestic servants*

Kitten: *very young girl*

Knock: *give*

Knock a fade: *go away, leave*

Knock out some vittles: *eat*

Knock somebody some skin: *shake hands with somebody*

Knowledge-box: *head*

Kyaw-kyaw: *sarcastic laughter*

Laine: *hick, innocent, sucker*

Lamp: *look at, see*

Latch on: *get hold of*

Late watch: *early hours of the morning*

Lay: *to give, do*

Lay down: *to recline and smoke opium*

Lay it: *do something masterfully, do a good job*

Lay it on somebody: *do something good for somebody*

Lay some iron: *tapdance*

Lay your racket: *perform, talk, give a good and convincing account of yourself*

Layout: *set of instruments used to smoke opium*

Lead: *melody, instrument that plays the melody in a band, solo chair of a section in a band*

Lead sheet: *topcoat*

Lean your affection on somebody: *to romance, to give a line to a girl*

Light up: *smoke marihuana*

Light up and be somebody: *smoke marihuana and make something of yourself*

Like Jack the Bear: *worthless, no-account, broke, insignificant*

Lily-whites: *sheets*

Lindy hop: *a Negro dance*

Line two: *one of anything (numbers are doubled to confuse outsiders)*

Line your flue: *eat*

Lip: *embouchure, muscular strength and control in the lips needed to blow wind instruments*

Liquor-head: *drunkard*

Loaded: *drunk or full of drugs*

Loot: *money*

Lowrate: *ridicule, show up*

Luck up on: *get by luck, come into possession of unexpectedly*

Lush: *to drink*

Lushhound: *drunkard*

Lushy: *drunkard*

Mac: *pimp*

Main saw on the hitch: *wife*

Main stash: *home*

Main stroll: *Seventh Avenue in Harlem*

Make: *rob, visit*

Make time: *beat a rhythm*

Make your love come down: *Arouse your passion, put you in a romantic mood*

Mammy jamming: *incestuous obscenity*

Mash: *give*

Mellow: *feeling good, especially after smoking marihuana*

Messerole: *corruption of mezzroll*

Mess-around: *dance in which hips are swung around in a circle*

The mezz: *the best brand of marihuana; anything unusually good*

Mezzroll: *fat sticks of marihuana, hand-rolled, with the ends tucked in*

The mighty mezz: *see the mezz*

Mooch: *beg, look for handouts*

Moo-juice: *milk*

Mop-mop: *modern corruption of jazz built up around mechanical riffs*

Moss: *hair*

Most anxious: *very fast or excited*

Motherferyer: *incestuous obscenity*

Much: *like, be in favor of*

Mudkicker: *streetwalker*

Mug: *making faces or subtly clowning during a performance*

Mugg: *associate with*

Muggles: *cigarettes of marihuana*

Murder Belt: *the South*

Murder State: *Mississippi, or any lynch state down South*

Mush: *kiss*

Muta: *marihuana*

Nappy: *kinky*

Nature: *potency, virility*

Nayo hoss: *no, buddy; that's wrong*

Never no crummy: *never in bad taste, never offensive*

Nix out: *eliminate*

No stuff: *no kidding*

Note: *notoriety, publicity*

Nowhere: *insignificant, broke*

Nympho kick: *nymphomaniac form of behavior, erotic exhibitionism*

Ofaginzy: *white person*

Ofay: *a white person (from the pig Latin for foe)*

Offtime: *out of harmony, old-fashioned, corny, offensive*

Old Fireball: *sun*

One-nighters: *one-night engagements*

Onliest: *only*

Oscar: *guy, especially a biased and narrow-minded one*

Out: *oust, get rid of, destroy*

Pad: *joint, place to enjoy yourself, bed*

Paddy: *cop*

Pay no rabbit: *ignore*

Peck: *see peckerwood*

Peckerville: *any Southern town*

Peckerwood: *any white Southerner*

Peepers: *eyes*

Pen: *penitentiary*

Penny one: *a single penny*

pick up on: *get, take, learn; also, smoke marihuana*

Pick up on what's going down: *understand what's happening*

Pick up on some vittles: *get some food, eat*

Pick up the tempo: *play faster*

Pigeon: *young girl*

Pill: *pellet of opium, also called yen pox*

Pink: *white*

Piss-ant: *a nobody, small fry*

Pitch a boogie-woogie: *get excited, get worked up*

Plant you now and dig you later: *got to go now, I'll see you later*

Play: *thing to do, program of action, the order of the day*

Play hip: *pretend to understand*

Playground: *see chippy's playground* . .

Poke: *pocket, wallet*

Politician: *trustee in a jail*

Poppa De-Da-Da: *New Orleans character who originated a strutting kind of dance*

Pounder: *cop on the beat*

Prayerbones: *knees*

Press roll: *a type of roll on the snare drums*

Psycho kick: *psychopathic form of behavior*

Pull a creep: *leave*

Pull a fade-out: *go away*

Pull somebody's coat: *enlighten, tip somebody off*

Pump: *heart*

Punk: *young man who plays the feminine role in a homosexual relationship*

Push: *sell, handle, purvey*

Put down: *do, be active in some way*

Put somebody on: *let him smoke some marihuana*

Queen: *woman, girl*

Quiet ones off the main drag: *sidestreets*

Quit it: *leave*

Raise: *arm (on your left raise=on your left)*

Raise sand: *make a fuss, create a stir*

Rap: *a criminal charge*

Razzmatazz: *anything old-fashioned, corny*

Ready: *competent, dauntless*

Recite: *play a good solo on your instrument*

Reefer: *cigarette of marihuana*

Rhyming: *verbal game in which an idiomatic conversation is conducted in rhythmic, rhyming phrases*

Riff: *n., musical phrase or passage; v., to play such distinctive phrases*

Righteous: *good, right, satisfying*

Righteous bush: *marihuana*

Righteous spiel: *correct, convincing and honest talk*

Rinky-dink: *antiquated, broken down*

Rip-bop: *corruption of jazz now in vogue, very fast, frenzied and mechanical type of music; also known as re-bop and be-bop*

Roach: *small butt from a cigarette of marihuana*

Rock: *dollar*

Rods: *long bars under a freight car*

Roost: *home*

Rooster: *buttocks*

Rubber: *automobile*

Rumble: *fight*

Run in: *arrest*

Run somebody away: *chase away*

Run with: *associate with*

Run your mouth: *talk a lot*

Salt and pepper: *cheap brand of marihuana*

Salty: *sour, hostile, unpleasant*

Sand: *an oldtime Negro dance*

Sawbuck: *Ten-dollar bill*

Scat: *sing nonsense syllables*

School: *teach*

Scoff back: *eat a lot*

Scraggy: *dilapidated*

Scratchpad: *verminous room or flophouse*

Screw: *prison keeper*

Scuffle: *struggle to get along*

Scuffle up: *raise, collect, get together*

Scumpteen: *a lot of*

Send: *give you a good feeling*

Sell out: *run away*

Shakes: *d.t.'s*

Shake-up: *mixture of corn whisky and wine*

Shark: *man with a good line that women fall for*

Sharp: *alert, dressed well, keen-witted*

Show: *to make an appearance*

Short-histe: *masturbatory, perverted*

Shroud-tailor: *undertaker*

Shying: *the technique of cooking opium pills*

Signify: *hint, put on an act, boast, make a gesture*

Simpy: *doped, imbecilic*

Skin-beater: *drummer*

Skullbuster: *brain-twister, a tough problem; also, something very good*

Sky-pilot: *preacher*

Slammer: *door*

Slave tip: *work*

Slot: *form of greeting*

Slow drag: *dance music in slow tempo*

Smeller: *nose*

Snagging: *verbal game in which person who has to say "What?" gets a mark against him*

Snap your cap: *go crazy*

Snatcher: *detective*

Snatchpad: *bed*

Sniffer: *nose*

Snow: *cocaine*

Solid: *good*

Sometimey: *unstable, unpredictable, neurotic*

Soundbox: *larynx, throat*

Spade: *Negro*

Spaginzy: *Negro*

Spike: *add alcohol to beer*

Splash: *rain*

Splinter your toupee: *go crazy*

Spring: *release from jail*

Square: *unenlightened person, a working man, an orthodox follower of the rules*

Square from Delaware: *unenlightened person*

Squinch-eyed: *heavy-lidded, with the eyes half closed*

Stash: *v., to hide or put away, to go to sleep; n., house, bed, hiding-place*

Stick of tea: *cigarette of marihuana*

Sticking: *having some or a lot, not destitute or empty-handed*

Stinchy: *stingy*

Stir: *penitentiary*

Stoolie: *stool pigeon, informer*

Storyville: *the old tenderloin district of New Orleans*

Straighten: *pay up, straighten out a debt*

Stretch your chippy's playground: *eat*

Strides: *pants*

Stringpost: *neck*

The Stroll: Seventh Avenue in Harlem; any main street

Strollers: pants

Struggle-buggy: jalopy

Stuff: a lie, a line, something suspect or unacceptable

Stuff with the dead one's pictures: paper money

Stud: guy, man

Study about: think about, contemplate

Suds: beer

Suspicion: suspect

Suzie-Q: a Negro dance

Tab: project, line of activity, program

Tail: somebody who follows you

Tailgate: New Orleans style of trombone playing

'Taint no crack but a solid fact: it's the truth

Take low: cower, act humble

Take some weight off somebody: relieve, cheer up

Talk behind somebody: believe and support what he says because he's honest

Tall: intoxicated, or stimulated by marihuana

Tea: marihuana

Tea-pad: place where you smoke marihuana

Teen-inetsy: teeny-weeny, tiny

Tell a green man something: enlighten me, put me wise

Tenth Street: ten dollars

Tick twenty: ten o'clock (times of day are doubled to confuse outsiders)

Tighten: sell a bill of goods, clinch a deal, win over

Tighten somebody's wig: let him smoke some marihuana

Tin: small amount of opium

Tinklebox: piano

Tip: way of acting, pattern of behavior, environment, program

Tipple ukelele: twelve-stringed ukelele

Tog: dress up

Tonsil-juice: saliva

Top: head

Tops: roofs of passenger trains

Torpedo: gunman

Toy: a quantity of opium

The Track: Savoy Ballroom in Harlem

Trail: walk

Trey: three

Trey of knockers: the three balls over a pawnshop

Trickeration: misleading words or acts

Trilly: walk in a carefree way

Troubled with the shorts: broke, poverty-stricken

Tubs: drums

Turf: street

Tush-hog: muscle man who touches people for protection money, bully

Twinklers: stars

Twister: key

Two's and fews: small change, a little money

Typewriter: machine gun

Unbooted: ignorant, naive, unenlightened.

Uncle's: a pawnshop

Uncle Tom: symbol of the bowing and scraping humility of the traditional Southern Negro

Unhip: naive, unenlightened, corny

The unlucky: Friday

Uppity: snooty, ritzy, conceited

Ups: the upper hand

Vine: suit of clothes

Viper: marihuana smoker

Walking bass: a bass part that moves up and down the chords

Waller: wallow

Wash away: kill

(Your) water's on and it's boiling: there's trouble brewing for you

Wear the green: have some paper money

Weave the four F's around somebody:
   high-pressure romancing (find 'em,
   fool 'em, frig 'em and forget 'em)
Weed: *marihuana*
Weight: *blues, depression*
Wet your tonsils: *drink*
White stuff: *cocaine, morphine and
   heroin*
Widen: *leave*
Wig: *head or hair*

Wig-trig: *idea*
Wooden kimono: *coffin*
Woodshed: *practise or study alone*
Wren: *young girl*

Yarddog: *low or uncouth person*
Yen hok: *implement used in cooking
   marihuana*

Zooty: *stylish, fashionable*

Index

Afterword by Bernard Wolfe

In the summer of 1968 D. J. Bruckner went to Chicago to cover a political convention for the Los Angeles *Times* and found himself a war correspondent. Time after time his thoughtful dispatches from the erupting sidewalk fronts dealt with the "Negroid" styles of the young white middle-class street fighters, the wholesale ways in which they mimicked their Black brothers in dress, hairdo, lingo, stance. What he was observing, Bruckner decided, was one more chapter in "a passionate love affair with the ghetto"—carried on by people far removed in color and circumstances from the ghetto.

That love affair in one form or another, sometimes flamboyantly, sometimes furtively, has been going on up and down this country, fired with utmost passion, since the founding days. It heaved up the national theatrical craze of the nineteenth century, the minstrel show, and a very great deal of our popular culture before and since. One of its interminable chapters, a short but meaningful episode, is the story of Mezz Mezzrow.

Mezzrow's obsessive and unrelenting embrace of the pariah nether world did, to be sure, take him to extremes. He was not unique in adopting the black man's music, slang, bearing, social and sexual modes—those cultural co-optations were and are to be observed in hundreds and hundreds of whites, sometimes in many millions. He was not alone in hanging around with blacks, moving physically into the closed black world, marrying a black girl and having a child with her. But search all the histories of personal "negrification" as you will, you'll never turn up another case of a man who after extended immersion in the ghetto came to believe he had actually, physically, turned black.

Mezzrow, after his long years in and under Harlem, did truly think his lips had developed fuller contours, his hair had thickened and burred, his skin had darkened. It was not, as he saw it, a case of transculturation. He felt he had scrubbed himself clean, inside and out, of every last trace of his origins in the Jewish slums of Chicago, pulped himself back to raw human material, deposited that nameless jelly in the pure Negro mold, and pressed himself into the opposite of his birthright, a pure Black.

When I first sought him out in a Greenwich Village jazz club somewhere around 1942, I knew nothing of this personal mythology. I thought he was simply an odd jazz musician who might be the subject for an interesting magazine article. After some nights with him on his home grounds in Harlem, I realized that it would take a lengthy book to do his reincarnation myth full justice. This is the book.

As the job was getting done, it dawned on me that though our ostensible subject was one very particular man it was really about an impersonal matter, a process that sweeps around and through many white American heads: Negrophilia. I began to wonder whether Negrophilia and Negrophobia were, as linear, one-way logic would suggest, polar opposites, or whether to get at the devious psychology of the thing you wouldn't have to see the two mindsets dialectically, in some other relationship than as mere opposites. After *Really the Blues* was published, I wrote two essays on the subject, in 1947 and 1948.

This kind of speculation was not in tune with the intellectual climate prevailing in our country just after the war. So I did not publish these theoretical articles in American magazines, except for *Commentary*. Jean-Paul Sartre and Simone de Beauvoir did, however, kindly make room for all of my meanderings on this subject in their Paris organ, *Les Temps Modernes*. Some time after they appeared a young medical student from Martinique, a black man named Frantz Fanon, showed up in Paris to continue his studies. He was reading everything he could get his hands on that had any remote bearing on race and racist psychology. He dug up the things I'd published in *Les Temps Modernes* and found, apparently, that they related to the problems he was thinking about.

Years later, when he came to write his first book, *Black Skin, White Masks*, he discussed these pieces of mine in detail, and intelligently. It was an instance of intellectual transculturation that pleased me—ideas do, somehow, however haltingly and by however circuitous a route, get around. Consider, if you will, that the theme of the speculations that follow is, *White Skin, Black Masks*.

This discussion deals with American popular culture up through the Forties. The scene today is admittedly a radically different one. All the same, I think my commentary has a defensible place alongside the original Mezzrow volume. It is my reaction to the world that Mezzrow was very much a part of. It is also my reaction to the experience of writing the Mezzrow book. In any case, the phenomenon of Negrophilia is still very much with us, though it has taken on stunningly new forms, some of them political. My tentative analysis of this totally remarkable matter may still have some validity—I suspect it does, however arguable it may be.

ECSTATIC IN BLACKFACE
The Negro as a Song-and-Dance Man (1947–48)

"The plaintive and derisive songs of an oppressed people," anthropologist Geoffrey Gorer notes, "... have become the background of the whole society's pleasures and distractions." And, according to one of our foremost dance critics, John Martin, the Negro "has certainly given us at least the basis for all our popular dances." Apparently, if happiness is "a kind of virtue" with us, song and dance are two of its most coveted forms—and these forms we consider almost a monopoly of the Negro, worth borrowing from wholesale.

Strange, this "aesthetic" commerce across the rigid barriers of caste. In two key areas, at least, the pursuit of happiness narrows down pretty much to a pursuit of the Negro; becomes, in fact, a mass touching—even fondling—of the Untouchable. . . .

We pride ourselves on knowing the "real" Negro, the "authentic" Negro; and, over long decades, we have come to equate him with one of our primary Europe-evading folk heroes—the ecstatic song-

and-dance man. But does the Negro "give" so freely, through his muscles and his mouth, simply because he is "being himself"? Or is it rather because white America, craving a song and dance it cannot generate itself, so ardently wants him to?

We sense the broader cultural backdrop that sprawls behind the Negro song-and-dance man: it is the whole formalized and institutionalized American joy-quest. The pursuit of happiness, of course, is far more than an abstract political guarantee; in living terms it is a mass striving which fans out to embrace; ultimately, all those things Americans pursue in the hope of being made happy. Under the fun-oriented sway of this mass endeavor come "the whole society's pleasures and distractions"—the sum-total of our activities over and above our food-getting and rent-paying. And almost everywhere in these "non-useful," "non-pecuniary" reaches of our culture the image of the Negro crops up with jumping-jack persistence, blithely hurdling caste fences.

It is no secret that our entertainment industries have always featured the Negro prominently, and nearly always in set "happifying" images. From post-colonial times on there has been a strong Negroid component, not only in our song and dance music, but in our vaudeville, drama, cartoons, popular humor, and related fields; and today it shows up, sometimes overwhelmingly, in movies, bestsellers, jukeboxes, dance halls, and so on. But this cultural Negrophilia spreads far beyond the amusement industries. If the entrepreneurs of these industries play up Negro themes it must be because there is a steady current of mass interest in them, and that interest must make itself felt in other areas too.

It does; standard amusement fare quite aside, America is inundated with many more tangible kinds of commodities to which one stock Negroid image or another is attached. One afternoon's browsing through any fair-sized shopping center will turn up an imposing array of these mass-produced images: on food labels, wallpaper, napkins, nylon stockings, perfumes, bandanas, charm bracelets, earrings, sweaters, men's shorts, lampshades, ash trays, figurines, the billboard and magazine ads for a wide variety of food and drink. A good deal of our standard décor, in fact, both modern and traditional, is dominated by the Negroid motif. All this, of course, in addition to the Negro's highly visible presence in many bestsellers, children's books, dolls, toys, and masks, on postcards and greeting cards.

In certain standard and stylized forms, then—most often radiating from an ecstatic grin—the Negro image is a central feature of our "pleasure" culture. And when such a motif endures so doggedly in the culture of a nation, we can guess that it is heaved up from the more profound "fun-loving" depths of the mass mind; there must be some deep-set mechanism behind its constant display.

What we have, then, is *the mass production and consumption of stock images of the Negro in the pleasure-culture of white America*—including, of course, the image of the Negro as an ecstatic song-and-dance man. From beginning to end this process is sparked by an intense, at times almost obsessive, cultural interest in the Negro—in the midst of a caste situation whose whole premise is that the Negro, as pariah, hardly deserves a second glance.

There are in our pleasure-culture certain areas in which whites produce images of the Negro for their own consumption, or hire Negroes to act out those images. And there are other areas in which the Negro appears as *himself*, creating himself in his *own* image. The Negro song-and-dance man is hailed as such a self-creation; his sounds and movements are taken to reflect only his own "insides." When this "uncued" ecstatic appears, it is alleged, the whites hug the sidelines as mere passive spectators, memorizing his ad libs for future use.

But in these pariah-elite exchanges the emotional traffic is not always one way; it sometimes happens that the "spectator" is really the star performer—by proxy. Most often, despite the claims of many whites to an uncanny sort of racial omniscience, their concept of "the Negro as he really is" turns out to be a coy fiction, designed to camouflage the Negro as the white world sees him and forces him to behave. By a devious interracial irony the "creative" Negro, far from being his own spontaneous self, may actually be dramatizing the white man's image of the "spontaneous" Negro "as he really is." Ad libs, too, can be cunningly cued; even ecstasy, or what passes for it, can be an extremely learned response.

No doubt the Negro sings and dances lavishly, unstintingly, to a degree that is unheard-of among other groups in America; and out of his "effortless" creations have come our most characteristic forms of song and movement, the only ones we did not import from Europe. But what we take, in the singing and dancing Negro, for his own self-portrait may very well be a composite portrait which the white world has slapped together haphazardly out of its own emotional leftovers and flung over the Negro. *We* may be creating, via the Negro's musculature and larynx, what we could not create in our own persons. So that the "happifying" Negro ecstatic we pursue so hotly may be a lot closer to us than we think; he may be our own phantom self—in blackface. More and more we are coming round to the view that the pariah in any caste society is in large part molded by the master's image of him. The anti-Semite, says Sartre, creates the Jew.

The pariah, it must be remembered, has few norms of his own to sustain him; the norms under which he is born and lives out his life are those laid down by his masters; it is a difficult matter not to see himself, to some degree, through his master's eyes. His master's eyes are mirrors; his sense of selfness is largely a reflex of what he sees there.

In part, then, "the" Negro must be a "reflex being"—what Gunnar Myrdal calls a "reactive personality"—led by the encompassing glare of his culture to think that he is, after all, something like the lowly thing his masters think he is. But the caste system has never taken such totalitarian hold of the American unconscious as it presumably did for long centuries of the Hindu; if it had, jazz, jitterbugging, and jive could never have evaded their cultural quarantine in slave quarters and ghetto. Nor would the white man mimic the Black man's culture as he has done and continues to do. It follows that there must also be a more conscious level of personality shaping—one unique with the American Negro—on which an entirely different order of "distortion" takes place.

In part, too, the Negro must sense that he deviates from his master's official picture of him, the one on which the whole structure of caste rests. He gleans that, far from being *merely* an abomination, he is in some way an object of considerable admiration and envy too. But in a world controlled by whites, he must conceal his inner departures from the official norms they have worked out for him; everything depends on it. If he is not wholly a "reactive personality," he must pretend to be. When the reflex falters, a false face must be clapped on.

Unless, of course, the white man will not take offense at such personality "lapses." That happens in very special cases, as when Br'er Rabbit turns into Bigger Thomas—or when New Orleans jazz, largely an accommodation to the mask, suddenly erupts into bop, a partial jibe at the mask.

There is, then, a nimble interplay of image, reflex, and false face across the caste lines which is death to all real spontaneity. It is nowhere more striking than in the entertainment fields, which feature the "spontaneous" Negro. In fact, most Negroes in our culture spend most of their lives "on"; the eyes of the white community seldom wander far from them. Every Negro is to some extent a performer.

Reflex, or the simulation of reflex—jazz, like most of the Negro's cultural creations, has traditionally teetered between these two extremes. Yet there are those who make a cult of this or that Negroidism without noting this dizzy shuttling between genuine robotism and mock robotism in the Negro performer; who consider the object of their interest, whether he acts reflexively or calculatedly, "the Negro as he really is."

Aren't they missing the whole point of the performance? Instead of grasping the phenomenon that unfolds before their eyes they themselves become part of the phenomenon—for their eyes cue the performance. The more they relish the Negro on the stage as "authentic," blinding themselves to the degree of calculation in the performance, the more must the Negro performer cling to the masks which they take for real faces. It makes no difference whether he feels at home in them or not. His audience does not recognize that order of subjective problem. The relationship across the footlights is not between subject and subject, but between subject and object.

Myrdal sums up this proliferating irony in a suggestive phrase: *the tyranny of expectancy*. The white man's expectant imaging is the tyrant that bludgeons the pariah's personality into being what it "really" is in a caste situation, whether as automaton or as masquerader. But anybody who does not see the subtle dividing line between reflex and false face, who overlooks the point at which *because* becomes *as if* and conscious intent creeps into the performance, has closed his eyes to the real meaning of most Negro art forms. At the same time, he guarantees that the Negro will continue to create himself in everybody's image *but* his own. The truth about the Negro performer is that he is required to be a *Negro impersonator*.

The purely passive, pliable, reactive side of the Negro is steadily losing ground to the consciously manipulated mask which he dons as part of a deliberate act. That is, the extent to which he really feels himself to be what the white man thinks he is is dwindling, and the extent to which he *pretends* to be this or that, to achieve certain effects among certain groups of whites, is on the rise. And in that murky inner space where the mechanical fades into the willful lies the source of most Negro art forms. If the shift is ever completed the mask will be thrown off entirely and a startling new crop of art forms will mushroom.

The American caste system, which never set too well on the national mind, is now losing its hold entirely on the Negro's inner life. If he still goes through the motions of caste ritual, on or off the stage, it is now a maneuver rather than a reflex, carried off with all sorts of subtle interpolations not called for by the script.

The unique thing about the American Negro is that he has *never* been fully able to take what he saw in his culture's mirror for gospel truth. All along, from the day the first slaver discharged its human cargo on American shores, his life has had overtones of *as if*. No doubt that not-quite-real quality of his daily experience has had a lot to do with crystalizing the Negro's engulfing sense of the absurd and his penchant for sheer nonsense. A burgeoning giggle can be traced in the Negro dance from the beginning—from the plantation shuffle and cakewalk to the triple lindy and the applejack. There was already a leavening of irreverent laughter in New Orleans jazz, even in the earlier blues; and bop is, above all, a satirical music.

Indeed, the stylized grin that motored the Negro's song and

dance, and which we took for a simple beam of ecstasy, may have been, from the start, less transparent and more enigmatic than we had imagined. The Negro must, in fact, impersonate the song-and-dance man said to be lurking in him. Whatever touches of his own he adds to the animated picture—sly interpolations, satirical asides, nihilistic nonsense, mock emotionalism, dabs of caricature—must be applied around the edges, blended imperceptibly into the background. These touches may also be applied by his Black brothers and sisters; in this sense the Black community itself tends to reinforce the Blackface image. Any outright flinging aside of the image, any wiping off of the standard grin, will be tolerated only in special circumstances.

In India the caste system was held to derive from the "natural" fact that Brahma created the noble Brahmins from his forehead, other intermediate castes from his arms, torso, etc., while the pariahs emanated from the god's lowliest anatomical portions or, indeed, from sources in no way divine. Accordingly the Brahmins could not be touched by the pariahs simply because the god's lowliest parts were not worthy to touch his loftiest ones. But a systematic vaulting of all barriers occurred in the *sakti-puja*, orgies among members of all castes, whose purpose was the wholesale venting of all taboo urges. *Sakti-puja* was also given a religious sanction: the orgy was actually organized as a celebration of *sakti*, "the power of the god in female form," and the taboo meat and drink consumed were first sanctified by offering portions of them to Vishnu, the goddess Sakti, and the female body representing Sakti.

Obviously it is possible to enforce caste protocol in public and violate it in private, along with other rigid regulations, only when a community is tightly organized around a set of myths with the aura of divine origination about them. Then both the prohibition and its disturbance can be attributed to the divine will, and ambivalence is projected out from the individual psyche into the remote control-room of the gods. Once the doubleness is defined as a dictate of supernatural powers it is no longer a human failing, the individual can wear one face in public and another in private without being disturbed by the *apparent* disparity between them. Consider, by way of contrast, the terrible guilt-ridden ambivalence that wracked the whole American South for two full centuries and more over the furtive sex relations between white men and Negro women.

We see where the "singlemindedness" of the Brahmin, and therefore of the Untouchable, comes from. It is ambivalence drained of guilt and uneasiness through being disguised as obedience to the manifold and unfathomable dictates of the gods, the supervisorial powers of the universe. Thanks to the device of divine sanction the Brahmin found it possible to be entirely consistent in the public and private departments of behavior without the two consciously clashing or even confronting each other. Hate was confined to one area, love to another; the linkage between the two was not at all apparent, one in no obvious way infiltrated the other. And because the Brahmin was so "together" in each department, the pariah, as a reactive personality, was too.

So there was no inconsistency noticeable between the Brahmin's socio-economic deportment and his cultural deportment. Socio-economically he defined the pariah as unworthy of notice; and in his official culture he did not notice him. Culturally the Untouchable was as untouchable as elsewhere, and so it came about that the Untouchable played his lowly flute and the Brahmin plunked his lofty lute and the two types of music (and the dance forms associated with them) remained as steadfastly separate as did the men who made them.

It is very much as though the Hindu Untouchable, breaking painfully out of the crust of his culture, had suddenly realized that for two thousand years he had been a sleepwalker enacting a vast lie as though it were gospel truth. If he decided to keep up the masquerade for quite practical reasons—or simply because, as yet, he had no fully composed face of his own in reserve for such emergencies—it would now be on the basis of *as if* rather than *because*. And no doubt he would inject a little "face-saving" satire into his rendition of the role.

We have never been able in our own caste dealings to develop this kind of *orderliness*, love here, hate there, of the Hindi. Ambivalence surfaces from minute to minute in our daily lives—the subterranean bobs up, the private permeates the public, the cultural attitude mocks the socio-economic. We are not a community in the tight, rigid, monolithic sense that the Indians were; we have no unilinear myths that we share to such a mass extent that we can use them to departmentalize our cleaved emotions and give to each department a sanction from on high.

Emotionally we are infinitely more fluid, turbulent, tossed, our loves and hates confusedly meshed. Unable to rid ourselves of the guilts attached to ambivalence—because we have no firmly enthroned myth figures onto whom we can project the whole both-and state—we can rarely take up any one attitude or sentiment with complete conviction, to the steady exclusion of its opposite. Without the "divine word" to steady it, our emotional polarity remains in constant uneasy motion, always reversing itself, turning now one face upward and now its opposite.

To be sure, there were many attempts made in the early days of slavery to work up theological principles that would sanction the enslavement of Negroes by Christians. But they were doomed to failure, first because of the ambivalence inherent in Christian doctrine itself (the doctrine of eternal damnation as the fate of all infidels as against the doctrine of all living things being the creatures of God and therefore deserving equally of charity), second because of the clash between a theology that was somehow made to justify slavery and the democratic ethos. So the taboos essential to the institution of slavery, and later to the institution of caste, never could receive any real divine sanction, and many whites must accordingly have suspected that they were entirely arbitrary, the rankest after-the-fact rationalizations.

In such a climate there must have been considerable impulse from the American beginning to violate these caste taboos, since restrictions that smack of the arbitrary never rest easily on people. But theological sanction could no more be found for the violations than for the taboos that men wanted to violate. The white man was caught, as a result of the never adequately motivated caste system, in the emotional trap of ambivalence.

And this ambivalence, because it could not be clamped in

position by mythic props, came constantly to the surface of daily life. Its first manifestations was our obsessive cultural-aesthetic curiosity about the Negro who, as pariah, was defined in socio-economic areas as beneath notice. From this early curiosity about the pariah, out of which was born last century's prime popular art form, the minstrel show, came many of the characteristic features of our present-day mass culture.

It might be said that in many significant respects our mass culture is now, and has always been, the form which *sakti-puja* takes in America. Jazz, jitterbugging, zoot, jive, Negrophilia in general—these are daily street-corner and hangout *sakti-pujas* taking place in the open because we have no techniques for draining off our all-at-once emotions about the beckoning Untouchable in private.

It follows that with us, Negrophilia and Negrophobia are not, or are not *just*, polar opposites. We may have to see them, before we're through, as the two sides of one coin, a coin we're forever flipping. We can't help ourselves. By the law of averages, it comes up now heads, now tails. By the law of association, every time one side shows up, we're acutely aware of the presence of the other just below.

The sociology of jazz, as of all cultural transactions between the castes, is clear enough. There is, first of all, the general phenomenon: the white world, violating all of its caste conceits about the pariah's worth, constantly places images of the Negro before itself or encourages the Negro to impersonate those images. Almost always, of course, these stilted pictures embody stubborn preconceived notions, rooted in a subsoil of *white* need and yearning which deserves the most careful study.

What if an elite poaches culturally on its own pariah over many decades? It can happen that the social effects of the pariah's creations seep back into them to infuse their aesthetic essences; that the social all but floods the aesthetic.

In Negro music and dance, assuredly, the profounder truths are more often sociological than aesthetic. That is precisely the cramping limitation of all pariah culture, especially of that intended for export across caste lines. For its content is ultimately the creation of its intended audience, and the apparent creator is most typically only a middleman between the white as tyrannical psychic impresario and the same white as passive sidelines consumer.

The Negro's role in all this is hardly one of "self-expression." He simply dispenses to his masters the wish-filled images that emanated from them in the first place—while adding more and more pointed comments under his breath.

In these very special joy areas the Negro is regarded as a capsule of undiluted "aestheticism," immune to the arrows of outer circumstance. Why it should be thought that the Negro, smothered by the harshest set of social circumstances in America, should be the only American fully insulated against circumstance, is a little difficult to understand; but perhaps what is wanted here is the most dramatic demonstration that can be had of the-subjective-conquering-the-social. Feeling crushed by the circumstances themselves, Negrophiliac whites prefer to see the Negro as a pre-social creature in whom the romping subjective is king; the Negro must be defined from "within" because we feel ourselves so thoroughly puppetized from "without." The theory would seem to be that the Negro is *lucky* to be a pariah: banished to the outskirts of the community, he thus evades all the pressures and batterings to which one is subjected at the center and which are lethal to the "inner spark."

In this view aestheticism—which here means little more than emotionality, instinct-release, the good time: in short, the stock forms of happiness we pursue—is a luxury of the periphery. It denotes a carefree, pleasure-bound state which must be given up when one becomes "serious" and enters into the life of the workaday community. In our wistful social geography, the aesthete is the dweller on the outskirts. The white aesthete, or would-be aesthete, is shocked, therefore, and even feels betrayed, when his fringe-Negro's joyous brow becomes furrowed by the sober concerns of the orthodox: by "serious" dance and "serious" music, among other things. This, to the white, smacks of selling a priceless birthright. It amounts to trading ecstasy for respectability, sex for prestige, spontaneity for technique, folk vigor for sophisticated gentility, the solar plexus for prefrontal lobe.

By turning to Negro art forms to sidestep harrying social

"irrelevancies" the white joy seeker helps to perpetuate an image of the Negro artist as a "natural" singing and dancing creature who is impervious to the pummelings of social forces. He seeks the mythological Negro—an inveterately thick-skinned idol who is nourished exclusively from "within," who lusts and exults come what may, whom "nothing gets down." And for the Negro jazz musician the presence of such an aesthete in the vanguard of his audience is a *social* fact he can't blink. This aesthete must be catered to, under penalty of splintering his pure-joy trance and driving him away.

Something of the sort, in fact, has happened to the white devotees of New Orleans. They are today mortally offended by bop, whose essential grimness and blatancy have unmistakable social overtones, echoing the strife of the restless ghetto; they miss the apparently unembattled, pre-social "complacency" of levee music, imbued with the I-don't-give-a-damn of the "serene" drifter on the fringe. And bop, as it expands its white audience, is progressively distorted by the squeamishness of many whites about "circumstantial" concerns. Originally an outcy against social circumstance, expressing the ghetto's hunger for the "serious" culture of the orthodox white community, bop is "self-determined" ecstasy. From its increasingly "unserious" antics one would never guess that the whole driving force of bop is an overpowering lust for respectability.

The "irrelevant" fact remains that jazz, the altogether astonishing creation of the American pariah, has a massive cult built around it by the white elite. And the aesthetic of any jazz form, as of any dance generated by it, must remain an enormous question mark until within its "frame of styles" is seen the interplay of image, reflex and masquerade which goes on constantly within the caste structure of America.

But this is to say that the Negro is not capable of true aestheticism? Quite so—for just so long as he continues to be so *circumstantially* mauled and hobbled that the Self he tries to focus on and explore is uniquely, every waking, harried moment, jostled, often crowded offstage entirely, by the Other. The aesthetic, in any really subjective sense, flowers only among those who, having passed freely through the community and tasted of all its sober concerns, can afford to turn their backs on it and commune with themselves. Sartre argues, perhaps too categorically, that the Jew, so long as he is surrounded and defined by anti-Semites, is perforce a social creature, and that his anxieties are social rather than metaphysical in nature: he cannot contemplate his relation to the universe so long as he is haunted by his daily relations with other men. But if this is an oversimplification about the Jew, who after all has some alternative norms of his own to fall back on if he chooses to use them, it must apply with full force to the Negro, who after three hundred years of slavery and pariahdom has few norms except those handed down to him from above.

In the situation of daily terror created for him by American caste life the Negro must be a uniquely harried being. A socially produced anxiety spread-eagles over his entire existence, negating in advance every attempt at a genuine plunge into the subjective. And the Negro produces unique sounds and movements of anxiety, rituals of tension and malaise; but social reality is their springboard, and social reality their target. Negro song and dance are, in their innermost frames, laments for the *smothered* subjective.

Very possibly the Negro has a breathtaking bent for the truly aesthetic, all the more remarkable for enduring in an environment which has never favored "non-useful" pursuits. But like the proletarian—we recall the many dismal Stalinist efforts to precipitate a "proletarian culture"—he will never be allowed the luxury of aesthetic preoccupation until he has groped his way to the very center of the community, feasted liberally on all its prestigious orthodoxies—and then, of his own volition, departed or at least turned his back. The social fringe can become a bohemia only for those who gravitate there out of choice, surfeited with the sober life behind, never for those who are exiled there from birth because of alleged incapacities.

There is some stubborn blind spot in the American mind which makes it easy for us to confuse bohemia with the ghetto: our cultural Negrophilia would be impossible without that fallacy. But the fallacy is much more easily maintained by the weekend tourist to the ghetto, who never relinquishes his social mobility, than by the permanent resident there, who is rooted to the despised spot.

The ghetto is always being eyed and eavesdropped on here. No pariah drenched in such cultural limelight is simply "spontaneous," just "being himself." His dance is designed for the ring of eyes peering over the caste fences, and his music is very subtly molded *at the source* by the white ears into which it will be funneled. And whatever the Negro adds of his own to these "creations" is by way of spiteful comment on those eyes and ears, not a spurt of the self-centered subjective.

To talk about "spontaneity" under such *circumstances* is to miss the point. And the reality.